The Act of Writing

Canadian Essays for Composition

Seventh Edition

RONALD CONRAD

McGraw-Hill Ryerson

Toronto Montréal Boston Burr Ridge, IL Dubuque, IA
Madison, WI New York San Francisco St. Louis Bangkok
Bogotá Caracas Kuala Lumpur Lisbon London Madrid
Mexico City Milan New Delhi Santiago Seoul
Singapore Sydney Taipei

To
Adele and Natalie

The McGraw·Hill Companies

McGraw-Hill Ryerson

The Act of Writing
Canadian Essays for Composition
Seventh Edition

ISBN: 0-07-095227-2

1 2 3 4 5 6 7 8 9 10 VH 0 9 8 7 6

Printed and bound in the U.S.A.

Care has been taken to trace ownership of copyright material contained in this text; however, the publisher will welcome any information that enables them to rectify any reference or credit for subsequent editions.

Sponsoring Editor: Karen Noxon
Marketing Manager: Marc Trudel
Developmental Editor: Christine Gilbert
Senior Production Coordinator: Jennifer Wilkie
Supervising Editor: Anne Nellis
Copy Editor: Rodney Rawlings
Cover Design: Dianna Little
Cover Credit: © Greg Stott/Masterfile
Composition: Valid Design
Printer: Von Hoffmann Press, Inc.

Library and Archives Canada Cataloguing in Publication
Conrad, Ronald, 1941–
    The act of writing : Canadian essays for composition/
Ronald Conrad. — 7th ed.

Includes bibliographical references.
ISBN 0-07-095227-2

1. English language — Rhetoric — Textbooks.
2. Canadian essays (English). I. Title.

PE1429.C66 2006   808'.0427   C2005-904303-2

CONTENTS

And then . . .

CHAPTER 1: NARRATION   17

For example . . .

CHAPTER 2: EXAMPLE   45

It's large and purple and . . .

Here's why . . .

It's just the opposite of . . .

CHAPTER 5:
COMPARISON AND CONTRAST   157

In a way, it's like . . .

CHAPTER 6:
ANALOGY AND RELATED DEVICES

There are three kinds of them . . .

CHAPTER 7: CLASSIFICATION

Here's how it's done . . .

CHAPTER 8: PROCESS ANALYSIS

Therefore . . .

CHAPTER 9:
ARGUMENTATION AND PERSUASION 271

CONTENTS BY SUBJECT

CHILDHOOD AND OLD AGE

WOMEN IN SOCIETY

OUTSIDERS

THE CITY

THE ENVIRONMENT

WORK

VIOLENCE IN SOCIETY

SCIENCE AND TECHNOLOGY

BUSINESS AND INDUSTRY

THE MEDIA

THE ARTS

LAUGHS

PEOPLES AND PLACES

MAINLY CANADIAN

ACKNOWLEDGMENTS

Doris Anderson: Activist, feminist, former editor of *Chatelaine* magazine. Reprinted with permission of the author.

Margaret Atwood: "Letter to America" from *Moving Targets: Writing with Intent, 1982–2004.* Copyright 2004 by O. W. Toad Ltd. Reprinted with the permission of House of Anansi Press.

Samantha Bennett: Copyright *Pittsburgh Post-Gazette,* 2005. All rights reserved. Reprinted with permission.

Mark Bernstein: Reprinted with permission of the author.

Dave Bidini: Taken from *For Those About to Rock.* Copyright 2004 by Dave Bidini, published by Tundra Books, Toronto.

Dionne Brand: Extracted from *Bread Out of Stone* by Dionne Brand. Copyright 1994 by Dionne Brand. Reprinted by permission of Alfred A. Knopf Canada.

Robert Christy: Reprinted with permission of the author.

Maria Coffey: From *Where the Mountain Casts Its Shadow* by Maria Coffey. Copyright 2003 by the author and reprinted by permission of St. Martin's Press, LLC.

Karen Connelly: Copyright 2001 Karen Connelly from *Touch the Dragon*. Reprinted with permission of Turnstone Press.

Roméo Dallaire: Extracted from *Shake Hands with the Devil: The Failure of Humanity in Rwanda* by Lt.-Gen. Roméo Dallaire. Copyright 2003 Roméo Dallaire, Lt.-Gen. (ret.) Inc. Reprinted by permission of Random House Canada.

Paul D'Angelo: Reprinted with permission of the author.

Kildare Dobbs: Reprinted with permission of the author.

Will and Ian Ferguson: Excerpt from *How to Be a Canadian*, by Will and Ian Ferguson, published 2001 by Douglas & McIntyre Ltd. Reprinted by permission of the publisher.

Sylvia Fraser: Reprinted by permission of Sll/Sterling Lord Literistic, Inc. Copyright 1989 by Sylvia Fraser.

George Gabori: Reprinted with permission.

Carol Geddes: Reprinted with permission of the author.

Ray Guy: Reprinted with permission of the author.

Charles Yale Harrison: Reprinted with permission of Annick Press.

Lawrence Hill: From *Black Berry, Sweet Juice: On Being Black and White in Canada*. Published by HarperCollins Publishers Ltd. Copyright 2001 by Lawrence Hill.

Martin Hocking: Reprinted with permission of the author.

Basil Johnston: Reprinted by permission of Basil Johnston.

Naomi Klein: Extracted from *No Logo* by Naomi Klein. Copyright 2000 by Naomi Klein. Reprinted by permission of Alfred A. Knopf Canada.

Joy Kogawa: Excerpt from *Obasan*. Reprinted with the permission of Joy Kogawa. *Obasan* originally published by Lester & Orpen Dennys in 1981 and currently published by Penguin Canada.

Albert Koehl: Reprinted with permission of the author.

David Lam: Reprinted with permission of the author.

Evelyn Lau: Reprinted with permission of the author.

Jack Layton: Published with permission from Key Porter Books. Copyright 2004 by Jack Layton.

Félix Leclerc: "The Family House" excerpted from *Pieds nus dans l'aube*, 1946, pp. 9–14. Collection "Bibliothèque Canadienne-française," Montréal.

Reprinted by permission of Gaétane M. Leclerc. Translated by Philip Stratford. Permission to reprint translation by Jacqueline Stratford.

Wendy Magahay: Reprinted with permission of the author.

Christie McLaren: Reprinted with permission from *The Globe and Mail.*

Leah McLaren: Reprinted with permission from *The Globe and Mail.*

Linda McQuaig: Extracted from *It's the Crude, Dude: War, Big Oil, and the Fight for the Planet* by Linda McQuaig. Copyright Linda McQuaig 2004. Reprinted by permission of Doubleday Canada Limited.

Naheed Mustafa: "My Body is My Own Business" from *The Globe and Mail,* June 29, 1993. Reprinted with permission of the author.

Rafi Mustafa: "The Bond of Nightmares" from the *Toronto Star,* 1991. Reprinted with permission of the author.

J. Kelly Nestruck: "The Importance of Email Punctuation: A Cautionary Tale" from *The McGill Daily,* November 15, 1999. Reprinted with permission of the author.

Patricia Pearson: "Avoiding the Big C: A Little Simple Advice" from *The National Post,* August 28, 1999. Reprinted with permission of the author.

Nathalie Petrowski: "The Seven-Minute Life of Marc Lépine" from *Le Devoir,* December 16, 1989. Reprinted with permission.

Catherine Pigott: "Adding Weight to the Image of Beauty" from *The Globe and Mail,* March 20, 1990. Reprinted with permission of the author.

Gordon Pitts: "Your New Job, Your New Life" from *The Globe and Mail,* September 15, 2001. Reprinted with permission from *The Globe and Mail.*

Mordecai Richler: "1944: The Year I Learned to Love a German" by Mordecai Richler, *New York Times Book Review,* 1986 © Mordecai Richler Productions Inc.

Rita Schindler: "Thanks for Not Killing My Son" from the *Toronto Star,* p. D3, December 30, 1990. Every effort has been made to contact the owner of this copyright material. The publishers will gladly accept any information that enables them to rectify any reference or credit for this item in subsequent editions.

Carol Shields: "Encounter," by Carol Shields, reprinted here with the permission of the Carol Shields Literary Trust.

Goran Simic: "Goodbye Muse, Hello Prada" from *The Globe and Mail,* February 24, 2000. Reprinted with permission of the author.

David Suzuki: "Hidden Lessons" from *The Globe and Mail,* February 7, 1987. Reprinted with permission of the author.

Drew Hayden Taylor: "This Boat Is My Boat" from *This Magazine,* July/August 2004, p. 23. Reprinted with permission of the author.

Catharine Parr Traill: "Remarks of Security of Person and Property in Canada" from *The Female Emigrant's Guide* by Catharine Parr Traill.

Margaret Wente: "Busy, Busy, Busy" from *An Accidental Canadian.* Reprinted with permission from *The Globe and Mail.*

Jan Wong: Reprinted with permission from *The Globe and Mail.*

TO THE STUDENT

We hope you like *The Act of Writing*. In our seven editions so far, we've put a lot of effort into developing material that is fun to read, that provides issues to debate in class, that inspires you to write about significant matters, and that suggests good books to keep you reading after the course is done.

The 50 selections between these covers provide some good reading right now. Notice, though, how the introduction to each author also lists more works by that person. And the "Explorations" feature after each selection suggests which of those books are probably most worth reading. Circle the most likely ones to try over the holidays, or next summer, or whenever else you have time. (Then keep this book, so you have a record of those choices!)

If our selection by Dave Bidini or Linda McQuaig or Mordecai Richler or Margaret Atwood or Naomi Klein especially appeals to you, then treat it like a movie preview: go on to a full-length feature as soon as you can. Remember that in addition to the fun you may have and the insights you may get, the act of opening a book is probably your most direct path to improving your own writing. Every time you read good writing, your mind is forming patterns that will help you produce your own.

"Explorations," the feature following each essay, also suggests several Web sites about this author and this subject. Check them out. You can read a poem by Goran Simic, or view Emily Carr's paintings, or check the latest investigation at David Suzuki's environmental Web site, or laugh at a spoof on SUVs after reading Linda McQuaig, or see a photo of Félix Leclerc and hear him sing a song in French. After reading Gordon Pitts you can visit a page of links to sites on terrorism, or after reading Dionne Brand you can see a list of everything else she has ever written. Use these references to keep you exploring. (If a Web site has disappeared since the book was printed, go to our own *Act of Writing* Web site given on the back cover, to see the current version with the newest sites.)

Finally, *The Act of Writing* teaches a philosophy of composition. We hope you consider carefully this book's advice about how good writing is produced in the real world: not just through blueprinting an essay before you write the first word, but through a process of discovery, of "thinking by writing." Do read our overview of the writing process, on pages 1 through 14, with close attention. Free yourself up to try the techniques it suggests, and free yourself from some of the inefficient or even harmful practices of the past. The methods we suggest are based on today's research, but they are also the same ones that most good writers have always used.

R.C.

TO THE TEACHER

How does an edition begin? There is a moment when you know. One day an extraordinary e-mail attachment arrived from Texas, then soon after again from Ohio. By the time I reached its author in Pennsylvania, I knew Samantha "Sam" Bennett had valuable things to say — both to Americans and to Canadians. And she said them with a delicious irony and humour. In that moment I saw our new edition.

Frankly, for about two years after 9/11, I wondered whether a seventh edition was even possible. Nothing was fun anymore. Nothing was being written in a nuanced way, nothing was being written with irony or balance, nothing was being written that could spark *The Act of Writing* again. My stack of clippings for the next edition had never been so thin.

But after about two years the curtains began to rise again. We had all grieved our neighbours' loss, and now were getting on again with life. Sam Bennett's zany analysis of opposite trends in America and in Canada ("It's Not Just the Weather That's Cooler in Canada", p. 208) was not the only fun to be had. Dave Bidini regaled us with a feast of rock band names; Margaret Wente showed us life in the fast lane; from across the ocean Leah McLaren praised the Canadian men she had left behind; Linda McQuaig poked fun at SUVs; Drew Hayden Taylor showed us the insanity of canoeists through native Canadian eyes; and Albert Koehl explained the fine points of male behaviour during hockey playoffs.

Yet despite joining together some of the most entertaining authors in a long time, we also plumbed the depths of major new issues, because a great deal of incisive analysis has also surfaced recently. Jack Layton demolishes our system of calculating economic progress; Maria Coffey reveals the dark side of extreme sport; Dr. Mark Bernstein dramatizes health care in a battle for life on the operating table; Margaret Atwood sends a heart-to-heart letter to America; and the truest Canadian hero of our time, General Roméo Dallaire, shows how the worst genocide since World War II could have been stopped but was not.

In summary, then, I believe this Seventh Edition of *The Act of Writing* offers one of the strongest combinations of authors we have ever had — and that is most of what an anthology is about.

Continuity

One aspect of designing a new edition is to conserve what readers have liked so far. Many reviewers have helped us in this task. We have stayed very close to their wishes, and we trust this means we have stayed close to your wishes too. In this edition a core of proven and familiar pieces stays in place, which we hope will provide many of your own favourites as you design your course.

In the core structure of the book, as well, we are not pursuing change for the sake of change. In earlier editions we have dropped and added chapters, in response to readers' wishes. This time we are maintaining the overall outlines of the book, because of the good degree of user satisfaction shown in the reviews. We have, however, made small adjustments to chapter size, for example boosting the much-used "Cause and Effect" chapter from seven essays to eight. Thus we hope to give the greatest choice to the greatest number of students and teachers. (Also note that at the end of each chapter introduction appears a list of essays in *other* chapters that also make use of the present means of organization — to give a still larger choice.)

Exploration

Of the 50 selections in *The Act of Writing*, Seventh Edition, about a third are new. But the newness lies even more in the selection of writers than in their number. We have many fresh voices this time — such as Dave Bidini, Margaret Wente, Leah McLaren, Linda McQuaig, Jack Layton, Maria Coffey, Drew Hayden Taylor, Ian and Will Ferguson, Dr. Mark Bernstein, Albert Koehl and General Roméo Dallaire — as a new generation of writers continues to take its place in Canada. A full 30% of our contributors are from Western Canada, to better balance our contents geographically. There is representation from Quebec and from the First

Nations population, and a large number of our contributors are New Canadians. As for gender, we offer a balanced proportion of 25 selections by women and 25 by men.

And we do resolutely maintain *The Act of Writing* as an anthology of all-Canadian essays, to provide an alternative for teachers and students who want more than a token selection of our own materials in the classroom. Yet at the same time you will find a strong international focus through Canadian eyes: Jan Wong samples the new China; Karen Connelly opens her eyes to Thailand; Catherine Pigott learns new body image in Gambia; Gordon Pitts foresees "Your New Job, Your New Life" after international terrorism; Margaret Atwood sees new directions in America; Naomi Klein investigates international sweatshop origins of the clothing worn by Canadians; and General Roméo Dallaire takes us to Rwanda, a paradise made hell by politics both local and international.

As times change, controversy keeps on emerging. A great many *Act of Writing* selections explore issues: globalization, war, terrorism, racism, homelessness, sexism, SUVs and their effects, prejudice against the disabled, and the challenges of being an immigrant. To reflect our strong emphasis on issues, the feature "Ideas for Discussion and Writing," which appears after each selection, is on the average fairly extensive, while "Structure" and "Style" are on the average more compact.

Finally, the feature "Explorations," at the end of each selection, has grown, to offer students a larger choice of books, Web sites and other sources that relate to the author and/or subject of that selection. We like to think of *The Act of Writing* as an index to independent readings students may wish to do: when they have been stimulated by a selection, they are given paths to continue on their own. Note, by the way, our own book Web site for "Explorations," which will be kept more current than any printed list can be, deleting dead links and adding new ones that appear between editions. It is at **www.mcgrawhill.ca/college/conrad**.

If You Are New to This Book

The Act of Writing, Seventh Edition, encourages flexibility and individualization. The combination of three to nine essays per chapter, with several more identified in cross-references, will yield more selections per unit than you are likely to use. Thus you can individualize, choosing readings that best suit the needs and interests of your particular class. This book also offers a range of difficulty, from essays that are very accessible to others that are challenging. *(Note: The "Table of Contents and Difficulty Ranking" of your Instructor's Manual rates all selections into three levels of difficulty, so if you are new to this book you can more quickly tailor a syllabus to your class.)*

The discussion topics after each selection offer themes for analysis and debate. "Explorations," as described earlier, suggests books and Web sites for independent investigation. And finally, the "Process in Writing" topic after each essay, the 30 essay topics at the end of each chapter, and the process "Guidelines" tailored for each chapter give a latitude of choice for the individual teacher, the individual class, the individual student.

See the two tables of contents. The first lists all selections in their chapters arranged by *form of organization* (you can choose from eight essays, for example, that all demonstrate organization through comparison and contrast). The second table of contents lists all essays by general *subject*, to help you choose selections of interest to your particular students, especially in a theme-based course.

An introductory essay, "The Act of Writing," starts the book off by putting to rest some common misconceptions about writing that plague students, then describes what it is that an essayist actually does. It emphasizes the individuality of the writer, the importance of motivation, the role of intuition as well as logic, and a balance of spontaneity and revision of the process of writing.

As we have seen, the essays are arranged in chapters that each demonstrate a fundamental pattern of thought — and therefore of organization. "Narration" starts the book off, because no approach is easier or more motivating for a first assignment than writing a story, in chronological order, about oneself. "Example" and "Description" follow, because these tools of development are used to some degree in almost all writing. "Cause and Effect" and its following chapter, "Comparison and Contrast," are at the centre of the essayist's organizational repertoire. "Analogy and Related Devices" and "Classification" follow "Comparison and Contrast," for they are both varieties of comparison. "Process Analysis," an approach used widely across the curriculum, follows. After all these *forms*, our largest chapter, "Argumentation and Persuasion," explores more fully the writer's most basic *purpose*: to make a point. It examines the dualities of deduction and induction, and of argumentation and persuasion, then illustrates their application with nine model essays.

Throughout the book each selection is prefaced by an introduction to the author, designed to interest the student, often to present the author as a role model, and to encourage further reading of his or her works. Then each selection is followed by pedagogical material entitled "Explorations," "Structure," "Style," "Ideas for Discussion and Writing," and in Chapter 9, "Argumentation and Persuasion." Note that in this material different questions serve different purposes. Some are directive, calling attention to major features of the essay. Some are technical, for example focusing on a specific point of language that illustrates a technique. Many are exploratory, encouraging open-ended response.

The Instructor's Manual answers those questions that are not open-ended and suggests responses to some that are. (Make sure to go to the text's Online Learning Centre at www.mcgrawhill.ca/college/conrad to download.) Read the manual's introduction: it gives more suggestions for using **The Act of Writing.** *For each essay, the manual also lists vocabulary that may need attention.*

Each of the nine chapters begins with a discussion of how and why to use the form at hand, and ends with a selection of 30 essay topics that complement that form. These topics have been chosen with care, to tap some of the students' deepest concerns and channel them into motivation for writing. The reason for this attention to topics is that no one problem is more destructive to the performance of both student and teacher than dull or superficial subject matter. How can writing be important if its content is not? And how can a teacher enjoy or even tolerate marking without an interest in what the students are saying?

A further "Process in Writing" topic is given after each essay. If class members have had a good discussion about the selection, their motivation and writing performance may be greatest if they explore these topics, which draw upon both the subject and the underlying form of the essay preceding them. And at the end of each chapter are the process guidelines mentioned earlier, individualized for the specific pattern of development in that unit.

Finally, a glossary at the book's end defines literary terms often used in the discussion questions; when one of these words is a key part of a passage, it appears in SMALL CAPITALS.

Your **Integrated Learning Sales Specialist** is a McGraw-Hill Ryerson representative who has the experience, product knowledge, training, and support to help you assess and integrate any of the above-noted products, technology, and services into your course for optimum teaching and learning performance. Whether it's using our test bank software, helping your students improve their grades, or putting your entire course online, your *i*Learning Sales Specialist is there to help you do it. Contact your local *i*Learning Sales Specialist today to learn how to maximize all of McGraw-Hill Ryerson's resources!

Finally, I would like to thank everyone who helped with this project: the many teachers who gave advice from their experiences in the classroom, and the many who reviewed both our previous edition and our new selections: Marian Allen, Grant MacEwan College; Sarika Bose, University of British Columbia; Julie Cairnie, University of Guelph; Elaine Chang, University of Guelph; C. Gordon-Craig, University of Alberta; Henry Heggie, Cambrian College; Rhonda Hustler, Centennial College; David Ingham, St. Thomas University; Carolyn Ives, University College of the Cariboo; Peter Miller, Seneca College; Elaine Mullen, Mount Royal College; David O'Rourke, Centennial College; Margaret Owens, McMaster University.

Thanks to my daughter Suzanne (who herself is a teacher) for her many valuable suggestions, and to my daughter Katherine (now a law student) for her excellent critical judgments as to our proposed new selections. Thanks also to my son Charles, who solved every computer problem, and to my son-in-law Lindsay, for consulting on hockey matters. And thanks to many others, such as Anne Bradley, Susan Harrison, Robert Hope, Lee Lybarger, Diana Madge, Charles Neuenschwander,

Alexandra Prasow and Larry Smucker for their suggestions. Thanks also to many of our authors, for their kind help in providing information for this book: J. Kelly Nestruck, Patricia Pearson, Naheed Mustafa, Doris Anderson, Catherine Pigott, Wendy Magahay, Samantha Bennett, Dr. Mark Bernstein and Albert Koehl. Most of all, I sincerely thank my wife Mary, who in fact is co-author of this book, though she declines to be named on the cover. Her hard work, lively interest and unerring judgment have helped shape every edition so far, especially this one.

R. C.

Introduction:
The Act of Writing

Writing is one of the most misunderstood of human activities. It is strange that after all the years we've spent in school, after all the hours we've spent reading other peoples' writing and producing our own, most of us can't say what really happens when we write. We can describe other complex tasks — driving a car, making pizza, building a house or searching the Web. But to many people the act of writing is a mystery. Not that we don't have theories, either those told us in school or those we have arrived at ourselves. But many of these theories are misconceptions that actually hinder our efforts to write. Let's look at some of them.

MISCONCEPTION: Writing is like following a blueprint: I figure it all out in advance and then just fill in the details. Of course an outline, used sensibly, will help. But our parents were taught in school that their best thinking should go into a logical and detailed outline — and that the writing itself was secondary. Thus they were reduced to carpenters or plumbers of the written word, who merely sawed, cut and fit pieces in place once the master plan was established. The problem with this reassuringly logical approach is that it views writing as a technology, not as the art that all our practical experience tells us it is. How many of us have given up

1

on a required outline, done our thinking mostly as we wrote the essay itself, then later produced the outline by seeing what we wrote? Or how many of us have painfully constructed a detailed outline in advance, only to find while writing the essay that our real message does not fit the plan?

Writing is exploring! We know which way we are headed and the main landmarks we hope to pass, but not every twist and turn of the path. What a dull trip that would be! Let's leave room for discovery, because our best ideas may occur in the act of writing. The Quebec poet Hector de St.-Denys Garneau actually said, "I cannot think except when writing." Some teachers reflect this fact of writing as discovery by calling a first draft the *discovery draft*.

But while avoiding the rigor mortis of overplanning, let's not go to the opposite extreme, like Stephen Leacock's famous horseman who "rode madly off in all directions." We do work best with an outline, five or ten or fifteen lines that define the main point and how we intend to support it. But our outline should be a compass on a journey, not the blueprint of a construction project.

MISCONCEPTION: *If I don't hit it right the first time, I've failed.* It's not hard to see where this idea came from: in school we write so many essays and tests within the limits of one class period that writing in a hurry begins to seem normal. But under such conditions, merely producing enough is hard; seriously revising it is even harder. Few people can "hit it right the first time." Professional writers know this; most of them take longer to write than we do. They tinker with words and sentences, they cross out and replace sections, they go through two or three or even five or ten drafts — and sometimes they throw the whole thing out and start over. These writers know by experience that writing is not a hit-or-miss affair with only one try allowed, but a *process.* They know that revision can yield amazing results.

MISCONCEPTION: *When I write, I am speaking on paper.* If you've heard a recording of yourself speaking, you were no doubt surprised at all the filler words you used. "Uh," "um," "well" and "hmmm" may fill the gaps between your thoughts very conveniently, but they hardly help to carry the message. And if you listened closely, you may have been surprised at the number of incomplete statements — fragments that by themselves made little or no sense. Fillers and fragments are accepted in speech because, after all, we're making up our message on the spot. There is no chance to plan, revise, edit or proofread.

But in writing there is, and this fact increases the expectations of your reader far beyond those of your listener. Language in written form can be planned. It is complete. It is precise and concise. It uses standard words. It has punctuation. It follows the rules. In short, it is a product of the time that its written form allows you to give it, not a spur-of-the-moment, hope-for-the-best effort like the speech that comes so easily from your mouth.

MISCONCEPTION: *The best words are the biggest words.* Variations on this theme are *If my writing looks scholarly it will impress the reader,* and even *If I make my essay so difficult that no one knows what I'm saying, everyone will believe me.* At the roots of these widespread ideas is a notion that writing is a kind of competition between writer and reader. A writer who is obscure enough will make the reader feel like a dummy and will thus win the game. But ask yourself: In real life do you *ambulate* or *walk? Expectorate* or *spit? Interdigitate* or *hold hands? Cogitate* or *think?*

Avoiding this game of writer vs. reader is not easy when so many leaders in business, education and government play it. The first step toward open communication, though, is to think of your reader not as an opponent but as a teammate. You are both moving toward the same goal, which is the reader's clear understanding of your ideas.

Another step is to admit that words small in size can be large in meaning. The best-loved writings in our language (think of the lines from Shakespeare you may have memorized for school) are filled with short words. Writing made of them is more concise, more vivid, and usually more profound than writing made of the elephantine words that some of us ransack the dictionary for. When a long word — like "elephantine" above — conveys your meaning best, by all means use it. But often the writer, like the architect, finds that *less is more.*

MISCONCEPTION: *I don't like to write.* For some unfortunate people this statement is true. But for most who say it, the truth is really "I don't like to *begin* writing." Who does? Staring at that blank page or screen is like staring from a diving board at the cold water below. But a swimmer and a writer both gather the courage to plunge in, and soon they both feel a new sensation: they don't want to come out. Teachers whose students write journals in class see the process at work every day. As class begins, the writers are filled with stress: they chew their pens and frown as they stare at the page to be filled. But in a while they are scribbling furiously, recording in an almost trance-like state their latest experiences, feelings and insights. If the teacher asks them to stop, in order to begin the next activity, they are annoyed: they sigh and *keep on writing* till asked a second or third time to stop.

Let's admit that most writers — and that includes professionals — dread the beginning. Let's also admit that most writers enjoy the rest of it, hard work though it may be.

With some of the most widespread misconceptions behind us now, let's take a fresh look at the act of writing. First, allow for personal differences. *Know yourself!* If you are a person whose desk is piled high with papers and books, whose closet is an avalanche waiting to happen, and whose shoes have not been shined in two years, you may write best by planning little and relying on your spontaneity. If you are a person who plans an August holiday in January, keeps a budget right down to the penny, and washes the car every Wednesday and Saturday whether it needs it or not, you may write best by planning fully.

On the other hand, your natural tendencies may have caused you problems and so may need to be controlled. If your spontaneity has produced writings that don't stay on topic, plan more: make a careful outline. If overorganizing has sucked the life out of your writing, free yourself up: leave more room for discovery as you write. Whatever the case, try to determine and use the approach that works for *you.*

Let's allow also for differences in assignments. If you are dashing off a short personal sketch, your planning may be no more than an idea and a few moments of thought. If you are writing a long research essay, the product of days in the library, you may need an outline two pages long. No single approach works for every person and every assignment. Keep in mind, then, that the process we are about to examine is a *starting point*, a basis but not a blueprint, for your own writing.

THE BEGINNINGS OF AN ESSAY CAN BE FOUND BY ANSWERING THESE QUESTIONS:

1.   *Why am I writing?* This most basic of questions too often goes unasked. If the answer is "to fill up five pages," "to impress" or "to get an *A,*" you begin with a severe handicap. The immediate reason to write may be a class assignment, but the real reason must be to communicate something of value. Otherwise your motivation is lost and so is your performance. So, from a list of topics, choose the one that means the most to you. If no topic seems significant, devise a way to *make* one significant. Probe the topic through the exercise of freewriting, explained later on. Look at your topic from a new viewpoint or approach it in some unusual way.

If that fails, and if your teacher is approachable, voice your concern and ask for an alternative topic. One teacher always made students analyze the relative merits of chocolate and vanilla ice cream, on the theory that a dull subject will not distract a writer from the real goals: grammar and style. He was wrong. Research shows motivation to be the single greatest factor in writing performance — and motivation comes from writing about things that matter.

When you write on your own, as in a personal journal, you may still need to answer the question *Why am I writing?* Just recording events may not be enough. Add your feelings, your perceptions, and your conclusions about those events. If you have problems, as most people do, confront them on the page. The more you discover yourself and your world through writing, the more important the writing becomes.

2.   *How big is my topic?* Classroom essays are shorter than most people think. A book may contain 100,000 words; a magazine article 2000 or 5000; a classroom essay as few as 500 or even 250. So narrowing the essay topic is more important than most people realize.

One student, who had been a political prisoner, chose to write about economic systems. He knew the subject well and was committed to it. But what he attempted was an analysis of communism, socialism and capitalism — all in two pages! A lack of focus spread his very short essay so thin that it approached the state of saying nothing about everything. It was the barest scratching of the surface, a summary of basic facts everyone already knows.

If the same person had focused on his arrest and imprisonment — or even on one day in his cell — he might have said far more about the system he opposed. It is in specifics that we best see generalities. Think of writing as photography. Putting aside the wide-angle lens that includes too much at a distance, look through the zoom lens that brings you up close to a small part of the subject. Select the part most meaningful to you, the part most characteristic of the whole, then take the picture.

Nearly all the essays in this book are close-ups: they explore one situation, one incident, one person or one process. Yet many of them are longer than the essays you will write. So when you choose a topic, judge its size — and if you have to, *change* its size.

3. *What message am I sending?* You may know your topic well. But unless you send a message concerning it, your reader will think *What's the point?* A message is often a value judgment: are robots dangerous? Will they take away our jobs or someday even rule over us? Or do they help us? Will they free us at last from the dehumanizing tyranny of manual labour? Most of the essays in this book take such a stance, either pro or con, toward their subjects. Some avoid judging their subjects directly, but send other messages: what it's like to be homeless, or what it's like to operate on a patient's brain.

If you have chosen a topic because it seems meaningful, you will no doubt have a message to send. What do you most feel like saying about the topic? Once you know, get it down in writing. This THESIS STATEMENT, as it is usually called, normally comes at or near the beginning of an essay. It is an introductory sentence or passage that does more than just tell what the topic is; it clearly states, as well, what you are saying *about* the topic. It lets your reader know what is coming — and, in the process, commits you to a purpose that all the rest of the essay must in one way or another support. It is your guide as you write.

4. *Who is my audience?* Do you talk the same way to a friend and a stranger? To an old person and a child? Probably not. Neither would you write the same way to all readers. In a personal journal you can write as freely as you think, for you are your own reader: omissions and excesses of all kinds will be understood and forgiven. In emails to a close friend you are nearly as free, because the reader knows you well enough to supply missing explanations or interpret remarks in the light of your personality. But your freedom shrinks when you write for others: a business person, a public official, a teacher. Now you must fight a misconception shared by many people: *Everyone is like me.*

This idea is seldom articulated but may lurk as a natural assumption in the back of our minds. It is a form of egotism. If you assume everyone is like you, many readers will not accept or even understand your message — because they are *not* like you. They did not grow up in your family, neighbourhood or even country. They are older or younger, or of the opposite sex. They have had different life experiences, so now they have different knowledge and temperaments and values.

Accept these differences as you write. You will never prove your point by quoting Marx to a capitalist, the Bible to an atheist, or Margaret Atwood to a male supremicist. Any argument built on a partisan foundation will collapse if the reader does not accept that foundation. Instead, build from facts or ideas that your reader probably *does* accept: killing is bad, government is necessary, women are human beings, and so on. Is your subject controversial? Then avoid an open display of bias. Calling police "pigs" or intellectuals "eggheads" or abortionists "hired killers" will appeal only to those who shared your view in the first place. (For more on these matters, read the introduction to Chapter 9, "Argumentation and Persuasion.")

Does the reader know what you know? If you write about statistics for a statistics teacher, use any technical terms customary to the field, and avoid the insult of explaining elementary points. But if you write on the same subject for a class exercise in English or a letter to the editor of your hometown newspaper, your reader will be very different: avoid most technical terms, define those you do use, and explain more fully each step of your argument.

The more open you become to the individuality of your reader, the more open your reader becomes to your message. It's a matter of mutual respect.

Prewriting

How do we begin the act of writing? By putting those first words on a page? The philosopher Lao-Tze said, "A journey of a thousand miles begins with the first step." In a way he was right: if we never take that official first step, we'll certainly never arrive at our destination. But how much daydreaming and planning do we do beforehand? Do we set out on a journey without consulting the map or the calendar or the tourist brochure or the travel guide — not to mention our wallet? And do we write an essay without somehow answering the questions we have just asked:

Why am I writing?
How big is my topic?
What message am I sending?
Who is my audience?

The process of writing, then, begins in thought. But thoughts do not come on command. Like the person on the diving board, we look down at the cold water and dread the plunge. Some writers like to "break the ice" by manipulating their environment: finding a quiet spot, going to a favourite chair with good lighting, or slipping a good CD into their stereo. Others fortify themselves with a good night's sleep, junk food or coffee. Any of these tricks may help, but they all avoid the real issue: How do we begin to *think?*

One direct approach, a variation on the old technique of outlining, is **brainstorming**. Once you have roughly identified your subject, just write down words or phrases that relate in any way to it, in a list going down a page. Put down anything that comes, letting one thought lead to another. Some entries will seem off-topic, trivial or even loony, but others may be just what you need: the keys to your essay. Circle them. Put them in order. As crude as this primitive outline may seem, it has served a purpose: your thoughts have begun to arrive. The process is in motion. You have taken that first "step" before even starting the first draft.

A similar but even more powerful "icebreaker" is *freewriting*. Put a blank page on the desk with your watch beside it. Think of your topic. Now write! Put down anything that comes: sentences, phrases, words — logical thoughts, hasty impressions, even pure garbage. Do not cease the physical act of writing, do not even lift the pen from the page, or your fingers from the keyboard, for at least five minutes. If your next thought doesn't come, write the last one over and over till the next one does come. What emerges may surprise you.

Like brainstorming, freewriting is an exercise in free association: the flow of your thoughts, the sudden leaps of your intuition, will "break the ice" so you can write. They may do even more: as in brainstorming, you may end up with a page of scribbling that contains the main points of your essay. Try to find them. Circle them. Put them in order. See if your intuition has led the way in answering the questions: *Why am I writing? How big is my topic? What message am I sending? Who is my audience?* If all goes well, you have already begun your journey.

The First Words

Once your thoughts are flowing comes the next step, the opening passage of your essay. In a very short composition your THESIS STATEMENT may serve also as the first words. In most longer essays it comes at the end of an introduction. Only about one-fourth of the selections in this book start right off with what could be called a thesis statement. What do the others start with?

Background information: About half the essays in this book lead off by telling the circumstances in which the topic is set. For examples, see the beginnings of our selections by Gabori (p. 25), Nestruck (p. 60), Simic (p. 73), Suzuki (p. 127), McQuaig (p. 136), Richler (p. 146), Lau (p. 258), Hocking (p. 278), Dobbs (p. 283), Atwood (p. 298), Schindler (p. 308) and Christy (p. 315).

Anecdote: A brief story, usually of a humorous or dramatic incident, can lead into the topic. See Nestruck (p. 60), Wente (p. 64), Pearson (p. 114), Pigott (p. 172), Rafi Mustafa (p. 177), Taylor (p. 182), Bernstein (p. 248) and Leacock (p. 264).

Quotation or allusion: The words of a philosopher, of a news report, of a recognized specialist in the subject, or of anyone with close experience of it can be used to break the ice. See Pearson (p. 114), Taylor (p. 182), Dobbs (p. 283) and Kogawa (p. 292).

Sense images: Vivid description can attract a reader's interest to the topic. See Fraser (p. 29), Geddes (p. 34), Christie McLaren (p. 88), Harrison (p. 92), Leclerc (p. 217), Klein (p. 303) and Dallaire (p. 319).

A striking comparison or contrast: Showing how things are like or unlike each other is a dramatic way to introduce a topic. See Shields (p. 20), Gabori (p. 25), Wong (p. 48), Suzuki (p. 127), Anderson (p. 160), Pigott (p. 172), Koehl (p. 254) and Hocking (p. 278).

Narrative: Several selections in this book begin by telling a story upon which the essay is based. See Carr (p. 99), D'Angelo (p. 118), Pigott (p. 172), Rafi Mustafa (p. 177), Dobbs (p. 283), Klein (p. 303), Brand (p. 312) and Dallaire (p. 319).

An unusual or puzzling statement: Such an opening appeals to the reader's curiosity. See Simic (p. 73), Carr (p. 99), Pearson (p. 114) and Layton (p. 164).

Figures of speech: A striking METAPHOR, SIMILE or PERSONIFICATION can spark the opening. See Hill (p. 191), Bennett (p. 208) and Leclerc (p. 217).

Most of these introductions are short: a couple of sentences or a paragraph or two at the most. And virtually all are designed to *interest* the reader, for a bored reader may not even finish the essay, let alone like or understand it. Writing is fishing. You throw in the line. Your reader tastes the bait (your introduction), bites, is pulled through the stream of your argument, and — if the line of thought doesn't break — lands in your net.

You, the writer, may also be "hooked." Once you have hit upon a strong introduction, one that shows off the drama or importance of your topic, the beginning may carry you along with it. And once you get going, the idea embodied in your thesis statement may pull you through the essay, enabling you to write freely as one page leads to another. You may become less and less aware of your surroundings as you become more and more immersed in your subject. By the time you develop a good beginning, you may experience the act of writing the way one student described it: "At first I couldn't start, but then I couldn't stop."

The Body

An introduction to an essay is like your head: it may decide to go somewhere but it needs your body to take it there. The "body" of your essay has the main work to do: following the direction set by your introduction, and especially by your thesis statement, the body explains, illustrates, and sometimes attempts to prove your point. But if it ever ignores the direction set by the head, it ceases to do its job. Even the best of explanations, without a purpose, is like one of those unfortunate football players who completes a spectacular run to the wrong goal. On the other hand, we know that writing is discovery. The acts of writing and revising will sometimes take us in a direction better than the old one decided by the introduction. When that happens, correct not the body but the "head" — so the two can move together in the new direction.

The easiest way to keep a direction is to choose a pattern for your essay — and that is what much of this book is about. As you read and discuss the essays that follow, and as you write your own essays, trying out the patterns other writers use, you will explore a range of choices:

Narration: In simple time order, from the first event to the last event, tell a story that illustrates the point.

Example: give one in-depth example that explains the point, or a number of shorter examples.

Description: Recreate for your reader, through vivid language, your own or someone else's experience with the subject.

Cause and Effect: Explain by showing how one situation or event causes another.

Comparison and Contrast: Explain by showing how two things are like or unlike each other.

Analogy and Related Devices: In comparing two things, use the one to explain the other.

Classification: Make a point by dividing your subject into parts, then explaining each in turn.

Process Analysis: Show how something is done or how something happens.

Argumentation and Persuasion: Using any pattern that works, make your point through logic and/or emotion.

Seldom does one of these methods appear alone. A *process analysis*, for example, is usually told as a *narrative*. Here and there it may use *examples*, *description* or any of the other patterns to help make its point. But these combinations occur naturally, often without the writer's knowing it. In most cases the only form actually chosen by a writer is the main one that organizes the whole essay.

How do you choose the right form? Let the subject be your guide. In architecture, form follows function. Rather than cram an office into a preselected structure, a designer likes to begin with the function of that office. How much space does it need? What shape? What barriers and passageways between one section and another? What front to present to the world?

An essay is much the same: the needs of its subject, if you are open to them, can suggest a form. If the main idea is to explain what something is like, you will tend to choose *examples* and *description*. If the subject is unusual or little known, you may *compare* or *contrast*, or make an *analogy* with something the reader does know. If its parts seem important, you may examine them one by one through *classification*. When some other need is greater, you may use still another form. If you stay open to the subject, whatever it is, this process can be so natural that you *recognize* a form rather than *choose* it.

If the process is natural, then why study these forms at all? Well, architecture students certainly study different kinds of building design, so their future condominiums or shopping centres don't collapse and kill people. Fortunately, readers are not killed by poorly organized essays, but the principle is similar: if the writer has a conscious knowledge of all the possibilities, his or her arguments will be easier to build and will be less likely to collapse.

Consider the longer essay — say, a major report or research paper. A jumble of notes sits on your desk. They are in chaos. Even with brain-storming or freewriting, knowing your purpose, having the facts, and com-pleting a thesis statement, you don't know how to coordinate all those facts. First give the natural process its best chance: *sort all your notes into groups of related material,* using a pair of scissors if necessary to divide unre-lated points. When everything is in two stacks, or three stacks or five, let your mind work freely. How do these groups relate to each other? Does one contradict another? Are they all steps in a process or parts of a whole? Now add your conscious knowledge of the forms: Do you see *narration, example, description, cause and effect, comparison and contrast, analogy, classifi-cation* or *process analysis?* It is rare that one of these forms cannot supply a structure to support your argument.

Right now you are practising them one by one, as the students in architecture school study different structures one by one — so that in all your future writing you will have choices. And for now, you may be using the topics at the end of the readings, or the larger list of topics at the end of each chapter, because they are coordinated to go with the form you have just read and discussed. But in your future writing you will go a step further, making the match yourself between topic and form.

Yet, even when you are looking over 30 choices at the end of a chapter, you are exercising choice: spend a good long time to pick the topic that strikes you as most interesting, most significant — and therefore most motivating. It is writing about things that matter that will most increase your performance — now and always.

Transitions

We have mentioned the passageways inside a building. Without them an office would be useless: no one could move from one room to another to have meetings. Yet some essays are built without passageways. One point ends where another begins, without even a "then" or "therefore" or "however" or "finally" to join them. Readers then have to break down walls to follow thoughts from one room to the next.

Help your readers. *You* know why one point follows another, but do *they*? Make sure by supplying transitions: say "although" or "but" or "on the other hand"; say "because" or "as a result" or "since"; say "first" or "next" or "last"; say "for example" or "in conclusion." And when moving readers from one main part of your essay to the next, devote a full sentence or even a paragraph to the job (one good example is paragraph 10 of Doris Anderson's essay).

Your plan may already be the right one, setting your points in their most logical order. Now let that logic show: give your readers a door between every room.

The Closing

A recent piece of email humour says that a conclusion is "the place where you got tired of thinking." Well, if you got some sleep last night and had your coffee, that doesn't have to happen! Every essay does have an ending — the place where the writing stops. But just halting the words is not enough. A closing in some way has to be deliberate, has to achieve a worthwhile purpose, has to let your reader know that this is where you have chosen to stop. If you end at just any convenient spot, without engineering an effect to fit your ending, the essay may trail off or even fall flat. But as preachers, composers, playwrights and film directors know, a good closing can be even stronger than a good opening. How do the essays in this book come to a close? They use a variety of devices:

Reference to the opening: Repeating or restating something from the opening gives a sense of culmination, of having come full circle. See the openings and closings by Wente (pp. 64 and 66), Simic (pp. 73 and 75), Leah McLaren (pp. 122 and 124), Coffey (pp. 168 and 169), Rafi Mustafa (pp. 177 and 179), Lam (pp. 227 and 229), Kogawa (pp. 292 and 295) and Christy (pp. 315 and 316).

Contrast or reversal: This ironic device exploits the dramatic potential of the closing. See the opening and closing by Wente (pp. 64 and 66).

Question: A question and its answer, or a question calling for the reader's answer, is a common means of closing. See Connelly (p. 84), Leacock (p. 264) and Christy (p. 315).

Quotation: A good quotation, of either prose or poetry, can add authority and interest to a closing.

Transition signals: Words, phrases or sentences of transition commonly signal the closing. See Gabori (p. 25), Bidini (p. 55), Nestruck (p. 60), Pigott (p. 172) and Johnston (p. 212).

Revealing the significance: Showing the implications or importance of the subject makes for a strong closing. See Shields (p. 20), Gabori (p. 25), Suzuki (p. 127), Petrowski (p. 141), Layton (p. 164), Johnston (p. 212), Pitts (p. 236), Dobbs (p. 283), Atwood (p. 298) and Dallaire (p. 319).

Summary: About a fourth of the essays in this book give a summary, either alone or in combination with other closing techniques, but one that is always short. See McQuaig (p. 136), Anderson (p. 160), Bennett (p. 208), Koehl (p. 254), Lau (p. 258) and Hocking (p. 278).

Conclusion: Although "conclusion" is often a label for the closing in general, more accurately it is only one of many closing techniques — the drawing of a conclusion from the discussion in the essay. See Geddes (p. 34), Nestruck (p. 60), Pearson (p. 114), Leah McLaren (p. 122), Suzuki (p. 127), Naheed Mustafa (p. 132), Richler (p. 146), Traill (p. 187), Atwood (p. 298) and Klein (p. 303).

Prediction: A short look at the subject's future can very logically close a discussion of that subject's past or present. See Geddes (p. 34), Suzuki (p. 127), Petrowski (p. 141) and Pitts (p. 236). Sometimes discussing the future takes the form of a call to action (Layton, p. 164).

You have probably noticed that some authors are named more than once; closings, like openings, can exploit more than one technique. In fact, the more the better. Stay open to techniques that appear while you write, even as you construct a closing using a technique you have deliberately chosen.

Any of these choices will be stronger, though, when used with the most fundamental technique of all: building your whole essay toward a high point or *climax*. Put your points in order from least important to most important, from least useful to most useful, or from least dramatic to most dramatic. (Sometimes you will not know this order till late in the writing. Just use your software to cut and paste; or if you write by hand, cut drafts apart with scissors to rearrange them.) When everything leads up to that climax, you have set the stage for a closing that applies all the dramatic power of the final position.

When you get there, apply the force of that closing to a real message. Techniques used just for their own sake are cheap tricks. Do not waste them. Instead, use them to underline your basic message, to impress upon your audience one last and most convincing time that what you have to say is significant. Your closing, more than any other part of your essay, can send the reader away disappointed — or moved.

The Process: How Many Drafts?

We have discussed the act of writing as a process in which, rather than trying to "hit it right the first time," we follow a number of steps in the journey toward a good essay. The rest of this book develops that approach. After each selection you'll find an assignment called "Process in Writing" that draws on the essay you've just read, suggesting a related topic for an essay of your own. The main steps of the process are given, individualized for each topic.

Then at each chapter's end you'll find a whole page of essay topics, designed for practice in the form of organization you've just studied. After them, in each chapter, appear sections called "Process in Writing: Guidelines" which give the steps of a process designed for the organizational form you've just studied. Whether you write on an end-of-essay topic or end-of-chapter topic, remember that these steps are only *guidelines* to the process; choose the steps that seem best for each case.

Our "process" of writing is flexible; it is not a blueprint like the elaborate outlines our parents were made to construct. Above all, the process is "recursive" — that is, while you may begin with brainstorming or freewriting, go on to a discovery draft, revise your argument in a further draft or drafts, and finally edit for spelling and punctuation, you may also double back or jump ahead at any time. Studies show that professionals writing all kinds of documents in all kinds of fields do this. While generating their "discovery draft" they may stop here and there to improve a word choice or fix punctuation — changes that normally occur later. Or, while they are in the middle of editing or even proofreading, a fine new idea may come thundering out of their mind; so they may back up a few steps, write it out, and add it to their argument, maybe junking something else they had thought was good. All this is consistent with the reality that *we think while writing.*

Do feel free to transgress the process "guidelines" in these ways, but not so often that you undercut the advantages of the process itself. For example, in writing your discovery draft you may detect some weak sentence structure. If you must, stop here to edit. But better yet, why not just mark the spot (at the keyboard, insert something easy to see, such as several asterisks), then come back to fix things later? For now, let the material keep rolling out uninterrupted. Then later on, while you are editing or even proofreading, a whole new idea may arrive. You could go back even now to fit it in — but this means work, maybe even reorganization. Proceed only if it is a real improvement and if you have the time.

Finally, how many drafts are we talking about? The "guidelines" later on are sometimes vague on this point — because what do we mean by a draft? Is every new copy a draft? If you write by hand, or edit by hand on hard copy, only a good many improvements added between the lines and in the margins qualify the next version as a new draft. And if you edit directly on the screen, it is true that a new copy can be printed at any point, but the document is still not a further "draft" until some in-depth editing has been done, and many little changes — or sometimes large! — have been made. In either case, whether writing on paper or keyboarding, seldom can you produce a good essay in only one draft. On the other hand, a total of four or five or six drafts may be a sign of time wasted just recopying, not really revising. You can often reach a point at least close to your best writing performance in two or three real drafts.

When do you reach the journey's end? You will know when you get there. It is the point where your response to a significant topic has become so direct, so exact, so forceful, that at last you know exactly what you think. It is clear that you were writing for others, but at this moment it is even clearer that you were writing for yourself.

CP/Winnipeg Free Press (Wayne Glowacki)

"I remember a lot of togetherness, a lot of happiness while we lived in the bush. There's a very strong sense of family in the native community. . . ."

— *Carol Geddes, "Growing Up Native"*

Narration

AND THEN . . .

Telling a story, or *narrating*, is an appealing and natural way to convey information. Every time you tell a joke, trade gossip, invent a ghost story or tell a friend what you did on the weekend, you are narrating. In both speech and writing, telling a story can also be the most direct way to make a point. If your idea or opinion was formed by an experience, a clear account of that experience can help others understand and believe your point.

When Sylvia Fraser sets out to explain her troubled past, she chooses narrative. Everything begins smoothly one morning at the local rink, with young Fraser carving circles and eights on the new ice. Then more skaters come, to play tag and crack the whip. By the time young Joe Baker asks her to skate with him, she is growing nervous, then as he walks her home and starts to hold her hand, she panics — and we wonder why. When her own family house comes into view, she yanks her skates from Joe and exclaims "I've got to go — by myself." She rushes inside, then as her father roars "Don't slam the door!," her panic explodes. By now Fraser's message to us is taking shape: something is really wrong. Then as this section of narrative ends, Fraser implies what the problem is: she describes her rage pouring out of her "like lava, devastating everything in its path. It flows around my father, implacable in his asbestos armchair." (Of course we realize the chair

17

is not of asbestos; Fraser is using images to show the power of her father, the dreaded source of her troubles.) Finally she goes into convulsions, *"releasing the rage my other self can no longer control."* Whether we realize yet that hers is a story of sexual abuse, we see that the result is serious indeed: the actions of the father are pushing her towards mental illness.

Of course narratives don't have to be violent or tragic or even dramatic. When Carol Shields in "Encounter" tells of her memorable walk in the rain, sharing an umbrella with a total stranger in Tokyo, we quickly grasp her underlying point that communication is a universal desire.

Narration is such an all-purpose tool that many authors in other chapters of this book use it too. Emily Carr narrates three painting expeditions to coastal Native villages. Rafi Mustafa narrates his escape, at age six, from one country to another. Evelyn Lau narrates her quest for a place to live. Dr. Mark Bernstein narrates a brain operation. And General Roméo Dallaire narrates an incident that, for him and for us, sums up the tragedy of genocide in Rwanda. (See below for page numbers.)

Many *examples* given by writers are really bits of *narrative*. To show how Canadians love risky water sports (in "This Boat Is My Boat," p. 182), Drew Hayden Taylor takes us out on the waves of the Georgian Bay, briefly narrating an experience that makes the point very clear.

In some ways narrating is easy. For example, the only research Shields required was her own experience. And her basic plan of organization was no more complicated than the chronological order in which the events occurred. (A flashback to the past or a glance at the future may intervene, but basically a narrative is the easiest of all writing to organize.) Yet a narrative, like any form of writing, is built on choices.

Choice of scope: Time stretches infinitely toward both the past and future — but where does your narrative most logically begin and end? Include only parts that develop your point. Do you need to dwell on getting dressed, eating breakfast, brushing your teeth and catching the bus, on the day you became a Canadian citizen? Or did the event really begin when you opened the courthouse door? When facts about the past or future are needed, sketch them in briefly so you interrupt the least you can.

Choice of details: Which details count? Reject random or trivial ones and seek those that convey your main impression or idea. When on page 29 Sylvia Fraser tells us that "the ice at Gage Park is best in the morning when it's flint hard and glass-smooth," that "all is possible" and that "you carve out circles and eights, and nothing exists until you put it there," she is not just making small talk as she begins her narrative. Rather, the cool fresh start of skating on new ice prepares a deadly contrast to the rage that later erupts when her "other self" confronts her old problems. Which details are most vivid? Reject weak ones and select those that help the reader *see, hear, feel, smell* or *taste* — in other words those which, by appealing to the senses, help readers live the event.

Choice of connections: Readers love to be "swept along" by narrative. How is this effect achieved? Partly just through a good story. Time signals, though, increase the impact of any narrative. Like road signs for the driver, terms like "at first," "next," "then," "immediately," "suddenly," "later," "finally" and "at last" show the way and encourage progress. Use these road signs, and others like them, at every curve. Choose carefully, so signals speed the reader to your chosen destination.

So far we have discussed only the first-person narrative. There are many advantages to writing about yourself. You know your subject well (in fact, is there any subject you know better?), yet in writing about yourself you may better understand your own ideas and actions. Your vital interest in your subject will motivate the writing. And finally, readers appreciate the authenticity of a story told by the very person who lived the event.

But of course it's not always possible or desirable to limit the subject to oneself. A third-person narrative, which tells the actions of others, opens up many more possibilities. Only by writing about others can one discuss past eras, places one has never visited, and events one has never experienced. Kildare Dobbs does this masterfully in his narrative "The Scar," in Chapter 9. He was not in Hiroshima the day it crumbled beneath an atomic blast, but his research and his imagination almost make it seem so; more importantly, reading his narrative almost makes us feel we were there too.

Note: Many authors in later chapters combine narration with other ways to develop their material. For more examples, see these selections:

CAROL SHIELDS

Encounter

American by birth, Carol Shields came at age 22 to Canada and went on to be one of our nation's best-loved authors. Though she taught at several universities, notably the University of Manitoba, and though she often wrote on academic subjects — as in her acclaimed 2001 biography of Jane Austen — Shields also became a novelist gifted in showing the mysteries of everyday life. Drawing richly on her own experience as wife and as mother of five children, and beginning to publish only after the children were all in school, Shields had a gift for uncovering what The Guardian *called "the dramatic in the domestic." Believing there is no such thing as "ordinary" life, Shields breathed such force into her everyday characters that to thousands of readers they came alive on the page. She also wrote and published poetry, but it is her fiction that raised her to the first rank of our authors. Her first novel,* Small Ceremonies, *appeared in 1976, then in 1987 her novel* Swann. *But it was in 1993 that she stunned the critics and won both the Pulitzer Prize in America and the Governor General's Award in Canada with* The Stone Diaries. *Many thousands of readers in 17 languages around the world followed its main character, Daisy Goodwill, through each stage of life as a woman in her society. Then in 1997 Shields depicted another "ordinary" character, this time a man, in her best-selling novel* Larry's Party. *The last novel before her untimely death in 2003 was* Unless. *Our own selection, from Katherine Govier's anthology* Without a Guide: Contemporary Women's Travel Adventures, *is autobiography — and, as always, examines the ordinary things of life, which in the vision of Carol Shields become remarkable.*

1   I was in Tokyo to attend a conference, one of a thousand or so delegates — and that probably was my problem: the plasticized name card and the logo of my organization marked me as someone who desired only to be cheerfully accommodated.

2   The allotted two weeks had passed. A single day in Japan remained, and at last I admitted to myself that I was disappointed. The terrible banality of tourist desire invaded me like a kind of flu. Walking the broad, busy boulevards, I caught myself looking too eagerly, too preciously, for minor cultural manifestations — the charming way the bank teller bowed when presenting me with my bundle of cash, the colourful plastic food in the windows of restaurants; these were items I was able to record in my travel journal, touching them up in the way of desperate travellers, shaping them into humorous or appreciative annotation on the Japanese people and the exotic city they inhabited.

But Tokyo with its hotels and subways and department stores was a modern industrial complex. Its citizens went to work in the morning, earned money, and travelled home again at night. These homes, to be sure, were impenetrable to me, but the busy working days bore the same rhythms as those found in any large North American city. The traffic noises, the scent of pollution, and the civility of people in the street made me think of — home. **3**

I had hoped for more; what traveller doesn't? Travelling is expensive, exhausting, and often lonely — the cultural confusion, the acres of concrete, the bitter coffee, the unreadable maps, and the rates of exchange that are almost always unfavourable. And then, like a punishment at the end of the traveller's day, there waits a solitary room, and a bed that, however comfortable, is not your bed. What makes all this worth the effort is the shock of otherness that arrives from time to time, rattling loose your bearings and making you suddenly alert to an altered world. But Tokyo was determinedly polite, fulsomely western, a city with a bland, smiling face, ready to welcome me not on its terms but on my own. **4**

I already know that the banquet that was to conclude the conference would be a model of French cuisine. Seven courses, seven different wines. No rice, no noodles, no sushi, no hot radish. It was to be held at the famous Imperial Hotel, which was fifteen or twenty minutes' walk from the somewhat less expensive hotel where I was staying. **5**

I started out in good time. It was a soft spring evening, and the thought of a leisurely stroll was appealing. I would be able to look around one last time, breathe in a final impression that I could perhaps test against my accumulated disappointment, acquiring some fresh point of perception with which to colour and preserve my Japanese sojourn. **6**

At that moment it began to rain. A few drops at first, then it came down in earnest, spotting the silk dinner suit I was wearing and threatening to flatten my carefully arranged hair. I looked about for a taxi or a roof to shelter under, but neither presented itself. The only thing to do, I decided, was to run as quickly as I could the rest of the way. **7**

But a tall man was standing directly in front of me, a man with an umbrella. He was smiling tentatively, and gesturing, and his mouth was moving. But what was he saying? I wasn't sure, since the accent was unfamiliar, but it sounded like "Imperial Hotel?" With a question mark behind it. "Yes," I said, nodding and speaking with great deliberation, "Imperial Hotel," and at that he lifted his umbrella slightly, and invited me under. **8**

The umbrella was large and black, resolutely standard, the sort of umbrella found in every city or backwater of the world. "Thank you," I said in Japanese — the only phrase I had mastered — but he only repeated what he had said earlier: "Imperial Hotel?" And tipped his head quizzically in an eastward direction. "Yes," I said again. And we began walking. **9**

10   It seemed only polite to make an effort at conversation. Where was he from? Was he with the conference? Was he a stranger in Japan like myself? He shook his head, uncomprehending, and released a shower of words in an unidentifiable language. Now it was my turn to shake my head. After that, smiling, we continued our walk in a contained silence, as though we had each admitted to the other that language was absurd, that rhetoric was a laughable formality that could be set aside for this brief interval.

11   Suddenly careless of social taboos, and because it's difficult for a short woman to walk with a tall man under an umbrella, I took the stranger's arm. (Thinking about this later, I theorized that he must have gestured minutely with his elbow, inviting my intimacy.) Now, arms linked, we were able to walk together smoothly, stepping over and around the puddles without losing our stride, pausing at traffic lights, stepping down from curbs.

12   We had arrived quickly at our congenial gliding pace, left foot, right foot, left foot again, a forward rhythm with a very slight sideways roll like a kind of swimming. Our mutually constrained tongues, the sound of the pelting rain, and our random possession of a random moment in time, seemed to seal us in a temporary vacuum that had nothing to do with Japan, nor with gender or age or with Hollywood notions about men and women walking in the rain. This was good walking, though, I knew that much — walking that transcended mere movement. Hypnotic walking. Walking toward the unimaginable. And I found myself wanting it to go on and on.

13   But there we suddenly were, at the brilliantly lit entrance of the Imperial Hotel, caught in a throng of people arriving and departing, people who had come from every corner of the globe, and trailing after them their separate languages, their lives, their ribbons of chance connection. The stranger with the umbrella abruptly disappeared. I looked around for him but was unable to recall his face, how he had been dressed. One minute he was there and the next minute he'd vanished, leaving me alone with that primary shiver of mystery that travellers, if they're lucky, hope to hang on to: the shock of the known and the unknown colliding in space.

● ●

Explorations:

Carol Shields,
   The Stone Diaries
   Larry's Party
   Swann
   Coming to Canada (poems)
http://oprf.com/Shields
http://schwinger.harvard.edu/~terning/bios/Shields.html

http://www.uwinnipeg.ca/~morton/Telecourse/Stone_Diaries/
eb_on_carol_shields.htm
http://www.nwpassages.com/author_profile.asp?au_id=1234
http://www.bookreporter.com/authors/au-shields-carol.asp
http://www.cbc.ca/news/obit/shields_carol

Structure:

1. This *narrative* is really two in one: a summary of the author's stay in Tokyo so far, then a real-time narrative of her "encounter" with the stranger. How does the first prepare us for the second? Where does the first end and the second begin? Which of the two phases of *narrative* is more powerful, and why?
2. How does Shields' two-part structure of *narrative* exploit the device of *contrast*?

Style:

1. Carol Shields is one of the nation's best-loved novelists. Does this non-fiction selection seem at all in the vein of fiction? If so, how?
2. Does Shields' STYLE excite admiration, or is it more like a clear window that shows us the events? Which approach do you prefer when you read? When you write? Why?
3. Point out the best FIGURES OF SPEECH in paragraph 12. Also analyze the power of the images that close this selection.

Ideas for Discussion and Writing:

1. "Encounter" narrates a small event, two strangers sharing an umbrella. In what ways, though, may this event be larger than it seems? What truths may it reveal about our lives in general?
2. Many writers seek sensational topics such as disaster, murder, adventure and romance. Were you attracted, though, by Shields' modest tale of "walking toward the unimaginable" (par. 12) with a stranger? If so, what does this show about focus and development in writing?
3. The two strangers of "Encounter" are thrown together by rain. When have you had close communication with strangers through events such as floods or earthquakes; ice, rain or snow storms; accidents; or power blackouts? *Narrate* an incident to the class. What does it show about life?
4. Shields discovers "the terrible banality of tourist desire" (par. 2) in a far place that turns out to be "fulsomely western, a city with a bland, smiling face, ready to welcome me not on its terms but on my own" (par. 4). Why do we become tourists? Why do we seek far places? Are they disappearing? If so, why?

5. Can you communicate, as Shields did, with people who do not speak your language? If your family has immigrated, can your own grandparents speak your language? Suggest techniques to the class.

6. **PROCESS IN WRITING:** *Shields' closing words describe the mystery that travellers seek, "the shock of the known and the unknown colliding in space." Freewrite on this topic for at least five minutes, never stopping the movement of your pen or keyboard, remembering a time when you felt this "shock." Now write the quick discovery draft of a* narrative *based on this material. Let your words cool off for a day, then take stock: Does your introduction prepare us for the story? If not, add. Have you described the persons and the place well enough to help us live the story too? If not, add SENSE IMAGES. Do TRANSITIONS speed us on? If not, add. And does the action sweep us towards a CLIMAX? If not, rearrange. Last of all, check for spelling and punctuation before you print off your best version.*

Note: See also the Topics for Writing at the end of this chapter.

GEORGE GABORI

Coming of Age in Putnok

Translated from the Hungarian by Eric Johnson with George Faludy

For much of his life George Gabori (1924–1997) drove taxi and ran a cab company in Toronto. Like many immigrants to this country, though, he had a past he would never forget. Gabori (pronounced Gábori) was born to a Jewish family in the village of Putnok, Hungary. His childhood was happy but short, for when the Germans overran Hungary and threatened the existence of the Jews, he joined the resistance. He led daring sabotage raids, blowing up German trains, till the Gestapo sent him, still a teenager, to a concentration camp. When later the Russians drove out the Germans, Gabori was as troublesome for the communists as he had been for the Nazis: soon after his release from Dachau, he was breaking rocks in a notorious Soviet labour camp. Always outspoken in favour of democracy, Gabori played a part in the 1956 Revolution, then escaped from Hungary to Canada, a "decent land," where years later he wrote his memoirs in Hungarian. With the help of Hungarian poet George Faludy, Eric Johnson condensed and translated the enormous manuscript, and in 1981 it was published. Since then, When Evils Were Most Free *has become a minor Canadian classic and has been translated into many other languages. Our selection is its opening passage.*

When I was nine years old my father, victorious after a long argument with my grandfather, took me out of our town's only *cheder* and enrolled me in its only public school. Overnight I was transported from the world of Hebrew letters and monotonously repeated texts to the still stranger world of Hungarian letters, patriotic slogans and walls covered with maps. 1

Grandfather rolled his eyes and predicted trouble, but it seemed he was wrong. I sat beside a boy my own age named Tivadar, a gentile — everybody was a gentile in that school except me. Tivadar and I got along famously until, after two or three weeks, he approached me in the schoolyard one day and asked me if it was true what the others were saying, that "we" had murdered Jesus. 2

Strange to tell — for this was 1933 and we were in Hungary — I had never heard about this historical episode, and I left Tivadar amicably enough, promising to ask my father about it. We met again the next morning and I told him what I had learned: that the Romans had killed Jesus, and that anyway Jesus had been a Jew, like me, so what did it matter to the Christians? 3

4   "That's not true," said Tivadar menacingly.

5   "My father does not lie," I replied.

6   By now a crowd had gathered around us and there was nothing for it but to fight it out. There were cheers and laughter as Tivadar hit me in the nose before I got my jacket off. It was not the first time I had tasted my own blood, but it was the first time a Christian had made it flow. Tivadar was flushed with pleasure and excitement at the applause and not at all expecting it when I lashed out with my fist and sent him sprawling backward on the cobbles. The crowd of boys groaned and shouted to Tivadar to get up and kill the Jew, but poor Tivadar did not move. Frightened, I grabbed my jacket and shoved my way through the crowd stunned into silence by this overturning of the laws of nature.

7   They were silent at home too when I told them what had happened. My father sent for me from his office in the afternoon, and I entered cap in hand. He always wore a braided Slovak jacket at work and looked more like a peasant than a Jewish wine merchant.

8   "Well, who started it?" asked my father, wearing an expression I had never seen on his face before. I was not at all frightened.

9   "He did. I told him what you said about Jesus and he challenged me."

10   My father clamped his teeth on his cigar and nodded, looking right through me.

11   "Jews don't fight," he finally said.

12   "Then why did you put me in a Christian school?" I asked in a loud, outraged whine.

13   "That's why I put you there, my son," he said at last, then swept me up and kissed me on the forehead. "You're learning fast; only next time don't hit him quite so hard."

14   Then he sent me out quickly and I stopped on the landing, startled to hear loud, whooping, solitary laughter coming out of my father's office.

• •

Explorations:

George Gabori, *When Evils Were Most Free*

George Faludy, *My Happy Days in Hell*

Adam Horvath, "Lives Lived: George Gabori," *The Globe and Mail*, December 7,1997

Anne Frank, *The Diary of Anne Frank*

Anne Michaels, *Fugitive Pieces*

http://www.bullying.org

http://en.wikipedia.org/wiki/1956_Hungarian_Revolution

http://ftp.nizkor.org/ftp.py?bibliographies/biblio.04

Structure:

1. What overall pattern organizes this selection?
2. Point out at least ten words or phrases in this *narrative* that signal the flow of time.
3. Scrutinize Gabori's opening paragraph: has he prepared us for the selection? Name every fact revealed about the setting and about the author.

Style:

1. How economical of words is this opening passage of Gabori's life story? How clearly does it reveal the author and his times? Would you predict with any confidence his character or fate as an adult? Do these pages tempt you to read the whole book? Why or why not?
2. *When Evils Were Most Free* is translated and condensed from the Hungarian original. Does this separate us from Gabori's thoughts? How exact can translations be? If you are bilingual or multilingual, how precisely can you put sayings from one language into another? Can translator Eric Johnson even be seen as a co-author of these pages?
3. In paragraph 6 Gabori states, "It was not the first time I had tasted my own blood. . . ." What makes this image strong?

Ideas for Discussion and Writing:

1. What exactly is the "overturning of the laws of nature" at the end of paragraph 6?
2. Was Gabori's father right to move the boy from a Hebrew *cheder* to a public school? In disproving the STEREOTYPE that "Jews don't fight" (par. 11), has the boy learned a worthy lesson? Or does he merely copy the worst traits of his opponents, thereby becoming like them?
3. Every ethnic group in Canada — including English Canadians — is a minority. Has your minority been persecuted here? If you have been a victim, *narrate* an actual incident, including your own reaction. Like Gabori, give many specifics.
4. In taunting and hitting his Jewish classmate, Tivadar is a bully. How much bullying have you seen in your own school years? Visit the *www.bullying.org* Canadian Web site given above (described on the CBC's *National* as one of the best sites in the world for children). Choose one of the many incidents described by victims. Summarize it to the class, then tell how you yourself would have reacted had you been the victim.
5. What are autobiographies for? What do you think writing your own life story would do for you? For others?

6. **PROCESS IN WRITING:** *Write a chapter of your own autobiography. Select one key incident in your life, then freewrite on it for a few minutes. Look over what you have produced, keep the best of it, and from this write your first draft. Have you begun and ended at just the right places,* narrating *the event itself but omitting parts that don't matter? Enrich the next draft with more IMAGES and* examples, *following Gabori's lead. Now share your* narrative *with a group of classmates, and adjust whatever does not communicate with this AUDIENCE. Finally, read your narrative aloud, with expression, to the whole class.*

Note: See also the Topics for Writing at the end of this chapter.

SYLVIA FRASER

My Other Self*

"Writing is healing," says Sylvia Fraser. Born in 1935 in Hamilton, Ontario, Fraser by the 1980s was an award-winning journalist and author of five novels (Pandora, 1972; The Candy Factory, 1975; A Casual Affair, 1978; The Emperor's Virgin, 1980; and Berlin Solstice, 1984). *But signs of trouble had also appeared. Her seemingly happy marriage had fallen apart. Her fiction grew darker in vision and increasingly filled with sexual violence. Then the dam broke: in 1983, Fraser consciously recalled what her other self had never forgot: that from her kindergarten year till almost the end of high school, her father had abused her sexually. Now it was clear how her novel* Berlin Solstice *had acquired its intimate and chilling insight into Nazi Germany. As Fraser put it, "Being victimized and essentially tortured by my father, I identified with the Jews. In trying to understand how the Germans could have done what they did, I was trying to understand my father — and I was preparing myself for my own truth"* (The Globe and Mail, *June 4, 1988). The book that followed,* My Father's House: A Memoir of Incest and of Healing *(1987), startled both the critics and the public with its honesty, clarity and emotion. The memoir not only helped "heal" its author, but ignited public debate on a hidden social problem, encouraging many other incest victims to deal with their past. From this book comes our selection, which dramatizes the victim's "other self" emerging. More recent works by Fraser include* The Book of Strange *(1992);* Ancestral Suitcase *(novel, 1996);* A Woman's Place *(anthology, 1997);* The Rope in the Water: A Pilgrimage to India *(2001); and* The Green Labyrinth: A Journey to the Amazon *(2003).*

The ice at Gage Park is best in the morning when it's flint-hard and glass-smooth. All is possible. You carve out circles and eights, and nothing exists until you put it there. Sometimes you just race around the rink, your legs sliding like they're on elastic bands, with your breath whistling through your teeth like steam from a locomotive, faster and faster. 1

Soon it's noon. The rink fills with kids in red and blue parkas playing tag or crack the whip. 2

"Hi!" It's Joe Baker from school. "Wanna skate?" 3

---

* Editor's title.

4   I prefer to play tag, but I don't want to hurt Joe's feelings and, besides, if I say no to him, maybe Perry Lord won't ask me. Such delicate weights and balances are the stuff of predating, as I am coming to know it. Giving my hand to Joe with a bright paste-on smile, I slow my racing pace to his stodgy rhythm. The sound system squawks out "Oh, How We Danced on the Night We Were Wed" as we skate around and around, like the needle on the record. Joe's silence rattles me. I make chattery conversation. "Did you see The Thing from the Deep?"

5   By bad luck, the record never ends. The needle hits a crack, repeats "we vowed our true love we vowed our true love we vowed our true love," then jerks into "Don't Fence Me In." Now Joe links arms, forcing me to even greater intimacy and an even slower beat, *and making my other self very, very nervous. She cannot bear to be held or confined.* The game of tag is breaking up. Joe speaks his only sentence, and it is a lethal one. "Can I ah take you home if ah you're not doing anything?"

6   At the word "home" a cold shiver passes through me. I ransack my head for an explanation for the unpleasant way I am feeling and, failing that, an excuse. "I'll check with Arlene. We came together."

7   The clubhouse is crowded and noisy and steamy, as always. We jostle for a place on the splintery benches closest to the wood stove. The air stinks of charred wool — someone's icy mittens left too long on top. Joe helps me off with my skates, then unlaces his own while I inform Arlene. "Joe wants to take me home."

8   "He's cute. You have all the luck."

9   I study Joe through the lens of Arlene's enthusiasm: brown cowlick in wet spikes from his cap, earnest face bent over the task of knotting skate laces. Cute? Now that I know how I'm supposed to feel, I am reassured. Well, maybe.

10   We leave the rink just as the gang takes off in a gossipy pinwheel for the Kozy Korner. I think about suggesting we go too, but I'm afraid Joe doesn't have any money and I don't want to seem like a gold digger. Perry Lord tosses a snowball at Cooky Castle but hits Arlene instead. Tonya Philpott zings one back overhand, the way a boy would. I yearn to take up the challenge, but being with a boy obliges me to conform to more ladylike standards. Trapped, I stick my fists in my pockets.

11   Crunch crunch crunch. Skates knotted over Joe's shoulder, we trudge through the chalky snow. I've already told Joe the plot of The Thing from the Deep, and since I saw it uptown it wasn't a double feature. The silence lengthens with the shadows. Joe doesn't seem to mind. I do.

12   "Arlene says you got a hundred in arithmetic."

13   "Yeah. So did you."

14   "Yeah. But our test was easier."

15   I make the mistake of taking my hand out of my pocket to brush a snowflake. Joe commandeers it. *My other self panics.* How long before I can brush another snowflake and get it back without seeming rude? As I am working out the etiquette of this, two dogs rush the season by

attempting to "do it" on the path in front of us. *My other self slips toward hysteria.* I burst into giggles. The blood rises up Joe's protruding ears. He fumbles with his backside: "Are you laughing at the rip in my ski pants?"

"No, it isn't that." But I can't stop giggling. 16

"Joker Nash cut it with his skate." 17

"Honest, I didn't even notice." I stifle more giggles in a sneeze. 18
"Ah-choo!"

We are approaching my house. The giggles stop. Now my anxiety 19
grows so intense I'm afraid I'll faint. Snatching my hand from Joe's, I pick up a stick and drag it ping ping ping along the fence around St. Cecilia's Home the way I used to as a kid, pretending this is the most important thing in the world. How can I let you hold my hand when I am busy doing this?

We turn the corner. Now I see it — a sour-cream frame listing with 20
snow like a milk bottle with the cap frozen off. *Home.* I stop, rooted to the spot. For reasons I can't explain, it's essential that Joe go no farther. I reach for my skates. "I live only a couple of doors away."

"I don't mind. I'll carry them to the —" 21

"No!" I yank the skates from Joe's neck, almost beheading him. "I've 22
got to go — by myself."

Again Joe blushes from his neck through his ears. "Is it because of the 23
rip in my ski pants? You don't want your parents to see —"

"No!" Then more humanely: "Honest. It has nothing to do with you." 24
Pushing past him, I sprint for my father's house, clearing the steps in a single bound. As I open the storm door, the wind catches it.

"Don't slam the door!" roars my father from his armchair. 25

My other self bursts into hysterical weeping. 26

"What's wrong?" asks my mother. 27

Again, I find myself overcome by an emotion for which I must find a 28
reason. Hurling my skates at her feet, I shout: "Why do I have to wear these old things? They hurt my feet."

Wiping her hands on her apron, my mother rallies. "Those skates 29
were new last winter."

"Secondhand from Amity. You said I could have new skates for 30
Christmas."

"You needed other things." By now I'm racked with weeping I can't 31
control. Not about the skates, though I hear a voice I hardly recognize go on and on about them. "I hate these skates." Rage pours out of me like lava, devastating everything in its path. It flows around my father, implacable in his asbestos armchair.

It's a relief to be sent upstairs without supper. Flinging myself onto my 32
bed, I pound the pillow till my body is seized with convulsions, *releasing the rage my other self can no longer control.*

• •

Explorations:

Sylvia Fraser,
> *My Father's House*
> *Pandora*
> *The Ancestral Suitcase*

Ruth Kempe, *The Common Secret: Sexual Abuse of Children and Adolescents*
Judy Steed, *Our Little Secret: Confronting Child Sexual Abuse in Canada*
http://www.wier.ca/sfraser.html
http://www.casac.ca/issues/myths_incest.htm
http://canada.justice.gc.ca/en/ps/fm/childafs.html

Structure:

1. Does Fraser *narrate* "My Other Self" in straight chronological order?
2. This sequence begins with ice (par. 1) and closes with lava (par. 31). Explain how Fraser's progression of IMAGES parallels her progression of emotion. How do these progressions add force to her narrative?
3. What does Fraser achieve by putting all references to her "other self" in italics?

Style:

1. If the events on these pages occurred when Fraser was young, why does she *narrate* in the present tense? Would "My Other Self" be stronger or weaker in the past tense? Why?
2. Where does Fraser use IMAGES that appeal to our senses of sight, touch, hearing and smell? Point out one of each.
3. In paragraph 9 our narrator says, "I study Joe through the lens of Arlene's enthusiasm. . . ." Point out two more METAPHORS in this selection. In paragraph 31 she says, "Rage pours out of me like lava. . . ." Point out two more SIMILES. What do these FIGURES OF SPEECH contribute to the total effect?

Ideas for Discussion and Writing:

1. Fraser stated in an interview, "I think of child abuse as being the AIDS of the emotional world. You cripple that child's emotional system so it can't deal with life" (*The Globe and Mail,* June 4, 1988). Point out all the ways in which our selection dramatizes her comment.
2. Why does Fraser refer to her "other self" in the third person as "she"? What does this usage seem to imply about young Fraser's mental state?
3. Some studies suggest that sexual abuse is an epidemic, with as many as one of every three or four children victimized. The place of these

offences has ranged from the home, to the hockey arena, to the orphanage, to the residential schools where First Nations children were once sent. What could be done to decrease such crimes? To rehabilitate the victims? To rehabilitate the offenders?

4. Fraser traces her fascination with the Holocaust to her feelings about her father (see the introduction to this selection). How fully does our relationship to our parents become a model for our relationship to the world? For example, do children of authoritarian parents grow up to resent authority in the form of employers or government?

5. Have you shared Fraser's experience of writing as healing? Analyze how the process might occur when we write an angry letter to tear up, when we send a letter to the editor, when we write a poem, or when we keep a personal journal.

6. **PROCESS IN WRITING:** *Think of a time when your own emotions carried you away. Experience it again by freewriting, never stopping the motion of your pen or keyboard for several minutes. Use the present tense, as Fraser does, to heighten the immediacy of your account. Now* narrate *a first draft, incorporating the best of your prewriting. In the next draft add more SENSE IMAGES and FIGURES OF SPEECH (remembering the "ice" and "lava" of "My Other Self"). Have you moved the action along with time signals such as "then," "next," "suddenly" or "at last"? Have you trimmed out deadwood? If you report dialogue, have you used quotation marks, and have you begun a new paragraph for each change of speaker? Finally, test your prose aloud before writing the final version.*

Note: See also the Topics for Writing at the end of this chapter.

CAROL GEDDES

Growing Up Native

Since Carol Geddes tells her own life story in the narrative that follows, we will not repeat it all here. Born into the security of her Tlingit First Nations family in the wilds of the Yukon, she was six when she first knew her country's majority culture and began to see the problems it causes for Native people. Since then she has spent her life integrating these two worlds. She celebrates the current "renaissance" of interest in Native culture, yet also values the rest of North American life. "We need our culture," she writes, "but there's no reason why we can't preserve it and have an automatic washing machine and a holiday in Mexico, as well." Hers is a success story. Despite the obstacles, she completed a university degree in English and philosophy (Carleton, 1978), did graduate studies in communications at McGill, and is today a successful filmmaker and spokesperson for her people. In addition to her films Place for Our People *(1981),* Doctor, Lawyer, Indian Chief *(National Film Board, 1986), and* Picturing a People: George Johnson, Tlingit Photographer *(NFB, 1997), she has produced some 25 videos on the lives and culture of aboriginal people in Canada. Geddes is a producer at Studio One of the National Film Board, and has taught other filmmakers at the Banff Centre for the Arts. She has also been a Director of the Yukon Human Rights Commission, the Yukon Heritage Resources Board, and the Women's Television Network Foundation, and is the first Northerner and first Native Person to be a Director of the Canada Council. In her spare time she does wilderness hiking and fishing, in the Yukon where she lives. Our selection, from* HomeMaker's *Magazine of October 1990, won the National Magazine Awards Foundation Silver Award.*

1   I remember it was cold. We were walking through a swamp near our home in the Yukon bush. Maybe it was fall and moose-hunting season. I don't know. I think I was about four years old at the time. The muskeg was too springy to walk on, so people were taking turns carrying me — passing me from one set of arms to another. The details about where we were are vague, but the memory of those arms and the feeling of acceptance I had is one of the most vivid memories of my childhood. It didn't matter who was carrying me — there was security in every pair of arms. That response to children is typical of the native community. It's the first thing I think of when I cast my mind back to the Yukon bush, where I was born and lived with my family.

2   I was six years old when we moved out of the bush, first to Teslin, where I had a hint of the problems native people face, then to Whitehorse, where there was unimaginable racism. Eventually I

34

moved to Ottawa and Montreal, where I further discovered that to grow up native in Canada is to feel the sting of humiliation and the boot of discrimination. But it is also to experience the enviable security of an extended family and to learn to appreciate the richness of the heritage and traditions of a culture most North Americans have never been lucky enough to know. As a film-maker, I have tried to explore these contradictions, and our triumph over them, for the half-million aboriginals who are part of the tide of swelling independence of the First Nations today.

But I'm getting ahead of myself. If I'm to tell the story of what it's like to grow up native in northern Canada, I have to go back to the bush where I was born, because there's more to my story than the hurtful stereotyping that depicts Indian people as drunken welfare cases. Our area was known as 12-mile (it was 12 miles from another tiny village). There were about 40 people living there — including 25 kids, eight of them my brothers and sisters — in a sort of family compound. Each family had its own timber plank house for sleeping, and there was one large common kitchen area with gravel on the ground and a tent frame over it. Everybody would go there and cook meals together. In summer, my grandmother always had a smudge fire going to smoke fish and tan moose hides. I can remember the cosy warmth of the fire, the smell of good food, and always having someone to talk to. We kids had built-in playmates and would spend hours running in the bush, picking berries, building rafts on the lake and playing in abandoned mink cages.

One of the people in my village tells a story about the day the old lifestyle began to change. He had been away hunting in the bush for about a month. On his way back, he heard a strange sound coming from far away. He ran up to the crest of a hill, looked over the top of it and saw a bulldozer. He had never seen or heard of such a thing before and he couldn't imagine what it was. We didn't have magazines or newspapers in our village, and the people didn't know that the Alaska Highway was being built as a defence against a presumed Japanese invasion during the Second World War. That was the beginning of the end of the Teslin Tlingit people's way of life. From that moment on, nothing turned back to the way it was. Although there were employment opportunities for my father and uncles, who were young men at the time, the speed and force with which the Alaska Highway was rammed through the wilderness caused tremendous upheaval for Yukon native people.

It wasn't as though we'd never experienced change before. The Tlingit Nation, which I belong to, arrived in the Yukon from the Alaskan coast around the turn of the century. They were the middlemen and women between the Russian traders and the Yukon inland Indians. The Tlingit gained power and prestige by trading European products such as metal goods and cloth for the rich and varied furs so much in fashion in Europe. The Tlingit controlled Yukon trading because they controlled the trading routes through the high mountain passes. When trading ceased to be an effective means of survival, my grandparents began raising wild mink in cages. Mink prices were really high before and during the war, but afterwards the prices went plunging down. So, although the mink pens were still there when I was a little girl, my father mainly worked on highway construction and hunted in the bush. The Yukon was then, and still is in some ways, in a transitional period — from living off the land to getting into a European wage-based economy.

6   As a young child, I didn't see the full extent of the upheaval. I remember a lot of togetherness, a lot of happiness while we lived in the bush. There's a very strong sense of family in the native community, and a fondness for children, especially young children. Even today, it's like a special form of entertainment if someone brings a baby to visit. That sense of family is the one thing that has survived all the incredible difficulties native people have had. Throughout a time of tremendous problems, the extended family system has somehow lasted, providing a strong circle for people to survive in. When parents were struggling with alcoholism or had to go away to find work, when one of the many epidemics swept through the community, or when a marriage broke up and one parent left, aunts, uncles and grandparents would try to fill those roles. It's been very important to me in terms of emotional support to be able to rely on my extended family. There are still times when such support keeps me going.

7   Life was much simpler when we lived in the bush. Although we were poor and wore the same clothes all year, we were warm enough and had plenty to eat. But even as a youngster, I began to be aware of some of the problems we would face later on. Travelling missionaries would come and impose themselves on us, for example. They'd sit at our campfire and read the Bible to us and lecture us about how we had to live a Christian life. I remember being very frightened by stories we heard about parents sending their kids away to live with white people who didn't have any children. We thought those people were mean and that if we were bad, we'd be sent away, too. Of course, that was when social workers were scooping up native children and adopting them out to white families in the south. The consequences were usually disastrous for the children who were taken away — alienation, alcoholism and suicide, among other things. I knew some of those kids. The survivors are still struggling to recover.

8   The residential schools were another source of misery for the kids. Although I didn't have to go, my brothers and sisters were there. They told stories about having their hair cut off in case they were carrying head lice, and of being forced to do hard chores without enough food to eat. They were told that the Indian culture was evil, that Indian people were bad, that their only hope was to be Christian. They had to stand up and say things like "I've found the

Lord," when a teacher told them to speak. Sexual abuse was rampant in the residential school system.

By the time we moved to Whitehorse, I was excited about the idea of living in what I thought of as a big town. I'd had a taste of the outside world from books at school in Teslin (a town of 250 people), and I was tremendously curious about what life was like. I was hungry for experiences such as going to the circus. In fact, for a while, I was obsessed with stories and pictures about the circus, but then when I was 12 and saw my first one, I was put off by the condition and treatment of the animals.

Going to school in Whitehorse was a shock. The clash of native and white values was confusing and frightening. Let me tell you a story. The older boys in our community were already accomplished hunters and fishermen, but since they had to trap beaver in the spring and hunt moose in the fall, and go out trapping in the winter as well, they missed a lot of school. We were all in one classroom and some of my very large teenage cousins had to sit squeezed into little desks. These guys couldn't read very well. We girls had been in school all along, so, of course, we were better readers. One day the teacher was trying to get one of the older boys to read. She was typical of the teachers at that time, insensitive and ignorant of cultural complexities. In an increasingly loud voice, she kept commanding him to "Read it, read it." He couldn't. He sat there completely still, but I could see that he was breaking into a sweat. The teacher then said, "Look, she can read it," and she pointed to me, indicating that I should stand up and read. For a young child to try to show up an older boy is wrong and totally contrary to native cultural values, so I refused. She told me to stand up and I did. My hands were trembling as I held my reader. She yelled at me to read and when I didn't she smashed her pointing stick on the desk to frighten me. In terror, I wet my pants. As I stood there fighting my tears of shame, she said I was disgusting and sent me home. I had to walk a long distance through the bush by myself to get home. I remember feeling this tremendous confusion, on top of my humiliation. We were always told the white teachers knew best, and so we had to do whatever they said at school. And yet I had a really strong sense of receiving mixed messages about what I was supposed to do in the community and what I was supposed to do at school.

Pretty soon I hated school. Moving to a predominantly white high school was even worse. We weren't allowed to join anything the white kids started. We were the butt of jokes because of our secondhand clothes and moose meat sandwiches. We were constantly being rejected. The prevailing attitude was that Indians were stupid. When it was time to make course choices in class — between typing and science, for example — they didn't even ask the native kids, they just put us all in typing. You get a really bad image of yourself in a situation like that. I bought into it. I thought we were awful. The whole experience was terribly

9

10

11

undermining. Once, my grandmother gave me a pretty little pencil box. I walked into the classroom one day to find the word "squaw" carved on it. That night I burned it in the wood stove. I joined the tough crowd and by the time I was 15 years old, I was more likely to be leaning against the school smoking a cigarette than trying to join in. I was burned out from trying to join the system. The principal told my father there was no point in sending me back to school so, with a Grade 9 education, I started to work at a series of menial jobs.

12   Seven years later something happened to me that would change my life forever. I had moved to Ottawa with a man and was working as a waitress in a restaurant. One day, a friend invited me to her place for coffee. While I was there, she told me she was going to university in the fall and showed me her reading list. I'll never forget the minutes that followed. I was feeling vaguely envious of her and, once again, inferior. I remember taking the paper in my hand, seeing the books on it and realizing, Oh, my God, I've read these books! It hit me like a thunderclap. I was stunned that books I had read were being read in university. University was for white kids, not native kids. We were too stupid, we didn't have the kind of mind it took to do those things. My eyes moved down the list, and my heart started beating faster and faster as I suddenly realized I could go to university, too!

13   My partner at the time was a loving supportive man who helped me in every way. I applied to the university immediately as a mature student but when I had to write Grade 9 on the application, I was sure they'd turn me down. They didn't. I graduated five years later, earning a bachelor of arts in English and philosophy (with distinction).

14   It was while I was studying for a master's degree in communications at McGill a few years later that I was approached to direct my second film (the first was a student film). *Doctor, Lawyer, Indian Chief* (a National Film Board production) depicts the struggle of a number of native women — one who began her adult life on welfare, a government minister, a chief, a fisherwoman and Canada's first native woman lawyer. The film is about overcoming obstacles and surviving. It's the story of most native people.

15   Today, there's a glimmer of hope that more of us native people will overcome the obstacles that have tripped us up ever since we began sharing this land. Some say our cultures are going through a renaissance. Maybe that's true. Certainly there's a renewed interest in native dancing, acting and singing, and in other cultural traditions. Even indigenous forms of government are becoming strong again. But we can't forget that the majority of native people live in urban areas and continue to suffer from alcohol and drug abuse and the plagues of a people who have lost their culture and have become lost themselves. And the welfare system is the insidious glue that holds together the machine of oppression of native people.

Too many non-native people have refused to try to understand the issues behind our land claims. They make complacent pronouncements such as "Go back to your bows and arrows and fish with spears if you want aboriginal rights. If not, give it up and assimilate into white Canadian culture." I don't agree with that. We need our culture, but there's no reason why we can't preserve it and have an automatic washing machine and a holiday in Mexico, as well. 16

The time has come for native people to make our own decisions. We need to have self-government. I have no illusions that it will be smooth sailing — there will be trial and error and further struggle. And if that means crawling before we can stand up and walk, so be it. We'll have to learn through experience. 17

While we're learning, we have a lot to teach and give to the world — a holistic philosophy, a way of living with the earth, not disposing of it. It is critical that we all learn from the elders that an individual is not more important than a forest; we know that we're here to live on and with the earth, not to subdue it. 18

The wheels are in motion for a revival, for change in the way native people are taking their place in Canada. I can see that we're equipped, we have the tools to do the work. We have an enormous number of smart, talented, moral Indian people. It's thrilling to be a part of this movement. 19

Someday, when I'm an elder, I'll tell the children the stories: about the bush, about the hard times, about the renaissance, and especially about the importance of knowing your place in your nation. 20

● ●

Explorations:

Carol Geddes, *Doctor, Lawyer, Indian Chief* (NFB film, 29 min., 1986)

Daniel David Moses and Terry Goldie, eds., *An Anthology of Canadian Native Writers in English*

Penny Petrone, ed., *First People, First Voices* (anthology of writings by First Nations people in Canada)

Julie Cruikshank, *Life Lived Like a Story* (interviews with Native Canadian women)

Brian Maracle, *Back on the Rez: Finding the Way Home* (memoir)

Basil Johnston, *Indian School Days* (memoir)

Hugh Brody, *Maps and Dreams* (anthropology)

Tomson Highway, *Kiss of the Fur Queen* (novel)

http://users.ap.net/~chenae/natlink.html

http://www.nativeweb.org

http://www.collectionscanada.ca/6/3/s3-201-e.html#a1

http://www.collectionscanada.ca/02/02012001_e.html

Structure:

1. "I remember it was cold . . ." says Geddes in her opening sentence, and "Someday, when I'm an elder . . ." she says in her closing sentence. Most *narratives* in this chapter relate one incident, but "Growing Up Native" tells the highs and lows of a whole life. Has Geddes attempted too much? Or has she got her message across by focusing on the right moments of her life? Cite examples to defend your answer.
2. Did you have the impression of being *told* a story, rather than reading it on the page? Cite passages where "Growing Up Native" comes across as oral history, as a tale told in person. Why do you think Geddes may have taken this approach?
3. Does Geddes *narrate* in straight chronological order? Point out any flashbacks or other departures from the pattern.
4. Read paragraph 12 aloud. Analyze its power as a TRANSITION between Geddes' past and present.

Style:

1. Geddes' paragraphs are well organized: most begin with a topic sentence, then clearly develop it with examples. Identify five paragraphs that follow this pattern.
2. Why are paragraph 10 and several others so long? Why is paragraph 20 so short?
3. In paragraph 2 Geddes tells of "the sting of humiliation and the boot of discrimination." Find other good FIGURES OF SPEECH in paragraphs 9, 12 and 15.

Ideas for Discussion and Writing:

1. Despite the hardships of living in the bush, does Geddes' childhood sound like a good one? If so, why? Give *examples.*
2. Geddes exposes various ways in which First Nations People have been STEREOTYPED. Point out the worst of these.
3. The white high school of paragraph 11 routinely put Native students in typing instead of science. How do the high schools of your province advise minority students as to course selection and career? Is a minority or working class student shut out from opportunity, or encouraged to try? Give *examples* from your own observation.
4. Geddes envisions First Nations People keeping their culture, yet also having washing machines and holidays in Mexico (paragraph 16). Discuss techniques for achieving such goals in the urban setting where most Native people now live.

5. **PROCESS IN WRITING:** *Interview someone who either grew up long ago, or who is from a culture very different from yours, to hear her or his life story. Tape the interview, then at home play it back, taking notes. Now choose either one main event of this* narrative *(such as the scene in which Geddes realizes she too can go to university), OR choose to give the overall sweep of the story. Also choose whether to just assemble the best excerpts from the tape to put in writing, OR to summarize the key events in your own words. Load your first draft with the best* examples *you have. Stay mainly in time order, but do use a flashback or flashforward if they enhance the story. Finally edit your version for things like spelling and punctuation. Read it aloud to the class. If there is time, also play the interview so the class can see how you chose and arranged the material of your* narrative.

Note: See also the Topics for Writing at the end of this chapter.

Topics for Writing

CHAPTER 1: NARRATION

WRITING ABOUT MYSELF

Choose one of these topics as the basis of a narrative about yourself. Tell a good story: give colourful details and all the facts needed to help your reader understand and appreciate the event. (See also the guidelines that follow.)

1. The Day I Tried an Extreme Sport
2. My Brush with the Law
3. My Worst (or Best) Restaurant Experience
4. The Day I Conquered a Fear
5. The Day I Began My First Job
6. My Encounter with a Wild Animal
7. My Escape from Another Country
8. The Day I Saved Someone's Life
9. My Best Day of Canoeing, Backpacking, Skiing or Cycling
10. The Day I Learned to Like (or Dislike) School
11. My Car Accident
12. My Moment of Glory in Sports
13. An Encounter with Gambling
14. A Little White Lie That Got Me in Trouble
15. The Day I Learned to Tell the Truth

WRITING ABOUT OTHERS

From this list of events, choose one that you witnessed in person. Narrate it, giving colourful details and all the facts needed to help your reader understand and appreciate the event. (See also the guidelines that follow.)

1. An Incident of Road Rage or Air Rage
2. An Example of Courage
3. A Disastrous Fire or Explosion
4. A Violent Incident at a Sporting Event
5. A Prank That Backfired
6. An Accident
7. A Crime in the Neighbourhood
8. An Incident of Bullying
9. An Incident Caused by Alcohol or Drugs
10. An Incident on Public Transit
11. A Case of Police Brutality
12. An Act of Sexism or Racism
13. A Success in the Life of a Teacher
14. A Wild Party
15. A True Act of Kindness

Note also the Process in Writing topic after each selection in this chapter.

Process in Writing: Guidelines

Follow at least some of these steps in the act of writing your narrative (your teacher may suggest which ones).

1. *Search your memory, or search any diary or journal that you keep, for an incident that could develop one of our topics.*

2. *When you have chosen an incident, test it by freewriting nonstop for at least five minutes. If the results are good, use the best parts in your first draft. If the results are weak, try another topic.*

3. *Write your discovery draft rapidly, letting the story just flow out onto the paper or the computer screen. Do not stop now to fix things like spelling and punctuation, for you will lose momentum. Consider narrating in the* present *tense, making the action seem to happen* now.

4. *Look this draft over: Does it begin and end at just the right places, narrating the event itself but omitting parts that don't matter? If you see deadwood, chop it out.*

5. *In your second draft, add more* SENSE IMAGES *to heighten realism. Add more time signals, such as "first," "next," "then," "suddenly" and "at last," to speed the action.*

6. *Read a draft to friends, family members or classmates. Does it sound good? Revise awkward passages. Does it communicate with your* AUDIENCE*? Revise any part that does not.*

7. *Finally, edit for spelling, punctuation and other aspects of correctness before printing off your best version.*

David Wiewel (www.davidwiewel.com)

"In almost every instance, a band's name will come back to haunt you. It's a label you invent at fourteen that you end up using at forty-four."

— *Dave Bidini, "The Fabulous Poodles, Etc.: Naming Your Band"*

Example

FOR EXAMPLE . . .

Many an audience, after struggling to grasp a speaker's message, has been saved from boredom or even sleep by the powerful words "*for example. . . .*" Heads lift up, eyes return to the front, bodies shift in their chairs, and suddenly the message is clear to all.

Writers, like speakers, use examples. Do you enjoy reading pages of abstract reasoning, generalizations, theory without application? You have probably heard the Chinese proverb "A picture is worth a thousand words." When the writer's words never form "pictures," how can you "see" the point? Of course generalizations have their place. For example your thesis statement is one, and so are subpoints, summaries and conclusions. These and others are needed, but cannot do the job alone. If you do not "show" as well as "tell," your reader will be like the people in the audience sinking into their seats — until you, like the speaker, say "for example. . . ."

Why not try for at least 50% example content in every essay, to avoid the hot-air approach to writing? The only trouble with using more examples is that you have to know the subject. Two suggestions:

- If you cannot think of examples, then you have probably chosen the wrong topic. Try another. The best essays are like icebergs: only a tenth of what you know shows above the surface, but it is supported by the other nine-tenths.

- If you cannot think of examples, *find* them. Read. Go to the library. Use the online catalogue and periodical indexes. Consult reference works such as the almanac or the encyclopedia. Search the Internet. In other words, do some *work*.

Examples take many forms:

Personal experience: To illustrate your point, narrate an incident you have experienced. Did an earthquake or tornado or ice storm or heat wave or flood show you the power of nature? Did your car accident illustrate the danger of drinking and driving, or did your fire show the danger of smoking in bed? Did a major success or failure demonstrate the importance of your work or planning or persistence?

The experience of others: To illustrate the point, narrate an incident you saw in person or heard about from others. Did your neighbour's unloved child run away from home or rob a milk store or get married at age 16? Did your cousin lose her job because of automation or downsizing or a corporate merger? Did a famous person succeed despite a physical disability or a deprived childhood?

Hypothetical examples: In a future-oriented society like ours, many arguments speculate about what might happen *if*. . . . Since the event or situation has not yet come to pass, use your best judgment to imagine the results. What would happen if street drugs were legalized? If the forests were all cut? If Quebec separated? If the national debt were paid off? If the polar ice cap melted? If our electricity came from windmills? If a world government were adopted?

Quotations: If the words of a poet, politician, scientist or other prominent person illustrate your point clearly and authoritatively, quote them (using quotation marks) and of course state who said them. What did Aristotle, Shakespeare, Marx, Einstein, Jane Jacobs, Warren Buffet, Nelson Mandela, Mordecai Richler or Margaret Atwood say about love or power or sex or money or old age or war? Start with the index of *Colombo's Canadian Quotations* or *Bartlett's Familiar Quotations* to find an apt statement on almost any important topic. Or go online to check out *Bartlett* at www.bartleby.com/100, entering key words for a search. Another good source is *Wikiquote* at en.wikiquote.org/wiki/Main_Page.

Statistics: These numerical examples lend a scientific, objective quality to your argument. Tell what percentage of marriages will end in divorce or how many minutes each cigarette takes off your life or how much energy a person consumes travelling by car as opposed to train, bus or

EXAMPLE **47**

airplane. Good places to find statistics are *The World Almanac and Book of Facts, Canada Year Book* and any good atlas. Be scrupulously honest, because everyone knows how statistics can lie (remember the statistician who drowned in the river that averaged two feet deep!).

Other devices: Later chapters in this book discuss cause and effect, comparison and contrast, and analogy. These devices may be used not only to plan the structure of an entire essay, but also to construct short and vivid examples within the essay.

Almost all good writing has examples, but some writing has so many that they become a means of organizing as well as illustrating. Ray Guy's essay "Outharbor Menu" has a brief introduction, a one-sentence closing, and a body made of nothing but examples. Such a collection could be a mere list of trivia, but Ray Guy — like anyone who writes well — has chosen his examples well for their colour and for the support they give his point.

Like Ray Guy, all the other authors in this chapter — Jan Wong, Dave Bidini, J. Kelly Nestruck, Margaret Wente and Goran Simic — have gone far beyond the suggested 50% example content for good essays. Though we could still disagree with their views, it would be astonishing if we did not at least *understand* them after "seeing" them so clearly in action.

Another way to use examples is to let one long one make the point. On page 141 of Chapter 4, Nathalie Petrowski develops one extended example of one young man who became a mass murderer. Yet through the single case of Marc Lépine, she helps us "see" the situation of many other Canadian youth who may also explode into violence if we do not reduce the pressures our society puts on them. Of course one example — or a hundred — will prove nothing. Statistics come close to proof, especially when based on a large and carefully designed study. But in general an example is not proof; it is a device of illustration and therefore an aid to both understanding and enjoyment.

Note: Authors in other chapters also use many examples, as well as other ways to develop their point. See especially these selections:

Patricia Pearson, "Avoiding the Big C: A Little Simple Advice," p. 114
Leah McLaren, "Canadian Guys Rule," p. 122
David Suzuki, "Hidden Lessons," p. 127
Doris Anderson, "The 51-Per-Cent Minority," p. 160
Jack Layton, "Measuring the New Prosperity," p. 164
Rafi Mustafa, "The Bond of Nightmares," p. 177
Laurence Hill, "Black + White = Black," p. 191
Samantha Bennett, "It's Not Just the Weather That's Cooler in Canada," p. 208
Gordon Pitts, "Your New Job, Your New Life," p. 236
Margaret Atwood, "Letter to America," p. 298

JAN WONG

Ten Things the Chinese Do Much Better Than We Do*

Jan Wong's life has been the stuff of fiction. Born in 1952 as a third-generation Chinese in Montreal, she was a gifted and popular high school student enjoying the lifestyle of a prosperous family. But once at McGill, Wong entered radical politics, a path that led her in 1972 to Chairman Mao's China, as the only Canadian university student in the country. There she mastered the language of her ancestors, studied Marxism, became an ardent revolutionary, volunteered for hard labour during the greatest excesses of the Cultural Revolution, and married the only American draft resistor to go to China during the Vietnam War. But after six years of seeing power abused in the "workers' paradise," Wong returned to Canada in disillusionment. She finished her degree at McGill, did a master's in journalism at Columbia, and entered the world of capitalism. Since then she has been a business reporter for the Montreal Gazette, *the* Boston Globe, *and the* Wall Street Journal. *She has also written extensively on China for* The Globe and Mail *(her eyewitness reporting of the historic 1989 Tiananmen Square massacre went on to be the runaway bestselling book of 1996,* Red China Blues: My Long March from Mao to Now). *Wong next gained notoriety as a trenchant interviewer of celebrities (which in 2000 resulted in another book,* Lunch with Jan Wong). *Today she is again reporting and writing feature articles for the* Globe. *Many of these, like our selection from October 23, 2004, are on China.*

1   Ah, those clever Chinese. First they invent gunpowder and a few other essentials of modern civilization. Now they're gunning their economic engines. Yet who would have thought that, after a millennium of poverty, they'd already do so many things better than we?

2   In fact, compiling a Top 10 list of what China does better than Canada isn't easy. There are so many items. To whittle it down, let's assume it's unfair to count anything related to cheap labour.

3   So we won't include the wonderfully thorough mop-ups of supermarket spills: The staff don't plunk down those yellow you-can't-sue-us caution signs. They actually fan the floor with a broken sheet of Styrofoam until it is dry.

---

* Editor's title.

Nor will we mention the exquisite, free head-and-shoulder massages that come with every shampoo and haircut.   4

And we will only sigh with envy over bicycle couriers speeding theatre tickets to you the same day — free.   5

Frequent travellers will love this one: Even remote rural hotels in China, not previously known for world-beating hygiene, now routinely slip blankets, quilts and coverlets into freshly laundered duvet covers. No more puffy bedspreads and nasty polyester blankets that cover guest after guest without being cleaned, which is still the practice in most of our hotel chains.   6

Considering how cheap labour is, it's astonishing that so many Chinese facilities offer free automated lockers now, the way European airports and train stations do. No more old-fashioned keys to form a lump in your pocket — just a slip of paper with a randomly chosen number that lets you retrieve your belongings. Stores like them because they cut shoplifting; customers like them because they reduce schlepping.   7

Not all progress is good. Taxis, subways, trains and elevators barrage you with non-stop ads on flat-screen videos. Some city buses feature live television. Who wants that? Pickpockets, probably.   8

For this list, we won't count minor things, either, like the narrow plastic bags that department stores and offices offer on rainy days to sheathe your dripping umbrella. Or the invention of the electronic fly swatter, which electrocutes without squishy messes (and is now available in dollar stores in Canada).   9

On this list, we won't count mega things, either, like the soaring architectural wonder of China's airports — even in provincial capitals like Fuzhou — awash in natural light. (Not to mention that you can understand the public announcements, and the restaurants are much better.)   10

We won't include the vast subway and highway systems and huge underground garages that Beijing, Shanghai and Canton have built in astoundingly little time. Or Shanghai's magnetic-levitation train, the first in the world, which accelerates to 431 kilometres an hour in 2 minutes and 53 seconds. Even the Germans who designed it can't afford one for themselves.   11

No, for this list we were looking for truly brilliant ideas, the forehead-slapping kind, the ones that make you say: Now why didn't we think of that?   12

1. Cellphones

By any standard you can think of — coverage, price, ubiquity — China's cellphone practices beat ours. You can use them in elevators, subways and parking garages. They work in Tibet, at the Great Wall, in remotest rural China, which is more than you can say for Ontario cottage country. Patients, doctors, nurses and visitors use them in hospitals, too, with no apparent ill effects.   13

14   It's a cheap, pay-as-you-go system, with no stupid monthly contracts or credit checks. The phones are so cheap — even sidewalk cabbage vendors have them — that China is now the biggest cellphone market in the world. With 300 million in use, each one telling time, wristwatch sales have plummeted.

15   "We're a nation of thumbs," a young Shanghai woman told me, meaning that Chinese use cellphones like BlackBerries, text-messaging friends 24/7, at 1.6 cents a pop. The Chinese never got used to voice-mail or answering machines; installing home phones was equivalent to two years' pay in the 1980s, so the country leapfrogged over landline technology right into cellular.

16   Chinese author Qian Fuchang even plans to transmit a novel — about an extramarital affair — via text-messaging, one 70-word chapter at a time.

2. Informative stop lights

17   In Tianjin, a city of 13 million people, traffic lights display red or green signals in a rectangle that rhythmically shrinks down as the time remaining evaporates. In Beijing, some traffic lights offer a countdown clock for both green and red signals.

18   During a red light, you know whether you have time to check that map; on a green light, you know whether to start braking a block away — or to stomp on the accelerator, as though you were a Toronto or Montreal driver. (That's probably why Montreal has a few lights with countdown seconds for pedestrians.)

3. Transit debit cards

19   Wouldn't it be great to have a single debit card for buses, subways — and taxis? That's how it works in Shanghai. Passengers don't have to fumble for exact change on buses and subways, or line up to buy tokens or tickets. Taxi drivers don't have to make change, or get ripped off by counterfeit bills, a real plague in China. And they aren't loaded down with cash, which would make them tempting targets for robbery.

20   (In another transit plus, forget those illegible handwritten taxi receipts we get in Canada. China's taxis automatically print out receipts with date, mileage, taxi medallion number, even the start and end times of the ride. That certainly would help you recover the Stradivarius you inadvertently left in the back seat.)

4. Adult playgrounds

21   Hate paying those gym club bills? Loathe huffing and puffing around buff bodies in spandex? Beijing provides free outdoor exercise equipment in neighbourhoods throughout the city: walking machines, ab flexers, weight machines and rowing machines in bright reds, blues, yellows and greens.

Adult playgrounds get everyone out in the fresh air, especially seniors who might stay shut in at home. Teens like to hang out there, too. And it sends a not-so-subtle propaganda message about the benefits of healthy living. 22

5. Anti-theft slipcovers

What do you do with a purse in a restaurant? It can slide off your lap, and looping the handle over the back of your chair is an invitation to a thief. In China, when you sling your purse or laptop or coat over your chair back, a waiter hurries to toss a tasteful slipcover over it. It foils thieves, and also protects coats from food spills. Some restaurants provide hooks under the table for purses. 23

6. Daily banking

We feel so lucky when a bank branch in Canada opens for a few hours on Saturday mornings. (Notice the long, long lines?) But Chinese banks are now open 9 to 5, seven days a week. Even on New Year's Day and other national holidays, at least some branches will open for business. The ones that are closed post helpful notices directing you to the closest open branch. And, yes, they do have a full network of ATMs. 24

7. Wireless service bells

Trying to flag down your waiter for a glass of water? Just press a made-in-China gizmo at your table. Your table number lights up on a panel inside the kitchen and your server is soon hovering by your side. The bell also eliminates that annoying waiterly interruption: "Is everything all right?" 25

The same gizmo in spas alerts masseuses when you're demurely under the sheet and ready for their attention. 26

8. Parking data

A celebrity I once lunched with was an hour late because he couldn't find an empty parking spot in downtown Toronto. He had driven to a dozen lots, each time finding a wooden sign plunked at the entrance smugly announcing that the lot was full. 27

In China, roadside electronic billboards not only give directions to nearby lots and garages, they crucially reveal how many empty spaces are left. 28

9. Computer seating maps

Canadian concert halls will tell you that Row DD, Seat 81 costs $74.95. But where on earth is it? At the Shanghai Grand Theatre, the black granite ticket counter is embedded with a Samsung computer screen which 29 lights up with the event you want to see, showing unsold seats, colour-coded by price, and the sightline to the stage. There is even a bar stool on which to perch while you consider your choices.

30   Movie theatres offer the same service. You choose which film and what showing, and the screen in the counter shows you what's unsold. After you make your choice, you can go shopping or enjoy a latte until show time. No one will take your seats.

10. Free hemming

31   This doesn't count as cheap labour because only three people service an entire department store. In Canada, hemming a new pair of trousers adds at least $10 to the cost, plus two trips to the tailor. And you have to try them on again while you get measured.

32   At the No. 1 Department Store in Shanghai, the salesclerk measures you while you are trying on the pants, asking: "Will you be wearing these with high heels or flats?" If you decide to buy them, she scribbles the length on your receipt. You head to what looks like a gift-wrapping station where a man measures and chalks the pants, scissors off the surplus and flings them to two women behind him. One hems the raw edge on a machine and tosses it to the other, who stitches the final hem on another machine and presses them.

33   Even with two customers ahead of me, I swear it took under three minutes in all to get two pairs back.

34   When I tell the woman ahead of me that stores in Canada don't do this, she's astonished. "Really?" she says. "How inconvenient."

• •

Explorations:

Jan Wong,
> *Red China Blues: My Long March from Mao to Now*
> *Jan Wong's China: Reports from a Not-So-Foreign Correspondent*
> *Lunch with Jan Wong*

Ha Jin, *Between Silences: A Voice from China* (poems)
http://www.dfait-maeci.gc.ca/china/menu-en.asp
http://www.china.org.cn/english
http://www.chinatoday.com

Structure:

1. Identify Jan Wong's THESIS STATEMENT.
2. Wong begins with a long introduction that points out kinds of things her argument will *not* cover. Why? How does this prepare us for her

main points she does cover? Which paragraph is her TRANSITION from the first part to the main part?

3. Have you ever tried Wong's technique of beginning subsections with subtitles? How does this work for you as Wong's reader?

4. If Wong is amassing examples of things the Chinese "do far better than we do," then how often does she complete the *contrast* to our less ingenious ways of doing things in Canada? Could this essay have appeared in the "Comparison and Contrast" chapter?

5. Do you believe "free hemming" is the best point to go last? Is there a stronger point that could go in this final position, to build a climax? Which point would you choose?

Style:

1. Does Jan Wong write like a typical newspaper journalist? Examine her vocabulary, sentence lengths, paragraphing, and level of objectivity before you give your answer.

Ideas for Discussion and Writing:

1. This selection was first published in a special "China Rising" issue of *The Globe and Mail*, which had huge Chinese characters on the front page, with this text in English: "If you can't read these words, better start brushing up. A profound global shift has begun, the kind that occurs once every few lifetimes. Don't be left behind." Do you believe it? Is China on track to soon dominate the world's economy? And if so, what are you doing to get ready?

2. In the same issue of the *Globe*, columnist Margaret Wente writes, "China's cities make the urgency of Manhattan look laid-back. Everybody's in a hurry, and everybody wants to get there first. They know that if they don't, they will be left in the dust." How does her view of the new China compare to your own view of the place where you live now? Give *examples*.

3. Jan Wong gives a picture of vast riches in the new urban China, yet rural areas remain in poverty, with almost half the population living on less than $2 U.S. per day. Another startling contrast is that this power-fully entrepreneurial country is still governed by the Communist Party. Should Wong have included other issues such as these, or would that just make her lose her focus and dilute her argument?

4. According to the World Bank, China contains 13 of the world's most air-polluted cities. Should we be happy that, in their new economic success, many Chinese are driving cars, and even Hummers, or should we fear for the environment? And what about our own country?

5. **PROCESS IN WRITING:** *Compile a list of 5 to 10 things that our own nation does very well, and make notes. Create a THESIS STATEMENT to give your list a purpose. Now arrange the items in order, starting with a major example to catch the reader's attention, next dropping back to the lesser items, and then working up to the most important example of all at the very end. Write the first draft, then the next day look it over. Is it concise? If not, trim. Is at least half your space taken by examples? If not, add. Finally do a quality control for punctuation and sentence structure, and print out your best version.*

Note: See also the Topics for Writing at the end of this chapter.

DAVE BIDINI

The Fabulous Poodles, Etc.: Naming Your Band

Dave Bidini is well known as rhythm guitarist for the quirky Rheostatics, who have played all across the nation in every venue from local bars to Maple Leaf Gardens, and who have so far made a dozen albums, such as Whale Music *(sound track to the film),* Music Inspired by the Group of Seven, *and* 2067. *Bidini also writes of his passions in books: anyone who has read his 1998 memoir* On a Cold Road *has experienced powerful insights into the life of a rocker: hardships of bus travel in winter, rivalries with other bands, funny and ridiculous incidents, and moments of defeat and glory onstage. As a boy Bidini wanted to be a sports writer, and now he is. An avid hockey player himself, he went to far corners of the earth to see how hockey is played there, and described his unusual findings in the 2001 book* Tropic of Hockey. *Then in 2004 he turned his attention to baseball, spending six months with a minor league team in Italy, where Canadian soldiers had introduced the sport during World War II. The resulting* Baseballissimo *(2005) is a portrait of a culture as well as a sport — enriched by Bidini's connecting with his own Italian roots. In 2005 appeared another hockey book,* The Best Game You Can Name. *Our own selection comes from Bidini's joyous 2004 guide for young musicians,* For Those About to Rock: A Road Map for Being in a Band. *Like all his writing it is compressed, polished, full of humour, full of life.*

Band names mean nothing. Okay, they don't mean nothing, but they mean very little. A group like the Barenaked Ladies benefited from the attention they got for their name, but if they hadn't been able to play, it wouldn't have mattered what they called themselves. Names are interchangeable, but character and quality is not. Nobody ever resisted the music of Neutral Milk Hotel, or Echo and the Bunnymen, or the Traveling Wilburys because they didn't like the name. And even though I spent countless hours in grade-eleven physics class drawing up lists of potential band names, I believe that our sound would have remained the same had we been called Shoot the Neighbours or Bring Home the Beaver (two other names on the list), instead of Rheostatics. Which is a pretty stupid name, if a little less stupid than those we didn't choose.

While there are no rules when it comes to choosing a band name, it's important to avoid certain clichés of the day. Every rock-and-roll epoch has been defined by what musicians called their groups. The 1950s, for instance, was a big time for bands named after birds and cars — the Robins, Orioles, Doves, Nightingales; the Fleetwoods, Cadillacs, GTOs, and Ventures — while '60s group names had the ring of characters from a Lewis Carroll° novel: the Electric Prunes, the We Five, the Strangeloves, Blues Magoos, Amboy Dukes, Chocolate Watchband, Sam the Sham and the Pharaohs, ? and the Mysterians, 1910 Fruitgum Company, Sir Douglas Quintet, Jefferson Airplane, the Grateful Dead, and the Incredible String Band, to name a few. This, in turn, spawned a movement towards simpler names: Poco, the Byrds, Love, the Band, the Move. As Richard Manuel suggested to Martin Scorsese in *The Last Waltz*, "When we were starting out, all of these bands had names like Chocolate Subway and Marshmallow Overcoat. So we just decided to call ourselves the Band."

3   The '70s gave way to an onslaught of groups whose names suggested a certain heaviosity of sound: Black Oak Arkansas, Foghat, Grand Funk, T.Rex, Led Zeppelin, Styx, FIST, Trooper, Motorhead, Black Sabbath, Anvil, Gong, Bachman-Turner Overdrive (BTO). Parallel trends saw bands using proper names, often of people not in the band (Max Webster, Jethro Tull, Barclay James Harvest, Norton Buffalo), acronyms (ELO, ELP, XTC, PIL, ZZ Top, X, M, CCR, DOA, and, once again, BTO), and the names of cities, countries, and occasionally continents (Boston, Chicago, Toronto, Chilliwack, Chelsea, New England, Kansas, UK, Europe, and Asia). At the end of the '70s, a Punk band just wasn't unless its moniker evoked the dread of modern life: Siouxsie and the Banshees, the Damned, the Sex Pistols, the Ruts, the Clash, the Slits, the Fall, Stranglers, the Dead Boys, Black Flag, Killing Joke, Fear, or Bad Brains.

4   New Wave bands of the 1980s favored themes of science or science fiction (the Space Invaders, Devo, Moon Martin, Wire, the Triffids, Oingo Boingo, Telex), or haughty globalism (Spandau Ballet, Classix Nouveaux, Depeche Mode, Duran Duran, Kajagoogoo, Eyeless in Gaza, Scritti Politti, Erasure, Bauhaus, X-Mal Deutschland, Bolshoi, Falco, China Crisis, Sigue Sigue Sputnik, Blancmange, Visage, Japan, Berlin, Cabaret Voltaire). The '90s featured a litany of numbered bands: Sum 41, Finger Eleven, blink-182, Matchbox Twenty, NC-17, Six Doors Down, 50 Cent, Buck 65, Galaxy 500, Nine Inch Nails, Sevendust, Sixpence None the Richer, Shed Seven, L7, Spacemen 3, Catch 22, Eve 6, 88 Fingers Louie, 7 Seconds, Mojave 3, Bran Van 3000, Andre 3000, and Powerman 5000, who, by dint of his name, was clearly at least 2000 better than anyone else. Most recently, the trend has been towards purposely misspelled band names (Staind, Linkin Park, Limp Bizkit, Phish, Outkast), names with the word "Super" in them (Superconductor, Supergarage, Superchunk, Superdrag, the Super Friendz, the

---

° Lewis Carroll (1832–98): author of *Alice's Adventures in Wonderland*.

Supersuckers, Super Furry Animals, Princess Superstar, Supersonic; strangely, Supertramp preceded this trend way back in the '70s) or, regrettably, bands linking the names of celebrities and mass murderers (Brian Jonestown Massacre, Marilyn Manson).

Then there are animal names. Young bands should approach this category with caution. It's not that I dislike many of these groups, but none of them would be mistaken for the Beatles, the Byrds, or the Animals (or, all right, the Eagles), which are the exceptions to the Curse of the Animal Name. Examples include Glass Tiger, Slaughter and the Dogs, Elephants Memory, Buffalo Tom, the Stray Cats, White Lion, the Monkees, Faster Pussycat, Hootie and the Blowfish, the Beaver Brown Band, Kid Koala, Babe the Blue Ox, Ducks Deluxe, Raising the Fawn, Alien Ant Farm, Whitesnake, Cats Can Fly, Flock of Seagulls, Budgie, the Fabulous Poodles, Ratt, Cat Power, Courage of Lassie, Toto, Mouse on Mars, Cobra, Armadillo, Adam and the Ants, the Bee People, Spiderbait, the Black Crowes, Counting Crows, and the Rainbow Butt Monkeys.

Some bands were lucky enough to be named accidentally. Before the Guess Who were called that — they were unofficially known as Chad Allen and the Expressions — they bombarded radio stations with brown paper packages containing their new single, "Shakin' All Over." In an effort to stir interest regarding the true identity of the group, only two words appeared on the sleeve: Guess Who? The resulting media frenzy never occurred because DJs decided that it didn't matter who was playing the song. That it sounded like a bona fide hit was good enough for them, so they just called the band the Guess Who, even though the name was strikingly similar to the name of another band of the time, the Who. The Who and the Guess Who actually met once, at the Marquee Club in London. The Who were upset because British audiences kept requesting "Shakin' All Over," while the Guess Who had been forced to deal with calls for "My Generation." Randy Bachman, the Guess Who's guitarist, remembers Pete Townshend asking the Guess Who to change their name. They told them to change theirs. Nothing was settled. Rock and roll was allowed to take its course.

Some bands have changed their names in an effort to distinguish themselves from the pack (Martha and the Muffins became M+M; Spizz Energi became Athletico Spizz 80; John Cougar reinserted his real name, Mellencamp), while many of those who might have considered getting a new handle actually thrived using their own names. Folksinger Loudon Wainwright III, who possesses one of music's most difficult-to-spell names, once arrived at a venue to find *Gordondon Wainwright* written on the marquee. In her early days, Ani Difranco was accidentally billed as Andy Difranco, and Led Zeppelin's name was forever butchered in club and concert listings. My band has also suffered the same fate. Over the years, we've been known as Red Static, Rheostapic, Riostatics, and Reostatics, as well as the constant Rheostat. After a while, I stopped taking it personally, and was happy that we were even listed.

8   In almost every instance, a band's name will come back to haunt you. It's a label you invent at fourteen that you end up using at forty-four. Very few songs from those early years survive, but a band's name remains. As you get older, it'll sound dated and old, and you'll have trouble saying it in public. But you'll learn to deal with it. There are a lot of other things you'll learn to deal with, too: bored crowds, or no crowds; ugly posters, T-shirts, album covers, and print ads; dumb things you told the press that you thought they wouldn't print, but did; radio DJs who ask stupid stuff like, "How'd you get your name?"; bummer tours, or bad colds, or throat nodes, or breakups with girlfriends/boyfriends in the middle of tours or album sessions; songs that won't hatch, bandmates who won't listen, muses that won't strike when you need them to most. Once you've dealt with all of these things, coming to terms with a stupid band name is the simplest of tasks. You go with it, mostly because you have no choice. Either that, or you rename your group after the author who warned you about this in the first place.

9   Go on.

10   I dare you.

Taken from *For Those About to Rock*. Copyright 2004 by Dave Bidini, published by Tundra Books, Toronto.

● ●

Explorations:

Dave Bidini,
> *For Those About to Rock: A Road Map to Being in a Band*
> *On a Cold Road: Tales of Adventure in Canadian Rock*
> *Tropic of Hockey: My Search for the Game in Unlikely Places*

http://www.popmatters.com/books/reviews/b/baseballissimo.shtml
http://www.rheostatics.ca/
http://zed.cbc.ca/go.ZeD?POS=3&CONTENT_ID=180179&FILTER_K
   EY=8727&page=content

Structure:

1. Bidini cites an extravagant number of *examples* (no less than 189 colourful names of rock bands). Is it fun? Does it illustrate his points? Or has he gone too far? Can there ever be too many? What other essay in this chapter gives a massive number of *examples*, and how do they work for you? Could your own writing use more?

2. Locate Bidini's THESIS STATEMENT. What overall point does his flood of *examples* support?

3. What simple and direct means does Bidini use to organize this enormous number of *examples*?

Style:

1. What AUDIENCE does Bidini aim for here? Profile it briefly. What STYLE of writing do these readers need? How far has Bidini gone to provide it? Give *examples* to back your point.
2. If this selection is on a pop topic such as rock, why are its paragraphs so long?

Ideas for Discussion and Writing:

1. What does it mean that Dave Bidini was able to collect such a huge number of band names? Is rock the dominant music of our time? Or does it have serious competitors? Name them. Which one or ones do you prefer? And why?
2. Bidini is a Canadian rocker. Name all the others you can think of, past and present. How important have they been on the world stage? And in what other areas of culture have Canadians made their mark?
3. Do you find it unusual that Bidini, rhythm guitarist for the Rheostatics, also writes very polished books about his passions, music and sports? Has he broken STEREOTYPES in doing so? Explain.
4. Bidini has been rocking for decades now. Around what age do rock musicians retire? Pro hockey players? Boxers? Ballet dancers? Movie stars? Writers? Classical musicians? Give *examples*, and give reasons.
5. **PROCESS IN WRITING:** *Bidini devotes real effort to analyzing names of rock bands, and to giving* examples. *What about our own names? Is there a large choice? Should parents pick their baby's first name carefully? Will a poor choice "come back to haunt you" as Bidini writes of band names in paragraph 8? Freewrite on all this, then let your notes lead to your THESIS STATEMENT. Now write a quick first draft to illustrate your point, using a flood of* examples *(name choices that may have various effects later in life). If you wish, categorize them (look ahead at the introduction to Classification, on pp. 225–226). Make useful recommendations in your closing. Finally check for CONCISENESS and punctuation before printing off your best version.*

Note: See also the Topics for Writing at the end of this chapter.

J. KELLY NESTRUCK

The Importance of Email Punctuation: a Cautionary Tale

Though in his essay he treats email with some humour, J. Kelly Nestruck is also very serious about it. "Anyone who wants to be a writer or improve his or her writing should write a lot of email," he advises, because "the more one writes the better one becomes at writing." He adds that "The Internet has totally altered what it means to be a writer. Whether on a blog or a fan site message board, it is a great place to be published and get feedback on your writing for the first time." It was in a campus newspaper, though, The McGill Daily, *that in 1999 the first-year McGill University arts student published his "cautionary tale." Later in his university years, Nestruck worked as culture editor at* The McGill Daily, *Quebec Bureau Chief for Canadian University Press, and eventually began freelancing to* The Montreal Gazette, The Globe and Mail, *and the* National Post. *Soon after graduating with a double major in English and history, Nestruck landed an internship at the* Post, *where he was eventually hired as an arts reporter. Nestruck is still drawn to electronic forms of communication, and has spoken about blogs at the University of Toronto, as well as Canadian Newspaper Association and Canadian University Press conferences. In his free time he blogs about politics at* www.nestruck.com *and theatre on* www.torontoist.com. *He also plays keyboards in the Bathtub Tafts, a jam band that may someday, he says, play a concert. Born in Winnipeg, Nestruck grew up in Montreal and now lives in Toronto.*

1
2
Never before in my life had I considered a colon so carefully. I spent a full 20 minutes staring at it at the very top of the message. Kelly, colon. It was perhaps the first time I had thought about the affective meaning of punctuation, particularly in email. Linguists have become increasingly interested in communication through email. This abbreviated, instant form of discourse has revolutionised the world. Even though I have only been using email for six or seven years, I can no longer imagine life without it. Classes now have discussion listservs. I can email an article minutes before a deadline from across the city. The relationship with my father in Winnipeg has become more personal than it had been with the alternating Saturday father-son telephone call. Because of its brief nature every single character in an email takes on enormous significance. This includes the colon that I found preceded by my name at the top of the email.

Previous emails from this person had begun with Kelly followed by a resounding exclamation point. My, how I savoured those exclamation points, each one echoing throughout my entire body. This correspondent of mine, whose slender fingers I imagine even now gently depressing the Shift key and then caressing the 1, is not one of those who overuses the exclamation point. She is not like others in my database who write valley girl messages littered with similes like, "Kelly! I just got a new garbage can! It has a pedal you push to make the lid go up!:) I'm going to Peel Pub later! TTFN!"°

Likewise, my slender-fingered email friend never adopted the punctuation of fakes, phoneys, and ostentatious schmucks: the semi-colon. The semi-colon, while popular outside of the cyberworld, should be relegated to formal modes of communication. A semi-colon in an email ("We should meet at Peel Pub; it is finally wet T-shirt night again.") is as out of place as an exclamation point in an essay ("The Miskitu Indians were subordinate to both the Nicaraguan state and the institution of American neo-colonialism!").

Occasionally, when my delicately digited correspondent's heart was heavy with some crisis or another, the exclamation point would disappear after my name. Short messages sometimes had my name followed by a comma. None of this bothered me. The colon however, shattered me. Colons are the punctuation of lawyers, bankers and junk emailers trying to get me to take out a $50,000 loan over the net. How cold and antiseptic that colon was. Two little bulletholes through my heart.

Then, later in the message, came the ellipsis. There is a world of difference between "We should get together to talk about stuff" period and "We need to get together to talk about stuff" period, period, period. I expected the ellipsis from the colon on down. The cautionary colon foreshadowed what was to come.

And now our relationship is in parentheses, as I await the anticipated appointment to talk about stuff, period, period, period. In person, the only commas will be drawn nervously in the air with her aforementioned slender fingers. The only dashes will be in her stilted, anxious speech. The only periods will be her small, black, intense pupils submerged in her beautiful green eyes, darting away from mine. And as she recedes into the distance, I will be left standing there like an ellipsis.

Two little bulletholes through my heart.

● ●

° TTFN: "Ta Ta for Now," an expression now replaced, the author says, by TTYL ("Talk to You Later").

Explorations:

Lynne Truss, *Eats, Shoots & Leaves* (humorous book about punctuation)
Ronald Conrad, *Process and Practice* (see coverage of punctuation)
http://www.webfoot.com/advice/email.top.html (advice on all main aspects of writing email messages)
http://everythingemail.net/email_help_tips.html (more advice on emails)
http://www.nestruck.com (J. Kelly Nestruck's blog, *On the Fence*)

Structure:

1. Did the beginning of this essay motivate you to read on? Why or why not? Point out every technique Nestruck uses in paragraphs 1 and 2 to gain your attention.
2. Identify Nestruck's THESIS STATEMENT.
3. To support his overall point that "every single character in an email takes on enormous significance" (par. 2), Nestruck constructs his argument as a series of *examples* of email punctuation. Identify each. Does every example further the point? Does his total of examples reach the recommended 50% of essay content?

Style:

1. This essay contains three sentence fragments. Identify them. Why is one repeated? Are they errors or are they just part of the author's STYLE? How FORMAL or INFORMAL is that style? Does it fit his subject?
2. The relationship of our author and his green-eyed email correspondent is now "in parentheses" (par. 7). Point out all his other METAPHORS involving punctuation marks. What TONE do they suggest? Should Nestruck be laughing about his endangered romance? If so, why?

Ideas for Discussion and Writing:

1. Have you ever had an online romance? How did it turn out? Are there advantages? Pitfalls? Dangers? Give an *example*.
2. Nestruck calls the semicolon, at least as used in emails, "the punctuation of fakes, phoneys, and ostentatious schmucks." Has he gone too far, or do you agree? Tell why. Do you use it in essays? In emails? Or do you avoid it? Why? And can you explain how it is correctly used in a sentence?
3. In his argument Nestruck names the colon, exclamation point, semicolon, comma, ellipsis, parenthesis, comma, dash and period. Which of these punctuation marks do you like most? Why? Which do you like least? Why? Give an *example* of each used correctly in a sentence.

4. In 2004 a humorous little book about punctuation, *Eats, Shoots & Leaves,* by British author Lynne Truss, became a huge international bestseller. Read it. How is Truss able to make a subject that some people dread into a topic of fascination and laughter? Do you share her view and Nestruck's, that choice of punctuation is crucial to written communication?

5. Has email led you to communicate more often in writing? Does it make relating to people easier, as it does for Nestruck and his father in Winnipeg? On the other hand, does the speed of email make you send messages you later wish you had not? Give an *example.*

6. Some office workers receive 100 or more emails a day. How do they deal with so much communication? How many do you get? How long do you spend answering? Tell your best technique for saving time doing so. All in all, do you believe email is saving your time or wasting it?

7. **PROCESS IN WRITING:** *Visit J. Kelly Nestruck's excellent blog* On the Fence, *at* www.nestruck.com. *Read several days' worth of entries till you hit on a topic that makes you feel strongly pro or con. Now write a fast reaction in your normal email style, format and punctuation. Send it to the blog, and print out a copy for yourself. Now translate the argument into a second version, this time in standard essay format. (Your teacher may suggest a length.) The next day look it over: Have you reached at least 50% example content, as Nestruck has in his essay? Is the vocabulary appropriate for an essay? Is the punctuation right for an essay? Finally, read both the email and essay versions aloud in class, and have volunteers identify the main differences between the two.*

Note: See also the Topics for Discussion at the end of this chapter.

MARGARET WENTE

Busy, Busy, Busy

An "accidental Canadian," as she puts it in the title of her book, Margaret Wente did not immigrate to Canada till her teens. She grew up in the fifties in a conservative suburb of Chicago, then when her divorced mother married a Canadian, moved with the family to Toronto. She found the city conservative as well, but was charmed by signs of change, such as the Yorkville expresso bars and the new music. After a B.A. from the University of Michigan and an M.A. in English literature from the University of Toronto, she began a career in journalism that led her to be editor of Canadian Business, ROB Magazines *and* The Globe and Mail's *business section. And from 1992 she has become known to a much larger audience, writing a quirky, humorous, brash and controversial column for the* Globe. *Not everyone is a fan. She steps on toes easily, for example in 2005 infuriating the whole province of Newfoundland with unflattering comments. And while she is often progressive on social issues, she is conservative on political ones, deflating Canadian cultural icons and often supporting American actions unpopular in Canada. Then in 2004 Wente collected many of her best columns in* An Accidental Canadian: Reflections on My Home and (Not) Native Land. *From it comes our selection.*

1   Not long ago, I phoned up an old friend of mine, a high-powered career woman who is usually on the road two or three days a week.

2   "How about lunch?" I said. "How does your calendar look for June?"

3   "How about today?" she said. "I'm totally free."

4   I was shocked. Nobody I know is free for lunch today. A person of average busyness is sometimes free the week after next. If you're trying to book a higher-status person, four to six weeks is normal, by which time you will be lucky to remember what it is you wanted to have lunch about anyway. This lunch will probably be rearranged a few times by various executive assistants, who will spend more time talking to each other, coordinating your respective calendars, than you will spend talking to your lunchee. If you are higher status (i.e., busier) than the other person, you will be allowed to reschedule at least twice.

5   That is, if you still do lunch. Busy people don't, and when they do, they tell you, "I really don't do lunch anymore," implying that you ought to be immensely honoured that they have broken the rule for you. And you'd better eat in a hurry. An hour and ten minutes is the most anyone spends on a business lunch now.

6   Whenever I run into someone I haven't seen for a while and ask how they are, they always say the same thing: "I'm really busy."

Want to get together for dinner some Saturday with another busy cou‐ 7
ple? Two months, minimum, before you can fit it in.

And when you do get together, you'll all brag about how much e‐mail 8
you get. "It's horrible," someone will say. "I took three days off and when
I got back to the office I had six hundred e‐mails!"

"That's nothing," the next person will say. "I had two thousand, and I 9
had forty‐seven voice mails."

The truly busy person, of course, will have answered all these voice mails 10
and e‐mails while on vacation so that she can get right back down to work.

Then comes the discussion about how early people get up in the 11
morning. If you sleep in after 5:30 on a weekday, your best strategy is to
lie about it so your friends don't think you're a slacker.

Recently, I took a few days off from work between assignments. It was 12
pleasant to spend all day reading the papers at my kitchen table, with the
sun streaming in, no places to go, no people to see. Pleasant — for about
five minutes. Then I started to get nervous. What if they had forgotten
all about me? So I got on the phone and called a few friends. The first
person I called had to take a call on his cellphone while he was speaking
to me. The second and third persons were in meetings and would call
me back just as soon as they were free.

Everyone was so busy! I recalled that just the day before I had been 13
that busy too, and in a few days' time I would be that busy again.
Meantime, I had the odd sensation that I was fading away. I quickly
invented a ridiculously complicated project that involved a great deal of
Internet searching and faxing things overseas at all hours of the day and
night, and immediately felt much better.

How did we get so busy? That's not too hard to figure out. The work 14
world has become a far more Darwinian° place in the past decade. Plenty
of middle managers with middling incomes are obligated to put in sixty
or seventy hours a week on the job. Workaholism? It's a condition of
employment. Job flexibility? Puh‐lease. New technology? Fabulous. It lets
us work all the time. To be is to do. And the more there is on your to‐do
list, the more reassured you are that you must count for something.

Of course, you don't get work overload without work stress, and everyone 15
I know has plenty of that. But people who suddenly aren't busy have more.

One man told me what happened to him after he had accepted a 16
gigantic buyout. He took his bag of money and set up a little office to
figure out what to do next. He showed up on Monday morning at eight.
His appointment book was blank. The phone didn't ring. Nobody
needed him. He says it was the worst moment of his life.

When I met my friend for lunch, I asked her what had happened to 17
her ultra‐busy schedule. She told me that she had put herself on a strict

---

° Darwinian: Referring to Charles Darwin (1809–82) who in 1859 published *The Origin of
Species*, a work arguing that stronger individuals and species survived and propagated
themselves through "natural selection," while the weaker died off.

new regimen. She was turning down at least three assignments a week. She was practising being a slacker. She had sworn off multitasking and was trying unitasking, though she confessed it was incredibly difficult. Then she invited me to go to the garden centre with her after lunch.

18   It would have been fun, I said. But I really had to get back to work.

• •

Explorations:

Margaret Wente, *An Accidental Canadian: Reflections on My Home and (Not) Native Land*

Carl Honoré, *In Praise of Slow: How a Worldwide Movement Is Challenging the Cult of Speed*

http://en.wikipedia.org/wiki/Karoshi

http://www.statcan.ca/english/studies/11-008/feature/star2002064000s 1a01.pdf

http://www.nsb.com/speakerbio.asp?name=Margaret+Wente

Structure:

1. What well-known technique does Wente choose to open her argument?
2. Roughly what proportion of her argument does Wente fill with *examples*? Have you ever used this many? Do you find it hard to think of them? Why? What is the solution?
3. Why does Wente choose to end her entire essay on the word "work"?

Style:

1. What is Wente doing when she uses the terms "lunchee" in paragraph 4 and "puh-lease" in paragraph 14? Are these usages appropriate for her topic and her treatment of it?
2. If overwork is a serious problem for Wente and the rest of us, why does she joke about it? Does her humorous TONE undermine the significance of her argument? Or can it be a valid approach to a real topic?
3. Explain the IRONY that in paragraph 18 powers Wente's closing: "It would have been fun, I said. But I really had to get back to work."

Ideas for Discussion and Writing:

1. Wente sums up the pressures to work with the words "To be is to do" (par. 14). Is this what our society believes? Is it what you believe? Are there alternative ways to "be"? Back your view with reasons and *examples*.

2. Is work addictive? (See the examples in paragraphs 12, 13, 15 and 16.) Are Wente and her friends hooked? Are you? If so, how does addiction begin? How serious does it get? How can it be beaten? What is withdrawal like?

3. In paragraphs 8–9, Wente's dinner companions say that when they took time off, they came back to 600 to 2000 emails, and as many as 47 voice mails. How many emails do you receive per day? Share your best techniques for dealing with them. Does digital communication increase or decrease our workload? Give *examples.*

4. The Japanese have a word for working oneself to death: *Karoshi.* Key the term into a search engine and visit some of the many Web sites on this topic. Report your findings to the class: How frequent and widespread is this problem? Does it happen only in Japan?

5 "The work world has become a far more Darwinian place in the last decade," reports Wente in paragraph 14. Explore this point. Draw an ANALOGY between humans competing in the workplace and animals competing in the wild.

6. One high-ranking employee of the World Bank says that if she leaves work before 7:30 p.m. she goes out the back door, to avoid being seen going home early. And in paragraph 11 Wente says that on weekdays one gets up at 5:30 a.m. to avoid being a slacker. How many hours do you think make a reasonable work week? And why? Give your best techniques for "having a life" while being an employee.

7. **PROCESS IN WRITING:** *You are probably among the majority of today's students who also have a part-time job. How busy is the combination of your studies and work? Write your own version of "Busy, Busy, Busy," giving large numbers of examples to illustrate your point. First freewrite or brainstorm to get ideas and examples safely down on paper, then look over these notes to make a short outline with a* thesis *statement. Write the draft quickly, not stopping now for corrections. Later look it over: Is there at least 50% of example content? Is the TONE consistent, whether serious or humorous? Have you used* logic signals *to speed your argument on? Are the words short and strong, or big and flabby? Edit for all these things. Finally, check the sentence structure and punctuation before printing off your best version.*

Note: See also the Topics for Writing at the end of this chapter.

RAY GUY

Outharbor Menu

Ray Guy's authentic and direct voice of the Newfoundland outports is witness that, despite globalization and standardization, Canada still includes peoples rooted in other ways, other views. Guy was born in 1939 at Arnold's Cove, an isolated fishing village on Placentia Bay. As a child he learned the self-reliance of a life little changed in centuries. Then after attending Memorial University for two years he went to Toronto, where in 1963 he earned a diploma in journalism at Ryerson. Back in Newfoundland he began reporting for the St. John's Evening Telegram, *but found that reporting was not enough. His distaste for the Liberal government of Joey Smallwood, and especially its policy of closing down the outports where for centuries Newfoundlanders had lived by fishing, led Guy to become a political columnist. His satirical attacks on Smallwood were so devastating that many credit him with the Liberals' defeat in the provincial election of 1971. Leaving the* Telegram *when the Thomson chain bought it, Guy went freelance, continuing to pour satire on his targets. Later Guy began to write plays, whose salty humour is much like that of his columns. Some of his best writings are collected in* You May Know Them as Sea Urchins, Ma'am *(1975);* That Far Greater Bay *(1976), which won the Leacock Medal for Humour, and from which our selection comes; and* Ray Guy's Best *(1987). In 1994 appeared* From the Straight Shore, *on Newfoundland's history. To honour Guy's lifetime of writing about Newfoundland, Memorial University made him an honorary Doctor of Letters in 2001.*

1   What feeds we used to have. Not way back in the pod auger days,° mind you. That was before my time. I mean not long ago, just before the tinned stuff and the packages and the baker's bread started to trickle into the outports.

2   Out where I come from the trickle started when I was about six or seven years old. One day I went next door to Aunt Winnie's (that's Uncle John's Aunt Winnie) and she had a package of puffed rice someone sent down from Canada.°

3   She gave us youngsters a small handful each. We spent a long time admiring this new exotic stuff and remarking on how much it looked like emmets' eggs. We ate it one grain at a time as if it were candy, and because of the novelty didn't notice the remarkable lack of taste.

° the pod auger days: a common Newfoundland expression meaning "the old days." A pod auger is an auger with a lengthwise groove.
° from Canada: Newfoundland did not join Confederation until 1949, after the time Ray Guy describes.

"Now here's a five cent piece and don't spend it all in sweets, mind." You never got a nickel without this caution attached.

4

Peppermint knobs. White capsules ringed around with flannelette pink stripes. Strong! You'd think you were breathing icewater. They're not near as strong today.

5

Chocolate mice shaped like a crouching rat, chocolate on the outside and tough pink sponge inside. Goodbye teeth. Bullseyes made from molasses. And union squares — pastel blocks of marshmallow.

6

Those mysterious black balls that were harder than forged steel, had about 2,537 different layers of color and a funny tasting seed at the centre of the mini-universe.

7

Soft drinks came packed in barrels of straw in bottles of different sizes and shapes and no labels. Birch beer, root beer, chocolate, lemonade, and orange.

8

Spruce beer, which I could never stomach, but the twigs boiling on the stove smelled good. Home brew made from "Blue Ribbon" malt and which always exploded like hand grenades in the bottles behind the stove.

9

Rum puncheons. Empty barrels purchased from the liquor control in St. John's. You poured in a few gallons of water, rolled the barrel around, and the result was a stronger product than you put down $7.50 a bottle for today.

10

Ice cream made in a hand-cranked freezer, the milk and sugar and vanilla in the can in the middle surrounded by ice and coarse salt. I won't say it was better than the store-bought stuff today but it tasted different and I like the difference.

11

Rounders (dried tom cods) for Sunday breakfast without fail. Cods heads, boiled sometimes, but mostly stewed with onions and bits of salt pork.

12

Fried cod tongues with pork scruncheons.° Outport soul food. Salt codfish, fish cakes, boiled codfish and drawn butter, baked cod with savoury stuffing, stewed cod, fried cod.

13

Lobsters. We always got the bodies and the thumbs from the canning factories. When eating lobster bodies you must be careful to stay away from the "old woman," a lump of bitter black stuff up near the head which is said to be poisonous.

14

I was always partial to that bit of red stuff in lobster bodies but never went much on the pea green stuff although some did.

15

We ate turrs° (impaled on a sharpened broomstick and held over the damper hole to singe off the fuzz), some people ate tickleaces° and gulls but I never saw it done.

16

° pork scruncheons: crisp slices of fried pork fat.
° turr: the murre, an edible seabird.
° tickleace: the kittiwake, a kind of gull.

17   We ate "a meal of trouts," seal, rabbits that were skinned out like a sock, puffin' pig (a sort of porpoise that had black meat), mussels and cocks and hens, otherwise known as clams, that squirt at you through air holes in the mud flats.

18   Potatoes and turnips were the most commonly grown vegetables although there was some cabbage and carrot. The potatoes were kept in cellars made of mounds of earth lined with sawdust or goosegrass. With the hay growing on them they looked like hairy green igloos.

19   A lot was got from a cow. Milk, certainly, and cream and butter made into pats and stamped with a wooden print of a cow or a clover leaf, and buttermilk, cream cheese. And I seem to remember a sort of jellied sour milk. I forget the name but perhaps the stuff was equivalent to yogurt.

20   There was no fresh meat in summer because it wouldn't keep. If you asked for a piece of meat at the store you got salt beef. If you wanted fresh beef you had to ask for "fresh meat."

21   Biscuits came packed in three-foot long wooden boxes and were weighed out by the pound in paper bags. Sultanas, Dad's cookies, jam jams, lemon creams with caraway seeds, and soda biscuits.

22   Molasses was a big thing. It was used to sweeten tea, in gingerbread, on rolled oats porridge, with sulphur in the spring to clean the blood (eeeccchhhh), in bread, in baked beans, in 'lassie bread.

23   It came in barrels and when the molasses was gone, there was a layer of molasses sugar at the bottom.

24   Glasses of lemon crystals or strawberry syrup or lime juice. Rolled oats, farina, Indian meal. Home-made bread, pork buns, figgy duff,° partridgeberry tarts, blanc mange, ginger wine, damper cakes.°

25   Cold mutton, salt beef, pease pudding, boiled cabbage, tinned bully beef for lunch on Sunday, tinned peaches, brown eggs, corned caplin.°

26   And thank God I was twelve years old before ever a slice of baker's bread passed my lips.

● ●

Explorations:

Ray Guy,
> *That Far Greater Bay*
> *Ray Guy's Best*

Farley Mowat, *This Rock Within the Sea: A Heritage Lost*

Al Pittman, *Once When I Was Drowning: Poems*

E. Annie Proulx, *The Shipping News* (novel)

Donna Morrissey, *Kit's Law* (novel)

° figgy duff: boiled raisin pudding.

° damper cakes: a kind of bannock made on the damper (upper surface) of a cookstove.

° caplin: a small and edible ocean fish often used by cod fishermen as bait.

http://www.wordplay.com/tourism/folklore.html
http://www.nflab.com
http://www.heritage.nf.ca/home.html
http://www.ncf.ca/ap/teach/teach99/wrt/nfld/guy.htm
http://www.gov.nf.ca

Structure:

1. How informative is Ray Guy's beginning? Identify every fact the opening sentence states or implies about the essay that follows.
2. At the end Ray Guy exclaims, "And thank God I was twelve years old before ever a slice of baker's bread passed my lips." What does this final sentence do that qualifies it to close the essay?
3. Roughly what percentage of this essay consists of *examples*? Are there enough to make the point? Are there too many?
4. Why does Guy tell the incident of the puffed rice (pars. 2 and 3)? How does it prepare us for the rest of the argument?

Style:

1. Do you find Ray Guy's vocabulary difficult? For what audience is he writing? If he had known people outside Newfoundland would read this essay, would he have done anything differently?
2. Does Guy waste words or save them? Give *examples*.
3. Find five sentence fragments. Do you consider them errors? Why does Guy use them?
4. Point out expressions that make the essay folksy and COLLOQUIAL. Does Guy's TONE fit his topic?
5. In paragraph 18 Guy describes root cellars: "With the hay growing on them they looked like hairy green igloos." Where else does he use SIMILES?

Ideas for Discussion and Writing:

1. Through newspaper columns Guy fought the Newfoundland government's policy of forcing people from outports — such as the one in this essay — to central locations where they would work in factories instead of fish. Should traditional cultures be preserved? Are governments ever right in forcing them to change? Or is this culturicide? Defend your answer with *examples*.
2. Fast-food chains have been Americanizing the eating habits not only of Canada but also of many other nations. In this process what have we gained? What have we lost?
3. The failure of the cod stock has been a severe blow to Newfoundland's tradition of fisheries. Discuss what could be done to

help replenish the cod, and what could also be done to create alternative employment in the outports.

4. **PROCESS IN WRITING:** *Guy refers to "outport soul food" (par. 13). In an essay, describe the "soul food" of your own childhood. Take notes over several days, letting one memory lead to the next. Then fill a draft with large numbers of examples. In further drafts add more SENSE IMAGES and FIGURES OF SPEECH, to bring this cuisine alive for readers who grew up elsewhere. Finally, read aloud to detect repetition or other weak style, before producing the final version.*

Note: See also the Topics for Writing at the end of this chapter.

GORAN SIMIC

Goodbye Muse, Hello Prada

*Born in Bosnia in 1952, Goran Simic had become a leading writer and intellec-
tual of his country by the early 90s, when civil war broke out in Yugoslavia. With
his Muslim wife and two young children, he spent a harrowing three years in the
siege of Sarajevo, living the appalling events he would later describe so vividly in
his poems. Then when in 1996 he and his family immigrated to this country, with
the help of PEN Canada, he had a rude awakening: as he relates in this selection,
what his new employers wanted was not his brain but his muscles. Yet despite the
drudgery he so wittily depicts on these pages, Simic found time to resume his real
career. In Yugoslavia he had edited several literary magazines, and published
many books of short stories, plays, radio dramas and lyrics for opera. Then in
1997 Oxford Press published a collection of his powerful Sarajevo poems,*
Sprinting from the Graveyard, *translated by David Harsent. More poems followed:* Peace and War *in 1998,* Immigrant Blues *in 2003, and* From
Sarajevo with Sorrow *in 2005. By now Simic has published eleven books, and
been translated into almost a dozen languages. He also writes essays, such as our
lively and ironic selection from the February 24, 2000* The Globe and Mail.*

"You shouldn't have gone to another continent just to be a
slave. You could get a better job here in Bosnia," my father
told me bitterly last month when we met.

It was his honest reaction to my honest need to inform him, which
I'd avoided for three years, about my job in Canada. I hadn't expected
he'd easily swallow the fact that I was no longer a bookshop owner or
a book columnist, as I'd been in Sarajevo, but just a worker in a Holt
Renfrew warehouse.

But I hadn't bargained with the words "labourer" and "North
America" summoning to his mind historical images of black slaves in
the American South toiling in the cotton fields, with me in the middle of them.

My brother was still a general in the army, my other brother was still a
professor, but I'd switched from being a respectable poet to being a
slave. What a disgrace to the family!

That moment I realized how much I'd erred in being honest with my
father. At his age — almost 80 — he accepted only good news. He'd had
enough bad news the past few years. After having fought as a partisan
during the Second World War and celebrated victory over fascism, he experienced the Bosnian war, which finished like a bad football game: 0-0, with
200,000 killed, and nothing to celebrate.

6   Instead of enjoying retirement in his own flat or in our family house in Sarajevo, he lives in a rented house in the middle of a nowhere village because a rural refugee family squatted in his flat and because our family home was plundered and destroyed by his former neighbours.

7   "You know why our neighbours will never invite me again to their homes?" he asked me sadly. "Because I would recognize some of my own furniture."

8   I didn't let him say all this happened just because he was a Serb, since I don't think there's a difference between Muslim and Serb thieves. They all have the same religion: robbery.

9   Then I tried to make him smile by putting all my effort into describing a Canada that is not the American South, and where there are no slaves.

10   After I came to Canada, it didn't take long to realize that poetry would not pay my bills. Moreover, judging by the public attention it received, poetry seemed like an unwanted pregnancy in the marriage between publishers and readers. "You're a poet, fine, but what's your real job?" I heard.

11   In my first Canadian job, I came to realize that the load of ideas and words I carried in my head was worth less than what I could lug on my back. At first I didn't understand this, not because of vanity or the feeling that a job labouring in a warehouse could ruin my poet's image, but because it didn't dawn on me that for $1,100 a month my muscles were going to be rented along with just 10 per cent of my brain. With the rest I could do whatever I wanted — but only at lunch break and after 4 p.m. Good-bye, muse. Hello, boss. I now understood that I was a replaceable wheel in a machine someone else made.

12   I got precious advice on how to save my soul from my old friend Sasha Bukvic, one of the best sculptors in the former Yugoslavia, who now worked at a job like mine. "Since you have to spend three hours on the commute, don't sleep on the buses or subway cars," he told me. "This is the time for who you are."

13   It wasn't easy to keep my eyelids open, but soon my favoured travelling companions were Milan Kundera, Jung Chang and Joseph Brodsky — all of them writers who lived outside their homelands. But the books didn't keep me from noticing how, at 6 a.m., the bus driving to Mississauga carried almost entirely first-generation immigrants. Only the driver was Canadian-born.

14   Alone among the 20 workers who came from all over the world — India, Iraq, Ethiopia — and who mostly worked scanning or marking down prices, I was the one who moved merchandise from world-famous clothing designers. Loading trucks, moving suits from one line to another, carting boxes, I soon realized how closely the prices of coats matched their weights.

15   On the one hand, I felt some designers had good fun searching for the quickest way to get money out of rich people's pockets. (Once I saw a Jamaican employee staring in disgust at the price tag of a Prada suit.

The price was higher than his entire year's earnings.) On the other hand, it was a pleasure to handle a wardrobe I imagined myself wearing.

After a while I could recognize designers by their styles, the same way   16
I would notice the difference between French surrealism and German symbolism, but I avoided saying this. Somebody might wickedly note that the difference between poetry and haute couture amounted to quite a few more zeros on the price tag.

The painter Johnny Cadiz, who worked with me for almost two years,   17
commented that our communication could be weirdly ambiguous:

"Where is Armani?"   18

"He's in the room with Donna Karan."   19

"Who hung up Calvin Klein on the rolling rack?"   20

"What's Prada doing in the same box as the Boss?"   21

I didn't spot any workers who weren't reading the horoscope in the   22
morning and weren't certain that next Friday they'd be Lotto 649 millionaires. It was amusing to listen to what they'd do with the money, but at the top of everybody's wish list was always: Quit this job immediately. What they'd say as a farewell to the managers was not generally to be found in dictionaries. But I heard worse cursing before Christmas when the managers announced that everyone would be laid off till the first week of the New Year.

To be honest, I didn't learn as much about the job as I learned about   23
my co-workers. You can learn quickly about a job, but you learn about people all your life. Some of them had lost everything, some had lost relatives, some held two jobs just to earn enough to bring their children here, or to feed their families. I asked myself who I was to think that my struggles were more important than theirs.

Once, at a PEN Canada° social gathering, I was introduced to Hilary   24
Weston, a nice woman who is Lieutenant-Governor of Ontario and married to the man who owns Holt Renfrew and many other enterprises. When I told her I worked in the Holt Renfrew warehouse she said, "Great! I hope one day you'll be manager." I didn't tell her I wanted to remain a writer.

As it happened, I met her again, two years later, this time on Canada   25
Book Day. After I told her I was quitting the job, she said, "Pity. But good luck."

I didn't tell my father any of this. He would have said, "What did I tell   26
you. There are still slaves in America!"

• •

° PEN Canada: The Canadian branch of International PEN, a world association of writers that defends freedom of opinion and "campaigns on behalf or writers around the world persecuted for the expression of their thoughts." See www.pencanada.ca.

Explorations:

Goran Simic,
>*Sprinting from the Graveyard* (poems, translated by David Harsent)
>*Immigrant Blues* (poems, translated by Amela Simic)

André Aciman, ed., *Letters of Transit: Reflections on Exile, Identity, Language, and Loss*

http://www.angelfire.com/poetry/goransimic
http://www.pencanada.ca/exile/bio.php?writerID=13
http://www.brickbooks.ca/BL-Simic.htm
http://www.cco.caltech.edu/~bosnia/bosnia.html
http://www.biblioasis.com/press/home.htm

Structure:

1. A good opening attracts the reader's attention. Does this one? Point out every technique Simic uses in paragraph 1 to get us reading.
2. How far does the rest of Simic's introduction extend? What does the rest of it achieve?
3. Identify the THESIS STATEMENT.
4. The body of the argument (starting in paragraph 11) appears in *chronological* order. Point out several time signals that move us on to each new part of the author's Canadian experience.
5. It is *examples* that do the main work of supporting Simic's argument. Point out two or three of your favourites. Has Simic reached the recommended 50% of *example* content for effective essays? Have you? Calculate this percentage for your own most recent essay, and report it to the class.

Style:

1. When in paragraph 11 Simic says "the load of ideas and words I carried in my head was worth less than what I could lug on my back," he uses the power of IRONY. Point out five more strong ironies in this essay.
2. If the subject of "Goodbye Muse, Hello Prada" is loss and hard times, why does Simic use so much humour? Does this strengthen or weaken his message?
3. Read paragraphs 17 through 21 aloud. What is so weird about this conversation, and why?

Ideas for Discussion and Writing:

1. Why does society pay Goran Simic more for lugging suits and coats around a warehouse than for writing poetry? Which activity do you see as having more value? Defend your answer with reasons.

2. Have you or your family, like Simic, risked your profession by immigrating to Canada? Give every reason you can think of why a doctor, lawyer, teacher or writer would come here if it means going to work as a labourer, security guard or janitor.

3. Have you, like Simic, been a "slave" renting your muscles and 10% of your brain? Tell the techniques you have found for coping with such a job.

4. Simic reports that he earns $1,100 a month. In your own town or city, how much must you make to rent housing? To buy a condo or house? To support a family? To buy the kind of clothes our author lugs around the Holt Renfrew warehouse? Do you buy lottery tickets, like all Simic's co-workers, to solve these problems? Why or why not?

5. Like more and more employees, our author commutes three hours a day (par. 12). How long is your own trip to school or work? Tell what you do to make it more pleasant or productive. Sleep? Read? How serious a problem is traffic and commuting time in the place where you live? What can individuals do about it? What can government do?

6. **PROCESS IN WRITING:** *Close your eyes, and think of the worst job you have ever had. Now taking notes, fill a page with colourful examples of what it was like. Looking these over, put your overall point into a THESIS STATEMENT, then write a discovery draft, packing the argument with your* examples. *The next day, look again. Have you reached at least a 50% con-*tent of examples? *If not, add. Does each* example *support the overall point? If not, cut or revise. Is your TONE consistent (either humorous and ironic, like Simic's tone, or serious)? If not, revise. Finally, hone the spelling and punctuation before printing your best version to show the class.*

Note: See also the Topics for Writing at the end of this chapter.

Topics for Writing

CHAPTER 2: EXAMPLE

Each topic below is a generalization that needs examples to bring it alive. Choose one that strikes your interest. Freewrite or brainstorm to see if the examples come (either many short ones or one or more long ones). If they don't, try another topic. If you disagree with what the topic says, reverse it and write from your own viewpoint.

1. Not Everyone Needs College or University to Be Successful
2. Love Is Blind
3. Working at a Job Reduces Performance in School
4. You Are What You Eat
5. Maintenance Is More Important Than Some Car Owners Think
6. Sports Imitate Life
7. Movies Teach False Values
8. Prison Is a School for Criminals
9. Hitchhiking Is Dangerous
10. Children Learn Best from Their Parents' Example
11. Money Cannot Buy Happiness
12. Opposites Attract
13. Hockey Is Becoming More Violent
14. Canadians Are Becoming Less Like Americans
15. Fast Food Is a Menace
16. Our Healthcare System Is Breaking Down
17. Superstition Is Widespread Even Today
18. We Learn Best from Our Mistakes
19. First Impressions Can Mislead
20. Men Still Run Our Society
21. Many Products Today Are Made to Fall Apart
22. Travel Is the Best Educator
23. No Pain, No Gain
24. You Usually Get What You Pay For
25. Honesty Is Still the Best Policy
26. The Cost of Living in the City Is Very High
27. Canada's Climate Is Changing
28. Peoples' Choice of Vehicle Reveals Their Personality
29. True Wealth Is Measured by What You Can Do Without
30. It Is Dangerous to Forget the Power of Nature

Note also the Process in Writing Topic after each selection in this chapter.

EXAMPLE   **79**

Process in Writing: Guidelines

Follow at least some of these steps in developing your essay through examples (your teacher may suggest which ones).

1. *Take time choosing your topic, then try it out through brainstorming or freewriting. Do you have something to say? Can you supply examples? If not, try another topic.*

2. *Visualize your* AUDIENCE: *What level of language, what* TONE, *what examples, will communicate with this person or persons? (Remember the kinds of examples listed in our chapter introduction.)*

3. *Do a rapid discovery draft. Do not stop now to fix things like spelling and punctuation; just get the material safely out on paper.*

4. *The next day, look this draft over. Do your examples make up at least 50% of the content? Or if you give one long example, do you explain in enough depth? If not, add. Does every example support your main point? If not, revise. Are examples in order of increasing importance? If not, consider rearranging to build a climax.*

5. *Check your second draft for* TRANSITIONS, *and if necessary add. Test your prose by reading aloud, then revise awkward or unclear passages. Now use the dictionary and style guide if you need them.*

6. *Proofread your final copy slowly, word by word (if your eyes move too fast, they will "see" what* should *be there, not necessarily what* is *there).*

EMILY CARR

British Columbia Archives PDP 00903

"The eyes were two rounds of black, set in wider rounds of white, and placed in deep sockets under wide, black eyebrows. Their fixed stare bored into me as if the very life of the old cedar looked out. . . ."

— *Emily Carr, "D'Sonoqua"*

CHAPTER THREE

Description

IT'S LARGE AND PURPLE AND . . .

Consider the writer's tools: words in rows on a page. The writer cannot use gestures, facial expression, or voice, as the public speaker does. The writer cannot use colour, shape, motion or sound, as the filmmaker does. Yet words on a page can be powerful. We've all seen readers so involved in the words of a book that they fail to hear their own name called for dinner, or pass their own stop on the bus. These people have entered another world, living at second hand what a writer has lived or at least imagined at first hand.

How does writing do this to us? How does it make experience come alive? There are many ways, and one of the best is description. In simulating real life, description makes frequent appeals to our senses:

sight
hearing
touch
smell
taste

In "D'Sonoqua," Emily Carr appeals to our senses of smell and sight together when she writes, "Smell and blurred light oozed thickly out of the engine room, and except for one lantern on the wharf everything else was dark." Then in the next paragraph she moves on to hearing and touch: "Every gasp of the engine shook us like a great sob."

In her first sentence alone, Christie McLaren shows us the "red hair and the purple dress" of her "Suitcase Lady" who sits "night after night" in the "harsh light of a 24-hour doughnut shop on Queen Street West." These details have already begun to "show" us one particular homeless person and her life.

Similarly, behind every descriptive choice you make, behind every image you give your reader, should be your own overall purpose. In a warmup exercise such as freewriting, or even as you begin a discovery draft, you may not yet know that purpose. But the act of writing should soon make it clear: Is your subject scary, inspiring, pitiful, exasperating, ugly, beautiful, calm or violent? Once you know, help your audience to know as well.

Figures of speech — such as the similes and metaphors discussed in Chapter 6 — are powerful tools of description. When Emily Carr writes that a person's face is "greeny-brown and wrinkled like a baked apple," we see old age clearly. In other places she uses onomatopoetic terms — words like "scuttled," "slithered," "grated" and "ooze" — which describe by sounding like what they mean. (See FIGURES OF SPEECH in the glossary.)

In a description not all words are equal. Use short and strong ones from everyday life, not the long and flabby ones that some misguided writers think are eloquent. Do we really "perspire" or do we "sweat"? "Ambulate" or "walk"? "Altercate" or "argue"? "Ponder" or "think"? "Masticate" or "chew"? "Expectorate" or "spit"? It is obvious that the second term in each case is stronger, more vivid, more descriptive. So why would we use the first?

Choose words that convey the right *feeling* as well as the right dictionary meaning. One student closed a pretty description of the ocean by saying "the water was as still as a pan full of oil." The image of water as oil may imply stillness, but this water is not exactly something we would want to dive into or even watch at sunset — we'd be too busy thinking of pollution! Another person described forest trees in autumn as being the colour of a fire engine. The colour may be right, but will the image of a large truck perched in the tree branches really give us that autumn feeling?

Spend the time, then, to *feel*, as well as *think*, your words. Search drafts for weak or inexact or inappropriate terms, and replace them. If the right word doesn't come, find it in a dictionary or thesaurus. And realize that your electronic thesaurus may be fast, but a desk-size book version offers far more choices to help your overall idea or feeling, whatever it may be, come through clearly.

Note: Many authors in other chapters use description to help make their point. See especially these examples:

Sylvia Fraser, "My Other Self," p. 29
Ray Guy, "Outharbor Menu," p. 68
Maria Coffey, "An Offering from the Dead," p. 168
Catherine Pigott, "Chicken-Hips," p. 172
Félix Leclerc, "The Family House," p. 217
Dr. Mark Bernstein, "Yes, It Is Brain Surgery," p. 248
Joy Kogawa, "Grinning and Happy," p. 292
Lt.-Gen. Roméo Dallaire, "*Cri de coeur*," p. 319

KAREN CONNELLY

August 4[*]

At age 16 Karen Connelly had become, as she later wrote, "painfully bored with high school and hungry for living knowledge of the world." So she applied to an exchange program and the next year left her home of Calgary, Alberta, for Denchai, a village in northern Thailand. There she lived a year of strong emotion: culture shock, wonder at the sights and smells and sounds of the tropics, pleasure at making new friends, and fulfillment in learning a language and culture and landscape so different from her own. So strong was her desire to live life that she later wrote, "I regret having needed to sleep in Thailand. I should have been awake constantly, I should have learned more." Though it took time from her new life, she wrote regularly in a journal, then for years afterward, living in several more countries, polished these notes till they became Touch the Dragon: A Thai Journal. *When the intensely lyrical work was published in 1992, Connelly became the youngest person ever to win the Governor General's Award for Nonfiction. From this book comes our selection, "August 4." Connelly's list of publications keeps growing: In 1990 she had won the Pat Lowther Memorial Award with a book of poetry,* The Small Words in My Body. *Then in 1993 appeared* This Brighter Prison; *in 1995 another travel memoir,* One Room in a Castle: Letters from Spain, France & Greece; *in 1997 more poems,* The Disorder of Love; *and in 2000* The Border Surrounds Us. *In it she reflects on her many crossings of "borders," and on her political engagement with countries such as Burma. In 2001 came another travel memoir of Thailand,* The Dream of a Thousand Lives. *Connelly now divides her time between Canada, Burma and Greece.*

1 Every day something happens and I don't have time to write it down. When an event goes unwritten, I think, I will not forget this day, that moment, the words from that laughing mouth. There is so much I haven't written down, and even more that I haven't touched. The days tear away so quickly now. I fear I'll wake one morning and discover I'm old. I will look backwards into the past and know that all the years I lived were only a few long moments, and that I never knew enough. I've called the airline in Bangkok to confirm my flight date, August 19, two days short of a full year. I don't want to go back.

2 Every roadside, every wild morning journey to Prae, to the market, even pedalling over the bridge in the morning — again and again, I meet stories and pass them by because there is not enough time to spin out the sensations and web them into words. I am too alive and the days are never still.

---

* Editor's title.

84

I ride into the fields and find two women. While they bathe at the well, 3 a blade of grass comes to life and glides onto the stones. The women shriek, the wind blows down from the sky and six sand-coloured dogs lope across the field. In movements from a dance, the women flay the pearled green snake with sticks. It is five feet long, thick as a sailing line, still and bloody on the stones. The women's long hair slides over their shoulders and into their eyes. The *pasins* they wear blossom vermilion, blue, yellow; the sky behind them bruises purple-grey with rain. When one of the women spears the snake with a stick and swings it over her head, the dogs leap barking into the air, underbellies creamy white. As the snake whips beyond them, they rush after it, growling and snapping their jaws.

All this splendid horror in seconds, in the rice field behind the 4 monastery. The women bend down again to the water. Was the twisting snake real? Did I see it?

Will I remember this sky and the people beneath it? Ajahn Champa° 5 was right when she said a year ago (a year! why so fast?) that Thailand would become a dream to me. It already is, but one I live daily. "Canada will soon be real again," she said the other day. Canada. Canada. I push the word over on my tongue. The country of cold rocks. Was I born there?

I believe everything now, take it literally when new market women ask 6 me where I've come from. Without thinking, I answer "the river" or "the school" or "the old temple." I don't even consider another country. This one is enough.

Canada? The word itself is a question now. 7

• •

Explorations:

Karen Connelly,
    Touch the Dragon: A Thai Journal
    One Room in a Castle: Letters from Spain, France & Greece
Peter Mayle, *A Year in Provence*
Barbara Hodgson, *The Tattooed Map*
Rosa Jordan, *Dangerous Places: Travels on the Edge*
Ronald Wright, *Time Among the Maya: Travels in Belize, Guatemala, and Mexico*
Isabella Tree, *Islands in the Clouds: Travels in the Highlands of New Guinea*
http://www.nectec.or.th/WWW-VL-Thailand.html
http://www.poets.ca/linktext/direct/connelly.htm

Structure:

1. How do the opening (par. 1) and the closing (5–7) of this selection reflect each other? What is the effect?
2. Point out the THESIS STATEMENT of this selection.

° Ajahn Champa: Connelly's teacher.

Style:

1. Why does Connelly write "August 4" in the present tense? Is this choice apt for a *description*?
2. When in paragraph 2 the author tells us "there is not enough time to spin out the sensations and web them into words"; when in paragraph 3 the "blade of grass comes alive"; when the women's garments, their *pasins*, "blossom vermillion, blue, yellow"; and when "the sky behind them bruises purple-grey with rain"; what FIGURE OF SPEECH is the author exploiting? How does it strengthen her *description*?
3. Analyze how ONOMATOPOEIA contributes to the view of Canada expressed in "Canada. Canada. I push the word over on my tongue. The country of cold rocks" (par. 5).

Ideas for Discussion and Writing:

1. Connelly was only 17 when she kept the journal that became *Touch the Dragon*. Yet in paragraph 1 she writes, "I fear I'll wake one morning and discover I'm old. I will look backwards into the past and know that all the years I lived were only a few long moments, and that I never knew enough." Do you find these words chilling? How does Connelly try to fight this fear of time passing? How would you?
2. "Every day something happens and I don't have time to write it down," says Connelly in her first words. Is writing the way to retain experience? To interpret and understand it? How does reading compare to direct experience? Do you keep a diary? A journal? What are the benefits? What are the limits?
3. Connelly sums up the episode of the women, the snake and the dogs as "all this splendid horror" (Par 4). Why "horror"? Why "splendid"?
4. In paragraphs 4 and 5 the author keeps wondering if the things she sees are "real," if she will "remember" them, and if returning from the "dream" of Thailand will make Canada "real" again. Do your own major experiences ever seem unreal? Give an example.
5. In the preface to *Touch the Dragon* Connelly describes her boredom at age 16 in Calgary, and how she hoped "to escape from Canada and go very far away." Have you gone on a student exchange, or had another long experience far away? Was it good or bad? *Describe* one event that gives the flavour of it. Or do you hope to stay right where you are? Tell why. Or have you already come here from another country? If so, have you begun to forget your first home, as Connelly in Thailand began to forget hers? Will you go back to visit? Why or why not?
6. **PROCESS IN WRITING:** *Developing question 5 just above, freewrite on your stay in a far place (for an* AUDIENCE *in Canada), or, if you have immigrated to Canada, freewrite on your first months here (for a hypothetical* AUDIENCE *in your first country). Do you see an overall point, like Connelly's observation that*

"I don't want to go back"? If so, put it into a THESIS STATEMENT *and incorporate it into your first draft. Now think of your readers: to help them "live" your experience, do what Connelly did. Pack your account with* examples, *with images, with appeals to the senses (sight, hearing, touch, smell and taste). Add these elements of* description *wherever you can. Finally, check for spelling and punctuation before you print off your best version.*

Note: See also the Topics for Writing at the end of this chapter.

CHRISTIE McLAREN

Suitcase Lady*

Christie McLaren lives in Canmore, Alberta, where she does freelance writing and editing, while developing her own book on the state of Canada's forests and forest industry. But when she wrote "Suitcase Lady" McLaren was a student at the University of Waterloo, reporting for The Globe and Mail *as a part of her English co-op work experience. After graduation she spent a year and a half at the* Winnipeg Free Press, *then returned to the* Globe, *where she continued to report on many issues. An avid hiker, skier and canoeist, McLaren channelled her love of the outdoors into several years of investigating forestry, energy and other environmental topics, as well as writing on national health policy and Ontario politics. McLaren has also published with* Nature Canada *and* Equinox, *and does photography as well. Though a professional journalist, she says that "writing is nothing but pain while you're doing it and nothing but relief when it's done. Any joy or satisfaction, I think, is a bit of fleeting luck." McLaren spent several nights with "the Vicomtesse" before hearing the story she reports in this selection. The article first appeared in the* Globe.

1   Night after night, the woman with the red hair and the purple dress sits in the harsh light of a 24-hour doughnut shop on Queen Street West.

2   Somewhere in her bleary eyes and in the deep lines of her face is a story that probably no one will ever really know. She is taking pains to write something on a notepad and crying steadily.

3   She calls herself Vicomtesse Antonia The Linds'ays. She's the suitcase lady of Queen Street.

4   No one knows how many women there are like her in Toronto. They carry their belongings in shopping bags and spend their days and nights scrounging for food. They have no one and nowhere to go.

5   This night, in a warm corner with a pot of tea and a pack of Player's, the Vicomtesse is in a mood to talk.

6   Out of her past come a few scraps: a mother named Savaria; the child of a poor family in Montreal; a brief marriage when she was 20; a son in Toronto who is now 40. "We never got along well because I didn't bring him up. I was too poor. He never call me mama."

7   She looks out the window. She's 60 years old.

---

* Editor's title.

With her words she spins herself a cocoon. She talks about drapes and   8
carpets, castles and kings. She often lapses into French. She lets her tea
get cold. Her hands are big, rough, farmer's hands. How she ended up
in the doughnut shop remains a mystery, maybe even to her.

"Before, I had a kitchen and a room and my own furniture. I had to   9
leave everything and go."

It's two years that she's been on the go, since the rooming houses   10
stopped taking her. "I don't have no place to stay."

So she walks. A sturdy coat covers her dress and worn leather boots   11
are on her feet. But her big legs are bare and chapped and she has a
ragged cough.

Yes, she says, her legs get tired. She has swollen ankles and, with no   12
socks in her boots, she has blisters. She says she has socks — in the suitcase — but they make her feet itch.

As for money, "I bum on the street. I don't like it, but I have to. I have   13
to survive. The only pleasure I got is my cigaret." She lights another one.
"It's not a life."

She recalls the Saturday, a long time ago, when she made $27, and   14
laughs when she tells about how she had to make the money last through
Sunday, too. Now she gets "maybe $7 or $8," and eats "very poor."

When she is asked how people treat her, the answer is very matter-of-   15
fact: "Some give money. Some are very polite and some are rude."

In warm weather, she passes her time at the big square in front of City   16
Hall. When it's cold she takes her suitcase west to the doughnut shop.

The waitresses who bring food to the woman look upon her with com-   17
passion. They persuaded their boss that her sitting does no harm.

Where does she sleep? "Any place I can find a place to sleep. In the   18
park, in stores — like here I stay and sit, on Yonge Street." She shrugs.
Sometimes she goes into an underground parking garage.

She doesn't look like she knows what sleep is. "This week I sleep three   19
hours in four days. I feel tired but I wash my face with cold water and I feel
okay." Some questions make her eyes turn from the window and stare hard.
Then they well over with tears. Like the one about loneliness. "I don't talk
much to people," she answers. "Just the elderly, sometimes, in the park."

Her suitcase is full of dreams.   20

Carefully, she unzips it and pulls out a sheaf of papers — "my concertos."   21

Each page is crammed with neatly written musical notes — the care-   22
ful writing she does on the doughnut shop table — but the bar lines are
missing. Questions about missing bar lines she tosses aside. Each "con-
certo" has a French name — Tresor, La Tempete, Le Retour — and each
one bears the signature of the Vicomtesse. She smiles and points to one.
"A very lovely piece of music. I like it."

She digs in her suitcase again, almost shyly, and produces a round   23
plastic box. Out of it emerges a tiara. Like a little girl, she smooths back
her dirty hair and proudly puts it on. No one in the doughnut shop
seems to notice.

24   She cares passionately about the young, the old and the ones who suffer. So who takes care of the suitcase lady?

25   "God takes care of me, that's for sure," she says, nodding thoughtfully. "But I'm not what you call crazy about religion. I believe always try to do the best to help people — the elderly, and kids, and my country, and my city of Toronto, Ontario."

• •

Explorations:

Jack Layton, *Homelessness: The Making and Unmaking of a Crisis*
Marlene Webber, *Street Kids: The Tragedy of Canada's Runaways*
George Orwell, *Down and Out in Paris and London*
Rohinton Mistry, *A Fine Balance*
http://ryandale.org/ryanlinks.html
http://www.nationalhomeless.org
http://aspin.asu.edu/hpn
http://www.homelessness.gc.ca

Structure:

1. "Suitcase Lady" was a feature article in *The Globe and Mail*. As newspaper journalism, how does it differ from a typical ESSAY?
2. What does the opening *description* achieve?
3. How do the many quotations help the *description*?
4. Explain the IRONY of the closing.

Style:

1. Why is the vocabulary of "Suitcase Lady" so easy?
2. "With her words she spins herself a cocoon," states McLaren in paragraph 8. How appropriate is this METAPHOR?
3. Point out at least five concrete details that help you picture this homeless woman's life. Now think about your own writing: do you also give details, or do you hide behind GENERALIZATIONS?

Ideas for Discussion and Writing:

1. "It's not a life," says "the Vicomtesse" in paragraph 13. Is your province currently making life easier or harder for homeless people? Give *examples*.
2. How do you react to people who, like the suitcase lady, "bum on the street"? How often do you give? What makes you give to one person but not another?

3. In paragraph 6 the suitcase lady speaks of her son in Toronto: "We never got along well because I didn't bring him up. I was too poor. He never call me mama." In the area where you live, how much money does a family need to stay together? To avoid quarrels over money? To be hopeful about the future?

4. **PROCESS IN WRITING:** *Tape an interview with someone who in economic status, age, values or some other respect is very different from you. Then write a profile. Like McLaren, portray your subject through her or his best comments. Now add many IMAGES of physical appearance to build your description. Edit for conciseness and finally correctness. Then read your best version, with feeling, to the class.*

Note: See also the Topics for Writing at the end of this chapter.

CHARLES YALE HARRISON

In the Trenches

Charles Yale Harrison (1898–1954) was born in Philadelphia and grew up in Montreal. His independent spirit revealed itself early: in grade four he condemned Shakespeare's The Merchant of Venice *as anti-Semitic, and when his teacher beat him he quit school. At 16 he went to work for the* Montreal Star *and at 18 joined the Canadian army. As a machine gunner in France and Belgium during 1917 and 1918, Harrison witnessed the gruesome front-line scenes he was later to describe in fiction. He was wounded at Amiens and decorated for bravery in action. After the war Harrison returned to Montreal but soon left for New York, where he began a career in public relations for the labour movement and for numerous humanitarian causes. He also wrote several books, both nonfiction and fiction. By far the best is* Generals Die in Bed, *an account of trench warfare that shocked the public and became the best seller of 1930. Spare in style, biting and vivid, this autobiographical novel was described by the* New York Evening Post *as "the best of the war books." From it comes our selection.*

1   We leave the piles of rubble that was once a little Flemish peasant town and wind our way, in Indian file, up through the muddy communication trench. In the dark we stumble against the sides of the trench and tear our hands and clothing on the bits of embedded barbed wire that runs through the earth here as though it were a geological deposit.

2   Fry, who is suffering with his feet, keeps slipping into holes and crawling out, all the way up. I can hear him coughing and panting behind me.

3   I hear him slither into a water-filled hole. It has a green scum on it. Brown and I fish him out.

4   "I can't go any farther," he wheezes. "Let me lie here, I'll come on later."

5   We block the narrow trench and the oncoming men stumble on us, banging their equipment and mess tins on the sides of the ditch. Some trip over us. They curse under their breaths.

6   Our captain, Clark, pushes his way through the mess. He is an Imperial, an Englishman, and glories in his authority.

7   "So it's you again," he shouts. "Come on, get up. Cold feet, eh, getting near the line?"

8   Fry mumbles something indistinctly. I, too, offer an explanation. Clark ignores me.

9   "Get up, you're holding up the line," he says to Fry.

10   Fry does not move.

11   "No wonder we're losing the bloody war," Clark says loudly. The men standing near-by laugh. Encouraged by his success, the captain continues:

"Here, sergeant, stick a bayonet up his behind — that'll make him move." A few of us help Fry to his feet, and somehow we manage to keep him going. 12

We proceed cautiously, heeding the warnings of those ahead of us. At last we reach our positions. 13

It is midnight when we arrive at our positions. The men we are relieving give us a few instructions and leave quickly, glad to get out. 14

It is September and the night is warm. Not a sound disturbs the quiet. Somewhere away far to our right we hear the faint sound of continuous thunder. The exertion of the trip up the line has made us sweaty and tired. We slip most of our accouterments off and lean against the parados. We have been warned that the enemy is but a few hundred yards off, so we speak in whispers. It is perfectly still. I remember nights like this in the Laurentians. The harvest moon rides overhead. 15

Our sergeant, Johnson, appears around the corner of the bay, stealthily like a ghost. He gives us instructions: 16

"One man up on sentry duty! Keep your gun covered with the rubber sheet! No smoking!" 17

He hurries on to the next bay. Fry mounts the step and peers into No Man's Land. He is rested now and says that if he can only get a good pair of boots he will be happy. He has taken his boots off and stands in his stockinged feet. He shows us where his heel is cut. His boots do not fit. The sock is wet with blood. He wants to take his turn at sentry duty first so that he can rest later on. We agree. 18

Cleary and I sit on the firing-step and talk quietly. 19

"So this is war." 20

"Quiet." 21

"Yes, just like the country back home, eh?" 22

We talk of the trench; how we can make it more comfortable. 23

We light cigarettes against orders and cup our hands around them to hide the glow. We sit thinking. Fry stands motionless with his steel helmet shoved down almost over his eyes. He leans against the parapet motionless. There is a quiet dignity about his posture. I remember what we were told at the base about falling asleep on sentry duty. I nudge his leg. He grunts. 24

"Asleep?" I whisper. 25

"No," he answers, "I'm all right." 26

"What do you see?" 27

"Nothing. Wire and posts." 28

"Tired?" 29

"I'm all right." 30

The sergeant reappears after a while. We squinch our cigarettes. 31

"Everything O.K. here?" 32

I nod. 33

"Look out over there. They got the range on us. Watch out." 34

35   We light another cigarette. We continue our aimless talk.

36   "I wonder what St. Catherine Street looks like —"

37   "Same old thing, I suppose — stores, whores, theaters —"

38   "Like to be there just the same —"

39   "Me too."

40   We sit and puff our fags for half a minute or so.

41   I try to imagine what Montreal looks like. The images are murky. All that is unreality. The trench, Cleary, Fry, the moon overhead — this is real.

42   In his corner of the bay Fry is beginning to move from one foot to another. It is time to relieve him. He steps down and I take his place. I look into the wilderness of posts and wire in front of me.

43   After a while my eyes begin to water. I see the whole army of wire posts begin to move like a silent host towards me.

44   I blink my eyes and they halt.

45   I doze a little and come to with a jerk.

46   So this is war, I say to myself again for the hundredth time. Down on the firing-step the boys are sitting like dead men. The thunder to the right has died down. There is absolutely no sound.

47   I try to imagine how an action would start. I try to fancy the preliminary bombardment. I remember all the precautions one has to take to protect one's life. Fall flat on your belly, we had been told time and time again. The shriek of the shell, the instructor in trench warfare said, was no warning because the shell traveled faster than its sound. First, he had said, came the explosion of the shell — then came the shriek and then you hear the firing of the gun. . . .

48   From the stories I heard from veterans and from newspaper reports I conjure up a picture of an imaginary action. I see myself getting the Lewis gun in position. I see it spurting darts of flame into the night. I hear the roar of battle. I feel elated. Then I try to fancy the horrors of the battle. I see Cleary, Fry and Brown stretched out on the firing-step. They are stiff and their faces are white and set in the stillness of death. Only I remain alive.

49   An inaudible movement in front of me pulls me out of the dream. I look down and see Fry massaging his feet. All is still. The moon sets slowly and everything becomes dark.

50   The sergeant comes into the bay again and whispers to me:

51   "Keep your eyes open now — they might come over on a raid now that it's dark. The wire's cut over there —" He points a little to my right.

52   I stand staring into the darkness. Everything moves rapidly again as I stare. I look away for a moment and the illusion ceases.

53   Something leaps towards my face.

54   I jerk back, afraid.

55   Instinctively I feel for my rifle in the corner of the bay.

56   It is a rat.

57   It is as large as a tom-cat. It is three feet away from my face and it looks steadily at me with its two staring, beady eyes. It is fat. Its long tapering tail

curves away from its padded hindquarters. There is still a little light from the stars and this light shines faintly on its sleek skin. With a darting movement it disappears. I remember with a cold feeling that it was fat, and why.

Cleary taps my shoulder. It is time to be relieved.   58

Over in the German lines I hear quick, sharp reports. Then the red-   59
tailed comets of the *minenwerfer*° sail high in the air, making parabolas of red light as they come towards us. They look pretty, like the fireworks when we left Montreal. The sergeant rushes into the bay of the trench, breathless. "Minnies," he shouts, and dashes on.

In that instant there is a terrific roar directly behind us.   60

The night whistles and flashes red.   61

The trench rocks and sways.   62

Mud and earth leap into the air, come down upon us in heaps.   63

We throw ourselves upon our faces, clawing our nails into the soft   64
earth in the bottom of the trench.

Another!   65

This one crashes to splinters about twenty feet in front of the bay.   66

Part of the parapet caves in.   67

We try to burrow into the ground like frightened rats.   68

The shattering explosions splinter the air in a million fragments. I   69
taste salty liquid on my lips. My nose is bleeding from the force of the detonations.

SOS flares go up along our front calling for help from our artillery.   70
The signals sail into the air and explode, giving forth showers of red, white and blue lights held aloft by a silken parachute.

The sky is lit by hundreds of fancy fireworks like a night carnival.   71

The air shrieks and cat-calls.   72

Still they come.   73

I am terrified. I hug the earth, digging my fingers into every crevice,   74
every hole.

A blinding flash and an exploding howl a few feet in front of the   75
trench.

My bowels liquefy.   76

Acrid smoke bites the throat, parches the mouth. I am beyond mere   77
fright. I am frozen with an insane fear that keeps me cowering in the bottom of the trench. I lie flat on my belly, waiting . . . .

Suddenly it stops.   78

The fire lifts and passes over us to the trenches in the rear.   79

We lie still, unable to move. Fear has robbed us of the power to act. I   80
hear Fry whimpering near me. I crawl over to him with great effort. He is half covered with earth and débris. We begin to dig him out.

° *minenwerfer*: mine-throwing trench mortars.

81   To our right they have started to shell the front lines. It is about half a mile away. We do not care. We are safe.

82   Without warning it starts again.

83   The air screams and howls like an insane woman.

84   We are getting it in earnest now. Again we throw ourselves face downward on the bottom of the trench and grovel like savages before this demoniac frenzy.

85   The concussion of the explosions batters against us.

86   I am knocked breathless.

87   I recover and hear the roar of the bombardment.

88   It screams and rages and boils like an angry sea. I feel a prickly sensation behind my eyeballs.

89   A shell lands with a monster shriek in the next bay. The concussion rolls me over on my back. I see the stars shining serenely above us. Another lands in the same place. Suddenly the stars revolve. I land on my shoulder. I have been tossed into the air.

90   I begin to pray.

91   "God — God — please . . ."

92   I remember that I do not believe in God. Insane thoughts race through my brain. I want to catch hold of something, something that will explain this mad fury, this maniacal congealed hatred that pours down on our heads. I can find nothing to console me, nothing to appease my terror. I know that hundreds of men are standing a mile or two from me pulling gun-lanyards, blowing us to smithereens. I know that and nothing else.

93   I begin to cough. The smoke is thick. It rolls in heavy clouds over the trench, blurring the stabbing lights of the explosions.

94   A shell bursts near the parapet.

95   Fragments smack the sandbags like a merciless shower of steel hail.

96   A piece of mud flies into my mouth. It is cool and refreshing. It tastes earthy.

97   Suddenly it stops again.

98   I bury my face in the cool, damp earth. I want to weep. But I am too weak and shaken for tears.

99   We lie still, waiting . . . .

• •

Explorations:

Charles Yale Harrison, *Generals Die in Bed*
Erich Maria Remarque, *All Quiet on the Western Front* (novel)
Ernest Hemingway, *A Farewell to Arms* (novel)
Colin McDougall, *Execution* (novel)
Timothy Findley, *The Wars* (novel)
Heather Robertson, ed., *A Terrible Beauty: The Art of Canada at War*

http://en.wikipedia.org/wiki/World_War_1
http://www.bbc.co.uk/history/war/wwone
http://canadaonline.about.com/od/canadaww1
http://www.rootsweb.com/~ww1can/index.html
http://www.firstworldwar.com
http://www.worldwar1.com
http://gutenberg.net.au/ebooks05/0500061h.html

Structure:

1. In *narrating* his description of trench warfare, does Harrison ever deviate from straight chronological order? If so, where and how?
2. Harrison uses SENSE IMAGES so often that throughout this passage *description* carries the main weight of development. Find one example each of a strong appeal to our senses of sight, hearing, touch, taste and smell.
3. Many of the paragraphs are small, some only a word or two long. Examine paragraphs 25–30, 53–56 and 60–68, determining in each passage why the paragraphs are so short.
4. This account of an artillery attack ends with the words "We lie still, waiting. . . ." Is the ending effective, and if so, how?

Style:

1. What degree of CONCISENESS has Harrison achieved in this selection?
2. Harrison tells of the rat: "I remember with a cold feeling that it was fat, and why" (par. 57). How does he convey so much horror in so few words?
3. Analyze the power of the deceptively simple events of paragraph 89: "A shell lands with a monster shriek in the next bay. The concussion rolls me over on my back. I see the stars shining serenely above us. Another lands in the same place. Suddenly the stars revolve. I land on my shoulder. I have been tossed into the air."
4. In describing, Harrison exploits FIGURES OF SPEECH. Point out at least one good SIMILE and one good METAPHOR.
5. Why is "In the Trenches" told in present tense, even though the book was published years after the war?

Ideas for Discussion and Writing:

1. Our narrator relates his first experience of war. What has it taught him?
2. Have you read books or seen films that show war in a positive light? Name them. In what ways does "In the Trenches" differ from those accounts?
3. "In the Trenches" is part of a book entitled *Generals Die in Bed*. Discuss the implications of this title.

4. If you have read "Coming of Age in Putnok," compare the conflict described by George Gabori with that described by Harrison. Does hostility between individuals contribute to hostility between nations?

5. **PROCESS IN WRITING:** *Have you lived through a violent or even life-threatening experience, as Harrison did? Close your eyes and remember it. Then in a rapid first draft,* describe *to your audience what it was really like. How did things look, sound, feel, smell or even taste? Use* SENSE IMAGES, *as Harrison does, to help your reader know too. The next day look your* description *over. Does it begin and end at the right spots, to emphasize the important things? If not, chop or add. Are there unimportant details? If so, chop. Are some parts "thin"? If so, add. Are paragraphs longer in the slower parts and shorter in the tenser parts, like Harrison's? If not, adjust them. Finally, edit for correctness and style before producing your final version.*

Note: See also the Topics for Writing at the end of this chapter.

EMILY CARR

D'Sonoqua

*Although Emily Carr (1871–1945) was born to a conservative family in the con-
fined atmosphere of 19th-century Victoria, British Columbia, she emerged as one
of the nation's most original painters and writers. Strong-willed and independent,
she turned down several offers of marriage because she believed men "demanded
worship" and would only hold her back. Instead she pursued her goal to San
Francisco, London and Paris, studying art. Home again, with a new way of seeing inspired by post-impressionist artists in France, she set out on solo expeditions
to remote Indian villages along the coast and in the Queen Charlotte Islands,
where she put on canvas the power she felt in the ruins of ancient cultures. Our
selection describes three such trips. The public laughed at her bold and free art, but
she kept on. Around 1929 Carr shifted focus to the paintings she is best known for
now, her looming, explosive visions of the coastal rain forest itself. Emily Carr lived
for years in poverty, because recognition came very late. For years she managed a
rooming house, and would often paint on cardboard because canvas cost too much.
In her last years, plagued by ill health, she abandoned painting for writing. Our
selection comes from her first and best book, published in 1941,* Klee Wyck *(the
title is her name, "Laughing One," given her by the Nootka people).* Klee Wyck *is
an extension of her painting: a collection of word sketches in language rich and
suggestive, yet pared to the bone. During her lifetime she published two more volumes,* The Book of Small *(1942) and* The House of All Sorts *(1944). Others
appeared after her death:* Growing Pains *(autobiography, 1946),* The Heart of
a Peacock *(1953),* Pause: A Sketch Book *(1953), and finally her journals,
published as* Hundreds and Thousands *(1966).*

I was sketching in a remote Indian village when I first saw her. The vil- 1
lage was one of those that the Indians use only for a few months in
each year; the rest of the time it stands empty and desolate. I went
there in one of its empty times, in a drizzling dusk.

When the Indian agent dumped me on the beach in front of the vil- 2
lage, he said "There is not a soul here. I will come back for you in two
days." Then he went away.

I had a small Griffon dog with me, and also a little Indian girl, who, 3
when she saw the boat go away, clung to my sleeve and wailed, "I'm 'fraid."

We went up to the old deserted Mission House. At the sound of the 4
key in the rusty lock, rats scuttled away. The stove was broken, the wood
wet. I had forgotten to bring candles. We spread our blankets on the
floor, and spent a poor night. Perhaps my lack of sleep played its part in
the shock that I got, when I saw her for the first time.

5   Water was in the air, half mist, half rain. The stinging nettles, higher than my head, left their nervy smart on my ears and forehead, as I beat my way through them, trying all the while to keep my feet on the plank walk which they hid. Big yellow slugs crawled on the walk and slimed it. My feet slipped, and I shot headlong to her very base, for she had no feet. The nettles that were above my head reached only to her knee.

6   It was not the fall alone that jerked the "Oh's" out of me, for the great wooden image towering above me was indeed terrifying.

7   The nettle-bed ended a few yards beyond her, and then a rocky bluff jutted out, with waves battering it below. I scrambled up and went out on the bluff, so that I could see the creature above the nettles. The forest was behind her, the sea in front.

8   Her head and trunk were carved out of, or rather into, the bole of a great red cedar. She seemed to be part of the tree itself, as if she had grown there at its heart, and the carver had only chipped away the outer wood so that you could see her. Her arms were spliced and socketed to the trunk, and were flung wide in a circling, compelling movement. Her breasts were two eagle heads, fiercely carved. That much, and the column of her great neck, and her strong chin, I had seen when I slithered to the ground beneath her. Now I saw her face.

9   The eyes were two rounds of black, set in wider rounds of white, and placed in deep sockets under wide, black eyebrows. Their fixed stare bored into me as if the very life of the old cedar looked out, and it seemed that the voice of the tree itself might have burst from that great round cavity, with projecting lips, that was her mouth. Her ears were round, and stuck out to catch all sounds. The salt air had not dimmed the heavy red of her trunk and arms and thighs. Her hands were black, with blunt finger-tips painted a dazzling white. I stood looking at her for a long, long time.

10   The rain stopped, and white mist came up from the sea, gradually paling her back into the forest. It was as if she belonged there, and the mist were carrying her home. Presently the mist took the forest too, and, wrapping them both together, hid them away.

11   "Who is that image?" I asked the little Indian girl, when I got back to the house.

12   She knew which one I meant, but to gain time, she said, "What image?"

13   "The terrible one, out there on the bluff." The girl had been to Mission School, and fear of the old, fear of the new, struggled in her eyes. "I dunno," she lied.

14   I never went to that village again, but the fierce wooden image often came to me, both in my waking and in my sleeping.

15   Several years passed, and I was once more sketching in an Indian village. There were Indians in this village, and in a mild backward way it was "going modern." That is, the Indians had pushed the forest back a little to let the sun touch the new buildings that were replacing the old community houses. Small houses, primitive enough to a white man's thinking,

pushed here and there between the old. Where some of the big community houses had been torn down, for the sake of the lumber, the great corner posts and massive roof-beams of the old structure were often left, standing naked against the sky, and the new little house was built inside, on the spot where the old one had been.

It was in one of these empty skeletons that I found her again. She had once been a supporting post for the great centre beam. Her pole-mate, representing the Raven, stood opposite her, but the beam that had rested on their heads was gone. The two poles faced in, and one judged the great size of the house by the distance between them. The corner posts were still in place, and the earth floor, once beaten to the hardness of rock by naked feet, was carpeted now with rich lush grass.

I knew her by the stuck-out ears, shouting mouth, and deep eye-sockets. These sockets had no eye-balls, but were empty holes, filled with stare. The stare, though not so fierce as that of the former image, was more intense. The whole figure expressed power, weight, domination, rather than ferocity. Her feet were planted heavily on the head of the squatting bear, carved beneath them. A man could have sat on either huge shoulder. She was unpainted, weather-worn, sun-cracked, and the arms and hands seemed to hang loosely. The fingers were thrust into the carven mouths of two human heads, held crowns down. From behind, the sun made unfathomable shadows in eye, cheek and mouth. Horror tumbled out of them.

I saw Indian Tom on the beach, and went to him.

"Who is she?"

The Indian's eyes, coming slowly from across the sea, followed my pointing finger. Resentment showed in his face, greeny-brown and wrinkled like a baked apple, — resentment that white folks should pry into matters wholly Indian.

"Who is that big carved woman?" I repeated.

"D'Sonoqua." No white tongue could have fondled the name as he did.

"Who is D'Sonoqua?"

"She is the wild woman of the woods."

"What does she do?"

"She steals children."

"To eat them?"

"No, she carries them to her caves; that," pointing to a purple scar on the mountain across the bay, "is one of her caves. When she cries 'OO-oo-oo-oeo,' Indian mothers are too frightened to move. They stand like trees, and the children go with D'Sonoqua."

"Then she is bad?"

"Sometimes bad . . . sometimes good," Tom replied, glancing furtively at those stuck-out ears. Then he got up and walked away.

I went back, and, sitting in front of the image, gave stare for stare. But her stare so over-powered mine, that I could scarcely wrench my eyes away from the clutch of those empty sockets. The power that I felt was not in the thing itself, but in some tremendous force behind it, that the carver had believed in.

32   A shadow passed across her hands and their gruesome holdings. A little bird, with its beak full of nesting material, flew into the cavity of her mouth, right in the pathway of that terrible OO-oo-oo-oeo. Then my eye caught something that I had missed — a tabby cat asleep between her feet.

33   This was D'Sonoqua, and she was a supernatural being, who belonged to these Indians.

34   "Of course," I said to myself, "I do not believe in supernatural beings. Still — who understands the mysteries behind the forest? What would one do if one did meet a supernatural being?" Half of me wished that I could meet her, and half of me hoped I would not.

35   Chug — chug — the little boat had come into the bay to take me to another village, more lonely and deserted than this. Who knew what I should see there? But soon supernatural beings went clean out of my mind, because I was wholly absorbed in being naturally seasick.

36   When you have been tossed and wracked and chilled, any wharf looks good, even a rickety one, with its crooked legs stockinged in barnacles. Our boat nosed under its clammy darkness, and I crawled up the straight slimy ladder, wondering which was worse, natural seasickness, or supernatural "creeps." The trees crowded to the very edge of the water, and the outer ones, hanging over it, shadowed the shoreline into a velvet smudge. D'Sonoqua might walk in places like this. I sat for a long time on the damp, dusky beach, waiting for the stage. One by one dots of light popped from the scattered cabins, and made the dark seem darker. Finally the stage came.

37   We drove through the forest over a long straight road, with black pine trees marching on both sides. When we came to the wharf the little gas mail-boat was waiting for us. Smell and blurred light oozed thickly out of the engine room, and except for one lantern on the wharf everything else was dark. Clutching my little dog, I sat on the mail sacks which had been tossed on to the deck.

38   The ropes were loosed, and we slid out into the oily black water. The moon that had gone with us through the forest was away now. Black pine-covered mountains jagged up on both sides of the inlet like teeth. Every gasp of the engine shook us like a great sob. There was no rail round the deck, and the edge of the boat lay level with the black slithering horror below. It was like being swallowed again and again by some terrible monster, but never going down. As we slid through the water, hour after hour, I found myself listening for the OO-oo-oo-oeo.

39   Midnight brought us to a knob of land, lapped by the water on three sides, with the forest threatening to gobble it up on the fourth. There was a rude landing, a rooming-house, an eating-place, and a store, all for the convenience of fishermen and loggers. I was given a room, but after I had blown out my candle, the stillness and the darkness would not let me sleep.

40   In the brilliant sparkle of the morning when everything that was not superlatively blue was superlatively green, I dickered with a man who was

taking a party up the inlet that he should drop me off at the village I was headed for.

"But," he protested, "there is nobody there."   41

To myself I said, "There is D'Sonoqua."   42

From the shore, as we rowed to it, came a thin feminine cry — the mew-   43
ing of a cat. The keel of the boat had barely grated in the pebbles, when the cat sprang aboard, passed the man shipping his oars, and crouched for a spring into my lap. Leaning forward, the man seized the creature roughly, and with a cry of "Dirty Indian vermin!" flung her out into the sea.

I jumped ashore, refusing his help, and with a curt "Call for me at sun-   44
down," strode up the beach; the cat followed me.

When we had crossed the beach and come to a steep bank, the cat ran   45
ahead. Then I saw that she was no lean, ill-favoured Indian cat, but a sleek aristocratic Persian. My snobbish little Griffon dog, who usually refused to let an Indian cat come near me, surprised me by trudging beside her in comradely fashion.

The village was typical of the villages of these Indians. It had only one   46
street, and that had only one side, because all the houses faced the beach. The two community houses were very old, dilapidated and bleached, and the handful of other shanties seemed never to have been young; they had grown so old before they were finished, that it was then not worth while finishing them.

Rusty padlocks carefully protected the gaping walls. There was the   47
usual broad plank in front of the houses, the general sitting and sun-ning place for Indians. Little streams ran under it, and weeds poked up through every crack, half hiding the companies of tins, kettles, and rags, which patiently waited for the next gale and their next move.

In front of the Chief's house was a high, carved totem pole, sur-   48
mounted by a large wooden eagle. Storms had robbed him of both wings, and his head had a resentful twist, as if he blamed somebody. The heavy wooden heads of two squatting bears peered over the nettle-tops. The windows were too high for peeping in or out. "But, save D'Sonoqua, who is there to peep?" I said aloud, just to break the silence. A fierce sun burned down as if it wanted to expose every ugliness and forlornness. It drew the noxious smell out of the skunk cabbages, growing in the rich black ooze of the stream, scummed the water-barrels with green slime, and branded the desolation into my very soul.

The cat kept very close, rubbing and bumping itself and purring   49
ecstatically; and although I had not seen them come, two more cats had joined us. When I sat down they curled into my lap, and then the strangeness of the place did not bite into me so deeply. I got up, deter-mined to look behind the houses.

Nettles grew in the narrow spaces between the houses. I beat them   50
down, and made my way over the bruised dank-smelling mass into a space of low jungle.

51   Long ago the trees had been felled and left lying. Young forest had burst through the slash, making an impregnable barrier, and sealing up the secrets which lay behind it. An eagle flew out of the forest, circled the village, and flew back again.

52   Once again I broke silence, calling after him, "Tell D'Sonoqua —" and turning, saw her close, towering above me in the jungle.

53   Like the D'Sonoqua of the other villages she was carved into the bole of a red cedar tree. Sun and storm had bleached the wood, moss here and there softened the crudeness of the modelling; sincerity underlay every stroke.

54   She appeared to be neither wooden nor stationary, but a singing spirit, young and fresh, passing through the jungle. No violence coarsened her; no power domineered to wither her. She was graciously feminine. Across her forehead her creator had fashioned the Sistheutl, or mythical two-headed sea-serpent. One of its heads fell to either shoulder, hiding the stuck-out ears, and framing her face from a central parting on her forehead which seemed to increase its womanliness.

55   She caught your breath, this D'Sonoqua, alive in the dead bole of the cedar. She summed up the depth and charm of the whole forest, driving away its menace.

56   I sat down to sketch. What was this noise of purring and rubbing going on about my feet? Cats. I rubbed my eyes to make sure I was seeing right, and counted a dozen of them. They jumped into my lap and sprang to my shoulders. They were real — and very feminine.

57   There we were — D'Sonoqua, the cats and I — the woman who only a few moments ago had forced herself to come behind the houses in trembling fear of the "wild woman of the woods" — wild in the sense that forest-creatures are wild — shy, untouchable.

●●

Explorations:

Emily Carr,
  Klee Wyck
  The Book of Small
Maria Tippett, *Emily Carr: A Biography*
Doris Shadbolt, *The Art of Emily Carr*
Susan Crean,
  The Laughing One
  Opposite Contraries
Germaine Greer, *The Obstacle Race*
http://collections.ic.gc.ca/totems
http://collections.ic.gc.ca/EmilyCarrHomeWork
http://collections.ic.gc.ca/EmilyCarr

Structure:

1. Carr's opening words are, "I was sketching in a remote Indian village when I first saw her." Why are we not shown "her" identity till paragraph 6?
2. Where do the three parts of this selection each begin and end? How do the three images of D'Sonoqua form a progression?
3. A voyage by water precedes Carr's visit to each image. Beyond its structural function, does it have a symbolic role? Consider this passage from paragraph 38:

> **There was no rail round the deck, and the edge of the boat lay level with the black slithering horror below. It was like being swallowed again and again by some terrible monster, but never going down. As we slid through the water, hour after hour, I found myself listening for the OO-oo-oo-oeo.**

Style:

1. Although Carr is esteemed as a writer, she is better known as a painter. What aspects of her PROSE remind you of the visual arts? Point out passages that illustrate your answers.
2. What does Carr gain by using words such as "scuttled" (par. 4), "slithered" (par. 8), "grated" (par. 43) and "ooze" (par. 48)?
3. Carr plays with words. Rather than describe the walk as "slimy," she writes that slugs "slimed" the walk. Find other words she uses in fresh ways.
4. What FIGURE OF SPEECH depicts the wharf's "crooked legs stockinged in barnacles" (par. 36)? Where else does it occur? How does it further the *description*?
5. The term "Indian," current when Carr published *Klee Wyck* in 1941, is going out of use. Why? Name all the reasons you can think of why now the preferred term is often "First Nations People."

Ideas for Discussion and Writing:

1. In paragraph 31 Carr states of the second D'Sonoqua, "The power that I felt was not in the thing itself, but in some tremendous force behind it, that the carver had believed in." Is skill itself enough to create art, or must the artist believe in some "tremendous force"?
2. What is art for? Think of these:

   - Monumental architecture, as in banks, cathedrals, train stations and airports
   - Pretty paintings and photographs on living room walls
   - Statues of generals on horseback or politicians orating
   - Nonrepresentational art in its many forms: impressionism, cubism, surrealism, expressionism, etc.
   - The images of D'Sonoqua carved in cedar

3. The narrator and others fear D'Sonoqua. Why have humans always imagined monsters such as the Minotaur, Grendel, Dracula, Frankenstein, King Kong, Godzilla and the Boogieman, not to mention the traditional witches and ghosts? Do we in some way need them?

4. In what ways can "D'Sonoqua" be considered a feminist essay?

5. **PROCESS IN WRITING:** *Visit the first Emily Carr Web site listed in "Explorations" above, and choose your favourite among the paintings that it shows. Take notes on the appearance of your favourite (colour, texture, form, etc.), and on your reaction to it. Now in a rapid first draft, write your own* description *of this painting. Use frequent sense images, as Carr does in "D'Sonoqua." Later when you edit, remember Carr's advice from her book* Growing Pains: *"... get to the point as directly as you can; never use a big word if a little one will do."*

Note: See also the Topics for Writing at the end of this chapter.

Topics for Writing

CHAPTER 3: DESCRIPTION

Applying techniques from our chapter introduction, describe one of the following as vividly as you can. (See also the guidelines that follow.)

1. A Line-up at the Airport or Border
2. A Funeral Parlour During Visiting Hours
3. A Dance Club on Saturday Night
4. A Pine Cone or Other Natural Object Observed Closely
5. My Attic or Basement
6. The Interior of a Police Station or Courtroom
7. The Interior of My Church, Synagogue, Mosque or Temple During a Service
8. The Kitchen of a Fast-Food Restaurant
9. A Thunderstorm, Blizzard, Ice Storm, Tornado, Hurricane, Flood or Earthquake
10. A Garage or Body Shop in Operation
11. The Youngest or Oldest Person I Know
12. Rush Hour on the Expressway, Subway, Streetcar, Bus or Sidewalk
13. A Food Store of a Culture Not My Own
14. My Pet
15. A Junkyard or Dump
16. A Spider Web
17. The Waiting Room of a Doctor's Office
18. One Square Metre of the Forest Floor, Observed Closely
19. The Hottest or Coldest Day I Remember
20. A Piece of Public Art in My Town or City
21. The Street I Most Dread Going On
22. The Entertainment District of My City on a Saturday Night
23. A Factory Assembly Line
24. A Building That Seems Out of Place in My Neighbourhood
25. A Pool Hall or Video Arcade
26. A Retirement Home or Nursing Home
27. The Seashore
28. A Concert Crowd
29. My Favourite Park
30. The Sky on a Clear Night

Note: See also the Process in Writing topic after each selection in this chapter.

Process in Writing: Guidelines

Follow at least some of these steps in the act of writing your description (your teacher may suggest which ones).

1. *If you can, take eyewitness notes for your description. If you cannot, choose a topic you know well enough to make good notes from memory.*

2. *Look these notes over. What is your main impression, feeling or idea of the subject? Put it into a sentence (this will be your THESIS STATEMENT, whether or not you will actually state it in the description).*

3. *With your notes and thesis statement before you, write a rapid first draft, getting your subject safely out on paper or on the computer screen, not stopping now to revise.*

4. *When your first draft has cooled off, look it over. Does every line of your description contribute to the main overall effect? If not, revise. Does each word feel right? When one does not, consult your thesaurus for another.*

5. *In the next draft add more SENSE IMAGES — appeals to sight, hearing, touch, smell and maybe even taste. Add more TRANSITIONS. Read aloud to hear flaws you did not see. Then revise.*

6. *Finally, look over the spelling and punctuation before printing off your best version.*

CP/Edmonton Sun (Preston Brownshlaigle)

"In an accident, an SUV is two and a half times more likely than a mid-size car to kill the occupants of the other vehicle. . . ."

— *Linda McQuaig, "Killing Machines"*

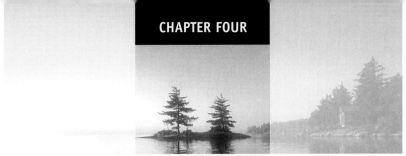

Cause and Effect

HERE'S WHY . . .

Have you heard the true story — and aren't they all supposed to be true? — of the philosophy prof who walked into class to give the final exam? He went to the blackboard and wrote one word: *Why?*
He knew that one of our most human traits is a desire to make sense of things by asking *why?* If something good happens, we want to know *why* so we can repeat it. If something bad happens, we want to know *why* so in future we can avoid it. On news reports of earthquakes, hurricanes, fires, floods, accidents, crimes and terrorist attacks, victims are always shaking their heads and asking "*Why?*"

In the financial world investors bite their nails guessing what makes stocks go up or down. Will a growing economy push stocks up? Or will it cause inflation, which will cause us to stop buying things we can't afford, which in turn will lower company profits and cause stocks to fall? Will a controversial election send stocks crashing? Or will it just clear the air of uncertainty, making stocks soar? Will a devastating earthquake harm the economy and the stock market? Or will the cleanup just create employment, sending stocks up? Using the same data, hundreds of experts reason that stocks will rise, while hundreds of others reason that they will fall. Do these experts, or do we, think cause and effect logic is easy?

Yet it is important. We use it in everyday life, and therefore many of our essays are based on it. So when you investigate causes and effects, think hard to get them right.

A church in Florida once began a campaign to burn records by Elton John and other rock stars. A survey had reported that 984 out of 1000 teenagers who had become pregnant had "committed fornication while rock music was played." The assumption was automatic: rock music causes pregnancy. Before they lit the first match, though, the church members might have asked what *other* causes contributed to the effect. How many of the music lovers had also taken alcohol or drugs? How many had not thought of birth control? Was the music played because sex usually takes place inside a building, where sound systems also happen to be? The church might also have investigated causes further in the past: What influences from family or society encouraged these teens to enter the situation in the first place? Finally, the church might have asked how often people this age have listened to Elton John and other musicians while *not* fornicating. Rock music may still be a factor — but who knows without a more objective and thorough search of *causes*? When you trace causes and effects, consider these principles:

Just because one event follows another, don't assume the first causes the second. If a black cat crosses the road just before your car engine blows up, put the blame where it belongs: not on the cat but on the mechanic who forgot to replace your crankcase oil.

Control your prejudices. If the bank manager refuses to give you a loan, is it because bankers are capitalist exploiters who like to keep the rest of us down? Or is it because this one had to call the collection agency the last time you took out a loan?

Explore causes behind causes. Your employer fired you because you didn't work hard enough. But *why* didn't you work hard enough? Because the job was a bore and the employer was a jerk? Or because you have two other jobs as well, and sleep only three hours a night? And if so, do you work these hours because the car you bought consumes every cent you earn? Finally, the real question may be *Why did you buy the car?*

Many events have multiple causes and multiple effects:

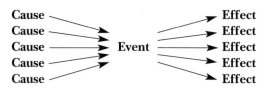

In addition, each cause may have one or more causes behind it, and each effect may produce further effects, leading to an infinite chain of causality receding into the past and reaching into the future.

Where, then, do you draw the boundaries as you plan an essay of cause and effect? The answer lies in your own common sense: include enough to make the point clearly and fairly, then stop. If your parents are workaholics, a description of their behaviour may help a reader understand your own. But do we need to hear about your grandparents as well? If we do, would a quick summary be enough, since we've already heard the details in your parents' case?

All the essays in this chapter show at least one clear-cut cause and at least one clear-cut effect. But while it is possible to give equal attention to both, constructing an essay is much easier if you focus *mostly* on cause or *mostly* on effect. Note also that while some essays in this chapter focus on one major cause or one major effect, others show several causes or several effects. For example, Patricia Pearson examines many possible causes of "the big C," while Linda McQuaig traces many effects of driving SUVs. As you choose your own approach to the organization of a cause-and-effect essay, remember above all your purpose: What kind of focus will most strongly explain and support your main point? Once you know, use it.

Note: Many essays in other chapters use cause and effect logic to help make their point. Among them, see especially the one by Gordon Pitts, which is among the strongest cause-and-effect arguments in this book:

Sylvia Fraser, "My Other Self," p. 29
Catherine Pigott, "Chicken Hips," p. 172
Catharine Parr Traill, "Remarks of Security of Person and Property in Canada," p. 187
Gordon Pitts, "Your New Job, Your New Life," p. 236
Dionne Brand, "Job," p. 312
Lt.-Gen. Roméo Dallaire, *"Cri de coeur,"* p. 319

PATRICIA PEARSON

Avoiding the Big C:
A Little Simple Advice

Patricia Pearson is the granddaughter of Lester B. Pearson, prime minister of Canada from 1963 to 1968, who won the Nobel Peace Prize for resolving the Suez Crisis of 1956 with his proposal to create a United Nations peacekeeping force. When Pierre Trudeau died in 2001, Patricia Pearson wrote a moving column in the National Post, *recalling how at age 8 she was devastated by the death of her beloved grandfather, and how, like Trudeau's family, hers had to hear the events broadcast on the public media, and share the state funeral with the nation. Later she lived several years in New York City, but now resides with her husband and two children in Toronto, where she has been a columnist for the* National Post, USA Today *and* Maclean's. *Pearson has also written for the* New York Times, *the* Guardian, *and the* Times of London. *Her article on the notorious killer Karla Homolka, "Behind Every Successful Psychopath," won a National Magazine Award, and in 1997 appeared her widely read book* When She Was Bad: Violent Women and the Myth of Innocence, *which demolished the myth that women, unlike men, are incapable of violence. Then in 2003 was published her comic novel* Playing House, *in 2005 its sequel* Believe Me, *and also in 2005 a book of comic essays,* Area Woman Blows Gasket and Other Tales from the Domestic Frontier. *Our own selection, a* National Post *column of August 28, 1999, showcases Pearson's witty and personal approach to journalism.*

1   The *New England Journal of Medicine* recently reported that "longer-legged people are significantly more prone to certain types of cancer." Indeed. Well, that's a huge relief for me. I can never see over anybody's head in a crowd. Guess I'll snicker at the supermodels and fry myself another burger.

2   What else, exactly, am I supposed to do with this information? Science, you may have noticed, pelts us daily with new studies on everything that causes cancer, everything that prevents it — and everything that they thought caused cancer before but they now realize actually prevents it.

3   At the moment, for example, I know that if I stay short, drink red wine, eat tomatoes and olive oil, avoid working in a coke foundry, avoid cigars, sleep more, take Aspirin, swallow Vitamin E, alter my estrogen levels, sip green tea, shun charcoal briquettes, dine on fish — but not from the Great Lakes — reduce my stress level and stay clear of Eastern Europe, my chances of dying from cancer will be reduced for the time being.

But it turns out that the sunblock that I've been slopping all over myself for five years may be carcinogenic, whereas sunburn is now thought to act as a cancer preventive. Meanwhile, the spinach and apples I've been eating all these years to bust cancer are laden with cancer-causing residues. 4

Likewise, Vitamin C, long touted as an antioxidant par excellence in megadoses, may actually change the structure of our DNA in such a way that . . . guess what? It makes us more susceptible to cancer. 5

And those soft plastic dishes I've been using to microwave my anti-cancer vegetable recipes? They cause cancer. 6

You may recall that a cancer-fighting diet book came out a while back. After chumps like me went out and bought it, an army of doctors charged forth and repudiated its findings. 7

Well, isn't that just great. I wanted to phone my mom to tell her how I've had it up to here (writer's hand slicing sideways at chin level) with trying to keep track of every eensy-weensy obscure bit of research on health dangers. But I'd just read that cell phones were being implicated in brain tumours. 8

It seems to me, the more I think about it, that what this whole explosion in medical research is actually discovering is that sooner or later people die. Of course, scientists are finding out other things that are useful to them, but they are not very useful to me. What all this research is generating in people is the expectation that somehow they don't have to die — that if they can only get *all the information* they can beat the odds. 9

If you talk to an insurance actuary, you'll be told what people actually die of, cancer-wise: smoking. Smoking is way, way up there with automobile accidents and heart attacks. And you don't need to read any more studies to know what to do about that one. Every other prevention strategy, in my opinion, is a crapshoot. 10

From now on, I follow the only recipe for longevity that's ever actually made sense to me: moderation in all things. A little wine, a nice walk, a good dish of pasta, a minimal amount of microwaving in Tupperware containers, a dash of olive oil, a soupçon of Vitamin C, a very brief visit to a foundry. Live life modestly — except during the holidays and when you've been dumped by your boyfriend — and hope for the best. It's all you can do. 11

Explorations:

Patricia Pearson, *When She Was Bad: Violent Women and the Myth of Innocence*
http://www.hc-sc.gc.ca/pphb-dgspsp/ccdpc-cpcmc/cancer/index_e.html
http://www.pearsonspost.com/bio2.html
http://www.pearsonspost.com

Structure:

1. Pearson starts right off with the odd idea that "longer-legged people are significantly more prone to certain types of cancer." What does this opening do for her readers?
2. Though Pearson informs us early as to her subject and point of view, her actual THESIS STATEMENT is kept in reserve till the first sentence of the last paragraph, where she advises "moderation in all things." Name one advantage of placing it at the end. Name one potential disadvantage. Why in most essays does it come at or near the beginning?
3. Roughly what percentage of her essay space does Pearson devote to *examples*? Tell two or three of your favourites. Has she reached the recommended 50% level? Point out which paragraphs are built entirely or mostly of examples.
4. In this essay of *cause and effect*, Pearson first questions current medical views on what does or does not *cause* cancer, before going on to her own advice. Have you tried to follow any of the popularly believed techniques in paragraph 3? Do her exposés of once-accepted but now rejected beliefs in paragraphs 4–7 seem to question the validity of the beliefs in paragraph 3? Finally, does the fact that she has made fun of formerly accepted beliefs help us to accept her own points that (in paragraph 10) smoking is the most obvious *cause* of cancer, and (in her closing paragraph) that "moderation in all things" is the main *cause* of longevity?

Style:

1. Does Pearson's humorous TONE work with the very serious topic of cancer?
2. In paragraph 10 Pearson calls most cancer prevention strategies "a crapshoot." Where else does she use very informal, COLLOQUIAL language? Does it work in her argument, or does it make us doubt her seriousness?

Ideas for Discussion and Writing:

1. Do you try to follow all the latest techniques to achieve the *effect* of good health, or do you just enjoy life and hope for the best? Argue for one of these points of view, giving reasons.
2. If you have read Stephen Leacock's essay "How to Live to Be 200" (in Chapter 8), compare the attitude of Jiggins, who "dumb-belled himself to death," with that of modern health seekers who try to reach the ideal diet and lifestyle.
3. Who in your extended family has reached a very old age? Do you think this longevity was *caused* by the person's lifestyle, or was the cause genetic? Give *examples*.

4. **PROCESS IN WRITING:** *Patricia Pearson's basic message is "modera-tion," but in our time we are more likely to encounter the "extreme." Why do so many of us seek extreme lifestyles, in areas such as food and drink, drugs, financial life, career, relationships, or in risky outdoor adventures? Fill a page with notes on this question, then narrow your focus down to one item — such as an "extreme sport" that you practise yourself. Analyze all the* causes *you can think of, or all the* effects, *and explain them in a first draft filled with examples. Examine it the next day. Does the* THESIS STATEMENT *unify your argument? Have you reached at least 50% example content? Do your points rise up to the most important at the end? After editing for content, polish the style, then bring your argument to class to read aloud.*

Note: See also the Topics for Writing at the end of this chapter.

PAUL D'ANGELO

The Step Not Taken

Paul D'Angelo's usual idea of writing is to tell fish stories, and he admits that his, like most, will stretch the truth. But one day the writer and TV critic for Outdoor Canada *magazine stepped into a Toronto elevator, and lived the true and sobering story that follows. When it appeared in* The Globe and Mail *of April 3, 1995, it struck a deep chord: dozens of readers sent replies, one of them 5000 words long. Several recounted tragic experiences they had just had themselves, and told how D'Angelo's confession had helped them face their own trials. The author of this thought-provoking essay has an unusual background for a writer. Born in Toronto, D'Angelo never went to university but always read a lot, an activity that gave him a way with words. After high school he spent seven years in Europe and Africa travelling, working here and there, and just living life. In the meantime, on a visit home he launched a seasonal greeting card business, which still left him seven months a year to roam. For some years, now, he and his family have lived in Toronto, where he thinks of himself mostly as an entrepreneur, but goes north to fish pike and bass for fun, and then writes about it in several columns a year. "Write what you live!" he says. Though D'Angelo usually finds writing to be slow and tough, he felt our selection so strongly that he just wrote it right off, to "get it off his chest." The* Globe *changed only one word. Though he "felt better," his hope that the young man in the elevator would see the article and respond never came true. Perhaps it still could, if that young man should happen to see the pages that follow.*

1 A few weeks ago I was followed into an office-building elevator by a well-dressed young man carrying a briefcase. He looked very sharp. Very buttoned-down. Wearing gold wire-frame glasses, he was of medium height and build with neatly trimmed brown hair and, I would guess, in his mid-20s. Typical junior executive material. There was nothing about him that seemed unusual. Nothing at all to indicate what was about to take place.

2 The elevator had only one control panel, and I excused myself as I leaned over to his side of the car and pushed the button for the 10th floor. He pushed the button for the 15th. The doors of the elevator closed and we began to ascend. Employing typical Toronto elevator etiquette, I stood staring up at the row of floor numbers above the doors while purposely ignoring my fellow passenger. Then it happened. A sudden strained gasp. Turning toward the noise, I was astonished to see the young man drop his briefcase and burst into tears. Our eyes met for a split second and, as if slapped, he averted his face from me, leaned his head against the wood-panelled wall of the elevator and continued to weep.

And what I did next still shames me. 3

The elevator stopped at the 10th floor and, without looking back, I 4
stepped out. I stood in the hallway, a bundle of mixed emotions, wondering what to do. A combination of guilt and uncertainty washed over
me. Should I go up to the 15th floor and make sure he's okay? Should I
search him out from office to office? Should I risk the embarrassment it
might cause him? Is he mentally disturbed? A manic depressive, perhaps? Is he a suicide just waiting to happen?

I didn't know what to do. So I did nothing. 5

And now he haunts me. Not with fear, of course, but with a sense of 6
regret. I see his face crumbling before he turns to the wall. I see his
shoulders heave as he sobs in a combination of sorrow and shame. I
wonder now what brought him to that moment in time. How long had
he been holding his pain inside before he could no longer contain it?
What could possibly have overwhelmed him to such an extent that he
was unable to keep from crying out?

Had he just visited the doctor and been told that he had an incurable 7
disease? Was he having marital problems? Was his wife ill? His child?
Had someone dear recently died? Was he being laid off? Was he looking
for a job and meeting with no success? Was he having financial woes?
Was he without friends in the city and crushed by loneliness?

The sorrows of this world are endless. 8

The few people I have told about the incident all say I did the proper 9
thing, the best thing, by leaving the young man alone.

But they are wrong. 10

Like so many things in life, I know now what I should have done then. 11
I should have thrown caution to the winds and done the right thing. Not
the big-city thing. The right thing. The human thing. The thing I would
want someone to do if they ever found my son crying in an elevator. I
should have given him the opportunity to unload his sadness onto my
shoulders. I should have reached out a hand and patted him on the
back. I should have said something like, "Why don't you let me buy you
a cup of coffee and you can tell me all your problems. There's no reason
to feel self-conscious. I'll listen for as long as you want to talk."

What would his reaction have been to that? Would he have turned 12
even further to the wall? Or would he have turned on me? Cursing
me? Telling me to mind my own damned business? Would he have
lashed out at me? Sorrow and insecurity turning to rage? Would he
have physically attacked me? Or would he have gone with me for that
cup of coffee?

I don't know. I'll never know. All I can be certain of is that I left him 13
in that elevator with tears streaming down his face. And that he was
alone. All alone.

I hope that somehow he gets to read these words, because I want him 14
to know that I'm pulling for him. That I hope things are looking up for
him. That I hope his sorrow is in the past. That I hope he is never again

burdened with such awful despair. That I am thinking of him. That I said a prayer for him. That I was wrong, dreadfully wrong, not to step forward in his time of need.

15   That I'm sorry.

● ●

Explorations:

Joseph Hartog *et al.*, eds., *The Anatomy of Loneliness*
John Glassco, trans., *Complete Poems of Saint Denys Garneau*
http://www.depressioncanada.com
http://www.nimh.nih.gov/healthinformation/depressionmenu.cfm
http://www.cfpc.ca/English/cfpc/programs/patient%20education/de
    pression/default.asp?s=1

Structure:

1. D'Angelo begins with an ANECDOTE. Is this a good technique? Do you see it often? How well does this one work as an introduction?
2. In paragraph 1 D'Angelo refers to "what was about to take place"; in paragraph two he says "Then it happened"; and in paragraph 3 he says "And what I did next still shames me." Why does he keep building suspense? What does this do for his AUDIENCE?
3. Identify D'Angelo's THESIS STATEMENT.
4. Tell how paragraph 10 works as a TRANSITION between parts. Why is it only one sentence long?
5. Where does D'Angelo ask himself *why*? Where does he ask *what if*? What *causes* does he imagine? What *effects*? And how important are these to the essay?

Style:

1. How CONCISE is this selection? Can you find any wasted words at all?
2. Read paragraphs 14 and 15 aloud in class. Why has D'Angelo given us a series of partial sentences? Why do most begin with "That ..."? Is this repetition accidental or deliberate? What effect does it achieve?
3. Why does D'Angelo's last paragraph contain only three words?

Ideas for Discussion and Writing:

1. If you were Paul D'Angelo, what would you have done when the young man on the elevator began to cry? Why do you think he was crying? Do you, like our author, live in the big city? Describe a time when the actions of a stranger made you wonder how to react. Did

you take the risk of involvement? Or did you do the "big-city thing"? Why? And now what do you think you should have done?

2. Did this selection bring tears to your own eyes? If so, in which parts? Is it good for an essayist to seek emotion in the reader?

3. Describe the favourite techniques of subway, streetcar, bus and elevator riders to preserve their solitude in rush hour. Arrange chairs as in a public transit vehicle, and role-play the situation in class.

4. Our essay title, "The Step Not Taken," is probably a reference to "The Road Not Taken," a poem by Robert Frost, in which the poet wonders what his journey would have been like had he taken the other fork in the path. Is this a universal theme? Describe a fork in your own path. Imagine to what destination "the road not taken" might have led you.

5. **PROCESS IN WRITING:** *You were the young man — or, if you like, a young woman — who was in the elevator that day, and you have just read Paul D'Angelo's article. Now answer him in a letter telling the* causes *of your pain, and responding to his shame at not helping. Look over your first draft: have you found all the main* causes? *Are there also important* causes *behind* causes? *Have you used* TRANSITION SIGNALS *to highlight the logic (words like* "because," "therefore," "as a result of," "so," *etc.)? Revise. Now check for punctuation and spelling before printing off your best version.*

Note: See also the Topics for Writing at the end of this chapter.

LEAH McLAREN

Canadian Guys Rule*

Fresh from Trent University, where she had won prizes as an English major, Leah McLaren arrived at The Globe and Mail. *She was 22. That summer of 1998 she wrote for the arts section, and was soon noticed for her brash and sassy commentary. The timing was right: McLaren's young and fresh appeal was what the* Globe *thought it needed in its competition with the new* National Post. *So at an unusually young age McLaren found herself penning a national column on style and lifestyle, drawing on her own experiences and those of her twenty-something generation. Not all the attention she got was good. Numerous commentators on Web sites and blogs resented her background of privilege, her movie star looks and glamorous lifestyle, her apparent lack of empathy for the poor, and the help she may have had in acquiring her own career (her mother was food editor at the* Globe *when McLaren arrived). A notorious 2003* Toronto Life *profile of her by Trevor Cole gave further expression to those resentments. McLaren does not seem to mind, and has replied, "I'm really, really bad at censoring myself."* The Continuity Girl, *her first novel, is expected in 2006. Our own selection, "Canadian Guys Rule," is her* Globe *column of August 3, 2002, written while she was on assignment for several months in London, England.*

1 Earlier this week, I was elbowing my way through Covent Garden on the way to meet a friend for coffee when I passed by London's Canada Shop. Located just a couple of doors down the street from the Molson-draft-slinging Maple Leaf pub, the Canada Shop is a sad little postage stamp stocked with Twizzlers and boxes of KD. The place is full of all the crap I didn't buy in Canada when I lived there. But walking by last week I did think of something from home I'd like to place on special order: a few good men.

2 I would like to take this opportunity to apologize to my male compatriots. Over the years, I have done you boys a great disservice. I have failed to appreciate you. Now that I am thousands of kilometres away, I hope you will forgive me. For all the years I rolled my eyes at your *Strange Brew* references, exploited your car-driving capabilities, sniffed at your ball caps, dismissed the Tragically Hip as a glorified bar band and generally took you all for granted, I am sorry. Well and truly so. In hindsight, I now see the truth: Youse guys is sure great.

---

* Original title: "Put It on the Front Page! Canadian Guys Rule."

During all my time in the nation of my birth, I never fell for a rotter.   3
(I still haven't over here, but there are plenty more of them around.) I
attribute this not to the idea that there are no bad Canadian men
(patently untrue) but to the fact that I had a great dad — one who
embodies all the virtues of his country (hockey skills, decency, unshake-
able sanity) and most of its vices too (a love of beer, tendency to bang on
about health-care reform).

It is an acknowledged truth that the constancy of a good father dur-   4
ing childhood goes a long way to prevent a girl from letting herself get
kicked around by jerkface male sadists later in life — and I am no exception to this rule.

When the undeniably cute thirty-something London surgeon pulls up   5
in front of my flat in his zippy little convertible and, instead of mounting the steps to ring the bell, *honks the horn*, my first thought is "Dad
would *hate* this guy." (Dad, in fact, would race out the door before me,
jump into the passenger side and deliver a pithy lecture on McLaren
Household Doorbell-Ringing Etiquette, with one menacing Dad-paw
placed on the cute surgeon's shoulder.)

Given my stringent Canadian standards, this surgeon doesn't get a sec-   6
ond chance. Horn-honking is bad practice in a 16-year-old prom date.
Coming from an educated 33-year-old, it's a sure sign of rotterdom.
Suddenly I have a sore throat.

Last week, *The Spectator*, a London weekly, published an article I wrote   7
on the romantic ineptitude of the English male. Since then, I've found
myself invited to slag off the chinless wonders on TV, radio and the
pages of various newspapers. But while it's true that English suitors leave
a lot to be desired, at heart I know the real problem lies with me. Over
the years, I've been spoiled silly by Canadian men.

Why do I love thee? Okay, let's count 'em . . . °   8

1. For your superior stature. Maybe it's the benefit of all those   9
Twizzlers and Hawaiian sprinkle doughnuts — Canadian boys, to my
eye, stand head and shoulders above the English competition.

2. For your feminism. Most with-it Canadian guys I know genuinely   10
like women; moreover, they tend to respect us as equals. The same cannot always be said of American men (who are well known to cynically
adopt New Man rhetoric in order to get chicks into bed) or English men
(who think feminism was a short-lived conspiracy to introduce salads
onto pub menus).

3. For your international character. Canadian men come from all over   11
the world — and you can tell. Even a couple of generations after their relatives landed, the Italians still shrug and look up at the ceiling, the Eastern
Europeans still kiss your hand, the Irish still set about getting you as drunk

---

° Why do I love thee?: a humorous reference to the Victorian poet Elizabeth Barrett
Browning's best-known sonnet, which begins "How do I love thee? Let me count the ways."

as humanly possible. These men don't assimilate as quickly in Canada because, unlike England or America, there is less of a culture to assimilate into. The result is a delectable international buffet of Canadian manhood.

12   **4. You smell good.** Like cedar chips and fresh sausages.

13   **5. You mean what you say.** Canadian men are pretty honest. In my experience, they tend to lie only when they feel they have to, rather than all the time, for fun, or just because they feel like it. Better yet, you can generally get the truth out of a Canadian guy just by looking him in the eye and asking him for it. Like most Liberal cabinet ministers, they make bad liars. Unlike most Liberal cabinet ministers, they don't try to pull it off in the first place.

14   **6. You know how to split wood — and snuggle.** In the far north of Canada, when winter begins to approach, single men and women begin pairing up like crazed rabbits. The reason being they need each other to get through the long and lonely winter, and they know it. Hibernating alone is a miserable business. I think some of this winter-induced romance has rubbed off even on urban Canadian men, who instinctively sense the importance of going out to woo when leaves start to turn colour.

15   **7. You remind me of home.** Funny how when you go away the first thing you feel nostalgic for is usually the same thing you complained about for years. I spent years in Toronto commiserating with girlfriends over the dearth of good men. How wrong I was. Forgive me, boys.

● ●

Explorations:

Leah McLaren,
> "The Tragic Ineptitude of the English Male," *The Spectator,* July 27, 2002
> *The Continuity Girl* (novel)

Trevor Cole, "Six Days with Leah," *Toronto Life,* July 2003, pp. 61–71
Douglas Coupland, *Souvenir of Canada*

Structure:

1. McLaren reverses the logical order of *cause and effect*, putting the main *effect* early on in paragraph 2 ("In hindsight, I now see the truth: Youse guys is sure great"), then listing all the *causes* in the second half of her essay. Why?
2. What all does McLaren achieve in her long introduction, before the *causes* begin in paragraph 9?
3. In paragraphs 9–15 McLaren numbers, subtitles and boldfaces the *causes* of her new realization that "Canadian Guys Rule." Do these

devices of formatting help you, the reader? Have you tried such devices in your own writing?

4. What proportion of McLaren's argument is made of *examples*? Has she reached the recommended 50%? Do you, in your own essays?

5. What techniques does McLaren use in closing? How do they add force to her argument?

Style:

1. In places McLaren uses academic sounding vocabulary such as "stringent" (par. 6), "ineptitude" (7) and "dearth" (15), but in other places conversational terms such as "KD" (1), "crap" (1), "jerkface" (4), "chicks" (10), or even "Youse guys" (2). Why? Profile the AUDIENCE you think she is aiming for.

2. McLaren says to Canadian men, "You smell good. Like cedar chips and fresh sausages" (par. 12). What device gives power to this statement?

Ideas for Discussion and Writing:

1. Once arrived in England, McLaren could appreciate the men of Canada. What changes in values or perceptions have your own travels *caused*? What principle lies behind travel as a learning device?

2. In paragraph 4 McLaren tells how "a good father during childhood goes a long way to prevent a girl from letting herself get kicked around by jerkface male sadists later in life," and in paragraph 5 she imagines her father's "Dad-paw" menacing the shoulder of the London surgeon who only honked instead of ringing the doorbell. How important do you believe the example of a father is to the future development of his daughters? Give *examples*.

3. Is it true that Canadian men "genuinely like women" and treat them as "equals" (par. 10), while American men "adopt New Man rhetoric in order to get chicks into bed" and while English men think that "feminism was a shortlived conspiracy to introduce salads onto pub menus"? Do we see STEREOTYPING here, or is it valid to generalize about groups of people?

4. Paragraph 6 tells Canadian men that "You know how to split wood — and snuggle." To what extent does our vast Canadian geography still influence our behaviour? Our worldview? Whatever your gender, do you know how to split wood? Do you go backpacking, canoeing, kayaking or skiing? Or if not, do you still thrill to Group of Seven paintings of the North? Or are you an urban person with urban interests and urban values? Give *examples*.

5. **PROCESS IN WRITING:** *Now write your own essay of cause and effect entitled "Canadian Women Rule" (OR substitute the women of any other country you know better). Whatever your own gender, close your eyes for a while*

and think of your subject. Then fill a page of notes. Choose the best of these, and from them write a quick first draft. Is there a THESIS STATEMENT*? Do you give at least one* example *for each point? Do you use* logic signals *such as "so," "because," "therefore" and "as a result" to highlight the* causes*? Are any words wasted? Read aloud to test your draft, then adjust whatever needs work. Finally check for grammar and punctuation, then print off your best version to share with the class.*

Note: See also the Topics for Writing at the end of this chapter.

DAVID SUZUKI

Hidden Lessons*

One of the most popular and enduring television shows anywhere is The Nature of Things, *a CBC series that has explained the natural world for over 35 years and is now seen in 40 nations across the earth. As its host since 1979, David Suzuki has become one of our country's best-known scientists and media figures. A third-generation Japanese-Canadian, born in Vancouver in 1936, he earned a Ph.D. at the University of Chicago in 1961, specializing in genetics, and soon gained an international reputation for genetic research on fruit flies. In 1969 he was named "outstanding research scientist in Canada," and since then has received many more awards and grants, and 15 honorary doctorates. In a 2004 CBC competition, he was voted one of the ten greatest Canadians of all time. Suzuki lectures internationally, writes a syndicated newspaper column, and has written some 30 books, among them* Metamorphosis *(autobiography, 1987),* The Japan We Never Knew *(1996),* Earth Time: Essays *(1998),* From Naked Ape to Superspecies *(with Holly Dressel, 1999), and 10 books explaining nature to children. In 1990 he created the David Suzuki Foundation (see its Web site given in "Explorations"), a think tank with some 15,000 supporters, whose goal is to influence environmental policy. In all these activities Suzuki rejects the narrow view of pure research, and instead works to educate the public about both the promise and dangers of science: the use of little-understood technologies; voracious economic and industrial expansion; and the resulting devastation of other plant and animal species through our consumption of their habitat. This "gladiatorial geneticist," as he has been called, is literally trying to save the planet. "If I didn't," Suzuki said in a CBC special about his life, "I couldn't look my children in the eye." The essay that follows, from* The Globe and Mail, *pursues this goal in an especially concrete way.*

In spite of the vast expanse of wilderness in this country, most Canadian children grow up in urban settings. In other words, they live in a world conceived, shaped and dominated by people. Even the farms located around cities and towns are carefully groomed and landscaped for human convenience. There's nothing wrong with that, of course, but in such an environment, it's very easy to lose any sense of connection with nature.

In city apartments and dwellings, the presence of cockroaches, fleas, ants, mosquitoes or houseflies is guaranteed to elicit the spraying of insecticides. Mice and rats are poisoned or trapped, while the gardener

---

* Editor's title.

wages a never-ending struggle with ragweed, dandelions, slugs and root-rot. We have a modern arsenal of chemical weapons to fight off these invaders and we use them lavishly.

3   We worry when kids roll in the mud or wade through a puddle because they'll get "dirty." Children learn attitudes and values very quickly and the lesson in cities is very clear — nature is an enemy, it's dirty, dangerous or a nuisance. So youngsters learn to distance themselves from nature and to try to control it. I am astonished at the number of adults who loathe or are terrified by snakes, spiders, butterflies, worms, birds — the list seems endless.

4   If you reflect on the history of humankind, you realize that for 99 per cent of our species' existence on the planet, we were deeply embedded in and dependent on nature. When plants and animals were plentiful, we flourished. When famine and drought struck, our numbers fell accordingly. We remain every bit as dependent upon nature today — we need plants to fix photons of energy into sugar molecules and to cleanse the air and replenish the oxygen. It is folly to forget our dependence on an intact ecosystem. But we do whenever we teach our offspring to fear or detest the natural world. The urban message kids get runs completely counter to what they are born with, a natural interest in other life forms. Just watch a child in a first encounter with a flower or an ant — there is instant interest and fascination. We condition them out of it.

5   The result is that when my 7-year-old daughter brings home new friends, they invariably recoil in fear or disgust when she tries to show them her favorite pets — three beautiful salamanders that her grandfather got for her in Vancouver. And when my 3-year-old comes wandering in with her treasures — millipedes, spiders, slugs and sowbugs that she catches under rocks lining the front lawn — children and adults alike usually respond by saying "yuk."

6   I can't overemphasize the tragedy of that attitude. For, inherent in this view is the assumption that human beings are special and different and that we lie outside nature. Yet it is this belief that is creating many of our environmental problems today.

7   Does it matter whether we sense our place in nature so long as we have cities and technology? Yes, for many reasons, not the least of which is that virtually all scientists were fascinated with nature as children and retained that curiosity throughout their lives. But a far more important reason is that if we retain a spiritual sense of connection with all other life forms, it can't help but profoundly affect the way we act. Whenever my daughter sees a picture of an animal dead or dying, she asks me fearfully, "Daddy, are there any more?" At 7 years, she already knows about extinction and it frightens her.

8   The yodel of a loon at sunset, the vast flocks of migrating waterfowl in the fall, the indomitable salmon returning thousands of kilometres — these images of nature have inspired us to create music, poetry and art. And when we struggle to retain a handful of California condors or

whooping cranes, it's clearly not from a fear of ecological collapse, it's because there is something obscene and frightening about the disappearance of another species at our hands.

If children grow up understanding that we are animals, they will look at other species with a sense of fellowship and community. If they understand their ecological place — the biosphere — then when children see the great virgin forests of the Queen Charlotte Islands being clearcut, they will feel physical pain, because they will understand that those trees are an extension of themselves.   9

When children who know their place in the ecosystem see factories spewing poison into the air, water and soil, they will feel ill because someone has violated their home. This is not mystical mumbo-jumbo. We have poisoned the life support systems that sustain all organisms because we have lost a sense of ecological place. Those of us who are parents have to realize the unspoken, negative lessons we are conveying to our children. Otherwise, they will continue to desecrate this planet as we have.   10

It's not easy to avoid giving these hidden lessons. I have struggled to cover my dismay and queasiness when Severn and Sarika come running in with a large wolf spider or when we've emerged from a ditch covered with leeches or when they have been stung accidentally by yellowjackets feeding on our leftovers. But that's nature. I believe efforts to teach children to love and respect other life forms are priceless.   11

●●

Explorations:

David Suzuki, *Metamorphosis*
Rachel Carson, *Silent Spring*
Annie Dillard, *Pilgrim at Tinker Creek*
Robert Ornstein and Paul Ehrlich, *New World, New Mind*
Henry David Thoreau, *Walden*
The Nature of David Suzuki (video, 44 min.), Harvey McKinnon Productions, 1997
http://www.davidsuzuki.org/Default.asp
http://collections.ic.gc.ca/heirloom_series/volume6/224-225.htm
http://www.sierralegal.org
http://archives.cbc.ca/IDD-1-74-663/people/david_suzuki
http://nccnsw.org.au/bushland/projects/Biodiversity/
19980123_suzuki.html

Structure:

1. What device of emphasis sparks the opening sentence, and how does it begin to introduce Suzuki's subject?

2. Does Suzuki explore more fully the *causes* or the *effects* of children's attitudes toward nature? Which paragraphs analyze mostly causes and which mostly effects? Is Suzuki right to place the causes first?

3. How long a chain of *cause and effect* does Suzuki show us? Point out each link.

4. Suzuki no doubt hopes his argument will spur us to action. Does his closing promote this goal? When he admits in paragraph 11 that "It's not easy to avoid giving these hidden lessons," are you discouraged or challenged?

Style:

1. Describe Suzuki's prose: Is it full of strategies calculated to affect us, or is it a plain and direct message? Which mode do you prefer when you read? When you write? Why?

2. Why is paragraph 6 the shortest one of the essay?

Ideas for Discussion and Writing:

1. Do you dread insects, worms, snakes, mice or weeds? If so, how did you learn to? How close are your attitudes to those of your parents? What actual dangers, if any, may these life forms pose to you?

2. In paragraph 8 Suzuki writes, "there is something obscene and frightening about the disappearance of another species at our hands." Elsewhere he has stated that two species an hour disappear from the earth, mostly because we "develop" natural habitats for our own profit. How important to you is a new paper mill, a logging project in the rain forest, a highway, dam, subdivision, ski resort, oil well or aluminum smelter — compared to the existence of a species? Defend your view.

3. First we learned to shun *racism*, and then *sexism*. Is *speciesism* next? Argue for or against our present belief that we are far more important than other members of our ecosystem.

4. How desirable is economic growth when it is based on exploiting nature? If you could save the rivers, the lakes and the rain forests by consuming less, how would you react? How large a cut in income would you accept to achieve the goal: 10%, 25%, 50% — or none at all? Defend your view.

5. Visit the David Suzuki Foundation Web site: www.davidsuzuki.org. Choose the example of a particular animal or plant in danger of extinction. Now write a concise letter or email to the prime minister and/or your Member of Parliament, telling what you believe should be done to save this species. Send the message (remember that letters to an M.P. or prime minister need no stamp). If you receive an answer, share both it and your original message with the class.

6. **PROCESS IN WRITING:** *Choose a current newspaper or newsmagazine article about an environmental problem. In response, write a short but hard-hitting letter to the editor exposing the* effects *of this problem. Since editors love conciseness, polish your second draft till every word counts. Cut deadwood. Use your thesaurus to replace vague or weak terms with exact and strong ones. "Show" through* examples *rather than "telling" through generalizations. Now try out a draft on an* AUDIENCE *of three or four classmates; incorporate their best advice before sending your final copy. Then watch the next issues to see if your message is published. If an editor has cut any part of your letter, analyze why: Was the part wordy? Off topic? General instead of specific?*

Note: See also the Topics for Writing at the end of this chapter.

NAHEED MUSTAFA

My Body Is My Own Business

Born in England, Naheed Mustafa moved as an infant to Canada. In 1992 she completed an honours degree in political science and philosophy at the University of Toronto, specializing in Third-World development. Then she studied journalism at Ryerson University. Mustafa currently lives in Toronto with her husband, and combines working as an editor with raising her three children. (For more about her family history, see on page 177 the introduction to Rafi Mustafa, Naheed's father, whose essay "The Bond of Nightmares" appears in this book as well.) "Almost anybody who's willing to work hard enough can learn to write very well," Naheed Mustafa says. It was on July 29, 1993 that "My Body Is My Own Business" appeared in The Globe and Mail. *She adds, "I see myself as being on something of a journey around this issue. . . ."*

1   I often wonder whether people see me as a radical, fundamentalist Muslim terrorist packing an AK-47 assault rifle inside my jean jacket. Or maybe they see me as the poster girl for oppressed womanhood everywhere. I'm not sure which it is.

2   I get the whole gamut of strange looks, stares and covert glances. You see, I wear the *hijab*, a scarf that covers my head, neck and throat. I do this because I am a Muslim woman who believes her body is her own private concern.

3   Young Muslim women are reclaiming the *hijab*, reinterpreting it in light of its original purpose — to give back to women ultimate control of their own bodies.

4   The Koran teaches us that men and women are equal, that individuals should not be judged according to gender, beauty, wealth or privilege. The only thing that makes one person better than another is her or his character.

5   Nonetheless, people have a difficult time relating to me. After all, I'm young, Canadian born and raised, university-educated — why would I do this to myself, they ask.

6   Strangers speak to me in loud, slow English and often appear to be playing charades. They politely inquire how I like living in Canada and whether or not the cold bothers me. If I'm in the right mood, it can be very amusing.

7   But why would I, a woman with all the advantages of a North American upbringing, suddenly, at 21, want to cover myself so that with the *hijab* and the other clothes I choose to wear, only my face and hands show?

8   Because it gives me freedom.

Women are taught from early childhood that their worth is proportional to their attractiveness. We feel compelled to pursue abstract notions of beauty, half realizing that such a pursuit is futile. 9

When women reject this form of oppression, they face ridicule and contempt. Whether it's women who refuse to wear makeup or to shave their legs or to expose their bodies, society, both men and women, have trouble dealing with them. 10

In the Western world, the *hijab* has come to symbolize either forced silence or radical, unconscionable militancy. Actually, it's neither. It is simply a woman's assertion that judgment of her physical person is to play no role whatsoever in social interaction. 11

Wearing the *hijab* has given me freedom from constant attention to my physical self. Because my appearance is not subjected to public scrutiny, my beauty, or perhaps lack of it, has been removed from the realm of what can legitimately be discussed. 12

No one knows whether my hair looks as if I just stepped out of a salon, whether or not I can pinch an inch, or even if I have unsightly stretch marks. And because no one knows, no one cares. 13

Feeling that one has to meet the impossible male standards of beauty is tiring and often humiliating. I should know, I spent my entire teenage years trying to do it. I was a borderline bulimic and spent a lot of money I didn't have on potions and lotions in hopes of becoming the next Cindy Crawford. 14

The definition of beauty is ever-changing; waifish is good, waifish is bad, athletic is good — sorry, athletic is bad. Narrow hips? Great. Narrow hips? Too bad. 15

Women are not going to achieve equality with the right to bare their breasts in public, as some people would like to have you believe. That would only make us party to our own objectification. True equality will be had only when women don't need to display themselves to get attention and won't need to defend their decision to keep their bodies to themselves. 16

• •

Explorations:

Elizabeth Warnock Fernea, *In Search of Islamic Feminism: One Woman's Global Journey*
Richard Gordon, *Anorexia and Bulimia: Anatomy of a Social Epidemic*
Naomi Wolf, *The Beauty Myth: How Images of Beauty Are Used Against Women*
Bharati Mukherjee, *Jasmine* (novel)
Salman Rushdie, *Shame* (novel)
Under One Sky: Arab Women in North America Talk About the Hijab (NFB, 43 min., 1999)
http://en.wikipedia.org/wiki/Hijab

http://www.usc.edu/dept/MSA/othersites

http://www.islamic-paths.org/Home/English/Discover/Poems/
Content/Hijab.htm

Structure:

1. Why does Mustafa open with two STEREOTYPES? Do they draw your attention? Do they go straight to her topic?
2. In her argument does Mustafa give more attention to *causes* or *effects*? Name the main causes. Name the main effects.
3. Why does Mustafa explore effects *first* and causes *after*, reversing the logical order of the two?
4. Identify the TRANSITION in which Mustafa actually asks "why" and answers with "because . . .," as she moves from *effects* to *causes*.

Style:

1. Ending on a key word is a powerful device of emphasis. Note the final word in each half of Mustafa's argument: What makes "freedom" and "themselves" good choices for these positions?
2. Language can speak through rhythm as much as through words. Read aloud the first sentence of paragraph 6, then analyze how its sound reinforces its meaning.

Ideas for Discussion and Writing:

1. Mustafa says male standards of beauty for women are "impossible" and that feeling the need to meet them is "humiliating" (paragraph 14). Is she right? Whether you are male or female, give examples of your own to defend or attack her view.
2. Examine the PARADOX of paragraph 8: that the effect of covering oneself with the *hijab* is "freedom." Do non-Muslims have means of shielding themselves, as well, from the unreasonable scrutiny and expectations of others? Name any such techniques you have used.
3. Though part of her background is the culture of another country, Mustafa is Canadian. If you too have origins in another culture, how fully do you plan to retain the clothes, the foods, the religion and language of that culture, while living in Canada? Predict the *effects* of your decision.
4. Mustafa confesses that as a teen she was a "borderline bulimic" (paragraph 14). What do you see as the main *causes* of bulimia and anorexia nervosa? What *causes* women, not men, to be the main victims?
5. At the library look through an illustrated history of art, taking notes on how the ideal of beauty in women has changed through the centuries. Then report your findings to the class, showing illustrations as evidence for your conclusions.

6. Watch your favourite television channel for one hour, taking notes on how women are presented both in programs and commercials. Then report to the class on the attitudes, especially any STEREOTYPES, which you detected. What *effects*, in both male and female viewers, do you think these attitudes will *cause?*

7. **PROCESS IN WRITING:** *Do number 6 above, except as an essay. Look over your notes, then choose a THESIS STATEMENT that expresses the main* effect(s) *on viewers of the* examples *you observed. Now write a rapid first draft, supporting your thesis statement with large numbers of these* examples. *When the draft has cooled off, look it over. Do the* causes *and* effects *seem reasonable? Have you tried to be objective, rather than interpret according to your own prejudices? Are there* causes behind causes, *or* effects of effects, *which might enrich your analysis? Do TRANSITIONS such as "since," "because" and "therefore" help the audience follow your logic? If not, add. Finally, edit for things like punctuation and spelling before doing the final version. Read it to the class, and be ready to answer questions from other points of view.*

Note: See also the Topics for Writing at the end of this chapter.

LINDA McQUAIG

Killing Machines*

Linda McQuaig is one of our nation's most hard-hitting social and economic critics. In her newspaper columns and in her books, she tirelessly battles vested interests such as big oil and other polluters, powerful transnational corporations, and governments that favour the wealthy over the poor. Bringing research, wit and a vivid writing style to bear upon her subjects, she excels at tracing webs of cause and effect, such as the thirst for oil that she argues lay behind the American invasion of Iraq. This and other petroleum-related subjects are exposed in her best-selling 2004 book It's the Crude, Dude: War, Big Oil and the Fight for the Planet. *(Our own selection, attacking gas-guzzling SUVs, comes from the same book.) Among McQuaig's many other published volumes have been* Behind Closed Doors: How the Rich Won Control of Canada's Tax System *(1987);* The Quick and the Dead: Brian Mulroney, Big Business and the Seduction of Canada *(1991);* The Wealthy Banker's Wife: The Assault on Equality in Canada *(1993);* Shooting the Hippo: Death by Deficit and Other Canadian Myths *(1995) and* The Cult of Impotence: Selling the Myth of Powerlessness in the Global Economy *(1998). McQuaig has also written regularly for* The Globe and Mail, *the* Toronto Star, Maclean's *magazine, the* National Post *and CBC Radio. She is also a popular speaker, bringing to her audiences the same sharp wit and vivid examples that fill her writings.*

1   Having paid insufficient attention to car advertisements in the 1990s, I somehow didn't get the concept of an SUV. I didn't realize, for instance, that it was a symbol of a bold, adventurous, sporty kind of life, driven by people with a tendency to go off-road — just as, elsewhere in their lives, they have a tendency to break with the pack, to do things their way, to think outside the box. To show how far out of the loop I was, I didn't even know there was a difference between an SUV and a minivan. They both just seemed like awkward, bulky, oversized versions of a car — useful, no doubt, for those trips to Price Chopper when one comes home laden with several extra cases of Coke and a year's supply of toilet paper.

2   Of course, I was dead wrong. I've leaned that there's a world of difference between a utilitarian minivan, which is designed for the Price Chopper trip as well as carting around children's soccer equipment, and an SUV, which is not only bold and adventurous but also glamorous, the

---

* Editor's title.

car of choice these days among Hollywood stars and others with limitless resources. Still, one can appreciate the role advertising has played in making this sort of distinction clear to people, in establishing the SUV as the symbol of everything chic. The sheer brilliance of this advertising coup can perhaps best be measured by the extent of the image transformation the SUV has undergone since its first incarnation as a vehicle with few uses outside the funeral business. As Keith Bradsher has noted in his book *High and Mighty*, the forerunner of the SUV — the Chevy Suburban — dates back to the 1930s, and it managed to survive in the early decades largely because its body was the perfect height and width for the easy loading and unloading of coffins. This feature is retained today but omitted from SUV advertising.

So effective has the advertising campaign been that the public seems largely unaware that SUVs are generally difficult to handle, with poor agility and manoeuvrability — exactly the opposite of the sports car, which of course, used to be the sexy car of choice. While a sports car, with its low-slung body and road-gripping tires, can zip around corners at great speed, the rigid, high-set body of the SUV makes its way around corners with considerably more difficulty, which explains why ads typically show SUVs motionless at the top of a mountain or charging straight ahead (got to get straight home with all that toilet paper), rather than driving on the kind of winding, exotic cliffside roads typically seen in sports car ads.

Much of the appeal of today's SUV may have less to do with sportiness and glamour, and more to do with security in an age of fear. Huge and growing ever larger, the SUV offers its riders a massive, wraparound steel exterior with the feel of a tank — a mobile version of a gated community. Bradsher reports that this is deliberate, that the tough, even menacing-looking appearance of many SUVs is intentionally and consciously designed by automakers for an era when civility on the roads has been replaced with unabashed hostility, a kind of me-first aggressiveness. In the age of everything from road rage to anthrax to SARS, you can't have too much steel between you and the rest of what's driving around out there.

And it's true: SUVs *are* a threat to others on the road — a fact that was appreciated as early as thirty years ago by researchers trying to draw attention to the dangers of designing vehicles with the sort of stiff, high front ends that are the hallmark of the SUV. In an accident, an SUV is two and a half times more likely than a mid-size car to kill the occupants of the other vehicle, due to the fact that SUVs are heavier (by a thousand pounds on average), stiffer and taller. These characteristics effectively turn SUVs into "battering rams in collisions with other vehicles," notes a recent report by the Union of Concerned Scientists. When an SUV hits a car from behind, it is more likely to ride up over the car's bumper, leaving the car (and its occupants) essentially defenseless. When an SUV hits a car from the side, it can ride up over the car's door frame and right into the passenger compartment. (Well, hello there!) This mismatch of sizes has been dubbed "vehicle incompatibility," but another possible name would be "vehicle homicide." And one-on-one against an unarmed pedestrian, an SUV is more lethal still, hitting the pedestrian higher up on the body, closer to vital organs, than a regular car does. Yet this greater height, stiffness and body weight seems to be something of a selling point, rather than a signal that perhaps something is seriously wrong with these oversized killing machines.

6   Even if the thought of killing others isn't a deterrent, one would think the thought of killing oneself and one's loved ones would count for something. But apparently not. SUV sales have skyrocketed despite the fact that they are also a danger to their own passengers because, with their considerable height, they have a tendency to roll over. More than 51,500 occupants of SUVs (and light trucks) died in rollovers from 1991 to 2001. The overall fatality rate for SUVs was 8 percent worse than for cars in 2000.

7   But the more far-reaching problem with SUVs — at least in terms of the survival of the planet — is the devastating amount of greenhouse gases they spew out into the air. An SUV produces roughly 40 percent more greenhouse gas emissions than a regular car does, and with SUV sales soaring — sales have increased seventeen-fold in the past two decades — their emissions have become a significant part of the problem of global warming. At a time when the dangers of global warming are blatantly evident and of serious concern to people all over the world, the breezy marketing of SUVs in North America makes a mockery of any claim that we are addressing the problem. While common sense would call for a special effort to move away from these over-emitting vehicles, exactly the opposite has been happening. Both the U.S. and Canadian governments have contributed to the SUV problem by offering SUVs regulatory controls far looser than those applied to regular cars. (The regulations were established in the U.S., but Canada has effectively adopted matching standards, which the automakers have agreed to deliver on a voluntary basis.) The extraordinary growth in SUV sales over the last two decades, then, can be attributed as much to government favouritism as to the massive advertising campaign that has left prospective SUV buyers thinking of off-road adventure rather than the ease of moving coffins.

8   The story of the SUV is in many ways a microcosm of the human folly that has led us to the brink of a climate change disaster. Perhaps it seems unfair to pick on the SUV. After all, it isn't, by any means, the only source of greenhouse gas emissions. It is, however, one of the fast-growing sources. SUVs now account for an astonishing 24 percent of all new cars sold, up from just 2 percent in 1980. (Overall, the transportation sector accounts for 26 percent of U.S. greenhouse gas emissions. Along with coal-fired power plants, transportation is one of the key sources of the global warming problem.)

9   I'm picking on the SUV partly because it somehow serves as a metaphor for the absurdity of the situation we find ourselves in, if for no other reason than that these enormous, awkward vehicles seem so . . .

well . . . unnecessary. There's another aspect to this story that makes it emblematic of the saga of global warming: how easily the problem could be corrected if there were any serious political will. The technology exists to make enormous strides in cutting back the greenhouse gas emissions currently spewing out of SUVs (and other vehicles, but particularly SUVs) on highways across North America. I'm not talking about exotic space-age cars that run on hydrogen in some dream scenario (that's likely a couple of decades or so down the road), but about technology that already exists — and currently sits on shelves — in the offices of our big automakers. This, then, is the story of how Luddites° in the auto sector, fearful of risking their dominant market position, have declined to take us to where any sane person can see we must go, hiding behind claims of technological "can't do," hoping the public won't realize that what we have here is, in fact, a tale of technological "won't do."

●　●

Explorations:

Linda McQuaig,
> *It's the Crude, Dude: War, Big Oil and the Fight for the Planet*
> *The Cult of Impotence: Selling the Myth of Powerlessness in the Global Economy*

Keith Bradsher, *High and Mighty*
http://www.rabble.ca/about_us/bios.shtml?x=814
http://www.randomhouse.ca/catalog/display.pperl?0385660103&
　view-print
http://slate.msn.com/Features/GodzillaSUV/page2.asp
http://www.suv.org/environ.html

Structure:

1. Why does McQuaig begin by confessing her former ignorance about sports utility vehicles (SUVs)?
2. Identify McQuaig's THESIS STATEMENT.
3. Point out how in paragraph 3 McQuaig exploits the device of *contrast*.
4. McQuaig explores both *causes* and *effects* of the SUV phenomenon. First point out all the *causes* she gives, then all the *effects*.
5. What technique does McQuaig exploit in closing on the very words "won't do"?

° Luddites: In 1811 in Nottingham, England, textile workers led by Ned Ludd revolted against factory owners who were replacing craftsmen with new technology. They smashed the weaving machines, to protect their own jobs, until authorities put down the uprising. Since then, those who oppose new technology have often been called Luddites.

Style:

1. In places Linda McQuaig uses academic words such as "emblematic," "microcosm" and "Luddites," but in other places more conversational language such as "got to get straight home with all that toilet paper" (par. 3) or, as the SUV is riding up over another car's door frame and into the passenger compartment, "Well, hello there!" (5). Is this mixture of TONE effective? Why or why not?

2. What FIGURES OF SPEECH does McQuaig apply when she likens an SUV to a "tank," a "gated community" (par. 4) and a "battering ram" (5)?

Ideas for Discussion and Writing:

1. In our era of consumerism, many people talk about "moving up" to a bigger car or house, rather than doing a "lateral move." Do you aspire to drive an SUV? What do you think would be the *effects* on your status level? Your driving habits? Your bankbook?

2. McQuaig argues that SUVs are two and a half times more likely to kill occupants of another vehicle (par. 5), are more lethal to pedestrians (5), are 8% more likely to kill even their own passengers (6), and emit 40% more greenhouse gasses (7), thus hastening planetary disaster. Why, then, do automakers promote these vehicles so heavily? And why do these "Luddites," as she calls them, refuse to take new technology off the shelf to improve the vehicles?

3. "I'm picking on the SUV," McQuaig openly states in paragraph 9. Has she gone too far in only criticizing and ridiculing? Should she have included positive points, in order to be fair? Or would that just diminish the whole idea of arguing a case?

4. In paragraph 7 McQuaig points out how Canada has followed the U.S. in adopting the same loose SUV emission standards. What are all the *causes* of this fact? What are the *effects*? Are we a nation of followers, or are there areas of public policy that are all our own?

5. What is the solution: Drive less? Car pool? Drive a small car? (Are they safe?) Use public transit? Cycle or walk? Give your own conclusions.

6. **PROCESS IN WRITING:** *Write an essay on the causes and/or effects of owning one of the following: a motorcycle, a very small car, a sports car, a pickup truck, a condo, a house, or a cottage. First rough out a page or two of notes. Then look to see if you have mentioned mostly causes, mostly effects, or both. Accordingly, plan your argument, arrive at a THESIS STATEMENT, and write a rapid first draft filled with examples. The next day look it over. Have you left out any obvious causes and/or effects? If so, add. Do logic signals such as "because," "therefore," "so that" and "as a result" highlight your cause-and-effect argument? If not, add. Finally, look over the punctuation and sentence structure before printing off your best version.*

Note: See also the Topics for Writing at the end of this chapter.

NATHALIE PETROWSKI

The Seven-Minute Life of Marc Lépine*

Translated from the French by Ronald Conrad

Born 1954 in Paris and educated in Montreal, Nathalie Petrowski is a radio and TV personality, and one of Quebec's favourite print journalists — quirky, personal, satirical. In 1995 she also published Maman Last Call, *and wrote the script for the book's feature film version released in 2005. In her newspaper column for* Le Devoir *of December 16, 1989 Petrowski had a special challenge: ten days before, a 25-year-old man had walked into an engineering class at the University of Montreal's École Polytechnique, shouted at the women students "You're all a bunch of feminists, and I hate feminists," ordered the men to leave — then lifted his rifle and shot the women. Six died. During the next minutes of terror he roamed the building, shooting. Altogether he gunned down 27 students, killing 14, all women. Then Marc Lépine turned the weapon on himself and died too. Canada felt a shock wave of anger and remorse, for this was the worst one-day mass murder in the nation's history, and its selectivity seemed to express a general sexism in society. In the next days, as the flag over Parliament flew at half-mast, citizens learned that Lépine's father had beat him and divorced the mother, and that the boy, though intelligent, had problems both academically and socially. He loved war movies, and from a paratrooper uncle had learned to handle firearms. His unemployment benefits were running out, the army would not take him, and the Polytechnique had refused him admission to its engineering program. Now on December 6 of every year, ceremonies across the nation honour the 14 young women, training for a profession still dominated by men, who were killed by a man whose suicide note blamed feminists for ruining his life. The essay that follows (originally entitled "Pitié pour les salauds") has a special poignancy, for Nathalie Petrowski wrote it in shock, as she and the nation first struggled to see meaning in the event.*

Pardon if I insist, pardon if I don't just mourn and forget, but it's stronger than I am, for a week I can't stop thinking about Marc Lépine. A psychoanalyst would say I'm identifying with the aggressor. But I'd say that inside every aggressor, every villain, there hides a victim.

I think of Marc Lépine to block out all the talk that just confuses things: Rambo, television, violence towards women, pornography, abortion, and firearms in display windows.

---

* Editor's title.

3   I think of Marc Lépine, still wondering what happened and exactly when the hellish countdown of his act was unleashed. Was it the morning of December 6, was it November 21 when he bought his rifle or September 4 when he applied for the firearm permit? Was it the day of his birth, the first time his father beat him, the day his parents divorced, the week when he suddenly quit all his courses, the night a girl didn't want to dance with him? What about all the hours, the days, the weeks, the years that passed before the bomb inside him went off?

4   Still, journalists have told us everything: where he lived, the schools he went to, the names of teachers and students he knew. We know how much he paid for his rifle and how he loved war movies. But once all this has been said, nothing has been said.

5   We know nothing of the ache that consumed him, of the torture inside him. We know nothing of the evil path he slipped into smiling the cruel smile of the angel of destruction, no longer himself, knowing only that he was put on earth to destroy.

6   I think of Marc Lépine but equally of Nadia,° his sister who was beaten, too, for singing out loud in the morning, Nadia who came from the same family but didn't fall prey to the same madness. Why Marc and not Nadia, why Marc and not another? That's what I ask myself when facts only deepen the mystery, when social criticism only confuses things.

7   No one remembers him from grade school, or from Sainte-Justine Hospital where he spent a year in therapy with his mother and sister. Until last week Marc Lépine did not exist. He was an unknown quantity, a number, an anonymous face in the crowd, a nobody who no one would even look at or give the least warmth, the slightest affection. In a few moments he went from a nothing to one of a kind, a pathological case who the experts claim in no way represents the society where he was born and grew up.

8   For a week I've been talking with these experts, hoping to understand. For a week all I've seen is that there is no one answer, there are a thousand. For a week I've dealt with the official and professional voices who keep their files under key, who keep repeating that there's no use wanting to know more, that Marc Lépine is dead, that he can no longer be healed or saved, that it's too late to do anything at all. Sometimes their excuses and justifications sound like lies.

9   But I refuse to hear the silence of death that falls like snow, the shameful silence that freezes my blood. Somewhere deep in the ruins of our private space we hide the truth, we try to protect ourselves saying that families — ours, his, the victims' — have been traumatized.

10   Forget about the past, say the authorities, let's move on and not let Marc Lépine's act dictate our choices. Yet the surest way to let this act dictate our choices is to hide it, to let it become a medical, psychologi-

---

° Lépine's sister Nadia Garbi later became a drug addict. In 1996 she died of cardiac arrest from an overdose.

cal and criminal secret, to push it into the smallest hollow of our collective memory till it's erased and we can say it never existed at all.

In this province where memory is reduced to a slogan on a licence plate,° we want to forget Marc Lépine like we forget all events that can disturb us and make us think. Though I know nothing of Marc Lépine's story, I've met enough young people in the high schools and colleges to know that chance as well as reasons, randomness as well as all the wrong conditions in one person's life, caused this act. His tragic destiny looks more and more like a tangle of shattered hopes, of frustrated dreams, of hopeless waits on a long and cold road without a single hand extended to help, and no guardrail.   11

Marc Lépine died the evening of December 6, but unlike his victims, he had died long before. In the end his life lasted just seven minutes. Before and after, he was forgotten.   12

So pardon my pessimism, but I cannot help believing that somewhere, at this moment, there are other Marc Lépines who won't ask for anything because they don't even know what to ask for — other children turned into monsters by abusive fathers and impersonal school systems, by a society so intent on excellence that every day it hammers the nail of Defeat further in, and plants seeds of frustration and violence in the fragile spirits of its children.   13

Though nothing can be done now for Marc Lépine, something can still be done for the others, whose inner clock has already begun the terrible countdown. It would be a mistake to forget them.   14

● ●

Explorations:

Nathalie Petrowski, *Il Restera toujours le Nebraska* (novel; available only in French)

Louise Malette and Marie Chalouh, eds., *Polytechnique, 6 décembre* (writings on the Montreal Massacre; available only in French)

Elliott Leyton, *Hunting Humans* (book on multiple murders)

Neil Boyd, *The Beast Within: Why Men Are Violent*

Heidi Rathjen and Charles Monpetit, *December 6: From the Montreal Massacre to Gun Control*

After the Montreal Massacre (NFB/CBC video, 27 min.)

Camilo José Cela, *Pascal Duarte's family* (novel, Spain)

Gabriel García Márquez, *Chronicle of a Death Foretold* (novella, Colombia)

Anne Hébert, *The Torrent* (novella)

http://www.whiteribbon.ca

http://dionysos.ulaval.ca/impact/ic/icart.951114.html

http://www.litterature.org/ile32000.asp?numero=373

° Quebec licence plates bear the motto "Je me souviens" ("I remember"); Quebeckers consider this a reference to their history, and especially the Conquest.

http://www.infoculture.ca/?page=5&view=2&numero=5223
http://www.radio-canada.ca/radio/indicatifpresent/Chroniques/
47790.shtml

Structure:

1. Identify Nathalie Petrowski's THESIS STATEMENT.
2. Tragic events leave people asking "why?" Point out all the reasons that Petrowski examines to explain Marc Lépine's acts. How fully is her argument built on *cause and effect* reasoning?
3. How does paragraph 6 use *comparison and contrast*?
4. What popular technique of conclusion gives force to the closing?

Style:

1. In paragraph 1 and elsewhere, Petrowski groups sentences together with commas. Do you view this as faulty punctuation, or is it a way for Petrowski to express strong feeling? Are we ever justified in breaking rules of punctuation and sentence structure?
2. Identify all the FIGURES OF SPEECH in paragraph 9. What do they contribute?
3. What feeling does paragraph 3 convey in its flurry of questions?

Ideas for Discussion and Writing:

1. After murdering 14 engineering students because they were women, Marc Lépine used the last bullet on himself. But in what sense had he "died long before" (par. 12)? In what sense did his life last only "seven minutes" (par. 12)?
2. Petrowski opens her essay with the belief that "inside every aggressor, every villain, there hides a victim." Can we and should we view Marc Lépine, the killer, as himself a victim? If so, a victim of who or what? What might have been done, and by whom, to help Lépine before it was too late?
3. In its issue covering the Montreal Massacre, *Maclean's* reported that in Canada one of every four women is harassed sexually at some time in life, and that a million women are abused each year by their husbands or partners. It also quoted a study by Rosemary Gartner who found that "as women move into non-traditional roles, they run a significantly higher risk of being killed." Do you see a link between this information and the act of Marc Lépine? Explain.
4. By the tenth anniversary of that terrible day, the number of female students in Canadian engineering programs had doubled. Are the problems being solved? Or do you believe women and their goals are still at risk?

5. In a *Fifth Estate* documentary, *Legacy of Pain*, marking the massacre's tenth anniversary, correspondent Francine Pelletier spoke of one survivor, Nathalie Provost, now an engineer and a mother. "The first time her little boy went bang-bang to her, she said she went white," reported Pelletier. "She took him by the arm and said, 'Don't you ever do that to me. Because mommy's been there.'" Would you allow your own children to have toy weapons? To play cops and robbers, or other traditional games of violence? What could be the *effects?* Defend your response with evidence.

6. On that day, Lépine carried one of the most popular rifles in Canada, a .223-calibre Sturm, Ruger semiautomatic, with two 30-clip magazines holding shells with expanding slugs. Are firearms such as this a danger in your city or town? Attack or defend the sale of arms, including handguns, over the counter. Are our strengthened gun laws an attack on civil liberties, as many hunters maintain, or are they still too weak to stop the next Marc Lépine?

7. **PROCESS IN WRITING:** *Lépine used a rifle, but handguns are the weapon of choice for shootings. At the library or at reliable Web sites, gather information on the role of handguns in crime in Canada. Research also our current regulations for their sale and use. Now decide on your THESIS STATEMENT: whether Canada should end, more severely limit, or continue to permit the sale of handguns to civilians. List your reasons. From this short outline write a fast discovery draft of your essay, developed mainly through* cause and effect *logic, not stopping now to fix things like spelling or punctuation. The next day look it over. Is every point backed by a reason or* example? *Does your* evidence *lead clearly to your* conclusion? *(Remember that many essayists will change a conclusion or even a thesis statement when the act of writing uncovers better ideas.) Finally, edit for correctness as you produce your final version.*

Note: See also the Topics for Writing at the end of this chapter.

MORDECAI RICHLER

1944: The Year I Learned to Love a German

One of Canada's most internationally known writers, Mordecai Richler (1931–2001) had, as critic Bruce McCall wrote, a "refreshingly low baloney threshold," and went "bellying through the saloon doors of life on our behalf in search of truths — about sex, sports, politics, culture. . . ." In his novels and essays both, Richler's well-crafted, ruthlessly satirical prose devastates its targets: hypocrisy, pretension, self-righteousness, prejudice, provincialism and nationalism (he attacks all these in our selection). Born to a working-class family in the Jewish quarter of Montreal, Richler left in 1951 for Paris, where he wrote his first novel. He returned to work at the CBC, then from 1954 to 1972 lived and wrote in England, returning to Quebec for good in 1972. He published many novels, among them Son of a Smaller Hero *(1955),* The Apprenticeship of Duddy Kravitz *(1959),* Cocksure *(1968),* St. Urbain's Horseman *(1971, Governor General's Award),* Joshua Then and Now *(1980),* Solomon Gursky Was Here *(1989) and* Barney's Version *(1997, Giller Prize and Stephen Leacock Award for Humour).* Duddy Kravitz *and* Joshua, *as well as his children's book* Jacob Two-Two Meets the Hooded Fang *(1975) were also produced as feature films. Richler gathered his essays and articles in collections such as* Shovelling Trouble *(1972),* Home Sweet Home *(1984),* Broadsides *(1990),* Oh Canada! Oh Quebec! *(1992), and* Belling the Cat: Essays, Reports & Opinions *(1998). Our own selection is from the* New York Times Book Review *of February 2, 1986. It is a revised version of his introduction to Erich Maria Remarque's classic antiwar novel,* All Quiet on the Western Front. *In it, Richler returns lovingly to the St. Urbain St. neighbourhood of his Montreal youth, but also looks outward to the "cities of light" which would soon also be his home.*

1   eading was not one of my boyhood passions. Girls, or rather the absence of girls, drove me to it. When I was 13 years old, short for my age, more than somewhat pimply, I was terrified of girls. They made me feel sadly inadequate. As far as I could make out, they were attracted only to boys who were tall or played for the school basketball team or at least shaved. Unable to qualify on all three counts, I resorted to subterfuge. I set out to call attention to myself by becoming a character. Retreating into high seriousness, I acquired a pipe, which I chewed on ostentatiously, and made it my business to be seen everywhere, even at school basketball games, absorbed by books of daunting significance.

Say, H. G. Wells's "Short History of the World" or Paul de Kruif's "Microbe Hunters" or John Gunther inside one continent or another. I rented these thought-provoking books for three cents a day from a neighborhood lending library that was across the street from a bowling alley where I used to spot pins four nights a week.

Oh, my God, I would not be 13 again for anything. The sweetly scented girls of my dreams, wearing lipstick and tight sweaters and nylon stockings, would sail into the bowling alley holding hands with the boys from the basketball team. "Hi," they would call out, giggly, nudging one another, even as I bent over the pins, "how goes the reading?"

The two women who ran the lending library, possibly amused by my pretensions, tried to interest me in fiction.

"I want fact. I can't be bothered with *stories*," I protested, waving my pipe at them, affronted. "I just haven't got the time for such nonsense."

I knew what novels were, of course. I had read "Scaramouche," by Rafael Sabatini, at school, as well as "Treasure Island" and some Ellery Queens and a couple of thumpers by G. A. Henty. Before that there had been Action Comics, Captain Marvel, Batman and — for educational reasons — either Bible Comics or Classic Comics. All these treasures I bought under the counter, as it were. They were passed hand to hand on dark street corners. Contraband. Our samizdat. The reason for this being that in 1943 the dolts who prevailed in Ottawa had adjudged American comic books unessential to the war effort, a drain on the Canadian dollar.

Novels, I knew, were mere romantic make-believe, not as bad as poetry, to be fair, but bad enough. Our high school class master, a dedicated Scot, had been foolish enough to try to interest us in poetry. A veteran of World War I, he told us that during the nightly bombardments on the Somme he would fix a candle to his steel helmet so that he could read poetry in the trenches. A scruffy lot, we were not moved. Instead we exchanged knowing winks behind that admirable man's back. Small wonder, we agreed, that he had ended up no better than a high school teacher.

My aunts consumed historical novels like pastries. My father read Black Mask and True Detective. My mother would read anything on a Jewish subject, preferably by I. J. Singer or Sholem Asch, though she would never forgive the latter for having written "The Nazarene," never mind "Mary" and "The Apostle." My older brother kept a novel, "Topper Takes a Trip," secure under his mattress in the bedroom we shared, assuring me that it was placed at just such an angle on the springs that if it were moved so much as a millimeter in his absence he would know and bloody well make me pay for it.

I fell ill with a childhood disease. I no longer remember which, but obviously I meant it as a rebuke to those girls in tight sweaters who continued to ignore me. Never mind, they would mourn at my funeral, burying me with my pipe. Too late, they would say, "Boy, was he ever an intellectual!"

9   The women from the lending library, concerned, dropped off books for me at our house. The real stuff. Fact-filled. Providing me with the inside dope on Theodor Herzl's childhood and "Brazil Yesterday, Today, and Tomorrow." One day they brought me a novel: "All Quiet on the Western Front" by Erich Maria Remarque. The painting on the jacket that was taped to the book showed a soldier wearing what was unmistakably a German Army helmet. *What was this,* I wondered, *some sort of bad joke?*

10   Nineteen forty-four that was, and I devoutly wished every German left on the face of the earth an excruciating death. The Allied invasion of France had not yet begun, but I cheered every Russian counterattack, each German city bombed, and — with the help of a map tacked to my bedroom wall — followed the progress of the Canadian troops fighting their way up the Italian boot. Boys from our street had already been among the fallen. Izzy Draper's uncle, Harvey Kugelmass's older brother. The boy who was supposed to marry Gita Holtzman.

11   "All Quiet on the Western Front" lay unopened on my bed for two days. A time bomb ticking away, though I hardly suspected it. Rather than read a novel, a novel written by a German, I tuned in to radio soap operas in the afternoons: "Ma Perkins," "Pepper Young's Family." I organized a new base-ball league for short players who didn't shave yet, appointing myself com-missioner, the first Canadian to be so honored. Sifting through a stack of my father's back issues of Popular Mechanics, I was sufficiently inspired to invent a spaceship and fly to Mars, where I was adored by everybody, espe-cially the girls. Finally, I was driven to picking up "All Quiet on the Western Front" out of boredom. I never expected that a mere novel, a stranger's tale, could actually be dangerous, creating such turbulence in my life, obliging me to question so many received ideas. About Germans. About my own monumental ignorance of the world. About what novels were.

12   At the age of 13 in 1944, happily as yet untainted by English 104, I couldn't tell you whether Remarque's novel was

a. a slice of life
b. symbolic
c. psychological
d. seminal.

13   I couldn't even say if it was well or badly written. In fact, as I recall, it didn't seem to be "written" at all. Instead, it just flowed. Now, of course, I understand that writing that doesn't advertise itself is art of a very high order. It doesn't come easily. But at the time I wasn't capable of making such distinctions. I also had no notion of how "All Quiet on the Western Front" rated critically as a war novel. I hadn't read Stendhal or Tolstoy or Crane or Hemingway. I hadn't even heard of them. I didn't know that Thomas Mann, whoever he was, had praised the novel highly. Neither did I know that in 1929 the judges at some outfit called the Book-of-the-Month Club had made it their May selection. But what I did know is that, hating

Germans with a passion, I had read only 20, maybe 30, pages before the author had seduced me into identifying with my enemy, 19-year-old Paul Baumer, thrust into the bloody trenches of World War I with his schoolmates: Müller, Kemmerich and the reluctant Joseph Behm, one of the first to fall. As if that weren't sufficiently unsettling in itself, the author, having won my love for Paul, my enormous concern for his survival, then betrayed me in the last dreadful paragraphs of his book:

"He fell in October 1918, on a day that was so quiet and still on the whole front, that the army report confined itself to the single sentence: All quiet on the Western Front. [14]

"He had fallen forward and lay on the earth as though sleeping. Turning him over one saw that he could not have suffered long; his face had an expression of calm, as though almost glad the end had come." [15]

The movies, I knew from experience, never risked letting you down like that. No matter how bloody the battle, how long the odds, Errol Flynn, Robert Taylor, even Humphrey Bogart could be counted on to survive and come home to Ann Sheridan, Lana Turner or — if they were sensitive types — Loretta Young. Only character actors, usually Brooklyn Dodger fans, say George Tobias or William Bendix, were expendable. [16]

Obviously, having waded into the pool of serious fiction by accident, I was not sure I liked or trusted the water. It was too deep. Anything could happen. [17]

There was something else, a minor incident in "All Quiet on the Western Front" that would not have troubled an adult reader but, I'm embarrassed to say, certainly distressed that 13-year-old boy colliding with his first serious novel. [18]

Sent out to guard a village that has been abandoned because it is being shelled too heavily, Katczinsky, the incomparable scrounger, surfaces with suckling pigs and potatoes and carrots for his comrades, a group of eight altogether: [19]

"The suckling pigs are slaughtered. Kat sees to them. We want to make potato-cakes to go with the roast. But we cannot find a grater for the potatoes. However, that difficulty is soon got over. With a nail we punch a lot of holes in a pot lid and there we have a grater. Three fellows put on thick gloves to protect their fingers against the grater, two others peel the potatoes, and the business gets going." [20]

The business, I realized, alarmed — no, *affronted* — was the making of potato latkes, a favorite of mine as well as Paul Baumer's, a dish I had always taken to be Jewish, certainly not a German concoction. [21]

What did I know? Nothing. Or, looked at another way, my real education, my lifelong addiction to fiction, began with the trifling discovery that the potato latke was not of Jewish origin, but something borrowed from the Germans and now a taste that Jew and German shared in spite of everything. [22]

I felt easier about my affection for the German soldier Paul Baumer once I was told by the women from the lending library that when Hitler [23] came to power in 1933 he had burned all of Erich Maria Remarque's books and in 1938 he took away his German citizenship. Obviously Hitler had grasped that novels could be dangerous, something I learned when I was only 13 years old. He burned them. I began to devour them. I started to read at the breakfast table and on streetcars, often missing my stop, and in bed with benefit of a flashlight. It got me into trouble. I grasped, for the first time, that I didn't live in the center of the world but had been born into a working-class family in an unimportant country far from the cities of light: London, Paris, New York. Of course this wasn't my fault, it was my inconsiderate parents who were to blame. But there was, I now realized, a larger world out there beyond St. Urbain Street in Montreal; a world that could be available to me, even though — to my mother's despair — I had been born left-handed, ate with my elbows on the table and had failed once more to lead the class at school.

24   Preparing myself for the *Rive Gauche*,° I bought a blue beret, but I didn't dare wear it outside, or even in the house if anybody else was at home. I looked at but lacked the courage to buy a cigarette holder. But the next time I took Goldie Zimmerman to a downtown movie and then out to Dinty Moore's for toasted tomato sandwiches, I suggested that instead of milkshakes we each order a glass of *vin ordinaire*. "Are you crazy?" she asked.

25   As my parents bickered at the supper table, trapped in concerns now far too mundane for the likes of me — what to do if Dworkin raised the rent again, how to manage my brother's college fees — I sat with but actually apart from them in the kitchen, enthralled, reading for the first time, "All happy families are alike but an unhappy family is unhappy after its own fashion."

26   Erich Maria Remarque, born in Westphalia in 1897, went off to war, directly from school, at the age of 18. He was wounded five times. He lost all his friends. After the war he worked briefly as a schoolteacher, a stonecutter, a test driver for a tire company and an editor of Sportbild magazine. His first novel, "Im Westen Nichts Neues," was turned down by several publishers before it was brought out by the Ullstein Press in Berlin in 1928. "All Quiet on the Western Front" sold 1,200,000 copies in Germany and was translated into 29 languages, selling some four million copies throughout the world. The novel has been filmed three times; the first time, memorably, by Lewis Milestone in 1930. The Milestone version, with Lew Ayres playing Paul Baumer, won Academy Awards for best picture and best direction.

27   Since "All Quiet on the Western Front" once meant so much to me, I picked it up again with a certain anxiety. After all this time I find it difficult to be objective about the novel. Its pages still evoke for me a back bedroom with a cracked ceiling and a sizzling radiator on St. Urbain Street, mice scrabbling in the walls, a window looking out on sheets

---

° *Rive Gauche*: the "Left Bank" of Paris, traditional quarter of students and intellectuals.

frozen stiff on the laundry line, and all the pain of being too young to shave, an ignorant and bewildered boy of 13.

Over the years the novel has lost something in shock value. The original jacket copy of the 1929 Little, Brown & Company edition of "All Quiet on the Western Front" warns the reader that it is "at times crude" and "will shock the supersensitive by its outspokenness." Contemporary readers, far from being shocked, will be amused by the novel's discretion, the absence of explicit sex scenes, the unbelievably polite dialogue of the men in the trenches.   28

The novel also has its poignant moments, both in the trenches and when Paul Baumer goes home on leave, an old man of 19, only to find insufferably pompous schoolmasters still recruiting the young with mindless prattle about the fatherland and the glory of battle. Strong characters are deftly sketched. Himmelstoss, the postman who becomes a crazed drillmaster, Tjaden, the peasant soldier, Kantorek, the schoolmaster. On the front line the enemy is never the Frogs or the Limeys, but the insanity of the war itself. It is the war, in fact, and not even Paul Baumer, that is the novel's true protagonist. In a brief introduction to the novel Remarque wrote: "This book is to be neither an accusation nor a confession, and least of all an adventure, for death is not an adventure to those who stand face to face with it. It will try simply to tell of a generation of men who, even though they may have escaped its shells, were destroyed by the war."   29

Since World War I we have become altogether too familiar with larger horrors. The Holocaust, Hiroshima, the threat of a nuclear winter. Death by numbers, cities obliterated by decree. At peace, as it were, we live with the daily dread of the missiles in their silos, ours pointed at them, theirs pointed at us. None of this, however, diminishes the power of "All Quiet on the Western Front," a novel that will endure because of its humanity, its honor and its refusal to lapse into sentimentality or strike a false note. It is a work that has earned its place on that small shelf of World War I classics alongside "Goodbye to All That," by Robert Graves, and Ernest Hemingway's "A Farewell to Arms."   30

• •

Explorations:

Mordecai Richler,
>   *The Apprenticeship of Duddy Kravitz*
>   *Barney's Version*
Erich Maria Remarque, *All Quiet on the Western Front*
The Apprenticeship of Mordecai Richler (NFB film, 57 min., 1986)
Misha Defonseca, *Misha: A Mémoire of the Holocaust Years*
Charles Yale Harrison, *Generals Die in Bed* (novel)
http://en.wikipedia.org/wiki/Erich_Maria_Remarque

http://www.kirjasto.sci.fi/remarque.htm
http://en.wikipedia.org/wiki/Mordecai_Richler
http://schwinger.harvard.edu/~terning/bios/Richler.html
http://www.worldwar1.com

Structure:

1. How does the long opening prepare us for Richler's argument? What do paragraphs 1 and 2 achieve? Paragraphs 3–6?
2. Why does Richler devote so little of his argument to the original *causes* of his reading, and so much to the *effects*?
3. Point out every *effect* on young Richler of reading novels, as shown especially in paragraphs 11, 13–17, 18–22, and 23.
4. Richler uses spaces to divide the essay in parts. What advantages does this technique have? Do you use it?
5. What technique does Richler exploit when in the closing he refers to nuclear weapons?

Style:

1. Richler's overall message is serious. Why, then, does he poke fun at adolescence, at his own and others' reading habits, at high school English, at the movies and at other targets? Do his humour and even SATIRE help or hurt the argument? Defend your answer with reasons.
2. A key technique of both novelists and essayists is to clothe abstractions in concrete IMAGES — to "show, don't tell." Point out how Richler does so in paragraphs 11, 24 and 27.
3. Explain the IRONY of calling Paul Baumer "an old man of 19" (par. 29). Using this example, analyze how irony promotes CONCISENESS.
4. Is the METAPHOR of Remarque's novel as a "bomb" (par. 11) well chosen for this topic?

Ideas for Discussion and Writing:

1. Almost every writer, like Richler, has read voraciously. Analyze the apparent *cause-and-effect* relationship: Why does reading other people's writing improve our own? Have you read enough? What are the *causes* of your attitude towards reading? What are the *effects*?
2. Richler admits that, as a Jewish boy growing up during the war, he "devoutly wished every German left on the face of the earth an excruciating death" (par. 10). Why *every* German? Do you see a STEREOTYPE behind this passage? Does it apply to those Germans who hid persecuted Jews? To those who fled Hitler's power, or even tried to assassinate him? Does it apply to Erich Maria Remarque? To Paul Baumer? Are other stereotypes more reliable? Those of women, teenagers, old people, Newfoundlanders, Quebeckers, Jews, Russians?

3. After reading 20 to 30 pages of *All Quiet on the Western Front,* Richler is "seduced" by the author into "identifying" with his "enemy," and even feels "betrayed" when, at the end, Paul Baumer dies. Cite another passage where Richler's reading of fiction dispels STEREOTYPES.

4. "I never expected that a mere novel, a stranger's tale, could actually be dangerous," says Richler in paragraph 11. How can a novel be "dangerous"? Why did Hitler burn this one and strip its author of citizenship (par. 23)? Name other books burned or censored. What may such cases reveal about the role of the writer in society?

5. Extend Richler's analysis to other media. List several films, TV serials, or Web sites you have recently seen. Which were "dangerous," challenging received attitudes? Which were "safe," propping up received attitudes? Argue, with examples.

6. **PROCESS IN WRITING:** *Choose either a "dangerous" or a "safe" film or TV series or Web site from the previous question. Now in an essay of* cause and effect, *show how the chosen work affected you: Did it just reinforce old opinions, or did it change your mind? First brainstorm: jot down scenes that either reassured or disturbed you. Now turn the best of these notes into a draft. Has the act of writing called up forgotten details? Add them. Has it challenged your view of the work's "danger" or "safety"? If so, change your* THESIS STATEMENT *and adjust the argument. Now strengthen* TRANSITIONS *to speed your argument and highlight its* causality. *Cut deadwood. Finally, test your prose aloud before writing the final version.*

Note: See also the Topics for Writing at the end of this chapter.

Topics for Writing

CHAPTER 4: CAUSE AND EFFECT

Analyze the cause(s) OR effect(s) of one of the following. (See also the guidelines that follow.)

1. Urban Sprawl
2. Vegetarianism
3. Internet Addiction
4. Road Rage
5. Moving to a New School
6. Pornography
7. Traffic Gridlock
8. Having a Cell Phone
9. Obesity
10. Being the Oldest, Youngest or Middle Child of a Family
11. Procrastination
12. The Underground Economy
13. Moving from a House to an Apartment, or Vice Versa
14. Popularity in School
15. Eating Junk Food
16. Being a Twin
17. Learning a Second Language
18. Being Tall or Being Short
19. Massive Popularity of the iPod
20. Holding a Job While in School
21. Gambling
22. Marrying as a Teenager
23. Moving to Another Country
24. Being Adopted
25. Divorce
26. The Underground Economy
27. Use of Credit Cards
28. Lying
29. Homelessness
30. Stress

Note also the Process in Writing topic after each selection in this chapter.

Process in Writing: Guidelines

Follow at least some of these steps in writing your essay of cause and effect (your teacher may suggest which ones).

1. *In the middle of a page, write the subject you wish to explore in your essay of* cause and effect. *Now around it write many other words that it brings to mind. Connect related items with lines, then use this cluster outline to discover your argument. Except for the introduction and conclusion, which may give background or look at the subject's future, focus down to EITHER the* causes *OR the* effects.

2. *Now write a quick first draft, getting it all out on the computer screen or the paper without stopping now to revise.*

3. *When this version has "cooled off," analyze it, referring to our chapter introduction: Have you begun and ended at the right places in the chain of causality? If not, cut or add. Have you found the* real causes *or the* real effects? *If not, revise. Do you also need* causes of causes, *or* effects of effects? *If so, add.*

4. *In your next draft sharpen the* TRANSITIONS, *using expressions like "since," "although," "because" and "as a result" to signal each step of your logic.*

5. *Share this version with a group of classmates. Revise any places where this* AUDIENCE *does not follow your logic.*

6. *Finally, edit for things like spelling and punctuation before printing out your best version.*

Mike Constable

"Women workers earn, on an average, only 70 cents for every $1 a man gets — even though on an average, women are better educated than men."

— *Doris Anderson, "The 51-Per-Cent Minority"*

Comparison and Contrast

IT'S JUST THE OPPOSITE OF . . .

You may have heard the old Chinese proverb, "I felt sorry for myself because I had no shoes, until I met a man who had no feet." How much more we suddenly know about both the shoes and the feet, thinking of them together! This is the power of comparison and contrast.

See Mike Constable's cartoon on the opposite page. What is happening? All the runners are in starting position, awaiting the same shot from the same referee, and no doubt aiming for the same finish line. These are the *comparisons* (similarities). Yet at the same time there are *contrasts* (differences). Three of the runners are men, but only one is a woman. The referee holding his gun is also a man, unlike the woman contestant. She will run in skirt and high heels, while the men clearly will not. Worst of all, the men will run straight ahead, while she must race uphill to reach their level. Is there any way the woman can win this race?

Though the cartoon has both comparisons and contrasts, clearly it is the contrasts that send the message — men have advantages in the race of life. In the essay that follows, Doris Anderson uses words to send the same message through the same logic. Though of course there are similarities between the lives of women and men, it is the differences, the *contrasts*, that build Anderson's point that women, though a "majority" in numbers, are a "minority" in power.

157

When using the logic of comparison and contrast in your own essays, you, too, may find both similarities and differences. Though it is possible to explore both, the need to focus means that using one is often better — and the choice is usually the more dramatic one: *contrast*.

You have experienced contrast if you have ever known culture shock. As you enter a new country, the look of the buildings and streets, the smells in the air, the sounds, the language and customs, all seem strange — because you are contrasting them to what you just left. And if you stay a long time, the same happens in reverse when you return: home seems strange because you are contrasting it to the place where you've just been. The cars may seem too big, the food too bland, the pace of life too fast. Travel is one of the great educational experiences: through contrast, one place puts another in perspective.

In a comparison and contrast essay, it is essential to choose two subjects *of the same general type*: two countries, two sports, two poems, or two solutions to unemployment. For example, a person who knows both Vancouver and Montreal might choose to compare and/or contrast these two cities: their cuisine, their night life, cost of rent, traffic, air pollution, crime, level of unemployment, level of multiculturalism, etc. By the end of the essay — whether or not we agree with the author's point of view or preference of city — we would have the impression of reading a logical argument. After all, Vancouver and Montreal are in the same category: major Canadian cities.

But suppose that instead of comparing two cities, the author had compared a city and an anthill. After all, there are similarities: both are crowded, both are highly organized, both have housing with many rooms located off corridors, etc. But no matter how much fun she might have had or what insights she might have got across, she would prove nothing — for the simple reason that people are not insects. The essay would be an *analogy*, a more imaginative but less logical kind of argument, which we will explore in the next chapter.

Once you have chosen your two subjects of the same general type, you face another choice: how to arrange them. There are two basic ways:

Divide the essay into halves, devoting the first half to Vancouver and the second to Montreal. This system is natural in a very short essay, because your reader remembers everything from the first half while reading the second half. It is also natural when for some reason the items are more clearly discussed as a whole than in parts.

Divide the subjects into separate points. First compare the cuisine in both cities, then the night life, then the cost of rent, and so on through your whole list of points. This system is most natural in long essays: putting related material together helps the reader to grasp comparisons or contrasts without the strain of recalling every detail from ten pages back.

Although "halves" are often best for short papers and "separate points" are often best for long papers, be open to the needs of your particular subject, treatment and purpose. Choose the approach that will most strongly deliver your message. For example, in this chapter Jack Layton chooses "halves" to contrast the Gross Domestic Product (GDP) and the Genuine Progress Indicator (GPI). The reason: both systems of measuring our economy take some explanation, and explanation works best when the details are not scattered.

Finally, the very act of comparing or contrasting means you need *examples* — either a large number of short ones or a small number of long ones. If these do not make up at least half the content of your essay, you are losing power. Add more.

To generate your examples and points, why not draw a line down the middle of a blank page and put the name of your subjects at the top of each column? Now brainstorm a list of points under each heading. Connect related items from left to right with lines, and, seeing relationships, decide on your thesis statement. Is cash better than credit? Is income tax fairer than sales tax? Are motorcycles more dangerous than cars? Whatever you believe is the truth, now write your essay, letting the many examples show your reader why.

Note: Many essays in other chapters use comparison and contrast to help make their point. See especially these:

Jan Wong, "Ten Things the Chinese Do Much Better Than We Do," p. 48
Leah McLaren, "Canadian Guys Rule," p. 122
Samantha Bennett, "It's Not Just the Weather That's Cooler in Canada," p. 208
Martin Hocking, "Capping the Great Cup Debate," p. 278
Kildare Dobbs, "The Scar," p. 283
Joy Kogawa, "Grinning and Happy," p. 292
Margaret Atwood, "Letter to America," p. 298

DORIS ANDERSON

The 51-Per-Cent Minority

Doris Anderson has always been a "rebel daughter" (to use the title of her autobiography). From a prairie childhood, with a tyrannical father but an independent mother, Anderson went on to teachers' college and taught in rural Alberta till she could put herself through university. With a B.A from the University of Alberta, she then went to Toronto and began her career in journalism. From copy editor and researcher, she moved in 1951 to Chatelaine, *where she rose through the ranks to become editor in chief in 1957, the same year she married lawyer David Anderson. Years before the rise of feminism, Anderson was shaking up her readers with articles on legalization of abortion, battered babies, divorce law reform, female sexuality, and practical advice for working women. Soon a million and a half women were reading* Chatelaine *every month, and in the process gaining a taste for new rights. As early as the 60s, Anderson agitated for a Royal Commission on the Status of Women. When it was created, with herself as chair, she scored the biggest achievement of her career: while the government debated the content of its new constitution, she saw there was nothing in it for women. So she suddenly resigned in 1981 from the Royal Commission; this sparked a massive campaign by women, a crisis in the government, and a result of full equal rights for women being enshrined in the new constitution. Anderson went on to head the National Action Committee on the Status of Women, as well as the Ontario Press Council. She has published novels,* Two Women *in 1978,* Rough Layout *in 1981 and* Affairs of State *in 1988. In addition to her many editorials and articles, she has written two nonfiction books,* The Unfinished Revolution *(on the status of women in Europe and North America) and her 1996 autobiography. Our own selection, "The 51-Per-Cent Minority," first appeared in* Maclean's.

1 In any Canadian election the public will probably be hammered numb with talk of the economy, energy and other current issues. But there will always be some far more startling topics that no one will talk about at all.

2 No one is going to say to all new Canadians: "Look, we're going through some tough times. Three out of four of you had better face the fact that you're always going to be poor. At 65 more than likely you'll be living below the poverty level."

3 And no one is going to tell Quebeckers: "You will have to get along on less money than the rest of the country. For every $1 the rest of us earn, you, because you live in Quebec, will earn 70 cents."

4 I doubt very much that any political party is going to level with the Atlantic provinces and say: "We don't consider people living there seri-

ous prime workers. Forget about any special measures to make jobs for you. In fact in future federal-provincial talks we're not even going to discuss your particular employment problems."

And no politician is going to tell all the left-handed people in the country: "Look, we know it looks like discrimination, but we have to save some money somewhere. So, although you will pay into your company pension plan at the same rate as everyone else, you will collect less when you retire."

And no one is going to say to Canadian doctors: "We know you do one of the most important jobs any citizen can perform, but from now on you're going to have to get along without any support systems. All hospital equipment and help will be drastically reduced. We believe a good doctor should instinctively know what to do — or you're in the wrong job. If you're really dedicated you'll get along."

As for blacks: "Because of the color of your skin, you're going to be paid less than the white person next to you who is doing exactly the same job. It's tough but that's the way it is."

As for Catholics: "You're just going to have to understand that you will be beaten up by people with other religious beliefs quite regularly. Even if your assailant threatens to kill you, you can't do anything about it. After all, we all need some escape valves, don't we?"

Does all of the above sound like some nihilistic nightmare where Orwellian forces have taken over? Well, it's not. It's all happening right now, in Canada.

It's not happening to new Canadians, Quebeckers, residents of the Atlantic provinces, left-handed people, doctors, blacks or Indians. If it were, there would be riots in the streets. Civil libertarians would be howling for justice. But all of these discriminatory practices are being inflicted on women today in Canada as a matter of course.

Most women work at two jobs — one inside the home and one outside. Yet three out of four women who become widowed or divorced or have never married live out their old age in poverty.

Women workers earn, on an average, only 70 cents for every $1 a man gets — even though on an average, women are better educated than men.

And when companies base pension plans on how long people live, women still pay the same rates as men but often collect less.

What politician could possibly tell doctors to train each other and get along without all their high technology and trained help? Yet a more important job than saving lives is surely creating lives. But mothers get no training, no help in the way of a family allowance, inadequate day-care centres, and almost nonexistent after-school programs.

No politician would dream of telling blacks they must automatically earn less than other people. But women sales clerks, waitresses and hospital orderlies often earn less than males doing the same jobs. It would be called discrimination if a member of a religious group was beaten up, and the assailant would be jailed. But hundreds of wives get beaten by their husbands week in and week out, year after year. Some die, yet society still tolerates the fact that it's happening.

16   Women make up 51 per cent of the population of this country. Think of the kind of clout they could have if they used it at the polls. But to listen to the political parties, the woman voter just doesn't exist. When politicians talk to fishing folk they talk about improved processing plants and new docks. When they talk to wheat farmers they talk of better transportation and higher price supports. When they talk to people in the Atlantic provinces they talk about new federal money for buildings and more incentives for secondary industry. When they talk to ethnic groups they talk about better language training courses. But when they think of women — if they do at all — they assume women will vote exactly as their husbands — so why waste time offering them anything? It's mind-boggling to contemplate, though, how all those discriminatory practices would be swept aside if, instead of women, we were Italian, or black, or lived in Quebec or the Atlantic provinces.

● ●

Explorations:

Doris Anderson,
    The Unfinished Revolution
    Rebel Daughter: An Autobiography
Simone de Beauvoir, *The Second Sex*
Naomi Wolf, *The Beauty Myth: How Images of Beauty Are Used Against Women*
Margaret Atwood, *The Handmaid's Tale* (novel)
http://www.nlc-bnc.ca/2/12/h12-295-e.html
http://www.cddc.vt.edu/feminism/can.html
http://www.writersunion.ca/a/adrsn_d.htm
http://www.cbc.ca/lifeandtimes/anderson.html

Structure:

1. Is this essay mainly a *comparison* or a *contrast?*
2. Does Anderson argue "point by point" or by "halves"?
3. Point out the passage of TRANSITION between Anderson's discussion of minorities and her discussion of women.
4. Why does this feminist essay never mention women until halfway through? How does this tactic help Anderson reach the potentially hostile 49% of her AUDIENCE which is male?
5. If you have read *1984* or *Animal Farm,* tell how the reference to George Orwell in paragraph 9 helps make Anderson's point.
6. Why does the closing offer a series of new *examples?* Why are they so short?

Style:

1. How important is the title of an essay? What should it do? How effective is this one, and why?
2. Anderson's essay first appeared in *Maclean's*, a magazine for the general reader. Name all the ways in which her essay seems designed for that person.

Ideas for Discussion and Writing:

1. Explain the IRONY of Anderson's claim: in what sense are women, 51% of the population, a "minority" in Canada?
2. Anderson states in paragraph 11, "Most women work at two jobs — one inside the home and one outside." Suppose that someday you and your partner both have full-time jobs. If you are a woman, how much of the housework will you expect your partner to do? If you are a man, how much of the housework will you expect your partner to do? Defend your view with reasons.
3. "The 51-Per-Cent Minority" first appeared in 1980. Revising it for this edition some 25 years later, Anderson was disappointed that she was able to raise from 61 cents to only 70 cents the amount that a woman now earns for every dollar a man earns (although in Quebec the figure is 75 cents). At this rate of change, equal pay will not arrive in Canada for over 75 years after the essay was written. Explain all the reasons why.
4. In paragraph 16 Anderson writes, "Women make up 51 per cent of the population of this country. Think of the kind of clout they could have if they used it at the polls." Do you agree that women have not yet used their votes to best advantage? If so, why not? How could they begin to?
5. **PROCESS IN WRITING:** *Write an essay that* contrasts *the way society trains girls to be women with the way society trains boys to be men. First divide a page into halves, one for each sex, and fill each half with* examples. *Now from these notes choose contrasting pairs. Decide whether to organize the pairs by "halves" or "point by point," then write a rapid discovery draft. In your next draft strengthen the* TRANSITIONS, *especially signals such as "but," "on the other hand," "however" and "yet," which point out* contrast. *Share a draft with classmates in small groups to see if all parts work. Revise any that do not. Finally, read your best version aloud to the whole class, and be ready to answer questions asked from other points of view.*

Note: See also the Topics for Writing at the end of this chapter.

JACK LAYTON

Measuring the New Prosperity

In his high school yearbook, Jack Layton declared that one day he would be prime minister of Canada. The charismatic and fluently bilingual politician is not there yet, but in 2003 became national leader of the federal New Democratic Party. Layton was born in 1950 in Hudson, Quebec, to a very political family. His blind great-grandfather was an activist for the blind, his grandfather a Quebec cabinet minister, and his father a Tory M.P. in the Mulroney government. But as a student at McGill, Layton was drawn to progressive causes, turned from his father's Conservative Party example, and joined the NDP. Completing a Ph.D. at York, Layton taught politics at Ryerson University. Then, winning an election, he served six terms as a Toronto city councillor (joining his wife Olivia Chow, also a councillor), working tirelessly for progressive causes: helping the homeless, the poor, gays and lesbians, families, neighbourhoods and the environment. He initiated the White Ribbon Campaign against male violence toward women, the deep lakewater cooling of major downtown office buildings, Canada's first municipal AIDS strategy, and the first urban wind turbine in Canada. To this day Layton's environmental principles mean he owns no car but rides a bicycle to work. Then in 2000 Layton became president of the Federation of Canadian Municipalities, and in 2003 was elected national leader of the NDP. Our selection, which reverses conventional thinking on economics, comes from one of his books, Speaking Out: Ideas That Work for Canadians *(2004).*

1   The way economists look at it, the 1998 ice storm, Nova Scotia's encounter with hurricane Juan, and British Columbia's forest fires and floods of 2003 were all good for the economy.

2   How's that? Because they all caused hundreds of millions of dollars of damage that needed to be repaired. They forced both governments and the private sector to spend money creating direct jobs. Those events resulted in a building boom. Stimulus! Spending! That has to be good.

3   Of course, they were horrible events for the people who had their homes destroyed, who went without power for a month or more, or who were forced into shelters until their communities could pick up the pieces — to say nothing of the people who died or the grieving families they left behind. But on the economic ledger, they go down on the plus side.

4   That's because our method of measuring the economy is nuts.

5   Automobile accidents stimulate the economy because they result in consumer spending (on repairs or a new car, and increased insurance premiums). Crime stimulates the economy because we pay more salaries for police officers and the criminal justice system. Divorce stimulates the

economy because people set up separate homes and buy more stuff. Spraying more pesticides on lawns is good for the economy, because people are buying and spending. If this produces increased health costs later, so much the better, as far as our economic measurements go. The absurdities go on and on.

Our common measure of economic activity is the gross domestic product (GDP). It simply adds up the total market value of goods and services produced in Canada. It attaches no value whatsoever to whether we actually want to be spending that money in the ways that we do; it draws no distinction between money spent on things that improve our well-being and those that diminish it. And, since the GDP measures only economic activity, where money changes hands, it leaves out everything to which no dollar value is attached.　6

The time you spend raising your family? Not measured. The contribution you make volunteering in your community? No value. If you spend $30 on a junk-food dinner in a fast-food restaurant, it's worth $10 more to the GDP than the $20 you might spend cooking a healthy meal at home.　7

And then there are all the detrimental things the GDP doesn't count at all. Damage to the environment? Not counted. Depletion of our natural resources? Not included. The GDP has no measure for strategies that might save the earth's ozone layer and protect us from damaging ultraviolet radiation. In fact, if suntan lotion and hat sales go up as a result, the economists are smiling. And if you walk to work instead of taking the car, that goes on the negative side, because you are not spending money on fuel, or on the wear and tear on your vehicle. Help Canada's economy — don't walk when you could drive!　8

Using the GDP as our economic measure gives us a completely false impression of the real costs and benefits of economic and social activity. It leads us to think that the economy is doing well, when what we're really doing is perpetuating costly mistakes. We need a different measure, one that acknowledges quadruple bottom line thinking and that measures our progress towards achieving the new prosperity.　9

One exciting idea being developed, largely in Canada, attempts to change these calculations so that they make more sense. Some economists are starting to use what they call the Genuine Progress Indicator (GPI). The GPI takes account of both plus and minus costs, and includes factors for which we've never assigned an economic value. In addition to personal consumption, it takes into account income distribution in a society, unemployment rates, and net capital investment. It factors in social costs, like family breakdown, and the contributions made by unpaid housework and child care. It takes away value for time spent commuting to work, for loss of farmland, wetlands, and forests, and for loss of leisure time.　10

Let's bring in new measurement techniques so we can honestly measure the new prosperity. The GPI adds value for additions to things we value, and subtracts value for the loss of things we value. If we used the　11

GPI instead of the GDP, we'd know better what was going on around us, and we could help shape our economy in ways that recognize the interconnections between the economy, the environment, and the people.

• •

Explorations:

Jack Layton,
>   *Speaking Out: Ideas That Work for Canadians*
>   *Homelessness: The Making and Unmaking of a Crisis*

http://ndp.ca/jack
http://politicswatch.com/layton-biography.htm
http://canadianeconomy.gc.ca/english/economy/gdp2.html
http://www.chebucto.ns.ca/CommunitySupport/NCC/GPI.html
http://www.gpiatlantic.org/

Structure:

1. Read paragraph 1 aloud in class. Does it make sense? What is a PARADOX? Analyze how Jack Layton uses this device to attract our attention and draw us into his topic.
2. Identify Layton's *thesis statement.*
3. Is Layton's essay a *comparison*, a *contrast*, or both?
4. Why do you think Layton has organized his argument by *halves* and not *point by point*? Where does the GDP section end and the GPI section begin?
5. What rhetorical strategy is Layton using when he ends his whole argument on the word "people"?

Style:

1. How INFORMAL or FORMAL is Layton's style? Who do you think is his intended AUDIENCE? Why?
2. Read paragraph 5 aloud in class. What phrase do you find repeated several times? Is this a weakness of style? Or a strength?

Ideas for Discussion and Writing:

1. When the logic of the gross domestic product (GDP) fails to include as benefits home child care, elder care, and volunteer work, and when it fails to include as losses resource depletion, pollution, crime, natural disasters and loss of leisure time, what sector of our society benefits? Labour? Families? Business?

2. The American nonprofit organization Redefining Progress (www.cyberus.ca/choose.sustain/Question/GPI.html) calculates that in the United States the Genuine Progress Indicator (GPI) has actually decreased about 45% since 1970, and that the annual rate of decline has increased from 1% in the 1970s to 2% in the 1980s and to 6% in the 1990s. What are your reactions to these figures?

3. About 6.5 million Canadians, 27% of the population, do volunteer work. At an average of 162 hours each per year, their efforts equal 549,000 full-time jobs, equivalent to the entire paid work force of Manitoba. Tell of the time you personally were helped by a volunteer. Tell of the time you, yourself, helped others. Tell what kind of volunteering you might like to do in the future.

4. Do you have more leisure time or less leisure time than your parents did at your age? Ask them whether they have more, or less, than their own parents did. And what are the reasons?

5. Jack Layton states humorously, "Help Canada's economy — don't walk when you could drive!" (par. 8). What is your own opinion? Can you see yourself, like Layton, riding a bicycle to work or walking instead of driving a car? Why or why not?

6. **PROCESS IN WRITING:** *Write a comparison and/or contrast of volunteer work and paid work. First draw a line down the centre of a page, then write "VOLUNTEER WORK" at the top left and "PAID WORK" at the top right. Now brainstorm, making notes. Next connect related items on both sides with lines, and from this make a brief outline. Create a* thesis statement *that establishes your overall main point. (Have clear in your mind whether the argument will be all contrast, all comparison, or some of each.) Write the first draft, and the next day look it over. Have you reached the recommended 50% level of* example *content? Have you used logic signals such as "by contrast," "on the other hand," "but" and "although"? Does everything support the thesis statement? Is the argument* concise, *like Layton's? Finally, check for grammar and punctuation, and print out your best version.*

NOTE: See also the Topics for Writing at the end of this chapter.

MARIA COFFEY

An Offering from the Dead*

Maria Coffey is an adventurer. As a child in England she devoured adventure books, then while a geography student at the University of Liverpool, devoted summers to her own adventures in Greece, Israel, Italy, Morocco and Russia. For a while she taught ESL, then was drawn to the hard-partying and risk-taking life of mountaineering. These exciting years ended when Coffey's partner Joe Tasker, world-famous mountaineer, died on the Northeast Ridge of the world's highest mountain. From this tragedy came Coffey's 1990 book Fragile Edge: A Portrait of Loss on Everest. *Looking for a change, she moved to British Columbia and met her future husband Dag. They built a house on an island, founded an adventure travel company, and have had many more adventures, recorded in both photography and writing. In 1995 appeared* A Boat in Our Baggage, *on kayaking around the world. And among their recent works has been* Visions of the Wild: A Voyage by Kayak Around Vancouver Island *(2001). So far Coffey has published ten books, as well as articles for* The Globe and Mail, *the* New York Times, Outdoors Illustrated, Sea Kayaker Magazine, *and* The Guardian. *Our own graphic and concise selection is from her 2003 book* Where the Mountain Casts Its Shadow: The Dark Side of Extreme Adventure. *It shook the world of mountaineering with its frank assessment of the risks, and the selfishness of adventurers who die and leave their families behind.*

1   Nanga Parbat.° Its summit guarded by the Rupal Face, the biggest mountain wall in the world. A murderous wall: sheer, beset by storms and avalanches. Four Japanese men are attempting it. They enter a steep chute called Merkl Gully. A storm breaks. The men do not return. At Base Camp the rest of their team wait . . . and wait. . . . Before abandoning the mountain, they climb the fixed ropes to 22,000 feet and leave a duffel bag filled with equipment, food, and shelter. A gesture beyond hope: an offering to the dead.

2   Some years later four North American men attempt the same mountain, by the same face. They are in Merkl Gully, 1,200 feet from the summit. One man is suffering from altitude sickness. A storm breaks. They retreat. Spindrift avalanches pour over them in waves. One, far bigger than the rest, sweeps them off the face. Their rope holds by a single ice

---

* Editor's title.

° Nanga Parbat: literally "Naked Mountain," at 8125 metres the world's ninth highest. Located in Pakistan. In 1953 Herman Buhl made the first ascent, losing 11 climbers and 15 porters.

screw. Dangling in panic from the mountain, choked by rushing snow, they expect the screw to fail at any moment, and death to follow. When the avalanche ceases, the sick man's face points upward, his eyelids frozen shut. "I was going to unclip," he tells his friends, "and get it over with."

Hour after hour they fight their way down. About ten at night, they emerge from Merkl Gully and reach a protective overhang. Two of the men remove the ropes from the final section of the gully. "I'm letting go of the ropes," shouts the man at the top. The wind blows away some of his words. His friend misunderstands. He hears a command. He obeys it. "Okay, I let go," he shouts back. Their ropes — their umbilical cords to the mountain, to life — sail away through space.

They have two choices. To stay where they are and freeze to death, or to attempt the impossible — descending the Rupal Face without ropes.

Morning. Four specks cling to a mountain by a few slivers of steel — crampons° and ice axes. No safety net. A single slip, and they fall 10,000 feet. Chances of survival: negligible. Then, they see it . . . . a duffel bag, clipped to the wall. Sun-bleached. Tattered. Emblazoned with Japanese writing. They cut it open. Sixty pitons° spill out. A dozen ice screws. Chocolate bars. A tent. A stove. Two new fifty-meter ropes. An offering from the dead.

● ●

Explorations:

Maria Coffey,
> *Where the Mountain Casts Its Shadow: The Dark Side of Extreme Adventure*
> *Fragile Edge: A Portrait of Loss on Everest*
> *Visions of the Wild: A Voyage by Kayak Around Vancouver Island*

Jon Krakauer, *Into Thin Air: A Personal Account of the Mt. Everest Disaster*
http://www.hiddenplaces.net
http://bcmc.ca/index.asp
http://www.annickpress.com/ai/coffey.html

Structure:

1. Is this selection mainly a *contrast*, a *comparison*, or *both* at once?
2. Clearly Maria Coffey organizes her comparison and contrast not *point by point*, but by what our introduction calls "*halves*." Where does the first part end and the second begin? Why is the one shorter and the other longer? Describe the effect when, despite the organization into "*halves*," these parts come together in the last five words of the piece.

° crampons: boot attachments with metal spikes, to give traction on ice.
° pitons: metal spikes, with an eye or ring at one end, to drive into cracks in ice or rock, as a support for ropes.

Style:

1. Hold this book at arm's length, and half close your eyes so you are not reading Coffey's words but just seeing them. How do they *look* together? And how does their visual appearance relate to Coffey's STYLE and to your own reading experience?
2. If these two expeditions occurred in the past, why does Coffey write about them in the present tense?
3. The opening paragraph has 4 partial sentences, and the closing paragraph has 13. Has Coffey forgot what she learned in Composition 101, or has she chosen to use these fragments? What effect do they have? And why are they placed in the opening and closing, with none between?
4. This passage, and especially the closing, are masterfully CONCISE. Read paragraph 5 aloud. Identify every factor you can think of that helps Coffey say more with less.
5. To what extent is the force of this selection powered by IRONY? Point out its major appearances here.

Ideas for Discussion and Writing:

1. Why do men and women climb mountains? What is the highest "mountain," actual or figurative, that you have climbed? Tell the story.
2. Are you a rock climber, backpacker, mountain biker, white water canoeist, kayaker or skier? Why or why not? *Contrast* your best experience and your worst experience of the sport.
3. Or do you have urban adventures? What are they? *Contrast* your best and your worst.
4. Coincidence in fiction is often criticized as unrealistic. Yet Coffey relates an actual occurrence as fateful as any in a novel. How big a role does coincidence really play in our lives? Give *examples* from your own experience, or that of family or friends.
5. In 1982 Coffey's partner, world famous mountaineer Joe Tasker, disappeared from the Northeast Ridge of Everest. Now Coffey has subtitled her book "The Dark Side of Extreme Adventure." Why do climbers and other extreme sport devotees risk all in pushing life to its limits? Why do so many narrowly escape death, only to return to the mountain? Are they heroic or are they selfish? Defend your view with reasons.
6. **PROCESS IN WRITING:** Contrast *the risks and the rewards of an outdoor sport you have tried. Draw a line down the centre of a page, writing "Risks" at the top left and "Rewards" at the top right. Make notes in each column, then draw lines to join related material. Put your overall point into a THESIS STATEMENT (such as "The exciting sport of rock climbing is less dangerous than it seems"). Now write a rapid first draft, organizing either by "halves" (as Coffey does) or point by point. Have you given enough examples?*

(Most student writers do not.) Are they linked by TRANSITIONS *to speed the argument? Later edit your writing: Is it* CONCISE *like Coffey's? Do you favour small and* CONCRETE *words, as she does? Also check sentence structure and punctuation before printing off your best version.*

Note: See also the Topics for Writing at the end of this chapter.

CATHERINE PIGOTT

Chicken-Hips[*]

How does a piece of writing begin? Here is an example. Seeing a documentary film about eating disorders, The Famine Within, *and interviewing its director Katherine Gilday for a magazine article, Catherine Pigott recalled her own time in Africa. It was several years earlier, while teaching English at a teachers' college, that she had shared the home and culture of a Gambian family. Then returning to Canada, she suffered culture shock: through African eyes she now saw North American ideas of eating and bodily appearance as cruel and misguided. In response to this mix of new experience and earlier memories, she wrote the essay that follows (*The Globe and Mail, *March 20, 1991), a celebration of the natural life she knew in Africa. Not only is its message cross-cultural but also its form: Pigott says "I was aware of speaking as I wrote," as in the oral tradition of African narrative. Now she applies this philosophy daily in her profession. After her return she worked for a time in print journalism, but then entered the world of radio: first the* CBC Radio News, *then the CBC's celebrated* Morningside, *where, as a producer, she found guests for host Peter Gzowski, and researched and developed a broadcast a day. From there she moved on to* Sunday Morning, *and to CBC Radio's national morning program,* This Morning. *Pigott thinks of her writing for radio as "not for the eye but the ear." It is direct, simple, natural. She offers similar advice to students writing essays: "Write for the ear as well as the eye."*

1   The women of the household clucked disapprovingly when they saw me. It was the first time I had worn African clothes since my arrival in tiny, dusty Gambia, and evidently they were not impressed. They adjusted my head-tie and pulled my *lappa*, the ankle-length fabric I had wrapped around myself, even tighter. "You're too thin," one of them pronounced. "It's no good." They nicknamed me "Chicken-hips."

2   I marvelled at this accolade, for I had never been called thin in my life. It was something I longed for. I would have been flattered if those ample-bosomed women hadn't looked so distressed. It was obvious I fell far short of their ideal of beauty.

3   I had dressed up for a very special occasion — the baptism of a son. The women heaped rice into tin basins the size of laundry tubs, shaping it into mounds with their hands. Five of us sat around one basin, thrusting our fingers into the scalding food. These women ate with such relish, such joy. They pressed the rice into balls in their fists, squeezing

---
[*] Editor's title.

172

until the bright-red palm oil ran down their forearms and dripped off their elbows.

I tried desperately, but I could not eat enough to please them. It was hard for me to explain that I come from a culture in which it is almost unseemly for a woman to eat too heartily. It's considered unattractive. It was even harder to explain that to me thin is beautiful, and in my country we deny ourselves food in our pursuit of perfect slenderness.

That night, everyone danced to welcome the baby. Women swivelled their broad hips and used their hands to emphasize the roundness of their bodies. One needed to be round and wide to make the dance beautiful. There was no place for thinness here. It made people sad. It reminded them of things they wanted to forget, such as poverty, drought and starvation. You never knew when the rice was going to run out.

I began to believe that Africa's image of the perfect female body was far more realistic than the long-legged leanness I had been conditioned to admire. There, it is beautiful — not shameful — to carry weight on the hips and thighs, to have a round stomach and heavy, swinging breasts. Women do not battle the bulge, they celebrate it. A body is not something to be tamed and moulded.

The friends who had christened me Chicken-hips made it their mission to fatten me up. It wasn't long before a diet of rice and rich, oily stew twice a day began to change me. Every month, the women would take a stick and measure my backside, noting with pleasure its gradual expansion. "Oh Catherine, your buttocks are getting nice now!" they would say.

What was extraordinary was that I, too, believed I was becoming more beautiful. There was no sense of panic, no shame, no guilt-ridden resolves to go on the miracle grape-and-water diet. One day, I tied my *lappa* tight across my hips and went to the market to buy beer for a wedding. I carried the crate of bottles home on my head, swinging my hips slowly as I walked. I felt transformed.

In Gambia, people don't use words such as "cheating," "naughty," or "guilty" when they talk about eating. The language of sin is not applied to food. Fat is desirable. It holds beneficial meanings of abundance, fertility and health.

My perception of beauty altered as my body did. The European tourists on the beach began to look strange and skeletal rather than "slim." They had no hips. They seemed devoid of shape and substance. Women I once would have envied appeared fragile and even ugly. The ideal they represented no longer made sense.

After a year, I came home. I preached my new way of seeing to anyone who would listen. I wanted to cling to the liberating belief that losing weight had nothing to do with self-love.

Family members kindly suggested that I might look and feel better if I slimmed down a little. They encouraged me to join an exercise club. I wandered around the malls in a dislocated daze. I felt uncomfortable trying on clothes that hung so elegantly on the mannequins. I began hearing old voices inside my head: "Plaid makes you look fat. . . . You're too short for that style. . . . Vertical stripes are more slimming. . . . Wear black."

13   I joined the club. Just a few weeks after I had worn a *lappa* and scooped up rice with my hands, I was climbing into pink leotards and aerobics shoes. The instructor told me that I had to set fitness goals and "weigh in" after my workouts. There were mirrors on the walls and I could see women watching themselves. I sensed that even the loveliest among them felt they were somehow flawed. As the aerobics instructor barked out commands for arm lifts and leg lifts, I pictured Gambian women pounding millet and dancing in a circle with their arms raised high. I do not mean to romanticize their rock-hard lives, but we were hardly to be envied as we ran like fools between two walls to the tiresome beat of synthesized music.

14   We were a roomful of women striving to reshape ourselves into some kind of pubertal ideal. I reverted to my natural state: one of yearning to be slimmer and more fit than I was. My freedom had been temporary. I was home, where fat is feared and despised. It was time to exert control over my body and my life. I dreaded the thought of people saying, "She's let herself go."

15   If I return to Africa, I am sure the women will shake their heads in bewildered dismay. Even now, I sometimes catch my reflection in a window and their voices come back to me. "Yo! Chicken-hips!"

● ●

Explorations:

Joan J. Brumberg, *Fasting Girls: The History of Anorexia Nervosa*
Richard Gordon, *Anorexia and Bulimia: Anatomy of a Social Epidemic*
Katherine Gilday, *The Famine Within* (video, 1990, 120 min.)
Jean Kilbourne, *Slim Hopes: Advertising and the Obsession with Thinness* (video, 1995, 30 min.)
Naomi Wolf, *The Beauty Myth: How Images of Beauty Are Used Against Women*
Joetta Schlabach, *Extending the Table: A World Community Cookbook*
http://www.mirror-mirror.org/eatdis.htm
http://home3.inet.tele.dk/mcamara/gam.html
http://ca.dir.yahoo.com/Health/Diseases_and_Conditions/Anorexia_ Nervosa

Structure:

1. "Chicken-Hips" is mainly a *contrast* of ideals of beauty in Gambia and Canada. Point out at least two other things that the essay *compares*.
2. Does Pigott organize her *contrast* mainly "point by point" or by "halves"?

3. How selectively does the author choose details from her year in Africa? In paragraph 1, for example, has she told anything at all that is not vital to her theme?

4. What classic techniques of organization does Pigott exploit in her opening and closing?

Style:

1. The Gambian women nicknamed our author "Chicken-hips" because of her relative thinness. Create five other METAPHORS they could have used to say the same thing.

2. Where do SENSE IMAGES most strongly help us "see" the author's point?

3. Judging by Pigott's vocabulary, what sort of *audience* is she aiming at in her essay?

Ideas for Discussion and Writing:

1. Review "My Body Is My Own Business" (p. 132), then *compare* and/or *contrast* the struggles of Naheed Mustafa and of Catherine Pigott with body image. Has either writer found a solution to the problem?

2. How important to you is the appearance of your body? Are you trying for an ideal size or shape? Describe it to the class. And what sources gave you this ideal?

3. Why, in Canada, is it mostly women who go on diets, and mostly women who suffer and die from anorexia nervosa?

4. In paragraph 5 thinness reminds Gambians of "things they wanted to forget, such as poverty, drought and starvation." On the other hand, the Duchess of Windsor once remarked, "Never too rich and never too thin." How do *you* see thinness? *Compare* or *contrast* your view to one of the above, and give reasons.

5. Have you, like Pigott, lived in another country? Tell the class one major thing the other culture taught you about life. Now that you are here, are you remembering or forgetting the lesson?

6. Many Canadians go abroad, as Pigott did, to teach in less developed countries. But imagine her Gambian friends coming to your school to teach you. What would some of their "lessons" be?

7. In paragraph 10, watching the "skeletal" Europeans at the beach, Pigott states "My perception of beauty altered. . . ." Examine the illustrations in a book of art history, taking notes on how our current view of human beauty differs from those of past periods. Report these differences to the class, showing illustrations as examples.

8. **PROCESS IN WRITING:** *Remember a time when you set out to change your body through a diet, athletics, aerobics, bodybuilding or other means. On a blank piece of paper draw a vertical line. Entitle the left column "BEFORE"*

and the right column "AFTER," then brainstorm to develop the contrast. *Now looking at these notes, decide your thesis: In which version of yourself did you actually feel happier, the before or after? Now write a rapid first draft, proceeding either by "halves" or "point by point." The next day look it over: Do images help your audience "see" you? If not, add. Is your draft at least 50% examples? If not, add. Are any words wasted? If so, cut. Finally, edit for things like grammar and spelling, then produce your good version.*

Note: See also the Topics for Writing at the end of this chapter.

RAFI MUSTAFA

The Bond of Nightmares

This essay was first published on the Internet. The week after thousands died in the 9/11 terrorist attack on New York City's World Trade Center, Rafi Mustafa expressed his anguish in "The Bond of Nightmares" and sent it to a Toronto newspaper. The letters editor was considering it, but several weeks went by. Really wanting his message to be heard, Mustafa then emailed it to friends. His daughter Naheed (see her own essay on page 132) also emailed it to her friends. They forwarded it to their own friends, till in a snowball effect thousands were reading it, and many were replying (see "Ideas for Discussion and Writing," no. 5, for one such message from an American Catholic to the Toronto Muslim author). Then the Network of Progressive Muslims *posted the essay, and so did several other Web sites such as* yespakistan.com. *Only after all this electronic publication did the* Toronto Star *also print it on October 28, 2001, and finally this book.*

Rafi Mustafa was born in India in 1943. After high school he became a private tutor, then in 1966 came to Canada as a student. Though at first he could not understand a word of his lectures, he did well, earning a Ph.D. in chemistry from the University of British Columbia. For the next decade he did research at the Universities of Toronto, Leicester and Windsor, and taught at Sind University and the University of Khartoum. Today Mustafa and his family live in the Toronto area, where he is active in charities and is president and CEO of a computer software company.

After all these years, the memory of my mother running for her life along a dirt road still haunts me in my nightmares. I was desperately running behind her but could not keep up. I was only six years old and could run only so fast. She had tied all our belongings in a bundle that she carried on her head. She stopped from time to time and looked back to see how far behind I was. "Hurry up, son!" she would scream, but I could not run any faster. My father was left behind somewhere and I kept looking back to see if he was anywhere in sight. I could see a long line of people — men, women and children running and walking with us. I knew that my father would eventually catch up.

We were running for our lives to cross the border from India into Pakistan.° I was told that Pakistan was our new country. We were Muslims, and for some reason did not belong to our homeland anymore.

° When the British left in 1947, India was divided into two countries: India for the Hindus and Pakistan for the Muslims. The resulting exodus in both directions led to social unrest and massacres, in which as many as a million people may have died.

We had spent terror-filled days and months, seeking refuge and spending sleepless nights. People stayed up all night guarding their homes and being on the lookout. We heard about trainloads of corpses entering Pakistan, stories of massacres of Muslim communities in neighbouring villages. We were always on edge.

3   As I am turning sixty, that dirt road is still a part of my life. I am still running desperately to get hold of my mother. In my nightmares I am always six years old.

4   I came to Canada as a student about 35 years ago. When I returned to Pakistan after my studies and joined my old teaching job at the university, I found that it was not the same country any more. I could not understand what had gone wrong in the four years I was away. The country was taken over by madness. People were killing people. They called it the language riots. The campus was taken over by rioters. They wanted to kick out every professor who didn't speak the right language. I was on the run again to save my family, but there was nowhere to go. Several days later I managed to visit the hospital in which many colleagues and their spouses lay with cracked skulls and broken limbs. My father told me I should go back to Canada.

5   Several months later, as we were going through the security check at Karachi airport, my son asked me why Grandma and Grandpa were not coming with us. I stopped for a moment and looked back at my parents. I could not leave them. They were old and needed my help. I wanted to turn back but then I saw my father waving goodbye. His long white beard was covered with tears. He could see my hesitation. He gestured with his hand asking me to go. I didn't know then that it was the last time I would see him.

6   That was the time when new nightmares were added to my stock. It is always pitch dark and I am running away from rioters. Sometimes I am on a runway, chasing a plane that is leaving us behind. My wife and children are following me. I turn back and ask them to hurry up, and then start running again. I am always missing flights, getting lost in a maze at an unknown airport or not having enough money to buy airline tickets for my family.

7   The other day my wife asked me if we might have to leave Canada one day. Hatred is in the air. I remembered a conversation in which someone said, "These Muslims are a cancer for humanity. They must be wiped out if humanity is to survive." I did not tell them I was a Muslim. The anger and frustration over the recent events is natural. But as a Muslim I refuse to accept any blame for it. I have accepted Canada as my country for only one reason. I am tired of being oppressed for who I am. I cherish my freedom and value it over everything else. This is where home is and will continue to be until I die. I am too old and too tired to start a new life one more time, and I don't need any new nightmares.

8   As I watched the World Trade Center come down, I was horrified to see the panic of those who were fleeing death. I know that they will relive this event again and again in their nightmares for the rest of their

lives. I also tried to visualize what was happening on the ground as we were watching the bombing of Baghdad ten years ago. At times I see an Israeli settler running for cover with his child under his arm. Are his nightmares any different from mine, or from those of a Palestinian mother carrying the lifeless body of her baby and crying with despair? I see images of a mother in strife-torn Africa carrying her child whose life is ending from starvation. I wish I could find out what kind of nightmares she has.

I once met a Holocaust survivor, the grandmother of someone I knew. I wanted to ask her about her nightmares. Then I remember the face of an Iraqi woman running on a deserted street in Baghdad during a bombing run. Her mouth is wide open and her eyes are bulging with terror. Does she have the same nightmares as that little Vietnamese girl with napalm burns, running naked on a street in Saigon, crying for help? 9

At times I feel that all these people are related to me. We share a common bond — the bond of nightmares. 10

• •

Explorations:

Denise Chong, *The Girl in the Picture: The Kim Phuc Story*
Salmon Rushdie, *Midnight's Children*
Rohinton Mistry, *A Fine Balance*
C. H. Philips and Mary D. Wainwright, *The Partition of India: Policies and Perspectives 1935–1947.*
http://en.wikipedia.org/wiki/Partition_of_India
http://www.terrorism.com/index.php
http://canada.gc.ca/SSC/SSC_e.html
http://www.meer.net/~johnl/e-zine-list/zines

Structure:

1. Point out Rafi Mustafa's THESIS STATEMENT.
2. The basic structure of this essay is a *comparison* of people around the world running from disaster. Point out every passage where this "nightmare" occurs to the author and to others. Does Mustafa succeed in showing these fleeing people of many nationalities, religions and locations as more *alike* than *different?* Do you see their mutual nightmare as a "bond"?
3. Though "The Bond of Nightmares" is mostly a *comparison*, Mustafa also uses every one of the following: *narration, example, description, cause and effect, analogy* and *persuasion.* Point out one example of each technique. Is his use of so many means of development a problem, or is it an advantage?

Style:

1. Mustafa's sentences are fairly short, averaging 13.4 words each. The words themselves are short, averaging 5 letters each. Give all the reasons you can think of why, for this topic, the author chose to go short.
2. How large a role do IMAGES play in the development of Mustafa's topic? Give examples.
3. What principle of style does the author exploit in placing the word "nightmares" at the very end?

Ideas for Discussion and Writing:

1. Perhaps the most famous news photo of all time shows the young Vietnamese girl of paragraph 9 running from a napalm attack, her clothes burned off. Kim Phuc later came to Canada as a refugee, and today lives in the Toronto area. Now tell the class a story of another refugee — if possible a family member, friend, or even yourself — who also came to Canada. *Compare* the similarities or *contrast* the differences between the two stories.
2. The author shows people around the world running from disaster. Many have "run" to Canada for safety as refugees. Has Canada's traditional welcome remained? Tell why or why not.
3. North America has long been considered safe, compared to places where wars and terrorism occur. To what extent has that belief changed since September 11, 2001? *Contrast* your own attitude before and after. Do you do anything differently now? Give an *example.*
4. On a certain street of the city where Mustafa lives, there are a synagogue, a mosque and a Buddhist temple all in a row, and down the street a Catholic church. Is this an image of the Canada you know? Tell why or why not.
5. One person who received Mustafa's essay by email, soon after the World Trade Center disaster, sent this message in return: "I read your letter that was forwarded to me and cried for your nightmares and the real nightmares of everyone you mentioned. I just wanted you to know the majority are with you in your sorrow during this time of tragedy. I do not know the full extent of what we are in for but I do know that hate and despair are the ultimate evil and I will pray that you and yours will find peace and that this very complicated world can come to deeper understanding. I am an American Catholic but recognize the faith of Islam is great and holy. I don't think this is a religious war and decry people who try to make it one. It's desperation and a power struggle. We can make a difference, and maybe in our own small ways it will help eventually. Take care. My prayers are with us all."

   Imagine that you, yourself, had received Mustafa's message. Write him your own reply. Then read it to the class.

6. **PROCESS IN WRITING:** *Our introduction tells how Rafi Mustafa sent this piece by email to people he knew, and they sent it to more people, till in a snowball effect thousands were reading it. Next it was published on several websites, including* yespakistan.com. *Only after all this did the* Toronto Star, *and finally this book, publish it on paper. Have you ever thought of writing for the Web? Try the following:*

Draw a line down the middle of a piece of paper. At the top of the left half write "terrorists" and at the top of the right half write "criminals." Now brainstorm to fill both columns with thoughts, examples, anything at all that might develop the key words. When you're finished, look over what you have produced. Have you compared *or* contrasted? *That is, do you believe terrorists are criminals, or are they something else, such as freedom fighters? You choose. Now put your main idea in a* THESIS STATEMENT, *do a rapid discovery draft using the best of your ideas, then the next day look it over. Does every point further your overall idea? If not, revise. Do you have enough* examples? *If not, add. Do* TRANSITIONS *speed your reader on? If not, add.*

After your final editing, go online and visit www.meer.net/~johnl/e-zine-list/zines, *which lists hundreds of "zines" and tells how to send them your writing. (Or, if the Web site has disappeared since this book was printed, there are several more like it. Do a search.) Now choose an appropriate zine, and send the essay in. Keep checking, and report any reactions, and especially publication, to your teacher and class.*

Note: See also the Topics for Writing at the end of this chapter.

DREW HAYDEN TAYLOR

This Boat Is My Boat

An Ojibway from the Curve Lake Reserve in Ontario, Drew Hayden Taylor has become one of Canada's most prolific Native writers. Whether in his short stories, his newspaper columns or his many stage plays, Taylor's trademark is a zany, satirical wit that leaves his audience both laughing and thinking. A time as Playwright-in-Residence, then Artistic Director for Native Earth Performing Arts confirmed Taylor's love of theatre. Since then there have been over 60 professional productions of his plays, such as Bootlegger Blues *(1991),* Someday *(1993),* AlterNatives *(2000),* The Boy in the Treehouse *(2001),* Girl Who Loved Her Horses *(2001), and* The Buz'Gem Blues *(2002). Taylor has also been a satirical columnist for the* Peterborough Examiner, *with his best pieces collected in a book,* Funny, You Don't Look Like One: Observations of a Blue-Eyed Ojibway *(1998). He has also written for* Maclean's, The Globe and Mail, Now *magazine and other periodicals; has written scripts for television series such as* The Beachcombers, Street Legal *and* North of Sixty; *and has directed documentaries on Native themes. In 1992 his anthology* Voices: Being Native in Canada *was published (with Linda Jaine), and in 1998* Fearless Warriors, *a collection of short stories. Our own essay selection, comic in tone but serious in theme, first appeared in the July/August 2004 issue of* This Magazine.

1   F Scott Fitzgerald once wrote "The rich are different from you and I,"° to which everybody usually responds, "Yeah, they've got more money." On a similar theme, it's been my Ojibway-tainted observation over the years that "middle-class white people are different from you and I." Yeah. They're insane.

2   Much has been written over the years about the differences between native people and non-native people, and the way they view life. I think there's no better example of this admittedly broad opinion than in the peculiar world of outdoor recreational water sports and the death wish that inspires them.

3   As a member of Canada's indigenous population, I've cast a suspicious glance at all these waterlogged enthusiasts for several reasons. The principal one is the now familiar concept of cultural appropriation — this

---

° "The rich are different from you and I": This best-known of all lines from the American novelist F. Scott Fitzgerald has been quoted in many slightly different forms. Probably the most accurate is "The rich are different from you and me," to which his friend Ernest Hemingway replied, in a memorable putdown, "Yes, they have more money."

time of our methods of water transportation. On any given weekend, Canadian rivers are jam-packed with plastic and fibreglass kayaks and canoes, hardly any of them filled with authentic Inuit or First Nations people, all looking to taunt death using an aboriginal calling card.

Historically, kayaks and canoes were the lifeblood of Inuit and native communities. They were vital means of transportation and survival, not toys to amuse bored weekend warriors. To add insult to injury and further illustrate my point, there is a brand of gloves used by kayakers to protect their hands from developing calluses. They are called Nootkas. To the best of my knowledge, the real Nootka, a West Coast First Nation, neither kayaked nor wore gloves.

Perhaps my argument can best be articulated with an example of the different ways these two cultural groups react to a single visual stimulus. A group of native people and white people sit in two separate canoes before a long stretch of roaring rapids — with large pointy rocks and lots and lots of turbulent white water. Watch the different reactions.

Granted, I'm generalizing, but I think I can safely say the vast majority of native people, based on thousands of years of travelling the rivers of this great country of ours, would probably go home and order a pizza. Or possibly put the canoe in their Ford pickup and drive downstream to a more suitable and safe location. And pick up pizza on the way. Usually, the only white water native people enjoy is in their showers. Hurtling toward potential death and certain injury tends to go against many traditional native beliefs. Contrary to popular assumption, "portage" is not a French word — it is Ojibway for "Are you crazy? I'm not going through that! Do you know how much I paid for this canoe?"

Now put some sunburned Caucasian canoeists in the same position, and their natural inclination is to aim directly for the rapids, paddling as fast as they can toward the white water. I heard a rumour once that Columbus was aiming his three ships directly at a raging hurricane when he discovered the Bahamas. I believe I have made my point.

I make these observations based on personal experience. Recently, for purely anthropological reasons, I risked my life to explore the unique subcultures of white water canoeing and sea kayaking. There is also a sport known as white water kayaking, but I have yet to put that particular bullet in my gun. So for three days, I found myself in the middle of Georgian Bay, during a storm, testing my abilities at sea kayaking. I, along with a former Olympic rower, a Quebecois lawyer who consulted on the Russian constitution, one of Canada's leading diabetes specialists, and a six-foot-seven ex-Mormon who could perform exorcisms, bonded over four-foot swells and lightning. All in all, I think a pretty normal crosscut of average Canadians. The higher the waves, the more exciting they found the experience.

Still, I often find these outings to be oddly patriotic in their own way. I cannot tell you the number of times I've seen people wringing out their drenched shirts, showing an array of tan lines, usually a combination of sunburned red skin and fishbelly-white stomachs. It reminds me of the red-and-white motif on the Canadian flag. Maybe that's where the federal government got its inspiration, back in the 1960s, for our national emblem.

10 But this is only one of several sports originated by various indigenous populations that has been corrupted and marketed as something fun to do when not sitting behind a desk in a highrise office building. The Scandinavian Sami, otherwise known as Laplanders, were instrumental in the development of skiing. Though I doubt climbing to the top of a mountain and hurling themselves down as fast as gravity and snow would allow was a culturally ingrained activity. The same could be said of bungee jumping. Originally a coming-of-age ritual in the South Pacific, young boys would build platforms, tie vines to their legs and leap off to show their bravery and passage into adulthood. I doubt the same motivation still pervades the sport, if it can be called a sport.

11 I have brought up the issue of recreational cultural appropriation many times with a friend who organizes these outdoor adventures. The irony is she works at a hospital. And she chews me out for not wearing a helmet while biking. She says there is no appropriation. If anything, her enthusiasm for the sports is a sign of respect and gratefulness.

12 That is why I think people should pay a royalty of sorts every time they try to kill themselves using one of our cultural legacies. I'm not sure if any aboriginal group has ever sought a patent or copyright protection for kayaks or canoes — that probably was not part of the treaty negotiations. But somebody should definitely investigate the possibility. Or better yet, every time a non-native person white water canoes down the Madawaska River, or goes kayaking off Tobermory, they should first take an aboriginal person to lunch. That is a better way of showing respect and gratefulness. And it involves much less paperwork.

● ●

Explorations:

Drew Hayden Taylor,
  The Buz'Gem Blues
  Funny, You Don't Look Like One: Observations of a Blue-Eyed Ojibway
  Voices: Being Native in Canada (co-edited with Linda Jaine)
Ronald Wright, *Stolen Continents: Conquest and Resistance in the Americas*
http://www.ammsa.com/classroom/CLASS3appropriation.html
http://www.ipl.org/div/natam/bin/browse.pl/A185
http://www.talonbooks.com/authors/Taylor.html
http://www.athabascau.ca/writers/dhtaylor.html
http://www.doollee.com/PlaywrightsT/TaylorDrewHayden.htm
http://wildernesscanoe.ca/index.htm

Structure:

1. Taylor's essay title is an ALLUSION to Woody Guthrie's well-known 1956 song "This Land Is My Land." Do you know the lyrics? (If not, find them at *www.arlo.net/lyrics/this-land.shtml.*) How does the meaning of Guthrie's song lead into Taylor's topic of cultural appropriation (par. 3)?
2. In paragraph 1 the common device of a quotation opens the essay. Where do you find good quotations for your own essays? How does the Fitzgerald quotation lead into Taylor's topic?
3. Identify Taylor's *thesis statement.*
4. Is Taylor's argument a *contrast* only, or does it also have elements of *comparison?* And is it done *point by point,* or by *halves?* Identify each main contrast that supports his overall argument.

Style:

1. In this essay Taylor is his usual zany and satirical self — as in paragraph 6 where the natives go for pizza while the Caucasians hurtle "toward potential death and certain injury," or where the word "portage" is said to be Ojibway for "Are you crazy? I'm not going through that! Do you know how much I paid for this canoe?" Does all his humour prevent Taylor from mounting a real argument against cultural appropriation? Or does it just make that argument more appealing?
2. Here and there Taylor uses conversational language, for example "Yeah. They're insane" (par. 1), or "chews me out" (11). Is this informal TONE appropriate to his essay? Why or why not?
3. How ABSTRACT or CONCRETE is Taylor's STYLE? Give examples. Has he attained the recommended 50% or more of *example* content?

Ideas for Discussion and Writing:

1. Do you admire thrill-seekers who sky dive, who scramble mountain peaks, do acrobatics on snowboards, run class five rapids in canoes and kayaks, or ski two months over ice to the North Pole? Why or why not? Why do people perform acts such as these? Have you attempted an extreme sport? Tell the class about it.
2. As an Ojibway, Taylor argues against "cultural appropriation." Do you agree with this view of many Native people that outsiders are not qualified to write about them and their lives? To make films about them? Even to attempt their sports? Or is making this subject matter off limits to others an attack on their personal liberties?
3. According to Ronald Wright in his book *Stolen Continents,* an estimated 100 million people, a fifth of the human race, were already living in the Americas when Columbus "discovered" the New World.

Within decades military conquest and epidemics of new diseases had killed most of them. The European invaders sacked cities, destroyed great works of art, shipped huge amounts of gold to Europe, and took the land. Was any of this "appropriation" justified? In our time what are the implications for land claim settlements with Native groups in Canada? To what extent can we and should we as a society make up for past wrongs?

4. **PROCESS IN WRITING:** *Think of any two sports that you play. First draw a line down the middle of a blank page, then make notes on sport A on the left and sport B on the right. Do you see mostly similarities or differences, or both? Let this help you decide whether to write a* comparison, *a* contrast, *or both. And does one sport emerge as better, more difficult, more dangerous, or what? Devise a THESIS STATEMENT that expresses this overall main idea. Now draw lines from left to right connecting related items, and when you are ready, organize these notes* point by point *into an argument. Write the first draft, and the next day look it over. Does every part develop the overall main idea in the* thesis statement? *Are there* plentiful *examples, as in Drew Hayden Taylor's essay? Do* transitional expressions *such as "on the other hand," "by contrast," "however" and "but" highlight the logic? Is there flabby language to trim? Finally, check the punctuation and print your best version.*

Note: See also the Topics for Writing at the end of this chapter.

CATHARINE PARR TRAILL

Remarks of Security of Person and Property in Canada

Catharine Parr ("Kate") Traill (1802–1899) exemplifies the best of Canadian pioneering life. She spent her early years in England, where she enjoyed the refinements of her father's estate near Southwold and published several books for children. But a reversal of family fortunes and her marriage to a retired half-pay officer meant immigration. In 1832 the Traills joined Catharine's brother Samuel Strickland (who would later write Twenty-Seven Years in Canada West*) near present-day Lakefield, Ontario, and soon they were joined by their sister Susanna Moodie and her husband (Moodie would go on to write a classic of pioneer life,* Roughing It in the Bush*). Catharine also wrote about Upper Canada. A collection of letters to her mother was published in 1836 as* The Backwoods of Canada, *and in 1854 appeared* The Female Emigrant's Guide, *her handbook of advice and techniques. Traill also wrote more books for children, and her professionalism as a botanist was widely recognized when in 1868 she published* Canadian Wild Flowers, *and in 1885* Studies of Plant Life in Canada. *Kate Traill's writing reflects her sunny personality: she was curious, observant, self-reliant — and above all optimistic about life in the New World. These qualities shine through our selection, from* The Female Emigrant's Guide.*

There is one thing which can hardly fail to strike an emigrant from the Old Country, on his arrival in Canada. It is this, — The feeling of complete security which he enjoys, whether in his own dwelling or in his journeys abroad through the land. He sees no fear — he need see none. He is not in a land spoiled and robbed, where every man's hand is against his fellow — where envy and distrust beset him on every side. At first indeed he is surprised at the apparently stupid neglect of the proper means of security that he notices in the dwellings of all classes of people, especially in the lonely country places, where the want of security would really invite rapine and murder. "How is this," he says, "you use neither bolt, nor lock, nor bar. I see no shutter to your windows; nay, you sleep often with your doors open upon the latch, and in summer with open doors and windows. Surely this is fool-hardy and imprudent." "We need no such precautions," will his friend reply smiling; "here they are uncalled for. Our safety lies neither in bars nor bolts, but in our consciousness that we are among people whose necessities are not such as to urge them to violate the laws; neither are our riches such as to tempt the poor man to rob us, for they consist not in glittering jewels, nor silver, nor gold."

2   "But even food and clothes thus carelessly guarded are temptations."

3   "But where others possess these requisites as well as ourselves, they are not likely to steal them from us."

4   And what is the inference that the new comer draws from this statement?

5   That he is in a country where the inhabitants are essentially honest, because they are enabled, by the exertion of their own hands, to obtain in abundance the necessaries of life. Does it not also prove to him that it is the miseries arising from poverty that induce crime. — Men do not often violate the law of honesty, unless driven to do so by necessity. Place the poor Irish peasant in the way of earning his bread in Canada, where he sees his reward before him, in broad lands that he can win by honest toil, and where he can hold up his head and look beyond that grave of a poor man's hope — the parish work house — and see in the far-off vista a home of comfort which his own hands have reared, and can go down to his grave with the thought, that he has left a name and a blessing for his children after him: — men like this do not steal.

6   Robbery is not a crime of common occurrence in Canada. In large towns such acts will occasionally be committed, for it is there that poverty is to be found, but it is not common in country places. There you may sleep with your door unbarred for years. Your confidence is rarely, if ever, abused; your hospitality never violated.

7   When I lived in the backwoods, out of sight of any other habitation, the door has often been opened at midnight, a stranger has entered and lain down before the kitchen fire, and departed in the morning unquestioned. In the early state of the settlement in Douro, now twenty years ago, it was no uncommon occurrence for a party of Indians to enter the house, (they never knock at any man's door,) leave their hunting weapons outside, spread their blankets on the floor, and pass the night with or without leave, arise by the first dawn of day, gather their garments about them, resume their weapons, and silently and noiselessly depart. Sometimes a leash of wild ducks hung to the door-latch, or a haunch of venison left in the kitchen, would be found as a token of gratitude for the warmth and shelter afforded them.

8   Many strangers, both male and female, have found shelter under our roof, and never were we led to regret that we had not turned the houseless wanderer from our door.

9   It is delightful this consciousness of perfect security: your hand is against no man, and no man's hand is against you. We dwell in peace among our own people. What a contrast to my home, in England, where by sunset every door was secured with locks and heavy bars and bolts; every window carefully barricaded, and every room and corner in and around the dwelling duly searched, before we ventured to lie down to rest, lest our sleep should be broken in upon by the midnight thief. As night drew on, an atmosphere of doubt and dread seemed to encompass

one. The approach of a stranger we beheld with suspicion; and however great his need, we dared not afford him the shelter of our roof, lest our so doing should open the door to robber or murderer. At first I could hardly understand why it happened that I never felt the same sensation of fear in Canada as I had done in England. My mind seemed lightened of a heavy burden; and I, who had been so timid, grew brave and fearless amid the gloomy forests of Canada. Now, I know how to value this great blessing. Let the traveller seek shelter in the poorest shanty, among the lowest Irish settlers, and he need fear no evil, for never have I heard of the rites of hospitality being violated, or the country disgraced by such acts of cold-blooded atrocity as are recorded by the public papers in the Old Country.

Here we have no bush-rangers, no convicts to disturb the peace of the 10 inhabitants of the land, as in Australia. No savage hordes of Caffres to invade and carry off our cattle and stores of grain as at the Cape; but peace and industry are on every side. "The land is at rest and breaks forth into singing." Surely we ought to be a happy and a contented people, full of gratitude to that Almighty God who has given us this fair and fruitful land to dwell in.

• •

Explorations:

Catharine Parr Traill,
> *The Female Emigrant's Guide*
> *The Backwoods of Canada*

Susanna Moodie, *Roughing It in the Bush*
Margaret Atwood, *The Journals of Susanna Moodie* (poems)
Marian Fowler, *The Embroidered Tent: Five Gentlewomen in Early Canada*
http://www.utpjournals.com/product/utq/671/catharine86.html
http://www.uwo.ca/english/canadianpoetry/eng%20274e/pdf/traill.pdf
http://www.collectionscanada.ca/moodie-traill/index-e.html

Structure:

1. The long first paragraph states all the main ideas of this essay. What, then, does the rest of the essay do?
2. In this *contrast* between the dangers of life in England and the security of life in Canada, why is so much more of the argument devoted to Canada than to England?
3. The main contrast, between Canada and England, occurs in paragraphs 7–9. Why is this detailed contrast followed, in the last paragraph, by very brief contrasts to Australia and the Cape?

Style:

1. Catharine Parr Traill published *The Female Emigrant's Guide* in 1854. Does her STYLE in this selection seem much different from the style of today's writers? Discuss the following:

    A. Word choice
    B. Sentences
    C. Paragraphs
    D. TONE

2. Discuss the meaning of "want" in the phrase "want of security" (middle of par. 1). Do you see other words in this essay that have changed meaning since 1854?

3. In paragraph 7, Traill writes that the Native people "never knock at any man's door." In paragraph 9 she states that "your hand is against no man, and no man's hand is against you." In fact, she mentions men so often that only once does she specifically refer to women — yet she entitled her book *The Female Emigrant's Guide*. Why in the past could "man" represent everyone? And why today have we rejected this usage?

4. In exactness, in vividness, and in poetic power, has our language improved or deteriorated since the time of Catharine Parr Traill?

Ideas for Discussion and Writing:

1. Does the Canada of today more closely resemble the new land that Traill describes in this essay, or the old land she left behind?

2. If you have moved to Canada from another country, as Traill did, have you experienced any of the benefits she describes?

3. Traill states that "it is the miseries arising from poverty that induce crime" (par. 5). Do you agree? Or does crime have other causes as well?

4. Traill states, "I, who had been so timid, grew brave and fearless amid the gloomy forests of Canada" (par. 9). The frontier has always been seen as a place to make a new start, leaving old problems in the past. In our increasingly crowded and industrialized world, do frontiers remain?

5. Can a "frontier" exist in the city? Are there new ways of living in old places, by which people can free themselves from problems of the past?

6. **PROCESS IN WRITING:** *Write an essay that compares and/or contrasts life in two countries, provinces, cities, towns or neighbourhoods. First divide a page in half with a vertical line; jot down facts about item A on the left and item B on the right. Looking over these notes, decide now on your THESIS STATEMENT and choose either the "halves" or the "point by point" method of organizing. After a rapid first draft, fine-tune your organization and add more concrete detail. Now read your paper aloud, to detect repetition and any other flaws of style, before doing the final version.*

Note: See also the Topics for Writing at the end of this chapter.

LAWRENCE HILL

Black + White = Black

In 2001 Maclean's *published an excerpt from Lawrence Hill's book of the same year,* Black Berry, Sweet Juice: On Being Black and White in Canada. *In the* Maclean's *version reprinted here, Hill tells much of his life story. There is more, though. Not only did his African-American father become Director of the Ontario Human Rights Commission, and later the province's ombudsman, but his brother Dan Hill became a celebrated singer/songwriter of the 70s and 80s. Lawrence himself moved from his upper-middle-class white suburb of Toronto to Quebec City, where in 1980 in French he completed a B.A. in economics from Université Laval. In 1992 he went on to an M.A. in writing from Johns Hopkins University in Baltimore. Having lived and worked abroad, Hill is fluent in both French and Spanish. In 1982 he began reporting for* The Globe and Mail, *then moved to the* Winnipeg Free Press. *Eventually he went on to write for ministries of the Ontario government. Meanwhile his own writing career took shape: in 1992 appeared Hill's first novel,* Some Great Thing, *then two nonfiction books about being black in Canada. His second novel,* Any Known Blood, *was published in 1997, and he is now at work on a third, to be entitled* Migration. *To learn more, read* Black Berry, Sweet Juice, *and see Hill's excellent Web site:* www.lawrencehill.com.

My childhood was punctuated with sayings about black people. My father's relatives sometimes said, "The blacker the berry, the sweeter the juice." On one level, the meaning is obvious: a raspberry or strawberry that is full and dark and pregnant with its own ripeness is sweeter than its pink, prematurely plucked counterpart. But there is also a sexual undertone to the saying, a suggestion of the myth of the overcharged, overheated, high-performing black body. Presumably, the blacker berry tastes richer, more full and is juicier. The trouble with this expression is that it has always struck me as a limp-wristed effort to help black people believe that it was OK to be black. It seemed to me sad and pathetic that we even felt a need to pass around a saying like that.

But I wasn't the only one who found that the words itched more than they tickled. My father bombed the pious saying to smithereens with his own sarcastic version: "The blacker the berry/The sweeter the juice/But if you get too black/It ain't no use." I absolutely loved that variation. Why? Because it turned self-affirmation on its head with a mere 10 additional words, offering a bittersweet reminder of the hopelessness of being black in a society that doesn't love — or even like — black people. There were many other sayings, such as "If you're white/You're all right/If you're brown/Stick around/If you're black/Stay back." Black people said these words and laughed. All the sayings underscored the utter futility of being black.

3   I discovered, very early, that some people had strange ideas about the children of interracial unions, and seemed inclined to believe that life for us would be miserable. When I was 12, my best friend was a white girl, Marilyn (as I shall name her), whose mother would embarrass the dickens out of me by singing my praises to her own children. "Look how well Larry does in school. Why can't you be like that, Marilyn?" Astoundingly, this same mother who thought I was doing so well once took me aside and said, "Frankly, Larry, don't you think it is terrible, mixing races like that? It ruins the children! How are they to make their way in life?"

4   As a child, my own experience of race, including my concept of my own racial identity, was shaded quite differently from that of my parents. They were both born and raised in the United States, and their racial identities were clearly delineated all their lives. The America of their youth and early adulthood was replete with laws that banned interracial marriages and upheld segregation in every domain of public life. One of the most telling details came to me from my mother, who was working as a secretary for a Democratic senator when she met my father in Washington in 1953: "When I started dating your father, even the federal government cafeterias were segregated." In the United States, there was never any doubt that my father was first and foremost a black man. Or that my mother was a white woman. And there is no question that, had my siblings and I been raised in the United States, we would have been identified — in school, on the street, in community centres, among friends — as black.

5   But my parents threw their unborn children a curveball. They came to Toronto right after they married, had us and we all stayed here. They had had enough of racial divisions in their country of birth. And although they spent their lives at the forefront of the Canadian human-rights movement, they were also happy and relieved to set up in suburban, white, middle-class Toronto, where race faded (most of the time) into the background.

6   When I was growing up, I didn't spend much time thinking about who I was or where I fit in. I was too busy tying my shoelaces, brushing my teeth, learning to spell, swinging baseball bats and shooting hockey pucks. But once in a while, just as my guard was down, questions of my own identity would leap like a cougar from the woods and take a bite out of my backside.

7   I found that race became an issue as a result of environmental factors. The average white kid growing up in a white suburb didn't have to think of himself as white. Gradually, my environment started talking to me and making me aware that I could never truly be white. There's nothing like being called "nigger" to let you know that you're not white.

8   Learning that I wasn't white, however, wasn't the same as learning that I was black. Indeed, for the longest time I didn't learn what I was — only what I wasn't. In the strange and unique society that was Canada, I was allowed to grow up in a sort of racial limbo. People knew what I wasn't — white or black — but they sure couldn't say what I was. I have black American cousins, of both lighter and darker complexions, who attended

segregated schools and grew up in entirely black communities. They had no reason to doubt their racial identity. That identity was wrapped around them, like a snug towel, at the moment of birth.

In 1977, when I decided to take a year off university, I went to visit my cousins in Brooklyn before flying to Europe, which must have appeared to them a quintessentially white thing to do. My cousin Richard Flateau took me under his wing, and was patient until I asked if he liked to play squash. An indignant retort exploded from his lips: "Larry! That's a white folks' game!" Today, looking back, I find irony in that memory. There I was, son of a black American Second World War veteran and a white American civil-rights activist, playing squash, a sport virtually unknown to inner-city blacks in the United States.

These days, I think of the factors that contributed to my sense of identity, and of how malleable that sense of identity was and still is. There were days when I went straight from my exclusive, private boys' high school to family events populated by black relatives or friends who idolized the icons and heroes of my childhood — Angela Davis, with her intelligence and her kick-ass Afro; sprinters Tommie Smith and John Carlos, with their black-gloved fists raised on the Olympic podium in Mexico City; Muhammad Ali, who stood up to the white man and spoke the words that moved the world: "I ain't got no quarrel with the Viet Cong." I bounced back and forth between studying Latin, playing squash and revering black American cultural icons, but who exactly was I?

Lately, I have been looking at some family photos and mulling over what they mean to me. In my home office, I have some 30 framed shots of relatives. There are my three children, running, cavorting, picking apples. The eldest, Geneviève, is 11, and I wonder how she will come to see herself, racially, as she moves into adolescence. She has been a ballerina for six years, and you don't find a world much whiter than that, not even in Oakville, where we live. She knows who she is, and has had much contact with the black side of her family — but the girl has blue eyes and skin even lighter than mine, and I can see that if she is going to assert her own blackness one day, she may have to work hard at it. Nine-year-old Caroline, the middle child, is the darkest of my three, and has that uncanny middle-child ability to relate to anybody of any age. I have noticed that she already bonds vigorously with black women. Andrew, who is 7, is about as interested in race as he would be in nuclear physics. Interestingly, though, he has already called out a few times, "I'm not black, I'm white," and shot a look my way to test for a reaction. He looks white, too.

Would you like to know how my children would once have been categorized, racially? Quadroons. They have a father who is supposedly half-black and a mother who is white, and that parentage, according to the traditional racial definition blender, would have made them quadroons. Quadroons, of course, were most definitely black, and enslaved like the rest of us in Canada and the United States. Quadroon women were favoured by slave owners for features deemed exotic and sexy but not too black, thank you very much. I shudder to imagine children who

9

10

11

12

looked just like mine dancing in the infamous Quadroon Balls in New Orleans, where hot-looking young women were bought and consumed until they were no longer young or beautiful.

13   Today in Canada, black people still contend with racism at every level of society. And yet, the way my children will define themselves, and be defined by others, remains up for grabs. Racial identity is about how you see yourself, about how you construct a sense of belonging, community, awareness and allegiance.

14   To this date, I have mostly seen myself as black. My black American relatives, who lived in Brooklyn, Washington, Baltimore and North Carolina, were much closer to us and much easier to visit than my mother's family. Apart from her twin, Dottie, whom we all adore, we never really got to know my mother's relatives. My mother spoke negatively of her brothers when we were young, describing how they gave her a hard time — one even questioned her sanity — when she announced that she would be marrying a black man. As a result, as a child I came to nourish a minor grudge against some of these relatives. On my father's side, however, family was like an extension of my own body and psyche.

15   My first sense of blackness, sprang from warm places. Our house boomed with jazz and blues on weekends. Dan, Karen and I watched — entranced, intrigued — as our parents danced in the living room to Ella Fitzgerald, Billie Holiday and Duke Ellington. Dad has an amazing voice. When he sang, he waltzed up and down the tunes with a playfulness and irreverence that we found absolutely infectious.

16   I remember being laid up with the flu when I was 5. My father asked: "Any musical requests, sir?" And I said, "Put on Joe Williams." *Every Day I Have the Blues* began to jump off the record player. I listened to my dad and Williams nailing the notes as Basie hammered the piano, and trumpets, trombones and saxophones erupted with glee. It's one of the happiest songs I've heard — even if it is about the blues. *Nobody loves me/nobody seems to care/between bad luck and trouble/well you know I've had my share.* Just about any words could have flown from Joe Williams's lips and soared, ecstatically, as if to prove that nothing could keep this man from living and loving. Jazz and blues were already showing me the sweet alchemy of trouble and joy that defined black musical expression, and black people themselves.

17   I don't recall early moments with family members that gave me a negative sense of race, but my siblings do. Perhaps because he was the firstborn, Dan had a rockier time with our father. Dan has no doubt that our father gave us mixed racial messages. When my brother was 11 or so, Dad gave him a stocking to wear on his head at night. The idea was to straighten out Dan's hair while he slept, or at the very least to keep it from getting too curly on the pillow. I asked Dan if Dad had told him why he had to wear it.

18   "It wasn't good to have curly hair. He'd pull a hair out of my head and put it on the table and say, 'See? This is curly. It's not good to have curly hair.' And I remember feeling extremely hurt and ashamed, and I started wearing the stocking cap. I remember feeling very concerned that my hair was curly, and I remember being frantic about straightening it."

Dan now attributes the incident to the strange paradoxes of human   19
nature. "I think that kind of behaviour is common among people like
our father, who have worked in the field of human rights. Very often,
people go into these fields as compensation for their own feelings of
inadequacy. That way, they can still bring those feelings of inadequacy
and self-hatred — self-racial-hatred — into the house."

Dan, Karen and I learned early that you can have a white parent and   20
still be considered black, but you can never have a black parent and be
considered white. It ain't allowed. You'll be reminded of your "otherness"
more times than you can shake a stick at it. This is one of the reasons why
I self-identify as black. Attempts at pleasant symmetry, as in "half-white,
half-black," trivialize to my eye the meaning of being black. This doesn't
mean I don't love my mother. I love her as profoundly as I love any person on earth. But I just don't see myself as being the same race as she is.
I raised this issue with my mother recently. "Listen," she told me, "when
I married your father, I knew that our children would be black. I would
have been an idiot to fail to see that. Look where we came from."

However, the suburb of Don Mills in which they eventually settled   21
became as suffocating for their children as D.C. had been for them. There
were no blacks in my school, on my street. Because I looked so different
from everyone else, I feared that I was ugly. I worried about having frizzy
hair, big ears, a big nose and plump lips. When I looked in the mirror, I felt
disgust. None of the people I admired looked the least bit like me.
Listening to stories of my father's working world instilled in us a measure
of black pride. We also derived a sense of connection from family moments
around the television, which is odd because we weren't that interested in
TV. But the late 1960s and the early 1970s featured big stand-up comedy
numbers by Bill Cosby and Flip Wilson. When I watched these shows, I felt
alive. I felt that there were people in the world who were speaking to me.

I had to find other ways to connect with them. So I ate up every bit of   22
black writing that I could find. Langston Hughes, Ralph Ellison, Richard
Wright — whom I approached gingerly because my mother confessed
that *Native Son* had upset her so much, it had made her vomit. James
Baldwin. Eldridge Cleaver — now that cat fascinated me, especially
when, in *Soul on Ice*, he speculated as to why black men and white women
end up together. I read Alex Haley's *Autobiography of Malcolm X*, and had
to struggle through the section of Malcolm X's life when he ardently
believed that white people were the devil incarnate. I knew this to be
false. My mother was white, and she was no devil.

Without knowing exactly what I was doing, I was forming my own   23
sense of blackness and my own connection to the black diaspora. Soon,
this exploration blossomed into creative writing. Every time I wrote, my
mind wandered into the lives of black characters. Slowly, I was developing
a sense of myself. These days, when I'm invited into schools with black
students, I feel a tinge of nostalgia for a past not lived. I can't help wondering what it would have been like to have black people around me
when I was young. I can't help wondering what it would have been like

to go out with black girls, or to drift into a friend's home and find myself surrounded by black people. What a different life that would have been.

• •

Explorations:

Lawrence Hill,
>   *Black Berry, Sweet Juice: On Being Black and White in Canada*
>   *Any Known Blood* (novel)

George Elliott Clarke, ed., *Eyeing the North Star: Directions in African-Canadian Literature* (anthology)

Frances Henry, *The Caribbean Diaspora in Toronto: Learning to Live with Racism*

Henry Gates and Nellie McKay, eds., *The Norton Anthology of African American Literature*

Richard Wright, *Native Son* (novel)

Toni Morrison, *Beloved* (novel)

Arnold Rampersad, ed., *The Collected Poems of Langston Hughes*

http://www.lawrencehill.com

http://www.blackvoice.com/high/default.asp?aID=893

http://www.wier.ca/lhill.html

http://www.thebukowskiagency.com/BookOfNegroes.htm

http://www.magenta.nl/crosspoint/cnd.html

Structure:

1. How do you interpret the equation in Hill's title, "Black + White = Black"? Is it a good start to the essay? What does it do? Compare another mathematical title in this book, Doris Anderson's "The 51-Per-Cent Minority."

2. Like many essayists, Hill opens with a quotation. Point out all the ways it moves us into his topic. Do you ever use this technique? If you don't have the right quotation to start your essay, where do you look for it?

3. Is Hill's argument all *contrast* between his black roots and white roots, or is there also *comparison*? If so, where?

4. In this argument of *contrast*, Hill organizes not by "halves" but "point by point." As a class, divide into 10 groups, each choosing a passage listed below. Examine your section in your small group, then report to the class what aspect of the total subject it analyzes through *contrast*: Paragraphs **1–2, 3, 4–8, 9, 10, 11–12, 14–19, 20, 21–22,** and **23.**

Style:

1. Why do you think Hill's paragraphs are longer than those of many other writers in this book? Are they too long? Are your own ever too short? What is a good typical length, and why?

2. In paragraph 8 Hill describes his American cousins growing up in black communities where "that identity was wrapped around them, like a snug towel, at the moment of birth." Where else does Hill use strong METAPHORS?

Ideas for Discussion and Writing:

1. Do you, yourself, have roots in two or more races or cultures? Do you, like Hill, identify more with one than with the others(s)? Try to explain why, giving examples.
2. With a father who was Director of the Ontario Human Rights Commission and later the province's ombudsman, Lawrence Hill had a privileged upper-middle-class childhood. Do working-class people have a different experience of racial issues? Give examples.
3. Canada — especially in its big cities — is said to be the most cosmopolitan, multicultural country in the world. Do you agree? Is your own neighbourhood multicultural? If so, name all the places where its different population groups have their roots.
4. *Contrast* the American and Canadian examples of racism that Hill gives. Was Canada the more open society when Hill's parents were young? Is it now? Give examples.
5. Do interracial couples, like Hill's parents, still face extra challenges in society, or by now has fairness been achieved?
6. *Compare* or *contrast* Lawrence Hill's portrayal of racism in society with those of George Gabori (p. 25), Carol Geddes (p. 34), Naheed Mustafa (p. 132), Mordecai Richler (p. 146), Rafi Mustafa (p. 177), Joy Kogawa (p. 292) or Dionne Brand (p. 312).
7. **PROCESS IN WRITING:** *If, like most Canadians, you have roots in more than one geographical area, language, culture or race, draw a line down the middle of a page. At the top left and right, name the two most important components of your own roots (such as "Iran" and "Germany," or "Mandarin" and "English"). Make sure that both items, as in these pairs, are from the same category: two countries, two languages, etc. Below them, on each side, make many notes on their characteristics. Now look over what you have produced: what* contrasts *do you see? Draw lines across the page to link the contrasting items. Next put your overall point in a THESIS STATEMENT, then write a discovery draft using your examples. (Choose to organize your contrast either by "halves" or "point by point.") When this draft has cooled off, look it over. Is it filled with examples, like Hill's essay? If not, add. Does it use transition signals like "but," "on the other hand," "however" and "by contrast" to heighten your contrast? If not, add. Finally, edit for correctness and conciseness before printing off your best version. Share it with the class.*

Note: See also the Topics for Writing at the end of this chapter.

Topics for Writing

CHAPTER 5: COMPARISON AND CONTRAST

Compare and/or contrast one of the following pairs. (See also the guidelines that follow.)

1. Living in a Hot Climate and Living in a Cold Climate
2. SUVs and Cars
3. Travel by Airplane and by Train
4. Small Families and Large Families
5. Roller Blading and Ice Skating
6. The Introvert and the Extrovert
7. Any Two Martial Arts
8. The Classical Music Fan and the Rock Music Fan
9. Commuting by Public Transit and by Car
10. Conventional Cars and Hybrid Gasoline/Electric Cars
11. A Desk Computer and a Notebook Computer
12. The Saver and the Spender
13. Living at Home and Living in Residence
14. Public School and Private School
15. Any Two Languages That You Speak
16. A Wedding and a Divorce
17. City People and Country People
18. The Morning Person and the Night Person
19. The Cuisine of Your First Country and of Your Second Country
20. Letters and Email Messages
21. Marriage and Living Common Law
22. The Novel and the Short Story
23. Acting Assertively and Acting Aggressively
24. Skiing and Snowboarding
25. TV News and the Newspaper
26. Eating at Home and Eating Out
27. Canoeing and Kayaking
28. Living in the Suburb and Living in the City
29. The Idealist and the Realist
30. The Stock Market and the Casino

Note also the Process in Writing topic after each selection in this chapter.

Process in Writing: Guidelines

Follow at least some of these steps in writing your essay of comparison and contrast (your teacher may suggest which ones).

1. *Spend enough time with the topic list to choose the item that best fits your interest and experience.*

2. *Draw a line down the middle of a blank page. Brainstorm: jot down notes for subject "A" on the left and for subject "B" on the right. Now join related items with lines, then take stock of what you have: Is A better than B? Is it worse? Similar? Opposite? Or what? Express their relationship to each other in a THESIS STATEMENT.*

3. *Now choose either "halves" or "point by point" to organize your argument, depending on the nature and size of your subject, then work your notes into a brief outline.*

4. *Write a rapid first draft, not stopping now to revise or edit.*

5. *Later analyze what you have produced: Does it follow your outline? If not, is the new material off-topic, or is it a worthwhile addition, an example of "thinking in writing"? Revise accordingly.*

6. *Try your prose aloud, to test the style. Cut all deadwood. Sharpen word choice. Add any missing examples. Strengthen TRANSITIONS.*

7. *Now edit for spelling and punctuation before printing off your good copy.*

CP/Chuck Stoody

"Yet as fast as the woodsmen cut, as much as they cut, it was never fast enough. The quantity always fell short of the expectations of the weendigoes, their masters."

— *Basil Johnston, "Modern Cannibals of the Wilds"*

Analogy and Related Devices

IN A WAY, IT'S LIKE . . .

One student wrote this childhood memory:

> **I heard and felt a rumbling from the ground, looked up and saw a huge red metallic monster with a tail on the end approach us. "Run, run," I said, "before it eats us." My mother reassured me that no fear was necessary. The monster slowly rolled up beside us, opened its mouth, and we went in.**

As adults, we know monsters have not roamed Canada for millions of years, and we know they were not red but probably green! We also know that monsters and streetcars have little in common. Yet who would say this *analogy* does not clearly express the child's first encounter with a streetcar? It may even help us, as adults, to view with new eyes something we had taken for granted. *(A warning, though: as explained below, what an analogy will **not** do for us is prove anything at all logically. An essay based on this device is more in the realm of creative writing than of factual argumentation.)*

In this chapter Basil Johnston describes another monster — the weendigo of Native American legend that eats humans who wander outside at night. In its new version the weendigo consumes not humans but pine, spruce, cedar and the wildlife that lives there. Though we know the forest industry is not staffed by monsters but by decent men and women trying to make a living, we cannot help but see, through Johnston's eyes, the "monstrous" destruction of clearcutting.

In the last chapter we discussed how two items from the same category — say, two cities — can be explained logically through comparison and contrast. By seeing how Vancouver and Montreal are alike or unlike, we gain a clearer understanding of both. An *analogy*, though, brings together two apparently *unlike* items from *different* categories (such as a monster and a modern industry). Instead of using the two to explain each other, it more often uses one as a device to explain the other. It is not the monsters we investigate but the monstrous aspects of the streetcar or the forest industry.

In the last chapter we speculated whether, instead of comparing two cities, we could compare a city and an anthill. To those of us who live in chambers along the corridors of apartment buildings or who each day crowd into holes in the ground to take the subway, the similarities may be all too clear. We do see right away that such an argument is hardly logical, for the very good reason that people are not insects. And we would certainly not want to base a factual paper, such as a research essay, on this device. Yet in a very informal or humorous paper, the analogy may be a fresh, thought-provoking way to express aspects of city life.

Topics that are unfamiliar or abstract almost cry out for analogies to explain them. Thus, a generation ago the term "computer virus" swept the world. These electronic "diseases" "infect" computer programs, "spreading" an "epidemic" of "contagion." The "outbreaks" of various "strains" feature names such as AIDS.II, Amoeba A, Anthrax, BW.Hepatitis, Cancer.2528, Cholera.A, Ebola 3000, Encephalitis, Leprosy, Measles.212, and Plague.2647.

These electronic diseases "contaminate" programs, erase memory and even attack hardware. Of course "antiviral" software to "vaccinate" the patient has been developed, with brand names like "Flu Shot +," "Data Physician," "Antidote," "AntiVirus," "Virus RX," "ViruSafe" and "Vaccine 1.0." In addition, "safe computing practices" have been recommended to avoid infection by viruses such as AIDS.II.

Have we already seen the first big analogy of the new millennium? In a 2005 *Globe and Mail* article, business reporter Andrew Willis wrote, "Spurned suitors, Unrequited passion. A final, joyful union. The latest round of takeovers is the stuff of romance novels.

"Just look at the flirting going on before Gillette finally fell into Procter & Gamble's waiting arms, and before SBC Communications got a ring on the finger of AT&T. . . . for years, chief executives at these companies met in secret spots or whispered into their phones late into the night. We've also learned they contemplated walking down the aisle with any number of other partners."

Apparently an optimist, Willis says nothing of divorce. But he has already exploited the power of the analogy. It comes not so much from its originality as its breadth, especially the heavy borrowing of vocabulary from the one item (romance) to the other (corporations). The further you develop such links between your two items, the stronger the analogy.

Yet even a brief statement, such as "A corporate merger is like a wedding," can have value. As a *simile* it is not much of an argument in itself, but is a concrete statement that can be used in support of another argument. While a *simile* states that one thing is *like* another, a *metaphor* states that one thing *is* another ("A corporate merger is a wedding"). Both devices occur often in poetry and fiction, and also occur in essays. This chapter's last selection, Félix Leclerc's description of his boyhood home, contains a steady stream of similes and metaphors that convey a vividly poetic sense not only of the place but also of the author's feelings about it. Though nothing objective has been proven, a message has certainly been given.

In closing, again a **WARNING:** *Do not confuse the pleasures of the analogy with the logic of argumentative devices such as comparison and contrast, or cause and effect. Save the analogy for personal essays, humorous pieces, and satires, where its free-wheeling poetic nature is appropriate.*

Note: For more examples of analogy and related devices, see these essays in other chapters:

Analogy:

Simile, metaphor and other figures of speech:

WENDY MAGAHAY

The Trail-Hiker's Guide to the Workplace

As you might guess from reading her essay, Wendy Magahay is a hiker as well as a manager. When in 1997 she moved to Victoria, B.C., one of the first things she did was to backpack the rugged West Coast Trail, along 75 km of the Pacific Ocean. Magahay has also lived and hiked in Toronto, Halifax, Montreal and Ottawa. She holds a B.A. in theatre and a Dip Ed in ESL, both from McGill, and an M.Ed in curriculum from the University of Ottawa. For 20 years Magahay has developed programs and resource materials for learners of all ages and their teachers. Before moving to B.C. this included 10 years with Carleton University, as well as projects with the University of Ottawa, Language Training Canada, and Citizenship and Immigration Canada. She has written numerous textbooks for young ESL students, and has published a great many articles in her field. "The Trail-Hiker's Guide to the Workplace" combines both her professional and leisure interests. It appeared first in the Careers *Section of the April 1, 2005* Globe and Mail, *then soon after was posted on* Workopolis.com. *"The most interesting thing to me," says Magahay, "is that I wasn't trying to write it. I was struggling with a piece on leadership for another audience when parts of this text just presented themselves." She then easily developed her hiking analogy, and the other essay too, because, as she puts it, she tries to stay "open and ready to write."*

1   While weekend and vacation hikes are meant to provide a break from the world of work, a number of rules to keep in mind on the trail have equally valuable application in the workplace.

2   So here's a trail-hiker's guide to the career world:

3   • **Hike with a buddy.** Whenever possible, you should travel with a companion; it can enhance the journey and, if something goes wrong, it just might save your life.

4   The same holds true at work, where some of our most important assets are our colleagues and the alliances and networks we build. Work teams, quality circles and formal and informal mentoring programs are all examples of powerful buddy systems at work.

5   • **Stay connected.** Sometimes a hiker prefers to commune with nature alone, but it's imperative that someone always knows where you are and your plans.

6   There are also times at work when the creative among us need to be alone to run with an idea. But if you don't want to end up isolating yourself or creating ill feelings, it's imperative to let your colleagues, bosses and support staff also know what you're up to — and keep

them in the loop. Don't shut out the rest of your team. That way, nobody gets left behind.

- **Have a map.** You might never take it out of your pocket, but you need   7
to know your starting point and where you want to go. You also need to have a career map for your own professional development and use it to track your progress.

    At the same time, whether on the trail or in the office, there are lots   8
    of different routes to choose from. It's all right to change plans as you go along, as long as you stay focused on your final destination.

    But don't be so fixed on staying the course that you forget to lift   9
    your head every so often and look around. Conditions both outdoors and indoors change, creating new opportunities or signalling a need to reassess where you're heading.

- **Break a long hike into manageable chunks.** If you don't want to get   10
overwhelmed, it's easier to reach for shorter-term goals and clearly measurable results to keep your enthusiasm from waning.

    The same goes for your job. Set work goals and benchmarks for   11
    yourself and your team that are realistic and can be easily achieved — and be certain to celebrate every success. Setting benchmarks will also let you know when things aren't working out as you projected and help you change course before it's too late.

- **It doesn't matter who made the mess — clean it up.** As you're walking   12
along a trail, you may come across droppings left by an irresponsible dog owner who failed to clean up after the pet. That leaves you with two choices: pick them up or leave them for someone else to step in.

    Similarly, in the office, you may also be faced with the "droppings"   13
    of someone else's mistakes, laziness or ineptitude. It doesn't matter the reason or whose fault it is. If you can clean up the mess, do it. Not only will you exemplify positive leadership to those around you, you'll also make your own life easier.

- **Share the load.** When hiking with a group, it's important to plan the   14
trip ahead of time, split up the work to be done and assign tasks that people enjoy. After all, the goal is for everyone to have a good time.

    Same goes at work. Advance planning, effective communication   15
    around roles and responsibilities, and recognition of everyone's strengths help to ensure that tasks get done, and done well — and, just as importantly, that people have fun and feel good about the work they're doing.

- **Practise etiquette.** On the trail, it's important to leave nothing but your   16
footprints behind. To keep your voice down. To use your cellphone only in an emergency because nobody wants to hear you talking to your broker while they're trying to commune with nature.

    That's the etiquette of hiking — and off the trail, all organizations   17
    have their own rules that reflect, govern and reinforce their culture and acceptable behaviour.

    Sometimes workplace etiquette is explicit — you can find it in mission   18
    and values statements or an employee manual. Other times, it is implicit

and learned through experience, observation and asking questions. Learn the rules of the organization where you work and apply them. Practising etiquette makes you a valued part of the workplace community.

19 • **Take care of your feet.** They support you and can easily suffer when you're hiking. Painful blisters and injuries can keep you off the trail so you need to keep yourself in shape for the trail.

20 It's the same at work, where your ability to do your best depends on taking care of yourself. Keep your life and work in balance. Job-sharing, flexible hours, health breaks, and participating in health and wellness programs inside and outside of work all help to keep the stress down and the morale up.

21 • **The person expending the most energy has priority.** When a hiker going uphill meets one heading down, it's usually the one going down who yields the right of way so the uphill climber can keep momentum and maintain aerobic level.

22 One of the best things you can do as a team leader and member is to recognize the hardest workers in your group and support them, sometimes by getting out of their way. Clear obstacles in their paths. Offer encouragement. Reward them and keep their momentum going, too.

23 • **Sometimes basic is beautiful.** Your battered, brown hiking boots might be the only footwear in your closet without wing tips or a three-inch heel. But there are times when absolutely nothing else will do.

24 In the workplace, solutions don't have to be complicated or experimental to be effective. Real innovation respects and builds on the things that are already working. What's most important is to gather the right people and the right tools for the job.

25 • **Exercise leadership.** Just as your leg muscles will be stronger if you make a point of exercising them year-round, your teamwork and leadership skills will also become stronger and work more effectively with regular use.

• •

Explorations:

http://www.nald.ca/wwestnet/PDFs/Btmline15.pdf
http://www.eastcoasttrail.com
http://www.torontobrucetrailclub.org//hikes-conrad-killarney/
    journal.htm
http://www.vancouverislandoutdoors.com/westcoasttrail

Structure:

1. Identify Wendy Magahay's THESIS STATEMENT.
2. How does Magahay's argument resemble a *comparison and contrast?* (If necessary, review the introduction to Chapter 5.) Yet why is her argument really an *analogy* instead?

3. What is Magahay's real subject: does the hiking explain the office work or does the office work explain the hiking?

4. The introduction to this chapter suggests a major way to build power in analogies: borrow vocabulary from the one item and use it to explain the other. To what extent has Magahay done this? Point out ten hiking terms that she applies to office work.

Style:

1. How FORMAL or INFORMAL is Magahay's STYLE (in areas such as vocabulary and sentence structure)?

2. The topic sentences that open each subpoint — telling the point of the section to come — are boldfaced. Is this visual feature useful to you the reader? Would you use it? Explain.

Ideas for Discussion and Writing:

1. As her biographical introduction states, the author knows both the hiking trail and the office. Do you too? If so, reverse her argument: describe an analogy you might construct using examples and vocabulary of the office to explain hiking.

2. The "Prewriting" section of this book's overall introduction (p. 6) quotes the philosopher Lao-Tze as saying "A journey of a thousand miles begins with the first step." Turn this idea into an *analogy* for something else, such as a career, a relationship, a search for ethics or spirituality, mastery of a sport or of an area of academic studies.

3. These days large numbers of hikers flood the West Coast Trail (Vancouver Island), the Bruce Trail (Ontario), the East Coast Trail (Newfoundland) and many others. Why have so many hiking and backpacking trails been developed, and why are they so popular?

4. "Take care of your feet," advises Magahay in paragraph 19, meaning stay fit for your office job. Describe at least five things an urban sedentary worker can do to stay in shape for work and life.

5. **PROCESS IN WRITING:** *"Have a map," advises Magahay in paragraph 7. As a student, have you made a "map" of your own academic journey? Close your eyes and think about this image, then write a page or two of brainstorming. From it choose the best* examples *and write your own* analogy, *making extensive parallels between following a map and progressing toward your educational destination. Later look it over. Have you applied the vocabulary of the one activity to the other? If not, add many more appropriate terms. Have you organized clearly, probably point by point? If not, revise. Does your quest rise in significance to your most important point last? If not, move the points around. Finally, edit for punctuation and sentence structure before printing off your best version.*

Note: See also the Topics for Writing at the end of this chapter.

SAMANTHA BENNETT

It's Not Just the Weather That's Cooler in Canada

When Samantha Bennett chose to write about Canada in her Pittsburgh Post-Gazette *column of July 30, 2003, she had no idea what was about to happen. Once her essay somehow got to Canada, and Canadians started emailing it across the country, she experienced what she calls "one of the more surreal and wonderful experiences I have ever had in my life. I got a marriage proposal. I made friends in Kingston, Ontario who put me up. . . . I have been offered more free beer, dinners, hotel rooms, city tours and guest beds than I could ever use. I feel like an unofficial national heroine." By the time the piece came out in the* Toronto Star, *the* Montreal Gazette *and the* Vancouver Sun, *Bennett was receiving "several e-mails an hour from places as distant as Newfoundland, Yellowknife, Northern Quebec and Vancouver Island." She says, "People would actually call me up from Toronto or even Vancouver just to ask if I was a real American journalist who really wrote that column. And to thank me."*

Not all the attention was positive. Some of the 1200 who replied were "furious Canadian patriots who didn't realize it was satire and thought I was bashing them." Quebeckers were miffed at a poor translation, and a few Westerners said their country was "going to hell in a handbasket. . . ." But the American lifestyle columnist — with a B.A. in English from Yale and an M.A. in professional writing from Carnegie Mellon University — is still wondering how she so totally "struck a chord."

1   You live next door to a clean-cut, quiet guy. He never plays loud music or throws raucous parties. He doesn't gossip over the fence, just smiles politely and offers you some tomatoes. His lawn is cared-for, his house is neat as a pin and you get the feeling he doesn't always lock his front door. He wears Dockers. You hardly know he's there.

2   And then one day you discover that he has pot in his basement, spends his weekends at peace marches and that guy you've seen mowing the yard is his spouse.

3   Allow me to introduce Canada.

4   The Canadians are so quiet that you may have forgotten they're up there, but they've been busy doing some surprising things. It's like discovering that the mice you are dimly aware of in your attic have been building an espresso machine.

5   Did you realize, for example, that our reliable little tag-along brother never joined the Coalition of the Willing? Canada wasn't willing, as it turns out, to join the fun in Iraq. I can only assume American diner

208

menus weren't angrily changed to include "freedom bacon,"° because nobody here eats the stuff anyway.

And then there's the wild drug situation: Canadian doctors are authorized to dispense medical marijuana. Parliament is considering legislation that would not exactly legalize marijuana possession, as you may have heard, but would reduce the penalty for possession of under 15 grams to a fine, like a speeding ticket. This is to allow law enforcement to concentrate resources on traffickers; if your garden is full of wasps, it's smarter to go for the nest rather than trying to swat every individual bug. Or, in the United States, bong.

Now, here's the part that I, as an American, can't understand. These poor benighted pinkos are doing everything wrong. They have a drug problem: Marijuana offenses have doubled since 1991. And Canada has strict gun control laws, which means that the criminals must all be heavily armed, the law-abiding civilians helpless and the government on the verge of a massive confiscation campaign. (The laws have been in place since the '70s, but I'm sure the government will get around to the confiscation eventually.) They don't even have a death penalty!

And yet . . . nationally, overall crime in Canada has been *declining* since 1991. Violent crimes *fell* 13 percent in 2002. Of course, there are still crimes committed with guns — brought in from the United States, which has become the major illegal weapons supplier for all of North America — but my theory is that the surge in pot-smoking has rendered most criminals too relaxed to commit violent crimes. They're probably more focused on shoplifting boxes of Ho-Hos from convenience stores.

And then there's the most reckless move of all: Just last month, Canada decided to allow and recognize same-sex marriages. Merciful moose, what can they be thinking? Will there be married Mounties (they always get their man!)? Dudley Do-Right° was sweet on Nell, not Mel! We must be the only ones who really care about families. Not enough to make sure they all have health insurance, of course, but more than those libertines up north.

This sort of behavior is a clear and present danger to all our stereotypes about Canada. It's supposed to be a cold, wholesome country of polite, beer-drinking hockey players, not founded by freedom-fighters in a bloody revolution but quietly assembled by loyalists and royalists more interested in order and good government than liberty and independence.

But if we are the rugged individualists, why do we spend so much of our time trying to get everyone to march in lockstep? And if Canadians are so reserved and moderate, why are they so progressive about letting people do what they want to?

Canadians are, as a nation, less religious than we are, according to polls. As a result, Canada's government isn't influenced by large, well-organized

---

° Freedom bacon: When France refused to join the U.S. invasion of Iraq, American fast-food restaurants changed the term "French fries" to "freedom fries." "Freedom bacon" is Bennett's humorous play on "Canadian bacon."

° Dudley Do-Right: From a 1961 television animation that spoofed early melodramatic portrayals of the RCMP. In 1969–70 it was lead feature of ABC's *The Dudley Do-Right Show.*

religious groups and thus has more in common with those of Scandinavia than those of the United States, or, say, Iran.

13   Canada signed the Kyoto global warming treaty, lets 19-year-olds drink, has more of its population living in urban areas and accepts more immigrants per capita than the United States.

14   These are all things we've been told will wreck our society. But I guess Canadians are different, because theirs seems oddly sound.

15   Like teenagers, we fiercely idolize individual freedom but really demand that everyone be the same. But the Canadians seem more adult — more secure. They aren't afraid of foreigners. They aren't afraid of homosexuality. Most of all, they're not afraid of each other.

16   I wonder if America will ever be that cool.

• •

Explorations:

Michael Adams, *Fire and Ice: The United States, Canada and the Myth of Converging Values*
Margaret Atwood, *The Handmaid's Tale* (novel)
Ian and Will Ferguson, *How to Be a Canadian, Even If You Already Are One*
Douglas Coupland, *Souvenir of Canada*
http://www.post-gazette.com/columnists/bio_bennett.asp
http://www.post-gazette.com/columnists/bennett.asp
http://www.parl.gc.ca/information/library/idb/forsey/can_am_gov_0
   1-e.asp
http://www.icomm.ca/emily

Structure:

1. Who was Bennett's original AUDIENCE? Why did it need such a dramatic introduction (paragraphs 1–3) to the subject of Canada?
2. Point out all the ways in which paragraphs 1–3 work as an ANALOGY. How strong an introduction does the analogy make to the essay? Point out at least five places later in the argument where Bennett's points develop the generalizations that the analogy first makes.
3. In paragraph 5 Canada is "our reliable little tag-along brother." Where else does Bennett use METAPHORS? Where do you see SIMILES? And how do all these FIGURES OF SPEECH contribute to the argument?
4. To what extent is Bennett's argument a *comparison and contrast*? Cite examples. Is it organized *by halves* or *point by point*?

Style:

1. Zany humour fills this essay and most of Samantha Bennett's other columns for the *Post-Gazette*. Yet this essay, like most of hers, examines

serious issues and comes to significant conclusions. Does her mix of light and serious work? Would it be acceptable in classroom essays? Why or why not?

2. Samantha Bennett received emails from "dozens of furious Canadian patriots who didn't realize it was satire and thought I was bashing them." When she makes observations such as "These poor benighted pinkos are doing everything wrong" (par. 7), did you at first mistake her meaning? Why is it sometimes hard to recognize IRONY?

Ideas for Discussion and Writing:

1. To what extent is Bennett's essay about Canada also about the United States? What messages does it have for its American readers?

2. Paragraph 5 looks at the "reliable little tag-along brother" who was however not willing to join "the fun in Iraq." Whether you were for or against that decision, how important do you feel it was in our history as a nation? Give reasons.

3. "It's supposed to be a cold, wholesome country of polite, beer-drinking hockey players," Bennett writes in paragraph 10. What other common STEREOTYPES of Canadians come to mind? Of Americans? Is there any truth here, or is it all image?

4. In paragraph 11 Bennett calls Americans "rugged individualists" and Canadians "reserved and moderate" — yet the former try to have everyone "march in lockstep" while the latter are "progressive about letting people do what they want to." How would you explain this PARADOX? Do you agree or disagree with her verdict? Give *examples.*

5. Samantha Bennett's essay is not the only one to be massively circulated by email. Review the introduction to Rafi Mustafa's selection on page 177, which snowballed across North America electronically. How has digital technology changed the whole idea of "publication"? How would you, yourself, go about publishing an essay this way?

6. **PROCESS IN WRITING:** *Samantha Bennett has discussed many things that Canada could teach her own country. Now do the reverse: brainstorm to think of things the United States could teach Canada. Begin as she does, with an* analogy *portraying the next-door neighbour as a person — then lead from this introduction to your points. Once you know those points, arrange them in increasing order of importance, with the strongest at the very end. The next day look over your draft. Does it have at least 50% example* content, *as hers does? Does it sparkle with* SIMILES *and* METAPHORS, *those little cousins of the* analogy? *Whether humorous or serious, is the* TONE *consistent? Do* TRANSITIONS *link the parts? Finally, check sentence structure and punctuation, before printing off your best version.*

Note: See also the Topics for Writing at the end of this chapter.

BASIL JOHNSTON

Modern Cannibals of the Wilds

Basil Johnston is well known as a writer, story teller and teacher of Ojibway (Anishinabe) language, mythology and history for 25 years in the Department of Ethnology of Toronto's Royal Ontario Museum. Born in 1929 on the Parry Island Reserve in Ontario, he went to Cape Croker public school, then at the Spanish Residential School lived the cultural dislocations of the residential school system which he later described in his book Indian School Days *(1988). He completed his education at Loyola College in Montreal and the Ontario College of Education. Johnston has long been a strong voice of First Nations People in Canada. Though he lectures widely on Ojibwa history, culture and language, it is his books that reach the largest audience:* Ojibway Heritage *(1976),* How the Birds Got Their Colours *(1978),* Moose Meat and Wild Rice *(1978),* Tales the Elders Told *(1981),* Ojibway Ceremonies *(1982),* By Canoe and Moccasin *(1986),* Tales of the Anishinaubaek *(1993),* The Manitous: The Spiritual World of the Ojibway *(1995),* The Bear-Walker and Other Stories *(1995),* The Star Man and Other Tales *(1997),* Mermaids and Medicine Women *(1998),* Crazy Dave *(1999) and* Honour Mother Earth *(2004). Our selection is from the August 1, 1991* The Globe and Mail. *In it Johnston goes beyond his usual role of imparting Ojibway culture; his portrait of the new "weendigo" cuts right to the heart of modern Canadian values.*

1   Woods and forest once mantled most of this land, this continent. It was the home of the Anishinabek (Ojibway, Ottawa, Potowatomi, Algonquin), their kin and their neighbours. It was also the home of the moose, the deer, the caribou, the bear, their kindred and their neighbours. It was as well the home of the thrushes, the sparrows, the hawks, the tanagers, the ravens, the owls, their cousins and their neighbours. Mosquitoes, butterflies, caterpillars, ants, moths, their kind and their neighbours had a place therein.

2   Not only was it home, but a wellspring from which all drew their sustenance, medicine and knowledge.

3   Also dwelling in the woods and forests were weendigoes, giant cannibals who fed upon human flesh to allay their perpetual hunger. They stalked villages and camps, waiting for, and only for, the improvident, the slothful, the gluttonous, the promiscuous, the injudicious, the insatiable, the selfish, the avaricious and the wasteful, to be foolish enough to venture alone beyond the environs of their homes in winter.

4   But no matter how many victims a single weendigo devoured raw, he could never satisfy his hunger. The more he ate, the larger he grew,

and the larger he grew, the greater his hunger. The weendigo's hunger always remained in proportion to his size.

Even though a weendigo is a mythical figure, he represents real human cupidity. What the old-time storyteller meant to project in the image of the weendigo was a universal and unchanging human disposition. But more learned people declared that no such monster ever existed, that he was a product of superstitious minds and imaginations.

As a result, the weendigo was driven from his place in Anishinabe traditions and culture, ostracized through disbelief and skepticism. It was assumed, and indeed it appeared as if, the weendigo and his brothers and sisters had passed into the Great Beyond, like many North American Indian beliefs and practices and traditions.

Actually, the weendigoes did not die out; they have only been assimilated and reincarnated as corporations, conglomerates and multinationals. They have taken on new names, acquired polished manners and renounced their craving for human flesh for more refined viands. But their cupidity is no less insatiable than their ancestors'.

One breed subsists entirely on forests. When this breed beheld forests, its collective cupidity was stirred as it looked upon an endless, boundless sea of green — as in greenbacks. They saw beyond, even into the future. Money. Cash. Deposits. Bank accounts. Interest. Reserves. Investments, securities, bonds, shares, dividends, capital gains, assets, funds, deals, revenue, income, prosperity, opulence, profits, riches, wealth, comfort.

They recruited woodsmen with axes, crosscut saws and Swede saws, sputters, shovels, cant hooks, grapples, chains, ropes, files and pikes, and sent them into the woods to fell, hew, saw, cut, chop, slash and level. The forests resounded with the clash of axes and the whine of saws as blades bit into the flesh of spruce, pine, cedar, tamarack and poplar to fill the demands of the weendigoes in Toronto, Montreal, Vancouver, New York, Chicago, Boston, wherever they now dwelt. Cries of "Timber!" echoed across the treetops, followed by the rip and tear of splintering trees, and thundering crashes.

And as fast as woodsmen felled the trees, teamsters delivered sleighload after sleighload to railway sidings and to the rivers. Train after train, shipload after shipload of logs were delivered to the mills.

Yet as fast as the woodsmen cut, as much as they cut, it was never fast enough. The quantity always fell short of the expectations of the weendigoes, their masters.

"Is that all? Should there not be more? We demand a bigger return for our risks and our investments. Only more will satisfy us. Any amount will do, so long as it's more, and the more the better."

The demands were met for more speed and more pulp, more logs and more timber. Axes, saws, woodsmen, horses and teamsters were replaced, and their blows and calls no longer rang in the forest. In their place, chainsaws whined, Caterpillar tractors with huge blades bulled and battered their way through the forest, uprooting trees to clear the way for automatic shearers that topped, limbed and sheared the trunks. These mechanical weendigoes gutted and desolated the forests, leaving death, destruction and ugliness where once there was life, abundance and beauty.

14   Trucks and transports operated day and night delivering cargo with a speed and quantity that the horses and sleighs could never have matched.

15   Yet the weendigoes wanted still more, and it didn't matter if their policies and practices of clear-cutting their harvest of timber and pulp resulted in violations of North American Indian rights or in the further impairment of their lives.

16   Nor does it matter to them that their modus operandi permanently defiles hillside and mountainside by erosion. They are indifferent to the carnage inflicted upon bears, wolves, rabbits, thrushes, sparrows, warblers. Who cares if they are displaced? What possible harm has been done? Nor does it seem as if these modern weendigoes have any regard for the rights of future generations to the yield of Mother Earth.

17   The new, reincarnated weendigoes are little different from their forebears. They are more omnivorous than their ancestors, however, and the modern breed wears elegant clothes and comports itself with an air of cultured and dignified respectability.

18   Profit, wealth, comfort, power are the ends of business. Anything that detracts from or diminishes the anticipated return, be it taking pains not to violate the rights of others, or taking measures to ensure that the land remains fertile and productive for future generations, must, it seems, be circumvented.

19   And what has been the result of this self-serving, self-glutting disposition? In 10 short decades, these modern weendigoes have accomplished what at one time seemed impossible; they have laid waste immense tracts of forest that were seen as beyond limit as well as self-propagating, and ample enough to serve this generation and many more to come.

20   Now, as the forests are in decline, the weendigoes are looking at a future that offers scarcity. Many others are assessing the weendigoes' accomplishments not in terms of dollars but in terms of damage — the damage they have inflicted on the environment and the climate and on botanical and zoological life.

• •

Explorations:

Basil Johnston,
>   *How the Birds Got Their Colours*
>   *Indian School Days*
Agnes Grant, ed., *Our Bit of Truth: An Anthology of Canadian Native Literature*
Linda Jaine and Drew Hayden Taylor, eds., *Voices: Being Native in Canada*

*The Limits to Growth: A Report for the Club of Rome's Project on the
    Predicament of Mankind*
Elizabeth May, *At the Cutting Edge: The Crisis in Canada's Forests*
M. T. Kelly, *A Dream Like Mine* (novel)
Margaret Atwood, *Strange Things: The Malevolent North in Canadian Literature*
http://www.for.gov.bc.ca/hfp/pubs/standman/atcc/atcc.htm
http://www.turtle-island.com/rolemodels.html
http://www.whetung.com/basil.html
http://www.hanksville.org/storytellers/BasilJ
http://queensu.ca/envst/a_new_design/events/symposium_poster.pdf

Structure:

1. Is "Modern Cannibals of the Wilds" a FABLE? (See this book's Glossary.) How do fables work? How does this one?
2. Why does Johnston open by listing so many animals, birds and insects whose "home" was once most of this continent?
3. Point out the paragraph of TRANSITION where we move from the old weendigo to the new one. Point out the THESIS STATEMENT.
4. Analyze how paragraphs 15 and 16 employ *cause and effect.*
5. Point out all the ways Johnston portrays the forestry industry as a monster and cannibal. How fully has he developed his *analogy?* Invent another *analogy* for those who support the forestry industry, and tell it to the class.

Style:

1. In what kind of writing do we more often see words like "mantled," "kindred," "improvident" and "slothful"? Describe Johnston's TONE. Why do you think he chose it for this subject?
2. Read paragraph 9 aloud to the class, with feeling, so all can experience its ONOMATOPOETIC language. Which words sound like what they mean? What is the overall effect?
3. How CONCISE is Johnston's analogy? What techniques make it so?
4. Why is the METAPHOR "flesh" of paragraph 9 appropriate to Johnston's portrayal of the weendigoes?

Ideas for Discussion and Writing:

1. If our human forestry industry is a "cannibal," then in what sense is it "eating" us as well as trees?
2. "The more he ate, the larger he grew, and the larger he grew, the greater his hunger" (paragraph 4). What if one day the monster's "food" runs out? When our forestry industry can no longer "eat" and "grow," will it "starve"? What can we do now to either reduce its appetite or extend its food supply?

3. Defend or attack the clear-cutting of forests that continues in British Columbia and most other provinces. Defend or attack the actions of environmentalists in convincing many European companies not to buy Canadian paper made through clear-cutting.

4. Conservationists often say that in Canada we do not "harvest" but "mine" the forests. Extend these images into *analogies*, by giving parallels. *Contrast* the philosophies behind both.

5. What particularly qualifies Basil Johnston, a First Nations person, to write on this subject?

6. **PROCESS IN WRITIN***G: In paragraph 16 Johnston refers to our "Mother Earth." Expand this widespread* metaphor *into an essay of analogy. First write the term "Mother Earth" in the centre of a page, then fill the surrounding space with other words it brings to mind. Connect related items with lines. Determine your main point. Now draw upon this cluster outline as you do a rapid first draft. When it has "cooled off," look it over. Do examples always help the reader "see" your point? If not, add. Does your TONE fit this important subject? If not, adjust. Is everything on topic? If not, cut. Finally, revise for spelling and punctuation as you produce your best version.*

Note: See also the Topics for Writing at the end of this chapter.

FÉLIX LECLERC

The Family House[*]

Translated from the French by Philip Stratford

Though as he grew older his own music went out of style, Félix Leclerc (1914–1988), Quebec's original chansonnier, *set the example for a generation of popular singers who, during the sixties and seventies, were a vital force in Quebec's "Quiet Revolution." As singer Gilles Vigneault put it, Leclerc was "the father of us all." Referred to by the media simply as "Félix," honoured by the annual "Félix" music awards named after him, Leclerc spent his last years as unofficial poet laureate of Quebec, a sage to whom the public turned for words in time of crisis. When Quebec mourned the death of nationalist leader René Lévesque, it was Leclerc whose words were carved on the tomb: "The first page of Quebec's true and beautiful history has been turned. Now he takes his place among the few liberators of their people." And when Leclerc died soon after, Quebeckers mourned another fallen leader, naming streets, roads, bridges and public buildings after him throughout the province. Leclerc was born in La Tuque. After announcing, acting and writing for Radio-Canada in the thirties and early forties, he acted for several years with a theatre company. Then in 1951 he arrived at Paris, where, singing his own rough-hewn songs in music halls, he won instant acclaim as "Le Canadien." But despite his success as songwriter and singer, Leclerc viewed himself primarily as a writer. He published more than a dozen books, including poetry, plays, fables, stories and novels. Among his most widely read are* Adagio *(1943) and* Allegro *(1944), two collections of his fables and stories written for radio;* Pieds nus dans l'aube *(1946), the autobiographical novel from which our selection comes; and his novel* Le fou de l'île *(1958), translated by Philip Stratford in 1976 as* The Madman, the Kite and the Island.

W̲e were all, brothers and sisters alike, born in a long three-storey wooden house, a house as humped and crusty as a loaf of homemade bread, as warm and clean inside as the white of the loaf.

Roofed over with shingles, harbouring robins in its gables, it looked itself like an old nest perched up there in the silence. Taking the north wind over the left shoulder, beautifully adjusted to nature, from the roadside one might also have mistaken it for an enormous boulder stranded on the beach.

---

[*] Translator's title.

3   In truth it was a stubborn old thing, soaking up storms and twilight, determined not to die of anything less than old age, like the two elms beside it.

4   The house turned its back squarely on the rest of town so as not to see the new subdivision with its shiny little boxes as fragile as mushrooms. Looking out over the valley, highroad for the wild St. Maurice river, it focused as if in ecstasy on the long caravan of blue mountains over there, the ones that flocks of clouds and the oldest seagulls don't seem able to get over.

5   With its rusty sides, its black roof and its white-trimmed windows, our common cradle crouched over a heavy cement foundation sunk solidly in the ground like a ship's anchor to hold us firm, for we were eleven children aboard, a turbulent, strident lot, but as timid as baby chicks.

6   A big, robust, rough fieldstone chimney, held together by trowel-smoothed mortar, began in the cellar near the round-bellied furnace just above that drafty little iron door that sticking a mirror into you could see the stars. Like the hub of a wheel it rose through the floors distributing spokes of heat, then broke through to the outside as stiff as a sentinel with a plumed helmet and smoked there with windswept hair, close to a grey ladder lying along the roof. The grey ladder and the sooty little door, we were told, were not for human use, but for an old man in red who in winter jumped from roof to roof behind reindeer harnessed in white.

7   From top to bottom our home was inhabited: by us in the centre like the core of a fruit; at the edges by parents; in the cellars and attics by superb and silent men, lumberjacks by trade. In the walls, under the floors, between the joists, near the carpets, and in the folds of the lamp-shades lived goblins, gnomes, fairies, snatches of song, silly jokes and the echoes of games; in the veins of our house ran pure poetry.

8   We had a chair for rocking in, a bench for saying prayers, a sofa to cry on, a two-step staircase for playing trains. Also other fine toys that we didn't dare touch, like the two-wired bird with its long beak and the bell in its forehead that talked to the grown-ups. A flower-patterned linoleum was our garden; a hook in the wall, a bollard to tie up our imaginary boats; the staircases were slides; the pipes running up the walls our masts; and armchairs miniature stages where we learnt with the hats, gloves and overcoats of our elders how to make the same faces that we wear today but without finding them funny.

9   A vast corridor divided the ground floor lengthwise. A few rung-backed chairs made a circle in one corner; above them a row of hooks like question marks disappeared beneath the coats of visitors who came to consult Papa, the biggest timber merchant in the valley. The living room and a bedroom for visitors stood side by side. The living room, with its black piano, its net curtains, its big blue armchair, its gold-framed pictures, a few old-style chairs upholstered in satin (particularly a spring-rocker dressed up like an old lady out of the past with tassels on the hem of her dress) gave our lives a quality of Sunday celebration. Our

parents' bedroom closed its door on impenetrable secrets. In its obscurity slumbered an old dresser full of camphor-scented sheets between which my mother hid mysterious notebooks, repositories of the exact hour of our birth, the names of godfathers and godmothers, and very private family events.

To the left of the hall a smoking room served as my father's study and as library for all of us. A door opened to the dining room — classroom would be more exact, for we only ate there once or twice a year. In the sewing room between the sewing machine and an enormous cupboard stood the sofa, ready to be cried on. At the back of the house, spreading the full width, was our gay and singing kitchen: the cast-iron stove with its built-in mirror, the red kitchen cupboards, the white muslin curtains hanging like fog in the narrow windows, and the patches of sunlight playing on the left of the long family table. There shone the ever-burning lamp, known to all people throughout all time as the soul of the home. There we were told of good news and bad. There Papa signed our school report cards. There in the high rocking chair we would often sit in silence to think of facts of creation discovered that day and ponder on the strange and marvellous world we had fallen into. 10

The first floor was lined with children's bedrooms. There were eight, I think, divided between girls and boys. In the girls' rooms it was cleaner, rosier, airier than the boys'. On the walls they pinned up tiny frames, graceful silhouettes and sprigs of flowers. On ours we stuck huge vulgar calendars, of hunters waiting for game and old gents smoking rubbed tobacco. 11

Our room, the most spacious on the floor, looked out on the garden, its black earth full as a cornucopia, and cut through with straight little paths that we walked down every evening, watering under the watching eyes of the cottontails. 12

We each had our own bed, a little white bed with a real straw mattress and iron bedposts ending in brass knobs where we hung our clothes, our slingshots, and our hands clasped in prayer. 13

On the second floor a screened veranda jutted out in a bow like a pilot-house. It was a veritable observation post dominating the waves of the valley like those of the sea: waves of snowstorms, waves of loggers in springtime, waves of poor families gathering wild fruit, waves of falling leaves, of showers of sunshine, of the beating of birds' wings, of paths traced by children, hunters and fishermen. On hot nights we slept there above the waves on that wooden porch which was also the children's playroom. Soldiers, teddy bears, drums, little wooden shoes, dolls seated at table before empty china plates, all keeping good company together. A tin bridge built long ago by my eldest brother served as access to this cardboard world. 14

On the floor above, behind a bull's-eye window, stretched the attic, a long deserted dusty cage, dormitory in winter for several lumberjacks. Between the three-legged chairs and the family portraits, these men on their mattresses, devoured by fatigue, tumbled headlong each night into sleep. 15

16   And like the crew of a happy ship, thinking neither of arrivals nor of departures, but only of the sea that carries them, we sped through childhood all sails set, thrilled with each morning and every night, envying neither distant ports nor far cities, convinced that our ship was flying the best colours and that we carried on board all necessary potions to ward off pirates and bad luck.

17   The house we lived in was number 168, rue Claire-Fontaine.

● ●

Explorations:

Félix Leclerc,
> *The Madman, the Kite and the Island*
> *Pieds nus dans l'aube* (available only in French)

Philip Stratford, ed., *Chez nous* (anthology of writings from Quebec, translated into English)

Félix-Antoine Savard, *Boss of the River* (novel)

Germaine Guèvremont, *The Outlander* (novel)

Jacques Ferron, *Tales from an Uncertain Country* (short stories, in translation)

Web sites in French:
> http://www.mef.qc.ca/felix.htm
> http://www.geocities.com/leclerc_felix
> http://www.litterature.org/ile32000.asp?numero=294
> http://www.comnet.ca/~rg/felix.htm
> http://www.chansonduquebec.com/bio/leclerc.htm
> http://www.felixleclerc.com/esp_espace.htm

Structure:

1. Leclerc packs this selection with FIGURES OF SPEECH, but develops only one image so fully as to make it an *analogy*. What is it? Which paragraphs develop it?
2. What is the overall point of this selection, and where does Leclerc most openly state it?

Style:

1. Do you see twice as many METAPHORS and SIMILES here as in most of the other selections? Four times as many? Ten times as many? What effect does this concentration of figures of speech give?
2. Point out ten SIMILES, ten METAPHORS and five cases of PERSONIFICATION in this selection. Are these figures of speech well chosen to build a single dominant impression?

3. Do you imagine "The Family House" was easy or hard to translate from French to English? Is an exact translation possible? If you speak two or more languages, how easy or hard is it to convert thoughts from one to another?

Ideas for Discussion and Writing:

1. In paragraph 8 Leclerc tells how the children imitated their elders, learning "how to make the same faces that we wear today but without finding them funny." Do you sense in "The Family House" a regret for lost childhood? Do you regret the loss of your own? Do most of us? Give reasons why or why not.
2. Almost everything Leclerc wrote expresses the same happiness and security that we see in "The Family House." Do happy children such as he depicts here usually become happy adults? Can troubled children also become happy adults? Give examples.
3. "Coming of Age in Putnok" is the opening of George Gabori's autobiography, while "The Family House" is the opening of Félix Leclerc's autobiographical novel. Compare the two. Which gives more facts? More feeling? More insight into the author's background and personality? Which would more strongly motivate readers to finish the book?
4. **PROCESS IN WRITING:** *Like Leclerc, depict your own childhood home in such a way as to strongly convey your feelings about it and your life there. First generate a page of* SIMILES, METAPHORS *and* SENSE IMAGES *that "show" your memories of home. Now search these notes for a common theme such as Leclerc's vision of a house as a ship. Next write a "discovery draft" to develop this analogy, using images from your notes, and new ones that come as you write. In further drafts chop out every word that does not in some way support the overall effect. Read your final version aloud, with feeling, to the class.*

Note: See also the Topics for Writing at the end of this chapter.

Topics for Writing

CHAPTER 6: ANALOGY AND RELATED DEVICES

Choose either a complete topic from items 1–15, or a subject from items 16–30 to complete. Then in an essay, extend your analogy as far as you can. (See also the guidelines that follow.)

1. Prejudice as a Wall
2. Hockey as War
3. School as a Factory
4. Life as a Road
5. Manners as a Mask
6. An Industrial Worker as a Robot
7. Television as a Drug
8. Music as a Drug
9. White Blood Cells as an Army
10. The Public Debt as a Cancer
11. A Career as War
12. A Person You Know as the Pet He or She Keeps
13. A Corporation as an Octopus
14. The City as a Jungle
15. Novels as Dreams
16. Television as _____
17. A Newborn as _____
18. Population Growth as _____
19. Dating as _____
20. Old Age as _____
21. Crime as _____
22. A Computer as _____
23. A Car as _____
24. Marriage as _____
25. Parents as _____
26. The Internet as _____
27. A City as _____
28. Pollution as _____
29. Money as _____
30. Planet Earth as _____

Process in Writing: Guidelines

Follow at least some of these steps in writing your essay of analogy (your teacher may suggest which ones).

1.   *Choose or devise a topic you really like, because motivation is the single greatest factor in writing performance.*

2.   *If you complete one of the topics from 16 to 30, be sure to invent an* analogy *(with two items from different categories),* not a comparison and contrast *(with two items from the same category). Know which item is your real subject, and which one exists merely to explain the other.*

3.   *Now freewrite on your topic, to achieve the spontaneity and originality that spark a good analogy.*

4.   *Incorporate the best of this freewriting into your first draft. Let the ideas flow, not stopping now to revise or edit.*

5.   *In your next version add any more points of comparison that come to you (a strong analogy is fully developed). Read your prose aloud to detect awkward passages, and revise. Trim deadwood. Heighten TRANSITIONS.*

6.   *Now edit for things like spelling and punctuation, before printing off your best version.*

AP/Marty Lederhandler

"... *amid the flames and wreckage of the World Trade Center, doomed people reached out by cellphones to their families, in order to know that they were loved right up to their last breaths.*"

— *Gordon Pitts, "Your New Job, Your New Life"*

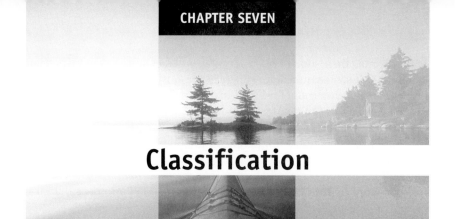

CHAPTER SEVEN

Classification

THERE ARE THREE KINDS OF THEM . . .

Our world is so complex that without classification we are lost. To call a friend we use an alphabetized phone book. To find mangos in the food store we head for the fruit section. To buy a used TV we go to the *classified* section of the newspaper. Putting things into categories is one of our most common methods of thought, both for good and for bad. Who would search the whole dictionary when the word in question begins with "T"? What student, *classified* into grade five, would look for the grade six *class*room?

Yet as Hitler and other racists have shown, classifying people can lead to stereotypes and stereotypes can lead to violence. Ethnic jokes may seem innocent *(Why does it take two WASPs to change a light bulb? One makes the gin and tonics while the other calls the electrician).* But such a characterization makes it hard for others to view a member of that group as an individual. If all WASPs (or all Texans or Quebeckers or women or Catholics or immigrants or stockbrokers or police) are classified as the same, we have dehumanized them. Dislike and even persecution are now possible. At its extreme, this process has led to genocides such as the bloody conquest of the Americas by Europeans, the extermination of the Jews by Nazi Germany, and the butchery of more recent "ethnic cleansing" in countries as diverse as the former Yugoslavia, Rwanda and the Sudan.

Be careful, then, not to let a classification become a stereotype. For example, our society may have practical reasons to group people by age, but let's always leave room for individuals: not all teenagers drive recklessly, not all 40-year-olds are divorcing, and not all 80-year-olds are in the rocking chair. In fact many teens don't even have a license, some 40-year-olds have never married, and a few people in their eighties still run marathons.

Whatever its subject, your essay of classification needs at least three categories, because only two would form a *comparison and contrast*. And it should have no more than you can adequately develop — seldom more than five or six. To be logical, a classification normally follows these guidelines:

Classify all items by the same principle. A study of major world religions would probably include Islam, Christianity, Judaism, Buddhism and Hinduism — but not atheism, which is the opposite of religious belief.

Do not leave out an obvious category, such as Buddhism, which has many millions of followers. On the other hand, if your neighbour proclaims a new religion that attracts five or ten people to its meetings every Wednesday night, grouping it with world religions would clearly not make sense.

Do not let categories overlap. Though a classification of world religions might include Islam, Christianity, Judaism, Buddhism and Hinduism, it would not include Catholicism — because that is a subgroup of Christianity.

Classifying is not easy; it's a real exercise in logic. Keep applying the guidelines.

Also observe the main principle of any essay: *Know your purpose.* Exactly *why* are you comparing the three kinds of parents or the four kinds of teachers or the five kinds of friends? Is it because you have a vision of what a good parent or teacher or friend is, and want to share it with others? Is it because bad experiences have led you to warn against certain kinds of parents or teachers or friends? Like any argument, an essay of classification makes a point — otherwise it is "pointless." Try freewriting or brainstorming for five or ten minutes to get thoughts flowing and ideas out in the open. Then look these over. Let them help you decide not only what the content of your classification will be, but also its overall point, its thesis statement. Since thinking is not easy, you need all the help you can get — and some of the best help comes from your own pen or computer: while it is writing, you are thinking.

Note: For more examples of classification, see these essays in other chapters:

Dave Bidini, "The Fabulous Poodles, Etc.: Naming Your Band," p. 55
Leah McLaren, "Canadian Guys Rule," p. 122

THE HONOURABLE DAVID LAM

Pulling Together

The Honourable David See-Chai Lam, born in Hong Kong in 1923, has had a long career in business and public life, culminating in his term from 1988 to 1995 as Lieutenant Governor of British Columbia. With a B.A. from Lingnam University and an M.B.A. from Temple University, he became in 1960 the CEO of Ka Wah Bank Ltd. of Hong Kong. Then, immigrating to the "golden mountain" which he celebrates in his essay, he became in 1968 the president of Canadian International Properties Limited. When Dr. Lam was invited ten years later to be the Lieutenant Governor of his new home, British Columbia, he underwent the uncertainties described in his essay below, at first declining because he was "living in a province with a history of discrimination against Chinese," because he was "getting old," and because English was not his first language. Reconsidering, though, he did accept the post, and, with the aid of his much-loved wife Dorothy Lam, found great fulfillment in the job through "building bridges" among the many population groups of British Columbia. Our selection, published in Maclean's *of January 30, 1995, reflects this experience in acceptance, belonging and contribution. Now retired from government, Dr. Lam lives in Vancouver, where he directs a charitable foundation that gives grants to universities, hospitals and other public institutions, and where he enjoys golf and boating.*

Once, Asians came to North America for jobs, albeit somewhat menial ones. Particularly in the West, there was ready work on the railway, in laundries and in chop suey houses. With the gold rush and its opportunity to strike it rich, this continent became known in China as the "golden mountain." 1

Today, Canada continues to attract Asians, although the lure is no longer gold. Instead, they come for things that a lot of us in Canada take for granted: stability, a peaceful life, law and order, education, generally friendly and understanding people. 2

As one of those who chose to settle in Canada over 28 years ago, I would like to offer a brief ABC for others hoping to make a new home here. 3

The A is for acceptance. And that goes two ways. Prospective immigrants must be accepted by the federal immigration department. But even if the government accepts you, your peace of mind and happiness will depend very much upon how you are accepted in your community. 4

Of course, newcomers could reject the broader Canadian community and choose to live only among their own people. But that choice is self-defeating: one becomes inward-looking, cut away from the mainstream of society. There is really no way to enjoy what Canada has to offer if one 5 lives in either a physical or psychological ghetto. So, it is a duty of sorts to strive for acceptance.

6   There are always difficulties arising from different value systems, a different cultural style. Speaking loudly, getting things done in the quickest manner, bragging about accomplishments and wealth — all might be commonplace in Hong Kong and totally acceptable in many other parts of the world. But they are not so in Canada.

7   Here, we try to minimize friction between people. We downplay displays of wealth. We respect good manners. Such simple courtesies as saying good morning and thank you are daily expressions of respect for others.

8   The B represents belonging. This is a very important feeling. People who do not belong always feel impermanent. As with people who reside in a hotel, no matter how beautiful it may be, they are constantly reminded that they are transients.

9   People who divide their time between Canada and another country become "astronauts" — flying too high and fast to put down real roots or to feel a sense of belonging. They are not found just among Chinese immigrants. Some Canadians who spend half of their time in California or in Florida might also be considered astronauts. When they are asked to become involved in community services, many say: "Ah, but in a couple of months I will return to Canada . . . ," or, ". . . I'll be leaving for the States."

10   If you want to feel that you belong, ask yourself: how much do I care about what happens in my community and related issues such as crime, a clean neighborhood, volunteering to pitch in.

11   The C stands for contribution. And this is the easiest thing of all to achieve. In this new country, in this new community, in this new neighborhood in which we have started to take root, commitment makes a strong statement that you belong. You can give without loving; but you cannot love without giving.

12   When I was initially approached to consider being nominated as lieutenant-governor of British Columbia, I turned it down. My negative side told me: "You are living in a province with a history of discrimination against Chinese. You are getting old. You speak English as a second language. Don't do it."

13   Fortunately, however, my positive side saw an opportunity to build bridges among people of different cultures, different ethnic backgrounds and different races. After 6½ years, I have experienced tremendous love and respect from the people of Canada as a whole, and particularly from those in British Columbia. I feel proud to be a Canadian, because I truly appreciate the quality of its people.

14   I was brought up in Hong Kong to be so conscious of racial differences that we had derogatory nicknames for everyone. That is no way to go through life. It is like carrying a little bit of poison in the mind. And the world is changing. The day is quickly coming when people with only one culture will find it difficult to compete, let alone to prosper.

Don't talk to me about "tolerance." Tolerating someone is like holding   15
your breath: you are telling the world that you can hold your breath longer
than anyone else. I say, let us celebrate differences — not tolerate them.

I believe in multiculturalism because it adds to our strength. The   16
Asia-Pacific region is the fastest-growing region in the world. And it is
just across the ocean from British Columbia. Let us turn the people of
all the races living in Canada into partners. Let us build a "golden mountain" for all of us.

● ●

Explorations:

Reginald H. Roy, *David Lam: A Biography*
Bennett Lee and Jim Wong-Chu, eds., *Many-Mouthed Birds: Contemporary
    Writings by Chinese-Canadians*
Wayson Choy, *Paper Shadows: A Chinatown Childhood* (memoir)
Sky Lee, *Disappearing Moon Cafe* (novel)
Amy Tan, *The Joy Luck Club* (novel; also made into a feature film and
    video)
http://www.asian.ca/community
http://www.ccnc.ca/toronto/history/timeline.html
http://www.vpl.ca/branches/LibrarySquare/his/StudyGuides/chinese_
    canadian_biographies.html
http://collections.ic.gc.ca/yipsang

Structure:

1. Why does David Lam both open and close his essay with the same
   expression, "golden mountain"? What effect does this repetition
   achieve?
2. How do you rate Lam's "brief ABC" as a *classification?* Are its three categories enough? Is any obvious category left out? Are all *classified* by
   the same principle? Do you think the organizational device of the
   "ABC" is a good fit for Lam's categories?
3. How does the device of *comparison and contrast* heighten the power of
   paragraph 9?
4. Why does Lam wait almost till the end to describe his own decision to
   become lieutenant governor of British Columbia?

Style:

1. How easy or hard is the vocabulary of "Pulling Together"? How short
   or long are its sentences? Its paragraphs? Who do you see as its
   intended AUDIENCE?

Ideas for Discussion and Writing:

1. While stating "I believe in multiculturalism because it adds to our strength" (par. 16), Lam also advises New Canadians not to live "in either a physical or psychological ghetto" (par. 5). What is your view? Do you prefer the traditional American "melting pot" which is supposed to assimilate immigrants, or the Canadian "mosaic," in which New Canadians are encouraged, even funded, to retain their first language and culture? Which path is better for the individual? For the nation?

2. David Lam's adopted home of British Columbia is part of the Asia Pacific rim, and is itself one of the most multicultural spots on earth. If you live there, describe how the cosmopolitan mix of its population has influenced your own life. Or if you live in Toronto, Montreal or another cosmopolitan place, apply this topic to your own city.

3. Lam says "The day is quickly coming when people with only one culture will find it difficult to compete, let alone to prosper" (par. 14). Do you think this is true for your own intended profession? Why or why not? If so, what have you done to prepare? If your family has immigrated, what are you doing to keep your first language and culture? If your family has earlier roots in Canada, what other languages, if any, have you learned to speak? And what experiences have you had to make yourself feel at home with other cultures?

4. **PROCESS IN WRITING:** *Whether you have immigrated, yourself, or only know others who have, think about the main challenges that face immigrants to Canada. Fill a page with brainstorming on this topic, then look it over. Circle or highlight the main points, choose your THESIS STATEMENT, then rearrange these thoughts into a short conventional outline that* classifies *the challenges. Are there at least three categories in your* classification? *Are any main ones missing? Are all* classified *by the same principle? Do any seem to overlap? Now write a rapid version of your essay of* classification. *The next day look it over. Does it have enough* examples? *If not, add. Do TRANSITIONS move the argument from one point to the next? If not, add. Finally, check the punctuation and spelling before printing out your best version.*

Note: See also the Topics for Writing at the end of this chapter.

IAN AND WILL FERGUSON

Theatre

Brothers Ian and Will Ferguson, writers of zany and colourful books about Canada, grew up in a family of seven children in the rugged fur-trapping town of Fort Vermilion in northern Alberta. Years later, Ian's book Village of the Small Houses *(Stephen Leacock Medal for Humour, 2004) would chronicle their childhood of material poverty but rich experience — such as the day their father drove their mother in a race against time, over logging roads to reach the hospital in Peace River, where she would give birth to the author himself. Ian went on to become a playwright, author of almost 20 works such as* Elephant Shoes *(1990),* Uncle Joe Again *(1991) and* Bonecrack *(1997). He also originated live improvised soap operas* Sin City *and* Die-Nasty, *and the CBC TV comedy show* Liquid Soapz. *Meanwhile his brother Will joined the Canadian volunteer program* Katimavik, *and in 1990 graduated from the York University Film Program. Stints of travel and teaching followed in Peru, Japan, Korea, Malaysia and China. He now lives in Calgary. Will has published many books of humour, such as* Why I Hate Canadians *(1997),* Bastards & Boneheads: Our Glorious Leaders, Past and Present *(1999),* Happiness *(a novel, 2001) and* Beauty Tips from Moose Jaw: Travels in Search of Canada *(2004). Our selection comes from* How to Be a Canadian, Even If You Already Are One, *written by both brothers. Published in 2001, it has sold over 100,000 copies.*

I n Canada, there are six different types of theatre company for you to choose from: 1

1. Commercial Theatre

2

Located in Toronto, Vancouver and Montreal only. Not to be confused with some of the larger non-profit theatres, which, despite their not-for-profit designation, are equally interested in making money. Commercial theatres offer epic musicals full of special effects and spectacle. Here's how to tell. If a helicopter lands onstage or a chandelier crashes from the ceiling at a key dramatic moment, chances are you are attending a commercial theatre production. If, however, the helicopter is portrayed by an actor running around frantically beating his fists against his chest or the falling chandelier occurs offstage with the actors pointing to the wing and shouting, "Look! A giant chandelier has fallen to the ground . . . just offstage!", you are probably at a smaller, non-profit theatre.

The tickets to commercial theatre cost a lot of money, more than the cost of an actual helicopter ride, in fact. But the good part is that you get 3 to feel very patriotic by saying things like "Wow, did you know that with the exception of the playwright, the composer, the director, the choreographer, the designer and the two lead actors, the rest of the cast and crew are completely Canadian?"

2. Government-Funded Regional Theatre, Large

Every big city has one, and they can usually be found in a convenient downtown location where parking costs — well, about as much as a helicopter ride. Large government-funded regional theatres function like big industrial bakeries. They're in the bulk business, and they present a consistent, if predictable, recipe of Neil Simon, Noel Coward, the odd musical and assorted plays that were hot on Broadway or in the West End four or five seasons ago. Tickets will cost you almost as much as you'd pay at a commercial theatre, but everybody involved in the show will be Canadian. Except the artistic director. He will be from England.

3. Government-Funded Regional Theatre, Small

Similar to above, only "edgier." And what, per chance, does "edgier" mean? It means they will build their season around a single play — that was hot off-Broadway four or five seasons ago. In Canada, this is considered cutting-edge. These theatres also commission new works by Canadian writers. By law, these plays will be set in the prairies. And they will have titles like *The Wheat Is High* or *42 Short Plays about Gabriel Dumont*. Tickets will be half the price of those at the larger theatres, and the artistic director will be Canadian and easily recognized. He (or she) will be the person who has to unplug the toilet during intermission.

4. Festivals, Large

These are, effectively, huge repertory theatre companies that specialize in the works of one particular playwright and related writings from around the same era. William Shakespeare or George Bernard Shaw. That kind of thing. Tickets cost an arm and a leg, but they're worth every limb, we say, if only because you'll be able to shout, "Hey! That guy from the Canadian Tire ad is playing Polonius.°" The artistic directors will be of British origin, but most of them will have taken out Canadian citizenship by now. Get them to autograph your copy of this book. They'll sign anything, including their life. Away. You will find them at the bar during interval, in a festive Faustian° funk, drinking with a certain raw desperation.

5. Festivals, Small

These are also called "fringe" festivals (as in "lunatic" or "benefits"). Fringe festivals are spreading across the country faster than fungus in a locker

---

° Polonius: a minor character in Shakespeare's *Hamlet*.
° Faustian: referring to Faust, who in works by both Christopher Marlowe and Goethe gains earthly power by selling his soul to the Devil.

room. Low ticket prices, independent productions, and lots of first-time playwrights, actors and directors: basically this type of festival functions like a farm team for the bigger houses. The artistic director of the festival will be a woman, and you will recognize her by the huge bags under her eyes and the constant use of her cell phone to deal with yet another emergency.

A warning. The quality and content of fringe shows can vary widely   8
(and wildly). Necrophilia and the true nature of love, that sort of thing. So don't attend if you're easily shocked and/or bored. Indeed, at many fringe shows you can be both — *at the very same time.* "I was never so shocked in my life! Or so bored!"

6. So-Called Dinner So-Called Theatre   9
Here, for around the same ticket price that a large government-funded regional theatre would charge, you not only get a show, you also get "food." (Note the use of quotation marks.) The play itself is probably going to be a tired old British farce with a title like *Ooh, That's Me Bum, Guv'ner!,* and it's going to feature some washed-up American sit-com star in the lead role, but hey . . . have you checked out the buffet? Some dinner theatres also have the actors waiting on tables "in character," which seems sensible, since most of the best waiters tend to be actors. And vice versa.

So get out there and become a regular theatregoer. If you don't believe   10
that the arts should be subsidized, then spend your money at a dinner theatre or go to your local fringe festival. Chances are nobody involved is making any money. Or, if you prefer to support individual artists, at the very least you can give the waiter a decent tip.

• •

Explorations:

Ian Ferguson, *Village of the Small Houses: A Memoir of Sorts*
Will Ferguson,
     Beauty Tips from Moose Jaw: Travels in Search of Canada
     Happiness (novel)
Ian and Will Ferguson, *How to Be a Canadian, Even If You Already Are One*
Paul Hiebert, *Sara Binks*
www.willferguson.ca
www.leacock.ca/win2004.html
http://www.banffcentre.ca/press/contributors/def/ferguson_w
http://www.banffcentre.ca/press/contributors/def/ferguson_i

Structure:

1. "Theatre" is one of the mostly clearly organized selections in this book. Point out all the techniques that make it so.

2. Have the Ferguson brothers reached the recommended 50% of *example* content?
3. In "Theatre" are all the categories *mutually exclusive*, or is there significant *overlap?*

Style:

1. In paragraph 7, "Fringe festivals are spreading across the country faster than fungus in a locker room." Point out five more vivid IMAGES in this selection. What do they achieve?
2. Point out five passages where the authors use IRONY to make their point.

Ideas for Discussion and Writing:

1. Have you ever acted in a student play, or served on the stage crew, built sets, done lighting or sound effects, done costumes or make-up, or done publicity and tickets? Describe your experience to the class.
2. Everyone has seen high school plays, but have you ever attended live professional theatre? Which of the Fergusons' categories did the most recent production fit into? Give reasons for your answer. Did you like the work and the performance? Why or why not?
3. As a playwright, should Ian Ferguson be poking fun at theatre in Canada? Why do you think he's doing so?
4. Can you afford to go to live theatre? How much do movies cost these days? Rock concerts? NHL hockey admissions? Did you know that many theatre productions are subsidized so highly, by government and by rich patrons, that you pay as little as one third of the real cost, especially at the student rate? Phone three local theatre companies, and report to the class what the cheapest seats go for at each.
5. In paragraph 2 the Fergusons write of commercial theatre productions, "Wow, did you know that with the exception of the playwright, the composer, the director, the choreographer, the designer and the two lead actors, the rest of the cast and crew are completely Canadian?" Are these satirical allegations true? And are the five other categories of theatre dominated by foreigners?
6. What percentage of the movies you see are Canadian, and what percentage are foreign? What percentage of the TV you watch is Canadian, and what percentage is foreign? Why?
7. In recent years Canada has become internationally known for its comedians and recording stars. Name some names.
8. Perhaps Canada's most striking success in the performing arts has been the *Cirque du Soleil*. Have you seen it? How and where did it begin? How has it redefined the idea of a circus? How big is it in the world now?

9. **PROCESS IN WRITING:** *Write an essay* classifying *one of the following: films, rock concerts, or classical concerts (focus your choice down as far as you wish, for example to kinds of action films, or kinds of love films). First do a page of brainstorming, then from these notes make an outline classifying the categories of your subject. Look it over: are there are least three categories? (Only two would be a* comparison and contrast.*) Do they overlap? If so, revise. Are they all* classified *by the same principle? Now devise a THESIS STATEMENT that makes your overall main point. Write a quick first draft, then the next day look it over. Have you supplied plenty of concrete* examples, *as Ian and Will Ferguson have? Is your language CONCISE, as theirs is? Do TRANSITIONS move your argument from one point to the next? Finally, check the sentence structure and punctuation before printing off your best version.*

Note: See also the Topics for Writing at the end of this chapter.

GORDON PITTS

Your New Job, Your New Life

On the fateful morning of September 11, 2001, The Globe and Mail *writer Gordon Pitts was at home working on a book. Despite news of two airliners crashing into the World Trade Center of Manhattan, he tore himself away from the TV to meet an important CEO for a planned interview. But both soon knew their topic was minor compared to the prospect of friends and colleagues being caught in the tragedy. So although he was on vacation, Pitts called the* Globe *to offer help with the "huge unfolding story." Grateful editors assigned him an essay for the weekend edition, that would, as Pitts says, "try to capture the changes in business and working life that would be spawned by the Sept. 11 attacks." The result was unusual: in a week when many journalists were dashing off hasty articles filled with shock, anger and hyperpatriotism, Pitts, only four days after the event, offered the compassionate yet highly reasoned analysis that follows. Though it was conceived as a business essay, its general impact was so great that on September 15 the* Globe *put it on the front page.*

Gordon Pitts holds a B.A. in history, politics and economics from Queen's and a Bachelor of Journalism from Carleton. From 1975 he was a business reporter and editor for the Ottawa Citizen, *then in 1981 joined the* Financial Post, *where he was managing editor of the weekend edition at the time the* Post *went daily. In 1990 was published his book on Canada and the European Community,* Storming the Fortress, *in 2000* In the Blood: Battles to Succeed in Canada's Family Businesses, *and in 2002* Kings of Convergence: the Fight for Control of Canada's Media. *At the* Globe *Pitts now writes features and profiles for the* Report on Business.

1   High-rise office employees shiver with dread as they begin their morning elevator ascents.

2   Nervous business travellers brace for long security checks at airports.

3   Children in school yards and daycares watch with anxious eyes as their parents drive away to work.

4   In the wake of this week's terrorist attacks, the mundane activities that make the global economy function have become more wrenching and more fragile.

5   The march of globalization, much heralded by management books, has not been halted, but it is undergoing a serious reality check. In important and trivial ways, business life will not be the same.

6   The crash of hijacked airplanes into New York's World Trade Center towers underlines the limitations of business. While your company can

reward you richly, even offer you warm collegiality, it is government that is ultimately responsible for protecting you from terrorism and external attack.

One of capitalism's great heroes, Jack Welch, retired the week before Tuesday's tragedy, ending the career of a man known as Neutron Jack for his mass firings. 7

That nickname seems like a sick joke now. The chief executive officer of General Electric doesn't kill people and he can't save them. CEOs are not about life and death. Terrorists and governments are. 8

The attacks in New York and Washington highlight another humbling reality for the capitalist system: We can't count on technology to protect us because human passion and fanaticism can still defeat the most advanced system. 9

This weekend, many of us are reassessing our lives and our work. Here are the themes of the new business world that awaits us. 10

Borders matter. It turns out that boundaries are still relevant after all, for better or worse. You have only to look at the 30-kilometre lineups at major border crossings between Canada and the United States to grasp that the economics of free trade and globalization have changed. The delays will get shorter but they will still be more protracted than before Sept. 11. 11

The restrictions augur badly for a North American economy already on shaky ground. They also signal a weakening of the free-trade assumptions that have powered the Canadian economy through the past decade. "Canada simply needs to have a porous border with the United States," warns Karl Moore, a McGill University business professor and co-author of *Foundations of Corporate Empire*, a history of globalization. 12

It has also relied on the relatively free movement of people. Management consultancies, already reeling from declining business, must now rein in their roaming staff. Think of the cost of one extra hour of unproductive delay, extended over a firm with tens of thousands of highly paid travellers. 13

More road warriors will stay home as flights are restricted to must-go situations. Working styles will change: TV ads that show a mother calling home from a nice hotel room or a father rushing to catch the tail end of a school concert will look sadly out of step. 14

Companies may bulk up on cross-border shipments, with fewer and larger loads. It may mean the reorganization of multinationals, as they move some functions back to branch plants or spread distribution centres across the continent. Inventories could rise to reflect a relaxation of just-in-time manufacturing schedules. 15

To assuage the anxieties of Americans, businesspeople will step up demands for greater standardization of Canadian and U.S. laws, particularly on immigration. 16

Rosabeth Moss Kanter, a Harvard Business School professor and student of global business, expects the border tightening to continue, but she views the attacks as further evidence of global interdependence. 17

18   When the World Trade Center is hit, the world shudders. The events will, in fact, spur wider sharing of intelligence and security resources, she argues.

19   "Let's not rush to assume the global economic system is going to be dismantled," says Prof. Kanter, author of the 1996 book *World Class: Thriving Locally in the Global Economy.* "There are forces that may make it more global, as well as things that temporarily seem to restrict movement."

20   **Work will change.** Until Tuesday, you might have assumed the worst thing that could happen at work would be a chewing out from the boss. Now, many offices and factories will feel a sense of heightened vulnerability. Expect much tighter workplace security, including demands for employee ID to be prominently displayed.

21   Cities and companies will re-examine their massive buildup of financial centres with vulnerable office towers and large concentrations of workers. The Cantor Fitzgerald experience is embedded in our consciousness. The New York bond trading company had 1,000 people working on the 101st to 105th floors of one World Trade Center tower. About 700 of them are believed to have perished.

22   Will skyscrapers still be built? Will companies take over, say 10 to 20 floors, in one of these towers? The powerful symbolism of being a tenant in one of the world's tallest office buildings will seem less appealing. Still, New York is New York, and there will be a strong civic determination to rebuild the financial centre.

23   "Ultimately, it comes down to economics," Richard Guy Wilson, a University of Virginia architectural historian, told Reuters. "The skyline of New York isn't created by architects, it's created by economics and the return on your dollar. That land is very valuable and that's the way to maximize it."

24   Even so, teleconferencing and videoconferencing, already on the rise, will become more widespread, especially as the technology gets better. Electronic transmission of data and video will look more attractive than face-to-face contact.

25   Telecommuting has been viewed as an unaffordable luxury in the recent economic malaise, but it too will stage a comeback. Many workers will simply demand it, just to work closer to their families.

26   **Government is still important.** Justified or not, many Americans feel that airline security has been exposed as severely deficient, that this life-and-death service has been privatized and left to low-wage, underqualified and often indifferent workers.

27   A massive re-regulation will not flow from the tragedies. But Prof. Kanter believes the events will make more Americans realize that governments need to be supported. The state, she says, has become more vulnerable "in terms of performing one of its primary objectives, to protect the safety of citizens."

28   Private capitalism, Prof. Kanter says, "only works if government is there to protect the public good."

The result will be some slowing or even reversal of privatization, in the same way that the water tragedy in Walkerton, Ont., has caused a reassessment of government out-sourcing and cutbacks in Canada.° 29

But the erosion of government over the past decade has badly under- mined talent in the public sector. While North Americans have fretted, perhaps excessively, about the shortage of young software engineers, they have allowed the decline of public-service work forces. Prof. Kanter urges a renewed policy emphasis on recruiting and keeping gov- ernment talent. 30

A sign of things to come: The International Air Transport Association, the airline trade group, said this week that the U.S. Federal Aviation Administration should consider taking over the passenger screening process rather than leaving it to the airlines. 31

It's about family. On Wall Street, careers are all-consuming. But amid the flames and wreckage of the World Trade Center, doomed people reached out by cellphones to their families, in order to know that they were loved right up to their last breaths. 32

There was a similar reaction among those who were stranded in air- ports. "In the midst of tragedy, where did everyone want to go?" asks Julian Barling, a professor of organizational behaviour at Queen's University, in Kingston. His answer is simple: "Home." 33

Former New Yorker Sandra Robinson, an associate professor at the University of British Columbia, says that grief teaches "perspective" — the feeling that everything that once obsessed you at work is suddenly minutely trivial. The challenge, she says, will be to hold on to that per- spective after the events have faded. 34

Some experts have warned that the balance between work and family in North America has tilted dangerously toward work, and that the job has become a substitute for home and social life. After Sept. 11, many employees will be less willing to accept that tradeoff. 35

• •

Explorations:

Kent Roach, *September 11: Consequences for Canada*
http://911digitalarchive.org
http://www.terrorism.com/index.php
http://www.bus.ualberta.ca/cefe/Events/gordon_pitts.htm
http://www.celebrityspeakersintl.com/pitts.html

° In May 2000 the water system of Walkerton, Ontario became contaminated with *E. coli 0157: H bacteria*. As a result, seven died and 2,300 became ill. Ontario Provincial Government cutbacks to water quality inspection were widely blamed for the disaster.

Structure:

1. What does a good title do? How good is this one?
2. Where does the introduction begin and end? What does it achieve? Point out its THESIS STATEMENT.
3. Pitts discusses four *categories* of effects on our jobs and our lives. Are all *classified* by the same principal? Do any overlap? And can you think of any obvious categories left out?
4. As well as being a classification, Pitts' argument is one of the strongest *cause and effect* essays in this book. Point out the *effects* of the WTC tragedy that will have the strongest influence on your own future life, and tell why. Now look back: point out at least five *causes* of terrorist acts such as that of September 11, 2001.
5. Why does Pitts save his point about family life for the last item of the classification?

Style:

1. Does the boldfacing of category titles help readers? Do you ever boldface, or use italics, or leave extra spaces, to help show the organization of your own essays?
2. The average paragraph of Pitts' newspaper essay is only 2.1 sentences long. Why so short? Does this aspect of style help or hinder the reader? Do your own school essays have longer paragraphs? Should they? If so, why?
3. Pitts supports several of his points with quotations. Should he have given references, as in a research paper? Or does journalism have different rules?

Ideas for Discussion and Writing:

1. Where were you when on September 11, 2001, two airliners hijacked and flown by terrorists destroyed the World Trade Center in Manhattan, another hit the Pentagon, and thousands of people died? Describe your reactions that day. Now that time has passed, do you view the event as you did then, or has your perspective changed? Has this and other terrorism changed your own value system in any way? Give specifics.
2. Has international terrorism affected your own actions? Are you more careful now in any way? Do you fly less? Has there been any career goal change or economic effect on your life?
3. Do you agree with Pitts that "Government is still important" (paragraph 25)? Have deregulation and privatization gone too far? Give examples from your own city or province.
4. Canada has long prided itself on its relatively open immigration policies, its multicultural programs, its cosmopolitan cities, and in gen-

eral its tolerance toward minorities. Have these qualities diminished in reaction to terrorism, or are they still with us?

5. In response to international terrorism, is Canada moving closer to America in areas such as border control, immigration policy, military cooperation, and looser sharing of resources? If so, are these changes good for Canada? Or do they threaten our nation's economic welfare and sovereignty?

6. In this essay on business, Pitts builds to his final point by saying "amid the flames and wreckage of the World Trade Center, doomed people reached out by cellphones to their families, in order to know that they were loved right up to their last breaths." Does it take disaster to provide "perspective" (paragraph 33)? How could we keep perspective, a focus on the truly important things, in our everyday lives as well? Suggest one concrete technique to the class.

7. **PROCESS IN WRITING:** *Brainstorm for a while on how Canada can protect its citizens against international terrorism. When your page is covered with notes, divide the suggestions into* categories. *Do a logic check: Are all items* classified *by the same principle? Is there too much overlap? Is any main category missing? If so, adjust. Now write a quick discovery draft, and when it has cooled off, edit. Are there enough* examples? *Do* transition words *move your reader from point to point? Is your style direct and clear (read the draft aloud to find out). Finally, print out your best version and share it with the class.*

Note: See also the Topics for Writing at the end of this chapter.

Topics for Writing

CHAPTER 7: CLASSIFICATION

Develop one of the following topics into an essay of classification. (See also the guidelines that follow.)

1. Landlords
2. Salespersons
3. Martial Arts
4. Street People
5. Internet Providers
6. Television Commercials
7. Gamblers
8. Loans
9. Drinkers
10. Bullies
11. Cell Phones
12. Police Officers
13. Bicycles
14. Drivers
15. Neighbours
16. First Names of Persons
17. Terrorists
18. Bosses
19. Roommates
20. Student Housing
21. Grandparents
22. Sports Fans
23. Parents
24. Music Lovers
25. Coaches
26. Sexism
27. Television Watchers
28. Junk Mail
29. Marriages
30. Teachers

Note also the Process in Writing topic after each selection in this chapter.

Process in Writing: Guidelines

Follow at least some of these steps in writing your essay of classification (your teacher may suggest which ones).

1. *Write a short outline, since the logic of classifying is difficult. Once you have chosen the principle on which to classify your topic, decide on the categories. Then ask: Do all relate to the same principle? If not, revise. Do any categories overlap? If so, revise. Is an obvious category missing? Add it.*

2. *Write your* THESIS STATEMENT. *Make it a significant point worth discussing.*

3. *Now arrange the categories in some climactic order that supports your thesis statement: smallest to largest, least important to most important, worst to best, etc.*

4. *Write a rapid first draft, not stopping now to revise or edit.*

5. *When this draft has cooled off, look it over. Does it follow the outline? If not, do the changes make sense? Does every part support the thesis statement? If not, revise the parts, the thesis, or both.*

6. *In your second draft sharpen word choice. Add missing* IMAGES *or examples. Heighten* TRANSITIONS. *Cut deadwood.*

7. *Finally, check for things like spelling and punctuation before you print off your best version.*

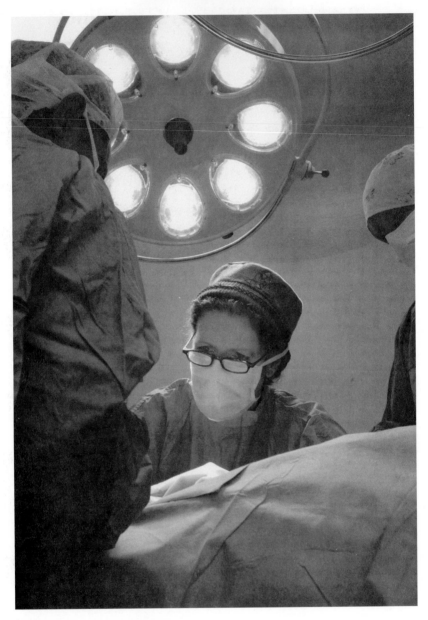

CP/Toronto Star (Andrew Stawicki)

"I look up at the clock on the wall. Three hours and 20 minutes have passed since we cut skin. It seems like 15 minutes. I feel exhilarated and at the same time spent — emotionally and physically."

— *Dr. Mark Bernstein, "Yes, It Is Brain Surgery"*

Process Analysis

HERE'S HOW IT'S DONE . . .

Whenever you enter a large bookstore, it won't be long before you notice titles like these: *Success Without College, How to Make People Like You in 90 Seconds or Less, Think and Grow Rich, Massage Made Easy,* and *The Complete Snowboarder.* Look a little further and you might see *Awaken the Giant Within,* or *Secrets of Power Persuasion,* or *Parenting Your Out-of-Control Teenager.* Then there are the "Idiot" and "Dummy" books: *The Complete Idiot's Guide to Plumbing, The Complete Idiot's Guide to Grandparenting,* and *Italian Cooking for Dummies* — not to mention *Norton for Dummies* and all the other computer titles for still more dummies. Clearly many people want to do things, and there is a great need to learn how. But the writer who tells how has some serious thinking and organizing to do.

Consider the last time you bought something in kit form and tried to assemble it. Maybe you were lucky and everything fit together. But more likely, you were sweating to make out tiny diagrams, to understand terminology you had never heard of, and to follow vague directions with spelling errors, that left out steps or got them in the wrong order. With your new exercise machine or computer desk or amplifier lying in parts on the floor, you wondered if you would *ever* get it together. And when you finally did, mysterious parts were left over.

It doesn't have to be this way. We are not "dummies," but we do need explanations that are clear and easy to follow. And so does your own reader. Writing that tells *how* to do things is often called *process analysis.* Sometimes we write an essay that gives what could be called a *directional* process analysis. It is a sort of *narrative,* taking readers from the beginning to the end of a task, usually in the time order required to grow tomatoes, write a résumé, tune up a car, or do whatever else readers set out to do. It includes every step, for each is vital to the success of the project. And unless it is written for the specialist, it includes all the details right down to the spacing and depth of seeds in the soil, the order of items in your résumé, or the size of the paint brush.

Did you ever eat something so good that you asked for the recipe? An experienced cook has a hard time explaining. Instead of giving quantities, temperatures and measurements of time that we can actually apply, the old pro will say things like "add some yeast" or "now put in a little salt" or "take it out of the oven when it's done." The writer of recipes in a book, though, puts his or her own experience in the background and thinks instead about what the *audience* needs to know. The result is a set of directions so exact that, even if we have never cooked before, the product is likely to turn out.

When you are writing directions, on whatever topic, this is the main challenge: keeping your *audience* in mind. If the subject is your area of expertise, you'll try to take shortcuts, skipping details you assume anyone would know. But remember your own encounter with the kit in the middle of the floor. Explain! And when you write from expertise you'll tend to fill your essay with technical terms. But think of the last time you tried to interpret Revenue Canada's directions on your income tax return. If you estimate your reader's level of knowledge and write accordingly, your directions will probably succeed.

Another kind of process analysis could be called *informational,* for it satisfies not our practical needs but our curiosity. We may wish to know how airliners are hijacked, how stockholders are swindled, how the greenhouse effect causes tornadoes and floods, or how the Second World War was won — knowing we will never do these things ourselves. Not every detail is given in this kind of armchair reading: only as many as it takes to inform and interest the reader. In this chapter Dr. Mark Bernstein tells how he saved a patient's life with a brain operation. His account is not a how-to-do-it set of directions, with the dose of every medication spelled out to the milligram — because he knows we're not going to operate on someone ourselves. But he does relate all the main points, and describes what happens with an almost scary vividness of imagery. He knows his *informational* process analysis will succeed if it keeps us on the edges of our seat.

Occasionally a writer will use the format of process analysis not really to instruct or inform, but as a means to other ends. When Stephen Leacock tells us "How to Live to Be 200," he advises us to eat cement — which seems a strange way to reach the goal, until we realize that his goal is not really longevity but humour.

Whether you aim to help the reader accomplish a task, to satisfy the reader's curiosity, or even just to entertain, your process analysis will work only if you realize *why* you are writing it: Are you giving directions? Then follow all the advice above, so your reader's efforts will be successful. Are you explaining a task that only specialists perform? Then interest the reader with a multitude of examples. Are you even just writing humour, like Leacock? Then do anything that is fun. But even then, you will probably find yourself making a serious point — like Leacock who advises us to enjoy life.

Note: For more examples of process analysis, see these essays in other chapters:

Mordecai Richler, "1944: The Year I Learned to Love a German," p. 146
Hon. David Lam, "Pulling Together," p. 227
Martin Hocking, "Capping the Great Cup Debate," p. 278

DR. MARK BERNSTEIN

Yes, It Is Brain Surgery

Dr. Mark Bernstein is a well-known neurosurgeon, author of some 200 medical papers and a book on brain tumours. Former head of the Division of Neurosurgery at Toronto Western Hospital, he is now Professor of Surgery at the University of Toronto, where he has won awards for his teaching of medical students and neurosurgery residents. He is charismatic as a surgeon, as a teacher — and, as we will see in the essay that follows, as a writer. Though Bernstein's main area of clinical interest is neuro-oncology (brain tumours), he is also concerned with the ethical side of medicine. He recently completed a Masters of Health Science in Bioethics; his main interests in that field are medical error, patient safety, ethical issues of surgical education, surgical innovation and research ethics. Bernstein also promotes the advancement of neurosurgery in the developing world, spending up to a month each year teaching and operating in Indonesia. In addition to his prolific medical publications, a few years ago he began writing "popular" pieces, and by now has published about 60 of them. (Our own selection is one of these, first appearing in the Maclean's *of October 14, 2002.) Reading Bernstein's fast-paced and gripping account of how he and his team saved a life on the operating table, we can begin to share in what he calls "the unbelievable thrill of brain surgery."*

1   Mike is enjoying his son's Saturday morning soccer game and kidding with the other soccer dads on the sideline when he falls over with a sudden headache, as if someone had hit him over the head with a baseball bat. An ambulance takes Mike (for the purposes of this article, a composite of typical aneurysm patients) to a local hospital. There a CT scan confirms a subarachnoid hemorrhage — a bubble on a blood vessel deep in his brain has popped. When he fully comes to, Mike discovers he's been taken to the neurosurgery unit at Toronto Western Hospital. As his neurosurgeon, I try to be as positive as possible as I tell him that an aneurysm that has ruptured in his brain has to be fixed. It's very risky surgery, but it has to be done.

2   Mike's wife sneaks away from the bedside and cries quietly. What would she and the three kids do without Mike, who's just three weeks shy of his 35th birthday? Called in on a Saturday for this emergency, I discuss the situation with my senior resident and the anaesthesiologist, and let the nurses in the OR know to get things set up. The thin blister on

the blood vessel deep in the brain lies in wait for us like a bomb ready to explode and take the patient's life with it. We suit up in our riot gear.

The patient has been anaesthetized and his head fixed in a metal clamp attached to the operating table. The left side of the scalp has been shaved, cleansed and draped in sterile sheets. The operation begins just after noon with a long, curved incision from in front of the ear to above the eye. Then the resident and I cut and peel the scalp and underlying muscle off the bone. Using an air-powered drill and saw, we remove a window of bone the size of a playing card. The brain is tense as we open the dura, the wet, leathery covering. The fluid surrounding the brain is stained from the blood that escaped from the aneurysm when it exploded a few short hours ago.

We peer at the arachnoid membrane, a wispy, translucent skin covering the brain like Cellophane. We can see the Sylvian fissure, cleft between the temporal and frontal lobes. We move the operating microscope into position on its ceiling track and the resident and I adjust our eyepieces. Focusing on the brain's surface, we use small forceps, dissecting tools and scissors to open the Sylvian fissure progressively down to two inches below the surface. Then we use the metal blades of retractors to pull the lobes apart, exposing the optic nerve and, just beside it, the internal carotid artery, one of the large vessels carrying blood to the brain. We have found our blood vessel highway, along which we will gently navigate in search of the enemy.

Step by step we dissect the brain off the carotid artery and exert more retraction. I hear one of the nurses talking about a social commitment she has this evening with her husband. I have been unaware of time and space for the last little while. I quickly wonder what my wife and daughters are doing on this beautiful weekend.

As we get about an inch along the carotid artery, we come to the place where it divides into the anterior cerebral and the middle cerebral arteries. The preoperative angiogram has shown us that the culprit aneurysm is on the middle cerebral. After more painstaking dissection under the operating microscope, we come to the point where that artery divides into many daughter branches. Now we can see the object of our pursuit. The aneurysm, the size of a small olive, is embraced by three good-sized daughter arteries which snake by to fulfill their vital task of providing oxygenated blood to the brain.

An aneurysm is a thin-walled blister that pouches out from the side of an artery because of a defect in its wall. The defect is present at birth, but it usually takes decades for the blister to expand and rupture. The dome of the aneurysm has a thin, transparent wall through which we can see the blood swirling violently. Viewed through the microscope, this is a frightening sight.

The object is to place a spring-loaded metal clip across the base of the aneurysm to exclude it from the general blood circulation and thus prevent rebleeding. If a patient is fortunate enough to survive the first rupture of an aneurysm, the second time is usually fatal. The challenge is to avoid leaving any of the aneurysm wall behind to collect blood, enlarge and bleed again, and to do so without pinching off any other arteries, some the size of a hair, because that could produce a devastating stroke for the patient.

9   So with delicate dissecting instruments we start to define the neck of the aneurysm, the narrow area where the bulb rises out of the artery. We do this by gently getting between the daughter arteries plastered to the aneurysm and the aneurysm itself with fine metal probes. The dissection goes slowly because if you're too rough or too fast, you can rip a hole in the aneurysm, instantly converting a controlled situation into a horrifying, potentially disastrous crisis. Your heart pounds, your eyes strain and every muscle in your body tenses to place your head and hands in a perfect position. Apart from the "beep-beep" of the anaesthetic machine, there is silence in the operating room as we work away.

10   The safest way to get the arteries off the aneurysm, we decide, is to be a bit rougher. First, though, we want to place a temporary clip across the trunk of the middle cerebral artery to decrease the pressure on the aneurysm and to ensure that bleeding would be non-catastrophic if it did rupture during our manipulations. We put the clip on and ask a nurse to monitor the time. Generally one only has a few minutes to work with a clip in place without risking a stroke. We continue to try to dissect off the daughter arteries, but it's tough going — it's like they were glued on. "One minute," announces the nurse. We continue, trying to establish a good enough slot for the clip to cut off the entire aneurysm but spare vital vessels around it. "Two minutes," says the nurse.

11   I'm not happy with our progress and decide to withdraw the temporary clip from the middle cerebral trunk. I become aware of my heart thumping painfully against my breast bone. My throat is dry as a chip as I whisper to my senior assistant, "I guess we'll have to take the bull by the horns and just do this without a temporary clip." I'm really seeking her endorsement and support, rather than dictating strategy.

12   We get up for a moment and walk over to the X-ray viewing monitor to look at the angiogram. We both know this is a stalling tactic to allow us to catch our breath. We return to our posts on either side of the microscope and pick up our weapons. I decide the only way to get a good look at one of the daughter arteries as it passes behind the aneurysm is to move the aneurysm dome with a flat, spatula-like dissector.

13   I picked this technique up from one of my senior, now-retired colleagues who helped me and many other neurosurgeons learn to do aneurysm surgery. It is a risk that has to be taken if we want to get on and clip this aneurysm. I start to gently but firmly retract the aneurysm — and then it happens. The beautiful, crystal-clear but surrealistic view of aneurysm, middle cerebral artery trunk, daughter vessels and brain disappears in a swirling sea of red that rises rapidly toward us. The aneurysm has ruptured.

Blood rushes into our operative field. Although not an uncommon occurrence during this type of surgery, it is truly frightening, something akin to the horror when your car hits a patch of ice and starts to slide at 100 km/h. There are some corrective measures you can take, but the outcome is unpredictable. At this pace of bleeding, the patient could die from blood loss alone in about 60 seconds, yet if we stop the flow too quickly, we could irreversibly injure the brain by damaging vital small arteries. My heart skips a few beats.   14

With two suckers vacuuming the blood, the resident and I work to compress the aneurysm with a bit of cloth about one centimetre square. "You better just put the clip across the aneurysm neck," I say, "and then we'll look around and make sure it's safe." After a few runs with the applicator forceps at different angles, she deftly slips the clip into place. I take the cloth off and there is no bleeding. We then retract the aneurysm to check whether the artery on the other side is free, only to find it squished in the blades of the clip. My heart skips a few more beats.   15

If we left it like this, the patient would have a serious stroke with speech problems and weakness of the right arm and leg. So again I press the cloth back on the aneurysm dome with a sucker tip to prevent bleeding, and the resident removes the clip and repositions it at a slightly different angle. Inspection now reveals that no vital artery has been trapped. The job is done.   16

I gasp and allow my muscles to relax a bit. I ask the anaesthesiologist how the patient is doing and he replies, "Solid as a rock." My head and the resident's move away from the eyepieces of the microscope and we make eye contact. Our brows are furrowed and our faces too stiff to move, but our eyes smile.   17

I look up at the clock on the wall. Three hours and 20 minutes have passed since we cut skin. It seems like 15 minutes. I feel exhilarated and at the same time spent — emotionally and physically. We remove pooled blood from the brain, make sure there are no active bleeding points, remove the retractors, stitch together the dura, replace the bone flap with little metal plates, and close the scalp.   18

Mike was cured. He woke up in fine shape and went on to be discharged a few days later. As he had slept through it all, and his wife did not witness this little war we waged in the operating room, they will never know just how close to death this husband and father had been.   19

• •

Explorations:

Tilda Shalof, *A Nurse's Story: Life, Death and In-Between in an Intensive Care Unit*
Ashish Goel, *Doctors Do Cry*
Oliver Sacks, *The Man Who Mistook His Wife for a Hat and Other Clinical Tales*

http://en.wikipedia.org/wiki/Aneurysm
http://www.ninds.nih.gov/disorders/cerebral_aneurysm/cerebral_ane
urysm.htm

Structure:

1. Not many readers of this essay will ever do brain surgery. So is Dr. Bernstein's *process analysis* any less interesting because it is *informational*, not *directional*? What can an account like this do for the reader? What gives it value? Name a process *you* could write about that probably none of your own readers would attempt, and tell why the piece could be worthwhile for those readers.
2. To what extent is this essay of process analysis also a *narrative*? Point out five TRANSITIONS that speed the action on.
3. How much concrete *description* does Dr. Bernstein give us? What are its effects? Point out five good examples of it.
4. What purposes does the introduction to this essay (paragraphs 1 and 2) accomplish? What does the closing (paragraphs 17–19) accomplish?

Style:

1. If the operation has taken place some time ago, why does Dr. Bernstein write in present tense?
2. A few years ago Dr. Bernstein wrote a medical article entitled "Practice Parameters in Adults with Suspected or Known Supratentorial Non-Optic Pathway Glioma." Do you know what this means? Why does he not use language like this in "Yes, It Is Brain Surgery"? What AUDIENCE does he have in mind for his *Maclean's* essay?
3. In paragraph 9 Dr. Bernstein writes, "Your heart pounds, your eyes strain and every muscle in your body tenses. . . ." Find five more good examples of SENSE IMAGES meant to put us into the scene.
4. In paragraph 2 the author writes, "The thin blister on the blood vessel deep in the brain lies in wait for us like a bomb ready to explode and take the patient's life with it. We suit up in our riot gear." Do you use SIMILES and METAPHORS like these in your own writing? What do they achieve? Point out at least five more good FIGURES OF SPEECH in this selection.

Ideas for Discussion and Writing:

1. Do we often think specialists or experts lack emotion when they go about their work? How do you react to Dr. Bernstein's showing his own emotions? Do you see it as a good sign for the health care system?
2. The author shows us a very positive example of our health care system in action. What has been your own experience with Canadian health care? Describe one example to the class.

3. A major point of debate in Canada is whether our health care system should remain universal, or whether a two-tier system should be allowed, so that those ready to pay for it can buy faster or better care from private sources. What is your view, and why?

4. **PROCESS IN WRITING:** *Think of something you know how to do well (such as a technical procedure, an athletic move, a social task, etc.). Now decide if the act is too difficult for the average person to learn (like brain surgery), or whether it is easy enough. Now accordingly, write the draft of an* informational *OR a* directional *process analysis. Next day look it over. Is the terminology too difficult? If so, revise for your* audience. *Have you shown* vivid *images, as Mark Bernstein does, to spark interest? If not, add. Do time signals speed the chronological steps of your process analysis? If not, add. And if your piece is actual instructions to be followed, have you given every step? Now edit for conciseness and punctuation, then share your* process analysis *with the class.*

Note: See also the Topics for Writing at the end of this chapter.

ALBERT KOEHL

Hockey Etiquette for the Beginner

Albert Koehl is many things: a Maple Leafs fan, a fluent speaker of many lan-
guages, a wilderness canoeist and hiker, a lover of the arts, and a high-powered
lawyer who hunts down and prosecutes corporate polluters. After graduating from
Queen's Law School in 1987, Koehl spent six years as a prosecutor for the Ontario
Ministry of the Environment, served in Guatemala as a volunteer human rights
observer and United Nations investigator and worked in Toronto community legal
clinics. Then in 2001 he joined Sierra Legal Defence, a powerful Canadian envi-
ronmental group that studies existing legislation to find new ways of bringing pol-
luters to justice. As if this were not enough, Koehl has found time to join the boards
of civic organizations for the poor; has run for political office; has travelled across
Africa by box car, bush taxi and barge; has studied Mandarin in China; is fluent
in French, German, Spanish and English — and also writes. (The essay that fol-
lows appeared in The Globe and Mail *of April 21, 2004.) Asked what changes*
he would like to see in his lifetime, Koehl replied, "We need to change our focus from
a right to pollute, to a right to clean air, water, and land. I believe a clean envi-
ronment is as crucial to a child as a good education and good health care."

1   It is a common mistake, especially for theatre, opera, and symphony
lovers, to conclude from the casual attire, beverage choice, and bois-
terous conduct of hockey fans that watching a game is a cultural event
of a lower social order. In reality, the etiquette expected of ice hockey afi-
cionados is quite refined. Ignorance of this etiquette risks turning an invitation to watch an NHL playoff game at the home of a friend, colleague
or business associate, into a social disaster. Fortunately, even the novice
can avoid embarrassing blunders by learning a few simple rules:

2   Arrive on time for the start of a game. Hockey fans may not make you
wait on the porch for the intermission, but if a goal is scored while you are
being greeted your punctuality faux pas may prejudice a future invitation.

3   Cheer for the host's team unless you have announced a contrary affil-
iation in advance, much like a vegan properly reveals a dietary preference before attending a pig-roast fundraiser for the opera. And
cheering for the other team simply because you like the colour of their
jerseys is considered uncouth.

4   Remember, each hockey fan considers his or her role as important to
the team's success as that of the players on the ice. Some fans contribute
to their team by a complex set of superstitions. While guests may not
believe in the power of the hockey gods, they are nonetheless expected
to participate. For instance, if the opposing team takes a lead you may

be asked to change seats. If you refuse, you can be blamed for the team's loss. In a recent game, our team was winning until my brother sent his toddlers to bed. Soon we were down by two goals. It turned out that the children's presence had been key to the team's lead and perhaps the reason they had so vigorously resisted bedtime. "I'll go wake up the kids," I volunteered.

Other fans contribute to the team by intensely concentrating on the game. It would be rude to mock this intensity, much like telling a mesmerized opera lover, "Relax, it's just singin' and yellin'." Hockey fans are willing to suffer tremendous anxiety for their team, even to pay the ultimate price. A recent study found that the anxiety suffered by fans during games sometimes brings on fatal heart attacks. At least the players have the chance to work off their nervous energy — a luxury the fan does not enjoy, except for the odd sprint to greet late arrivals at the door.

If the opposing team scores, quietly gauge the host's reaction. At the very least, allow the host to move uninterrupted through feelings of guilt, denial, anger, and acceptance. Later, it is always helpful to blame the referee, the seating arrangement or bad luck for the team's misfortune. On the other hand, remarking on the skill of the opposing team's scorer can be dangerous and is in any case considered déclassé, like hooting at a sexy stagehand at the theatre.

However, when the home team scores there are few rules to the proper conduct of the celebration, although damaging walls, smashing light fixtures (unless your host is a tenant) or interfering with the electrical cord to the TV are frowned upon. The euphoric mood of the host is also a perfect opportunity for a business associate or friend to bring up a delicate subject, such as the loss of a major contract or running over the family dog on the rush into the driveway to avoid being late.

Conversation during a game is properly limited to superficial topics. Generally, matters that can be answered with "yes" or "no" are acceptable, except during commercial breaks. Attempting to engage the host in a discussion about the war in Iraq, for example, would be like phoning your stockbroker during a symphony. It is worthwhile noting, however, that hockey fans are eager to share their extensive repertoire of trivial statistics. A fan may not remember his wife's birthday but would be happy to field a question such as, "Hey, do you know how much [Maple Leafs Captain] Mats Sundin weighs?" or "How tall is [Calgary star] Jerome Iginla?"

Similarly, telephone calls to a hockey fan during the playoffs are best kept to a minimum and, of course, restricted to the intermission. Never phone a hockey fan after 9:30 p.m. during the playoffs, since an overtime period may be in progress. If in doubt, do not call during evening hours until late June, when the playoffs end.

If the host's team is eliminated from the playoffs, behaviour that is appropriate at a funeral home is expected. For instance, you would never say "Look on the bright side, you still have other relatives." By the same token, clichés like "There's always next season" are not appreciated. Instead they expect the passing of their team from competition to be marked with profound solemnity. In fact, intimacy that might otherwise raise eyebrows is perfectly acceptable. A tender hug, even for a business associate, is remembered with fondness.

11   It is even acceptable for men to weep on the demise of their team. As one caller to a hockey talk show recently admitted, "I have cried only twice in my life, each time when the Maple Leafs were eliminated from the playoffs." To belittle a man at such a time is like mocking a person moved to tears by fair Juliet's plight.

12   By mastering these simple rules, a playoff game can become an enjoyable, even rewarding, cultural experience.

● ●

Explorations:

Ken Dryden, *The Game*
Dave Bidini, *Tropic of Hockey*
Brian McFarlane, *Brian McFarlane's World of Hockey*
http://www.hhof.com/index.htm

Structure:

1. If Albert Koehl's essay is a process analysis, why does he begin paragraph one with a *comparison and contrast?*
2. Point out where else, throughout this selection, Koehl uses comparison and contrast.
3. Where is Koehl's thesis statement?
4. Is Koehl's essay a *directional* or an *informational* process analysis?
5. Does Koehl give his process analysis in the usual chronological order?
6. What common technique of closing does Koehl employ?

Style:

1. Parts of this piece are formal (big words, big sentences, big paragraphs), while other parts are informal ("Relax, it's just singin' and yellin'"). What is Koehl doing through this contrast of styles?

Ideas for Discussion and Writing:

1. One fan in paragraph 11 admits "I have cried only twice in my life, each time when the Maple Leafs were eliminated from the playoffs." Why do spectator sports move us? Tell of the time when you were most deeply affected by watching a sport.

2. Which does more for us, watching a sport or playing it ourselves? Give reasons.

3. Ken Dryden, one of the great goalies of all time, played for the Montreal Canadiens from 1971 to 1979, when they won six Stanley Cups. He also did a law degree (like Albert Koehl), wrote four best-selling books, became president of the Toronto Maple Leafs, then went on to be a federal MP and cabinet minister. Is his a rare story, or do sports build a character and ability that help athletes later in life?

4. Do high salaries, high ticket prices and the recent labour-management conflicts mean NHL hockey is in trouble? Suggest long-term solutions to strengthen our national sport. And do you think hockey will remain our national sport?

5. Paragraph 4 describes typical superstitions of sports fans. Why, in an age of science, do we still believe things like these? Tell your own strongest superstition, and give evidence whether it works or not.

6. Do you prefer watching sports, or going to the symphony, theatre or opera? Or, like Albert Koehl, do you like them all? Argue why or why not.

7. **PROCESS IN WRITING:** *Write a humorous process analysis, like Koehl's, entitled "Concert Etiquette for the Beginner." (The concert may be of any kind, from classical to heavy metal.) Start with a page of notes, then put them in time order and select the best. Are there plenty of actual techniques? How do concertgoers do each thing? (Include such acts as obtaining tickets, entering the hall, finding one's place, enjoying the event, dealing with annoying neighbours, showing appreciation for the performance, etc.) Now do a quick draft. The next day look it over. Are words wasted? Then cut. Do examples fill at least half the essay? If not, add. Is word choice exact? If not, see your thesaurus. Do you move the reader on with transitions such as "first," "then," "next," "at last" and "finally"? Is the punctuation accurate? If not, edit. Finally, read your process analysis, with feeling, to the class.*

Note: See also the Topics for Writing at the end of this chapter.

EVELYN LAU

I Sing the Song of My Condo

At age 18 Evelyn Lau caused a sensation with her memoir Runaway: Diary of
a Street Kid. *She had grown up in Vancouver, in a middle-class conservative
home where her parents had urged her to study hard and become a doctor. From
age 6, though, Lau knew she wanted to be a writer. When her parents ordered her
to stop writing, the honour student left at age 14 for the street, where she spent
several years in prostitution, drug addiction and depression. Then one day she
entered the office of a literary agent with a 900-page diary of her life as a runaway. It was edited down, published in 1989, became a bestseller, then was made
into a two-hour CBC television movie entitled* The Diary of Evelyn Lau. *Today
Lau has left the street, makes a living from writing and has built a reputation as
one of the nation's finest crafters of both poetry and prose. Among her subsequent
publications are* You Are Not Who You Claim *(poems, 1990),* Oedipal
Dreams *(poems, 1992),* Fresh Girls and Other Stories *(1993),* In the
House of Slaves *(poems, 1994),* Other Women *(novel, 1995),* Choose Me
(stories, 1999), Inside Out — Reflections on a Life So Far *(2001), and*
Treble *(poems, 2005). Though Lau's schooling ended at grade 9, she has educated herself through serious reading, paying close attention to the style, even the
sound, of the words on the page. This fine ear for language, and her success in
putting it on her own page, shines through the prose of our selection, which first
appeared in* The Globe and Mail.

1   Late in the spring of last year, my fancy turned to thoughts of real
estate and I joined the growing ranks of Canadians in their 20s
who were looking for their first homes.

2   I had been a renter since I was 16 and I never wanted to deal with a
landlord again. Instead, I wanted to know what it was like to worry if I
spilled wine on my carpet, to agonize over the exact placement of a picture before pounding a nail in my wall, to open a closet door or rest my
forehead against a kitchen cabinet and think, "I own this."

3   I went to the bank with a bundle of tax returns under my arm to pre-
qualify for a first mortgage. After a long meeting during which the bank
manager and I peered morosely at a computer screen and juggled numbers for savings, RRSPs and a writer's erratic income into a yearly figure, I walked out with a brochure titled *Information for First Homebuyers*
in my hand.

4   The people depicted in the brochures were not like anyone I knew.
The women were blond, with sunny smiles, and their husbands looked
both chiselled and paternal. They were engaged in chummy family

activities, like washing the dog or puttering in the garden, with the help of their model children. A white picket fence stood in soft focus in the background.

I knew then I wanted to live in the world of the mortgage brochures, which never showed these middle-class people lying awake among twisted sheets in their new master bedrooms or throwing up into their ceramic sinks from panic at hefty mortgages and rising interest rates. I wanted to sing the love song of the middle class. I wanted this to be the song of myself — a litany of mortgage payments and car payments, the weeping and gnashing at tax time, maximum RRSP payments and mutual funds, credit cards and credit's twin, debt.

Laura Cavanagh, the real-estate agent I acquired through a friend's connections, was an outgoing woman with tanned skin, long hair and hips so slim it seemed impossible she had two teenaged children. The male realtors we met in front of apartment buildings always held her hand for a beat too long and fastened their eyes upon hers with much intent and private meaning.

Together we toured a depressing number of 500-square-foot one-bedrooms listed by young married couples who had just had their first baby. Their apartments smelled of sour milk and spoiled food, and in the bedroom a crib took up whatever space the double bed did not already occupy. The vendor's agent would gamely point out that new carpets weren't that expensive, really, and if I enlisted the help of friends I could easily strip away the velvet-textured and dung-coloured wallpaper. He would flick on all the light switches and then exclaim, "And look at how bright this unit is!"

I became increasingly dejected at what my savings could afford in Vancouver, when I knew the same amount could buy a house, with acreage attached, in Saskatoon. Laura, however, remained true to her business card's slogan — "The realtor with a positive attitude" — and came to my apartment several times a week to show me yet another suite.

Over the months I grew fond of her. She was different from some of the other agents we encountered, who drove gold Mercedes and who staggered about in high heels and silk scarves, arrived late for appointments and then whipped us through the apartment while their pagers and cell phones incessantly beeped and rang. Laura held my hand when I made my first offer — and my second, third and fourth, all unsuccessfully — and comforted me after I had spent another sleepless night over interest-rate calculations.

As summer passed into fall, I discovered that acquiring a real-estate agent was like acquiring a stray kitten or a runaway child — it was a lifetime commitment. She reminded me of little Gertrude in John Cheever's *The Country Husband,* with her uncanny knack of showing up in places I did not expect. I would open my front door on a Saturday morning to pick up the paper and there she would be, showered and perfumed, standing in the hallway and proffering the latest figures on a suite in which I had expressed a moment's interest. See, here's its sales history, its current assessment. Would I like to see it in 15 minutes? She would be wearing such a brave smile that I could only admire her and never find it in my heart to turn her away.

11   Meanwhile, my friends, who were older and therefore wealthier, were actually buying places. I went to a friend's housewarming party with a smile of congratulations on my face and envy in my heart. My former foster parent bought a penthouse with 12-foot ceilings in a new building; another friend purchased an actual house with the help of his well-off parents. I went to a cocktail party at his parents' home, where a hundred guests fit neatly into the kitchen. I was surrounded by half-a-dozen empty bedrooms, Jacuzzis and soaker tubs and murderous chandeliers in the marble foyer. Resentment blazed in me.

12   Now when I walked the streets of Vancouver, I glared up at the high windows of the condominiums and felt the owners were not as special as me, nor as deserving. When I gave poetry readings, I looked out at the audience and wondered how many of them owned their own homes. It came to me that I had rarely wanted anything this much before.

13   One afternoon Laura took me to the opening of a converted building where she said the suites were priced below market value. Balloons were tied to the gates and hedges, and dozens of would-be buyers stood about the grounds, gazing up at the suites with their brochures shielding their eyes.

14   The display suite was bustling with activity — realtors wearing suits and flustered smiles, the women with green eye shadow and trailing a scent of White Shoulders. They paced back and forth with their clients, pulling out calculators to demonstrate price per square foot and the amount of monthly payments. Even as I sat there, someone called out that suite 312 had just been sold and 105 down the hall and they were expecting an offer on 210.

15   The cell phones rang and rang and the anxiety of the buyers became a frenzy of panic. It was a fever that sparked smiles on the faces of the realtors. Offers were recklessly written, and a slim-waisted woman in a floral dress who represented the financing company stepped forward to give or withhold her approval.

16   I was tempted by the display suite, which was small but fully renovated, boasting a marble fireplace and slate tiles. Loden wallpaper in the bathroom was printed with female Greek statues clutching scraps of fabric to their breasts. I realized that the suite was a good bargain, but as I sat on the rented leather couch I found I could not pull out my chequebook and write an offer, not without at least a night's reflection.

17   "In all good conscience, I can say you aren't going to lose money on this one," Laura said, but I was immobilized with terror. An hour later she drove me home. I spent the evening drinking heavily and calculating my finances.

The suite was priced within my range and by the light of morning I 18
had decided I would make my move. I went back to the suite where I had
sat on the couch and looked around my new home — this was where I
would put my desk, my bed. I approached the sales agent — a beefy,
blond man with a distracted air and an incessantly warbling pager —
and said I would buy the display suite.

"Oh. That was sold yesterday," the man said, already turning away. 19

I surprised myself with my own reaction — it was grief. I very nearly 20
heard the crack of my heart breaking. This was not the relief I felt when
one of my previous offers had fallen through; this was my *home* being
taken away.

I stumbled out in a daze and walked the three kilometres home, wip- 21
ing away tears with the back of my hand the whole way. It seemed my
song would be a different one after all, it would be the song of Rainer
Maria Rilke's *Autumn Day:* "Whoever has no house now will never have
one." It was all very well for Rilke — he had owned houses. He had written his famous elegies while staying in Princess Marie von Thurn und
Taxis-Hohenloe's castle. I wished bankruptcy, illness and death upon
whoever had bought my suite.

What surprised me for weeks afterward was how entirely alike this feel- 22
ing of bereftness was to losing the person you love. Somehow, the real,
intelligent, sensible desire to buy a first home and stop paying rent had
mutated over the months into an obsession that was like a woman's
obsession for a man who had deserted her, whom she could love only at
a distance.

When I slept I was tortured by dreams in which I walked through 23
beautiful apartments that were within my price range, then just as I
pulled out my chequebook I would wake up. Several times I dreamed
I bought an apartment with three balcony doors but no balconies, and
I knew that one day I would open the doors, step out and fall to my
death. In another, I had just moved into a new condominium and discovered that with the removal of the previous owner's furniture and
pictures, I could see that the walls were pocked with holes the size of
my fist.

Over the course of a year, my realtor and I saw 50 suites, I sat on 50 24
strangers' sofas, looked into their cupboards, sniffed inside their refrig-
erators, inspected their drapes and light switches. I checked the drains
in their balconies and flushed their toilets. I looked for my own books
on their bookshelves and was dismayed by the rows of American best-
sellers or educational texts I found there. I peered into their closets and
discovered if the owners were people who shopped in vintage stores or
Sears or Holt Renfrew.

Once I saw the apartment of a little old lady whose obsession was tur- 25
tles — troops of ceramic, glass and jade turtles filed across every available counter and desktop. She owned an aquarium of turtles, posters of
turtles, a bedspread with a turtle stitched on it.

26   After 12 months of searching, I no longer believed I would purchase anything soon. I had visions of my realtor and me setting out at the turn of the millennium to look at our 300th suite.

27   When at last I found the right place, it happened so suddenly that the frustrations of the year vanished overnight. I went to an open house on Sunday and on the Monday Laura presented my offer. It was accepted that afternoon. She stopped by to give me the news and when she came down the hallway her eyes were shining.

28   "You have a home now," she said.

29   The rest of the week flashed by in a blur of telephone calls and meetings with the bank manager. I signed contracts, read bylaws and city council meeting minutes and certified deposit cheques. It was so stressful that I felt disconnected from reality. I vacillated between happiness, numb panic and a great, swelling pride. I had never been in debt for anything before, had never even owned a car or a computer, and now here I was committing myself to a $100,000 mortgage for 650 square feet. I had made a decision that was going to affect the rest of my life.

30   I take possession of the suite at the end of June, just days before my 24th birthday. I may never sleep again. But at last I am a homeowner.

● ●

Explorations:

Evelyn Lau,
> *Runaway: Diary of a Street Kid*
> *Other Women* (novel)
> *In the House of Slaves* (poems)
> *Inside Out — Reflections on a Life So Far* (memoir)

http://www.ucalgary.ca/UofC/faculties/HUM/ENGL/canada/poet/
   e_lau.htm
http://www.ryerson.ca/library/events/asian_heritage/lau.html
http://www.athabascau.ca/writers/elau_biblio2.html

Structure:

1. Lau presents her process analysis as a *narrative*, in almost pure chronological order. Identify at least ten words or phrases of TRANSITION (often at the beginnings of paragraphs) that speed us along. Is Lau's organizational choice a good one for her topic of buying a condo?
2. You've just read how Evelyn Lau found and bought her new home. Is her *process analysis* detailed enough that you could now do the same? Or is it more informational than directional? Is it both?
3. In paragraph 22 does Lau go too far in equating a deserted lover with a renter yearning for property? Or has the emotion of her essay risen to the point where this *comparison* works?

Style:

1. Has Lau reached the recommended 50% or higher level of *example* content? In which paragraphs does she offer especially vivid ANEC-DOTES and SENSE IMAGES? If you didn't know, might you guess from this essay that she also writes poetry and fiction?
2. In paragraph 23 Lau uses the device of dreams to portray her own state of mind. How effective is this passage?
3. Read paragraph 24 aloud in class. Where do you hear *repetition*? Does it come across as an error of style, or as a deliberate technique? What effect does it have?

Ideas for Discussion and Writing:

1. In paragraphs 3, 12 and 24, Lau hints at the economic perils of her own career as writer. And if you have read her autobiography *Runaway: Diary of a Street Kid*, you know the insecurities of the life she had escaped not long before writing this essay. Do these facts explain the strength of her desire to own a home? Or does everyone want to be an owner? Do you? What are your own future plans for shelter?
2. In the eighties Canadian real estate prices shot up, then in the early nineties fell by about a third. As of this writing, houses and apartments are rising in value again. Is buying a house or apartment still a good investment? Or is it now more of a lifestyle decision?
3. Lau vividly portrays her real estate agent Laura Cavanagh at work. Now using this example, summarize to the class, in a verbal *process analysis*, how a good agent helps her or his client to find and purchase a property.
4. Are there advantages to renting? Name them. Are there disadvantages? Name them.
5. Lau states that she "had never even owned a car or a computer" (par. 29), yet was now signing a $100,000 mortgage. Is your attitude toward ownership more like that of Lau *before* or *after* her decision to buy real estate? What are your own economic goals as you look into your future?
6. **PROCESS IN WRITING:** *Think about the time you selected and bought one of the following: a computer, a motorcycle, a used car, or a new car. Fill a page with brainstorming. Now look over what you have produced, circle or highlight the best items, and arrange them in a short outline. Do you have all the steps of the* process *you performed? Are they in time order? Do plentiful and exact details — without intimidating jargon — make the* directions *useful to your* AUDIENCE? *Or if not, are there enough* ANECDOTES *and examples* to make *your* informational process analysis *entertaining? Now write a quick first draft. The next day look it over. Has it reached the 50% level of example content? Have you, like Lau, sped your reader on with* TRANSITIONS? *Does the* whole process *rise at the end, like hers, to a* CLIMAX? *Edit for these things, then finally for spelling and punctuation, before you print out your best version.*

Note: See also the Topics for Writing at the end of this chapter.

STEPHEN LEACOCK

How to Live to Be 200

During his lifetime Stephen Leacock became the world's best-known humorist writing in English, a Canadian successor to the American writer Mark Twain. Reading in person, Leacock was so funny that once a member of his audience literally died laughing. Though he was for decades Canada's favourite author, Leacock has slipped into undeserved neglect. Born in England in 1869, at age 6 he came with his family to Ontario. He studied at Upper Canada College, the University of Toronto and the University of Chicago, where in 1903 he received a Ph.D. That year McGill hired him to teach economics and political science, and from 1908 till his retirement in 1936, he served as head of his department. He died in 1944. Leacock wrote over 60 books, many on academic subjects, but of course it is for his books of humour that he is remembered. The best-loved have been Literary Lapses *(1910),* Nonsense Novels *(1911),* Sunshine Sketches of a Little Town *(1912),* Arcadian Adventures with the Idle Rich *(1914) and* My Remarkable Uncle and Other Sketches *(1942). Our selection, from a later version of* Literary Lapses, *is vintage Leacock: through exaggeration and incongruities, it reduces to absurdity a topic that many people, today as in Leacock's time, take seriously. It may be worth noting that Leacock himself shunned the "health mania" to spend large amounts of time enjoying his favourite brandies in the McGill Faculty Club.*

1   Twenty years ago I knew a man called Jiggins, who had the Health Habit.

2   He used to take a cold plunge every morning. He said it opened his pores. After it he took a hot sponge. He said it closed the pores. He got so that he could open and shut his pores at will.

3   Jiggins used to stand and breathe at an open window for half an hour before dressing. He said it expanded his lungs. He might, of course, have had it done in a shoe-store with a boot stretcher, but after all it cost him nothing this way, and what is half an hour?

4   After he had got his undershirt on, Jiggins used to hitch himself up like a dog in harness and do Sandow exercises. He did them forwards, backwards, and hind-side up.

5   He could have got a job as a dog anywhere. He spent all his time at this kind of thing. In his spare time at the office, he used to lie on his stomach on the floor and see if he could lift himself up with his knuckles. If he could, then he tried some other way until he found one that he couldn't do. Then he would spend the rest of his lunch hour on his stomach, perfectly happy.

In the evenings in his room he used to lift iron bars, cannon-balls, 6
heave dumb-bells, and haul himself up to the ceiling with his teeth. You
could hear the thumps half a mile.

He liked it. 7

He spent half the night slinging himself around the room. He said it 8
made his brain clear. When he got his brain perfectly clear, he went to
bed and slept. As soon as he woke, he began clearing it again.

Jiggins is dead. He was, of course, a pioneer, but the fact that he 9
dumb-belled himself to death at an early age does not prevent a whole
generation of young men from following in his path.

They are ridden by the Health Mania. 10

They make themselves a nuisance. 11

They get up at impossible hours. They go out in silly little suits and run 12
Marathon heats before breakfast. They chase around barefoot to get the dew
on their feet. They hunt for ozone. They bother about pepsin. They won't
eat meat because it has too much nitrogen. They won't eat fruit because it
hasn't any. They prefer albumen and starch and nitrogen to huckleberry pie
and doughnuts. They won't drink water out of a tap. They won't eat sardines
out of a can. They won't use oysters out of a pail. They won't drink milk out
of a glass. They are afraid of alcohol in any shape. Yes sir, afraid. "Cowards."

And after all their fuss they presently incur some simple old-fashioned 13
illness and die like anybody else.

Now people of this sort have no chance to attain any great age. They 14
are on the wrong track.

Listen. Do you want to live to be really old, to enjoy a grand, green, 15
exhuberant, boastful old age and to make yourself a nuisance to your
whole neighbourhood with your reminiscences?

Then cut out all this nonsense. Cut it out. Get up in the morning at a 16
sensible hour. The time to get up is when you have to, not before. If your
office opens at eleven, get up at ten-thirty. Take your chance on ozone.
There isn't any such thing anyway. Or, if there is, you can buy a Thermos
bottle full for five cents, and put it on a shelf in your cupboard. If your
work begins at seven in the morning, get up at ten minutes to, but don't
be liar enough to say that you like it. It isn't exhilarating, and you know it.

Also, drop all that cold-bath business. You never did it when you were a 17
boy. Don't be a fool now. If you must take a bath (you don't really need to),
take it warm. The pleasure of getting out of a cold bed and creeping into
a hot bath beats a cold plunge to death. In any case, stop gassing about
your tub and your "shower," as if you were the only man who ever washed.

So much for that point. 18

Next, take the question of germs and bacilli. Don't be scared of them. 19
That's all. That's the whole thing, and if you once get on to that you
never need to worry again.

If you see a bacilli, walk right up to it, and look it in the eye. If one flies 20
into your room, strike at it with your hat or with a towel. Hit it as hard as
you can between the neck and the thorax. It will soon get sick of that.

21   But as a matter of fact, a bacilli is perfectly quiet and harmless if you are not afraid of it. Speak to it. Call out to it to "lie down." It will understand. I had a bacilli once, called Fido, that would come and lie at my feet while I was working. I never knew a more affectionate companion, and when it was run over by an automobile, I buried it in the garden with genuine sorrow.

22   (I admit this is an exaggeration. I don't really remember its name; it may have been Robert.)

23   Understand that it is only a fad of modern medicine to say that cholera and typhoid and diphtheria are caused by bacilli and germs; nonsense. Cholera is caused by a frightful pain in the stomach, and diphtheria is caused by trying to cure a sore throat.

24   Now take the question of food.

25   Eat what you want. Eat lots of it. Yes, eat too much of it. Eat till you can just stagger across the room with it and prop it up against a sofa cushion. Eat everything that you like until you can't eat any more. The only test is, can you pay for it? If you can't pay for it, don't eat it. And listen — don't worry as to whether your food contains starch, or albumen, or gluten, or nitrogen. If you are a damn fool enough to want these things, go and buy them and eat all you want of them. Go to a laundry and get a bag of starch, and eat your fill of it. Eat it, and take a good long drink of glue after it, and a spoonful of Portland cement. That will gluten you, good and solid.

26   If you like nitrogen, go and get a druggist to give you a canful of it at the soda counter, and let you sip it with a straw. Only don't think that you can mix all these things up with your food. There isn't any nitrogen or phosphorus or albumen in ordinary things to eat. In any decent household all that sort of stuff is washed out in the kitchen sink before the food is put on the table.

27   And just one word about fresh air and exercise. Don't bother with either of them. Get your room full of good air, then shut up the windows and keep it. It will keep for years. Anyway, don't keep using your lungs all the time. Let them rest. As for exercise, if you have to take it, take it and put up with it. But as long as you have the price of a hack° and can hire other people to play baseball for you and run races and do gymnastics when you sit in the shade and smoke and watch them — great heavens, what more do you want?

• •

Explorations:

Stephen Leacock,
  Sunshine Sketches of a Little Town
  Literary Lapses
  My Remarkable Uncle and Other Sketches

° hack: a kind of horse-drawn carriage.

Robertson Davies, *Stephen Leacock*
D. Staines, *Stephen Leacock: A Reappraisal*
http://archives.cbc.ca/IDD-1-41-615/sports/fitness
http://schwinger.harvard.edu/~terning/bios/Leacock.html
http://www.library.utoronto.ca/utel/rp/authors/leacock.html
http://www.nlc-bnc.ca/3/5/index-e.html
http://archives.cbc.ca/IDC-1-74-645-3540-20/that_was_then/people/
   stephen_leacock_obit

Structure:

1. This essay has two main parts. Where do they join? How do they differ?
2. We begin with Jiggins. How is his story organized? Were you surprised at his death in paragraph 9? Why? What literary device lies behind this effect? How does the death of Jiggins lead into Leacock's main argument?
3. Are Leacock's health tips given in order of application?
4. What is our first clue that Leacock's *process analysis* is meant more to entertain than to instruct?

Style:

1. Leacock writes "eat" ten times in paragraph 25. Read the passage aloud in class, with feeling. Is the repetition accidental? What effect does it have? In which other paragraph does Leacock exploit repetition?
2. Paragraph 25 states, "That will gluten you, good and solid." What effect does Leacock's unusual use of "gluten" have here?
3. Reduction to absurdity is a comic device Leacock often uses, as in the "bacilli" as insects to swat or as a favourite dog run over by a car. Where else in this essay has he reduced something to total absurdity?

Ideas for Discussion and Writing:

1. Do you have the "Health Habit," like Jiggins, or do you prefer comfort and luxury, like our narrator? Give reasons.
2. Update Leacock's argument for our times. Which kinds of "Health Mania" would you drop? Which would you keep? Which might you add?
3. To women in the class: Why does Leacock refer only to men pursuing the "Health Mania"? Give a *process analysis* of your own actions to keep healthy and fit.
4. **PROCESS IN WRITING:** *Write a* process analysis *of how to reach old age in good health. First brainstorm or freewrite, then do a fast discovery draft. When it has cooled off, analyze it: Are the steps of your process in order? Are the instructions clear for your intended* AUDIENCE? *Have you supplied examples? Revise accordingly. Now sharpen word choice as well. Heighten* TRANSITIONS. *Cut deadwood. Finally, test the prose aloud before printing your best version.*

Note: See also the Topics for Writing at the end of this chapter.

Topics for Writing

CHAPTER 8: PROCESS ANALYSIS

Tell your reader how to perform one of these processes. (See also the guidelines that follow.)

1. Decorate a Room on a Low Budget
2. Survive the School Cafeteria
3. Keep a Dog in the City
4. Do Without a Car
5. Keep an Old Car Running
6. Update Your Wardrobe
7. Avoid Criminal Attack in the Big City
8. Avoid Bear Attacks in the Wilderness
9. Make Friends in a New School
10. Cure Insomnia
11. Fight Pollution in Your Daily Life
12. Get Along in a Blended Family
13. Choose an Apartment
14. Study Better in Less Time
15. Snorkel
16. Avoid Getting Colds or Flu
17. Choose a Used Car
18. Get Along with Roommates
19. Survive as a Homeless Person
20. Protect Yourself Against Terrorism
21. Protect Yourself Against Computer Viruses
22. Choose Your Style in Clothing
23. Avoid Road Rage
24. Enjoy Winter
25. Pay Off a Student Loan
26. Make Wine or Beer
27. Eat Better for Less
28. Control Stress During Exams
29. Flirt
30. Break Off a Romance

Note also the Process in Writing topic after each selection in this chapter.

Process in Writing: Guidelines

Follow at least some of these steps in writing your essay of process analysis (your teacher may suggest which ones).

1. *Spend time deciding which topic you like best, so your motivation will increase your performance.*

2. *Visualize your audience (see step 6 below), and choose the level of terminology accordingly.*

3. *Fill a page with brief notes. Scan and sort them to choose the steps of your process analysis, and their order.*

4. *Write a rapid first draft, not stopping now to revise or edit. If you do notice a word that needs replacing or a passage that needs work, insert a signal so you can find and fix it later.*

5. *When this draft has cooled off, look it over. Are all steps of the process given? Do TRANSITIONS introduce them? In technical topics, have you defined terms that may puzzle your audience? Revise accordingly.*

6. *Now share the second draft with a group of classmates. Do they believe they could actually follow your directions? If not, revise.*

7. *If you have consulted books or periodicals to write this paper, follow standard practice in quoting and in documenting your sources. Remember that plagiarism is a serious offence.*

8. *As you produce your good copy, edit for things like spelling and punctuation before printing off your best version.*

"It is time that I tell the story from where I stood — literally in the middle of the slaughter for weeks on end."

— Lt.-Gen. Roméo Dallaire, with Major Brent Beardsley, "Cri de coeur"

Argumentation and Persuasion

THEREFORE . . .

So far the essays in this book have taken many paths in developing their subject. They have narrated events, they have described, they have explained, and some have entertained. But you have surely realized that in one way or another, whatever else they do, almost all the selections have tried to make a point. After all, an essay without a point is "pointless." The very use of a thesis statement implies a main idea or opinion. In this final chapter, we now focus more closely on how the writer makes that point. The process takes two complementary forms: *argumentation* and *persuasion*.

ARGUMENTATION

This word has a broad set of meanings, but here we will consider it the writer's attempt to convince the reader *through logic*. This stance implies respect: it considers the reader a mature individual capable of independent thought. It assumes the reader will also respect the thoughts of the writer, if those thoughts are presented in a logical way. In summary, the writer and reader are *partners*: since the writer does not play on the reader's emotions, the reader considers the argument with a more open mind. If the logic makes sense, the reader may be convinced.

271

Argumentation through logic takes two opposite forms, *deduction* and *induction*. Let's look at each.

Deduction

Deduction accepts a general principle as true, then applies it to specific cases. For over two thousand years logicians have expressed this process in a formula called the *syllogism*. Here's a well-known example:

Major premise: All men are mortal.
Minor premise: Socrates is a man.
Conclusion: Socrates is mortal.

This chain of reasoning is about as foolproof as any: since no human in the history of the world has yet lived much longer than a century, we feel safe in assuming that no one ever will; therefore "all men are mortal." And since all historical records about Socrates portray him as a man — not, say, as a rock or horse or tree — we accept the minor premise as well. Logic tells us that if both the major and minor premises are true, then the conclusion will inevitably be true as well.

But now let's look at a syllogism whose logic is not as clear:

Major premise: Progress is good.
Minor premise: The automobile represents progress.
Conclusion: The automobile is good.

At first glance the argument may seem all right: it certainly reflects values common in our society. But let's examine the major premise, the foundation on which all the rest is built: is it true that "progress is good"? Well, how do we know until we define "progress"? Is it more jobs? More production? More cars? Higher sales? More consumption? A rising stock market? Or are all these the opposite of true "progress" because our natural resources are dwindling, our highways are choked with traffic, our lakes and forests are dying of acid rain, the greenhouse effect is already disrupting our climate, and around the world several species of life per hour are becoming extinct? Our values will determine our response.

If we cannot agree on what "progress" is, how can we say it is "good"? And how could we go on to our minor premise, saying that "the automobile represents progress"? How could we build even further on this shaky foundation, claiming in our conclusion that "the automobile is good"? Within its own framework the argument may be "valid" (or logical). But only those who accept the original premise will view the conclusion as true. Those who do not will reject it as false.

And that is the problem with deduction: not always can we agree on premises. A thousand years ago society ran almost entirely on deduction: the King or the Church or our parents told us what to believe, and we simply applied those principles to any case that came up. But in our millennium many of us do not accept being told what to think. Not only do many people now question systems of belief such as Marxism or codes of religion, but scientists even question the previously accepted "laws" of nature. How is a person to know what is true? It is therefore no coincidence that most contemporary essays argue not through deduction but through induction.

Induction

We have discussed how deduction applies a general rule to explain particular cases. Induction is the opposite: it first observes particular cases, then from them formulates a general rule. This is the basis of the scientific way, the procedure that enables humans to conquer disease, multiply food production and travel to the moon. It can produce faulty results, just like deduction, but the open mind required to use it appeals to our modern sensibilities. Let's take an example:

> **After a summer in the factory Joan thought she could afford a car, so the week before school began she bought a sporty red three-year-old Japanese model. Speeding around town with the stereo turned up was so much fun that she didn't mind the $350-a-month payments. But when the insurance company hit her for $2800 as a new driver, her savings took a dive. Each month she found herself paying $150 for gas and $200 for parking. A fall tuneup set her back $180, and new tires $500. Then came the repairs: $250 for brakes, $325 for a clutch, $225 for an exhaust system, and $380 for a timing belt. In desperation Joan took a part-time job selling shoes. That helped her bankbook but took her study time. Two weeks after exams, holding a sickly grade report in her hand, Joan decided to sell the car. Nobody could have told her to, since, like most people, she likes to make up her own mind. But the long string of evidence did the teaching: now Joan knows, through *induction*, that as a student she cannot afford a car.**

Induction is not infallible. Conceivably Joan's next car might never need a repair. Next year insurance might somehow drop from $2800 to, say, $75. Gas stations might sell premium for 10 cents a litre, and on Boxing Day a good tire might cost $1.99. Anything is possible. But Joan feels that the consistency of her results — the steady high cost of her car ownership — will *probably* not change. Likewise, the scientist believes that her or his years of research have yielded results that will not be disproved by the very next experiment. But in all humility both Joan and the scientist must consider the new principle not a fact, not an unchangeable law, but simply an idea with a very high probability of being true.

Finally, suppose that Joan analyzes her experience in an essay. If she sets up her paper as most essayists do, we will read her thesis statement near the beginning — even though the principle it states is the *result* of the evidence still to come. This positioning is not a flaw of logic: Joan simply *introduces* the main idea so we can see where we are going, then tells us how she arrived at it, letting her evidence lead inductively toward the main point which will be restated at the end. You will find this pattern at work in several of this chapter's inductive essays, for example the one by Martin Hocking.

You will also find that, although deduction and induction represent opposite methods of logic, sometimes both are used in the same argument (when the writer's original opinion is confirmed by the evidence). This does not necessarily mean weakness in logic either. Another link between these opposites is that most principles which we accept as true, and upon which we base our own deductions, originated in someone else's induction. (Newton arrived inductively at his theory of gravity, through evidence such as the famous apple that fell on his head; almost all of us now believe Newton and his theory without waiting for an apple, or anything else, to fall on our own heads.) Similarly, a conclusion we derive from our own induction could become the premise of someone else's deduction — a link in an ongoing chain of logic. To keep this chain from breaking, the individual has a double task: to check over any links provided by others, then to make her or his own link as strong as possible.

PERSUASION

We have just seen how *argumentation* seeks to convince through logic. But, whether deductive or inductive, is logic enough? Now let's look at the complementary approach of *persuasion*, which attempts to convince through emotion. A century of inductive research into psychology has shown that we humans are seldom rational. Even when we think we are "reasoning," we are often building arguments merely to justify what we thought or felt already. It is possible to write an argumentative essay with enough restraint to be almost purely logical. But to most people the effort is difficult and unnatural, requiring a great deal of revision, and the result may seem cold and uninviting to those who have not spent years reading the almost pure argumentation of scholarly journals. Most professional writers would say that a little feeling and a little colour can help an essay. But how do we take this approach without slipping into dishonesty? Let's look now at the major techniques of *persuasion* — both their uses and abuses.

Word choice: Is a person "slim," "thin" or "skinny"? Is a governmental expenditure an "investment," a "cost," a "waste" or a "boondoggle"? Is an oil spill an "incident," an "accident," a "mistake," a "crime" or an "environmental tragedy"? Essayists tend to choose the term that reflects their feeling and the feeling they hope to encourage in the readers. While deliberate choice of words is one of the central tasks of all writers, including essayists, let's not abuse the process. Bertrand Russell once quipped, "I am firm; you are stubborn; he is pig-headed." If too many of your word choices follow the model of "pig-headed," you will alarm an alert reader and unfairly overwhelm a careless one.

Example: Although examples form the basis of logical induction, they can also add colour and feeling to a persuasive essay. Choose vivid ones. An attempt to show old people as active may be helped by the example of your grandmother who skis. But avoid dubious cases like that of the man in Azerbaijan who is rumoured to have ridden a horse at age 155.

Repetition: Although we try to cut accidental repetition from our writing (as in the case of one student who used the word "tire" 55 times in an essay about, you guessed it, tires), intentional repetition can build feeling. Stephen Leacock builds emphasis by using the word "eat" over and over in paragraph 25 of his essay (see p. 266), and in paragraphs 14–17 of her selection (see p. 293) Joy Kogawa builds feeling by starting a whole string of sentences with the contraction "it's."

Hyperbole (exaggeration): A humorist can exaggerate and get away with it, as Stephen Leacock does when he tells us "How to Live to Be 200." By contrast, an essay with a serious subject should stay strictly with the truth.

Analogy and figures of speech: You have seen in Chapter 6 how we can suggest a point by comparing one thing with another from a different category: a monster with the forestry industry, or a house with a ship at sea. Analogies, and their shorter cousins similes and metaphors, are powerful tools of persuasion; avoid abusing them through name-calling. Think twice before casting a politician as a dinosaur, entrepreneurs as piranhas, or police officers as gorillas. Remember, above all, that neither analogies nor figures of speech are logical proof of anything.

Irony: When in Chapter 2 the poet Goran Simic tells of his job moving clothes in a warehouse; when in Chapter 4 Naheed Mustafa covers herself with the traditional *hijab* in order to be free; when in Chapter 5 Maria Coffey shows how the death of some mountain climbers saved the lives of others; and when in this chapter Rita Schindler "thanks" her son's assailants for not killing him — we feel the power of irony. A writer can use this device for a lifetime without exhausting its emotional power; yet irony lends itself less easily to abuses than do many tools of persuasion, for both its use and its appreciation demand a certain exercise of intelligence.

Appeal to authority or prestige: Opponents of nuclear weapons love to quote Albert Einstein on their dangers; after all, since his discoveries made this hardware possible, he should know. We also invite our reader to believe what a famous economist says about money, what a judge says about law, or what an educator says about education. This approach appeals to our reader's ethical sense: he or she believes these people know the facts and tell the truth. But avoid the common abuse of quoting people on matters outside their competence — a terrorist on peace, a disgraced politician on honesty, or a convicted murderer on religion.

Fright: You can be sure that a frightened reader is an interested reader, for fright is personal: what you say in your essay could be important! Avoid cheap effects, though. Frighten a reader only with facts that really are scary (such as the number of times computer error nearly launched World War III).

Climax: Whatever your argument, don't trail off from strong to weak. After a good introduction, drop to your least important or least dramatic point, then progress upward to your strongest. This very rise produces an emotion in the reader, like that of the concertgoer who thrills to the final dramatic chords of "The Hallelujah Chorus."

PLAYING FAIR IN ARGUMENTATION AND PERSUASION

We have looked at some abuses both of argumentation and of persuasion. Now read the following communication, an actual chain letter that arrived one day in the mail. (Versions of it are also sent on the Internet; you may have seen one.) What attempts does it make at *deduction* or *induction*? Are they logical? What attempts does it make at *persuasion*? Are they fair? (For your information, the person who received this letter did not send it on. So far he has not died or been fired — but then, neither has he won a lottery!)

KISS SOMEONE YOU LOVE WHEN YOU GET THIS LETTER
AND MAKE SOME MAGIC

> **This paper has been sent to you for good luck. The original copy is in New England. It has been around the world nine times. The luck has sent it to you. You will receive good luck within four days of receiving this letter, provided you send it back out. THIS IS NO JOKE. You will receive it in the mail. Send copies to people that you think need good luck. Don't send money as fate has no price. Do not keep this letter. It must leave your hands within 96 hours. An R.A.F. officer became a hero. Joe Elliot received $40,000, and lost it because he broke the chain. While in the Philippines, Gene Welch lost his wife six days after receiving this letter. He failed to circulate the letter. However, before her death she had won $50,000.00 in a lottery. The money was transferred**

to him four days after he decided to mail out this letter. Please send twenty copies of this letter and see what happens in four days. The chain came from Venezuela and was written in South America. Since the copy must make a tour of the world you must make copies and send them to your friends and associates. After a few days you will get a surprise. This is true even if you are not superstitious. Do note the following: Constantine Dias received the chain in 1953. He asked his secretary to type twenty copies and send them out. A few days later he won a lottery of $2,000,000. Aria Daddit, an office employee, received the letter and forgot that it had to leave his hands within 96 hours. He lost his job. Later, finding the letter again, he mailed out twenty copies. A few days later he got a better job. Dalen Fairchild received the letter and not believing, threw it away. Nine days later he died. PLEASE SEND NO MONEY. PLEASE DON'T IGNORE THIS. IT WORKS!

Note: No essay in this chapter adopts a stance of pure logic to the exclusion of emotion, or of pure emotion to the exclusion of logic. The nine essays represent different proportions of both elements, and are arranged in approximate order from most argumentative to most persuasive.

For more examples of argumentation, see these essays in other chapters:

Jan Wong, "Ten Things the Chinese Do Much Better Than We Do," p. 48
David Suzuki, "Hidden Lessons," p. 127
Doris Anderson, "The 51-Per-Cent Minority," p. 160
Jack Layton, "Measuring the New Prosperity," p. 164
Laurence Hill, "Black + White = Black," p. 191

For more examples of persuasion, see these essays in other chapters:

Nathalie Petrowski, "The Seven-Minute Life of Marc Lépine," p. 141
Rafi Mustafa, "The Bond of Nightmares," p.177
Drew Hayden Taylor, "This Boat Is My Boat," p. 182
Samantha Bennett, "It's Not Just the Weather That's Cooler in Canada," p. 208

MARTIN HOCKING

Capping the Great Cup Debate

Few scientists could be better equipped to investigate the subject of our selection than Martin Hocking. With a Ph.D. in organic chemistry from the University of Southampton (1963), experience as research chemist in industry, then extensive research and publication as professor of chemistry at the University of Victoria, Hocking is a prominent voice in his field. He has advised government on scientific issues; has long taught industrial and environmental chemistry; holds many patents in the fields of monomers, process chemistry and medicine; has over 70 scientific papers to his credit; and has published a major reference book: Handbook of Chemical Technology and Pollution Control *(second edition, 1998). It was his comparative analysis in the journal* Science *that in 1991 sparked debate on the environmental effects of paper cups and foam cups. Hocking concluded that, contrary to public opinion, foam was better. Some scientists questioned his emission figures and his view of paper mill energy use; others commended his open revealing of data sources, a practice not all scientists follow, and the relevance of his "cradle-to-grave" scope: from logging the raw resources to discarding the old cups in landfills. Then Hocking adapted his article for a general audience; in 1991* The Globe and Mail *published this selection. In 2000 Hocking again made the news: circulation of fresh air is so slow in the new airliners, he announced in a report, that passengers risk exposure to colds, flu, measles, chicken pox and even tuberculosis. The air industry and the House of Lords reacted angrily, but on the BBC Hocking defended his findings with statistics. Now retired since 2004, Hocking enjoys orienteering and long-distance running.*

1   The polystyrene foam cup has long suffered contempt from an environmentally aware public that assumes paper cups are ecologically friendlier. It's easy to understand why: paper cups are made out of a wood product, a renewable resource, and therefore would seem to be the proper conservationist choice.

2   In fact, foam cups are proving to be the environmentally better choice.

3   For one thing, people overlook the fact that logging necessary for the paper industry has adverse effects on the landscape that range from the construction of roads to clear-cutting practices that typically increase the likelihood of flood and drought in immediate watershed areas.

4   In addition, a review of other factors does not support the use of paper. A comparative analysis of paper versus polystyrene conducted by us at the University of Victoria leads to the inevitable conclusion that foam cups are better from a range of standpoints.

Here are the principal findings of the analysis:

5

Hydrocarbons
The extraction and delivery of oil and gas hydrocarbons have a significant impact on sensitive ecosystems. A polyfoam cup is made entirely
from hydrocarbons, but a similar amount of hydrocarbons are also used
to produce a paper cup.

6

Paper cups are made from bleached pulp, which in turn is obtained
from wood chips. Although bark, some wood waste, and organic residues
from chemical pulping are burned to supply part of the energy required
in papermaking, fuel oil or gas is used to provide much of the rest. Even
more petroleum is needed if the paper cup has a plastic or wax coating.

7

Inorganic chemicals
In the making of paper cups, relatively small amounts of sodium hydroxide or sodium sulphate are needed for chemical pulping makeup requirements, since the recycling of these in the kraft pulping process is quite
efficient. But larger amounts of chlorine, sodium hydroxide, sodium
chlorate, sulphuric acid, sulphur dioxide and calcium hydroxide are
normally used on a once-through basis to the extent of 160 to 200 kilograms per metric ton of pulp.

8

The total non-recycled chemical requirement works out to an average
of about 1.8 grams per cup.

9

Polystyrene is far superior to wood pulp for cup construction; only
about one-sixth as much material is needed to produce a foam cup.
Chemical requirements for the polystyrene foam cup are small because
several of the stages in its preparation use catalysts that nudge the
process along without being consumed themselves.

10

Alkylation of benzene with ethene (ethylene) also uses aluminum
chloride catalytically to the extent of about 10 kilograms per metric ton
of ethylbenzene produced.

11

The spent aluminum chloride is later neutralized with roughly the
same amount of sodium hydroxide. Further small amounts of sulphuric
acid and sodium hydroxide are also consumed to give a total chemical
requirement of about 33 kilograms per metric ton of polystyrene.

12

This works out to 0.05 grams per cup, or about 3 per cent of the chemical requirement of the paper cup.

13

Utility consumption
In terms of energy consumption, polystyrene cups also appear to come
out ahead. One paper cup consumes about 12 times as much steam, 36
times as much electricity, and twice as much cooling water as one polystyrene foam cup, while producing 58 times the volume of waste water.

14

The contaminants present in the waste water from pulping and
bleaching operations are removed to varying degrees, but the residuals
(with the exception of metal salts) still amount to 10 to 100 times those
present in the waste-water streams from polystyrene processing.

15

Air pollution

16   The wholesale price of a paper cup is about 2.5 times that of polyfoam since it consumes more in terms of raw materials and energy. But their respective purchase prices are not so closely linked to the environmental costs of productions and recycling or final disposal. Air emissions total 22.7 kilograms per metric ton of bleached pulp compared to about 53 kilograms per metric ton of polystyrene.

17   On a per-cup basis, however, this comparison becomes 0.23 grams for paper versus 0.08 grams for polyfoam.

Emissions

18   In terms of mass, the 43 kilograms of pentane employed as the blowing agent for each metric ton of the foamable beads used to make polystyrene foam cups is the largest single emission to air from the two technologies.

19   Pentane's atmospheric lifetime is estimated to be seven years or less, about a tenth that of the chlorofluorocarbons formerly used in some foamable beads. Unlike the chlorofluorocarbons, pentane would tend to cause a net increase in ozone concentrations, both at ground level and in the stratosphere.

20   However, its contributions to atmospheric ozone and as a "greenhouse effect" gas are almost certainly less than those of the methane losses generated from disposal of paper cups in landfill sites.

21   If the six metric tons of paper equivalent to a metric ton of polystyrene completely biodegrade anaerobically in a landfill, theoretically the paper could generate 2,370 kilograms of methane along with 3,260 kilograms of carbon dioxide.

22   Both are "greenhouse gases" that contribute to global warming.

Recycling

23   The technical side of recycle capability with polystyrene foam is straightforward. All that is required is granulation and washing, followed by hot-air drying and re-extrusion of the resin for re-use. Though recycled resin may not be used in food applications, this only partially limits the many possible uses for recycled polystyrene products.

24   Such uses are in packaging materials, insulation, flotation billets, patio furniture and drainage tiles.

25   An improved collection infrastructure is all that is needed to make this option a more significant reality and convert this perceived negative aspect of polyfoam use to a positive one.

26   Paper cups use a non–water soluble hot melt or solvent-based adhesive to hold the parts together.

27   For this reason, cups are technically excluded from paper recycling programs because the adhesive resin cannot be removed during repulping.

28   If the paper is coated with a plastic film or wax, this too prevents recycling, at least for renewed paper products.

Final disposal

Polystyrene is relatively inert to decomposition when discarded in land-fill. However, there is also increasing evidence that disposal of paper to landfill does not necessarily result in degradation or biodecomposition, particularly in arid regions.   29

In wet landfills, where degradation occurs, the paper cup produces methane, a gas which has five to 20 times greater global-warming effect than carbon dioxide. Water-soluble fragments of cellulose from the decomposition also contribute biochemical oxygen demand to leachate (any water that percolates through the land-filled waste) from the landfill.   30

Leachate may be treated to remove contaminants to control environmental impact on discharge, or may be lost to surface waters or underground aquifiers (a porous rock layer that holds water) to exacerbate the oxygen demand in these raw water sources.   31

Thus, as a result of our analysis, it would appear that polystyrene foam cups are the ecologically better choice.   32

At the very least, they appear to be no worse than paper in one-use applications, contrary to the instinctive consumer impression.   33

●●

Explorations:

Peter Kruus, *Chemicals in the Environment*
Rachel Carson, *Silent Spring*
http://www.ec.gc.ca/ecocycle
http://communications.uvic.ca/ring/01oct04/air.html
http://news.bbc.co.uk/1/hi/health/1523619.stm
http://www.science.ca/scientists/scientistprofile.php?pID=46
http://www.chemistry.uvic.ca/newsletters/newsletter7.pdf

Structure:

1. How does the opening prepare us for Hocking's argument?
2. Identify the THESIS STATEMENT.
3. Hocking's argument is a model *comparison and contrast* of paper and foam cups, organized *point by point*. Identify each of these major points.
4. Find three passages where Hocking reasons through *cause and effect*.
5. Do the subtitles help? Have you tried subtitles yourself?

Style:

1. What AUDIENCE does Hocking write for in this condensation of a scientific journal article? Are the many technical terms a barrier to these readers? Are they to you? Why or why not?

Argumentation and Persuasion:

1. Written by a scientist, "Capping the Great Cup Debate" is the most *argumentative* essay of this chapter. Can you find any passage at all that appeals to *emotion* rather than *reason*? Does all the logic reduce your interest in this essay, or does the quality of thought increase it?
2. As the introduction to this chapter suggests, science is based on *induction*. In saying "A comparative analysis . . . leads to the inevitable conclusion that foam cups are better," (paragraph 4), scientist Martin Hocking in fact labels his argument as *inductive*. Is he right? How fully does he base his conclusion on evidence? Does he successfully avoid reasoning from prior values or assumptions?
3. How much of this argument consists of *examples*? How many are numeric (statistics)?
4. *Comparison and contrast, cause and effect,* massive *examples* and *process analysis* all help Hocking make his point. Do you think he planned to use these all, or did some just appear as he wrote? How fully *should* we organize before writing?

Ideas for Discussion and Writing:

1. Did you think paper cups were better for the environment? Do you still, or did Hocking change your mind? Tell why.
2. "Think globally, act locally," say environmentalists. Consider the pollution caused by disposable pens, lighters, razors, towels and tissues, plastic wrap, diapers, paper plates — and cups, whether paper or foam. What "acts" could you perform to help "globally"?
3. Name one act you already perform to reduce pollution.
4. Is science outside the realm of values? Or are scientists responsible for the good and bad effects of their discoveries? Defend your view with examples, including Hocking.
5. Which is more important to you right now, the economy or the environment? Which will seem more important by the time you have grandchildren? What implications can you *deduce* from your answer?
6. **PROCESS IN WRITING:** *At the library, read and take notes on how vitamin C affects humans, making sure your* evidence *comes from the work of scientists, not health faddists. Let this collected evidence lead to your* THESIS STATEMENT: *whether or not taking large doses of vitamin C improves our health. Now write your* argument *of* induction, *using any form(s) of organization that work, but basing your argument very heavily on evidence. (Your teacher may advise whether to document informally or use full MLA style.) Proofread any quotations word for word against the originals, and be sure to enclose them, even short phrases of two or three words, in quotation marks. Now read your draft aloud. Does its* STYLE *promote thought or does it promote feeling? Replace any loaded or very* INFORMAL *words with more* OBJECTIVE *ones. State your* conclusion *clearly. Finally, edit for things like spelling and punctuation as you produce the final version.*

Note: See also the Topics for Writing at the end of this chapter.

KILDARE DOBBS

The Scar*

Kildare Dobbs was born in Meerut, Uttar Pradesh, India in 1923, was educated in Ireland, then during World War II spent five years in the Royal Navy. After the war he joined the British Colonial Service in Tanganyika, then, after earning an M.A. at Cambridge, came in 1952 to Canada. Dobbs has been a teacher, editor for Macmillan, *managing editor of* Saturday Night, *and book editor of the* Toronto Star. *He was one of the founders, in 1956, of the* Tamarack Review. *He is also the author of numerous books, among them* Running to Paradise *(essays, 1962, winner of the Governor General's Award);* Canada *(an illustrated travel book, 1964);* Reading the Time *(essays, 1968);* The Great Fur Opera *(a comic history of the Hudson's Bay Company, 1970);* Pride and Fall *(short fiction, 1981);* Anatolian Suite *(travel, 1989);* Ribbon of Highway *(travel, 1992);* The Eleventh Hour: Poems for the Third Millennium *(1997);* Casablanca, the Poem *(1997); and* Historic Canada *(1998). Many of Dobbs' books are about far places, whether travel writing, serious analysis, or both mixed. In a millennium project he visited 24 countries, logging over 27,000 miles, filing regular reports by satellite to the CBC. Our own selection, from* Reading the Time, *tells of an event Dobbs was not there to see, yet the vivid details that support his argument show all too clearly what that tragedy must have been like.*

This is the story I was told in 1963 by Emiko Okamoto, a young Japanese woman who had come to live in Toronto. She spoke through an interpreter, since at that time she knew no English. It is Emiko's story, although I have had to complete it from other sources.

But why am I telling it? Everyone knows how terrible this story is. Everyone knows the truth of what von Clausewitz said: "Force to meet force arms itself with the inventions of art and science." First the bow-and-arrow, then Greek fire, gunpowder, poison-gas — and so on up the lethal scale. These things, we're told, should be considered calmly. No sweat — we should think about the unthinkable, or so Herman Kahn suggests, dispassionately. And he writes: "We do not expect illustrations in a book of surgery to be captioned 'Good health is preferable to this kind of cancer.' Excessive comments such as 'And now there is a lot of blood' or 'This particular cut really hurts' are out of place. . . . To dwell on such things is morbid." Perhaps the answer to Herman Kahn is that if surgeons hadn't dwelt on those things we wouldn't now have anaesthetics, or artery forceps either, for that matter.

---

* Editor's title.

3 To think about thermonuclear war in the abstract is obscene. To think about any kind of warfare with less than the whole of our mind and imagination is obscene. This is the worst treason.

4 Before that morning in 1945 only a few conventional bombs, none of which did any great damage, had fallen on the city. Fleets of U.S. bombers had, however, devastated many cities round about, and Hiroshima had begun a program of evacuation which had reduced its population from 380,000 to some 245,000. Among the evacuees were Emiko and her family.

5 "We were moved out to Otake, a town about an hour's train-ride out of the city," Emiko told me. She had been a fifteen-year-old student in 1945. Fragile and vivacious, versed in the gentle traditions of the tea ceremony and flower arrangement, Emiko still had an air of the frail school-child when I talked with her. Every day, she and her sister Hideko used to commute into Hiroshima to school. Hideko was thirteen. Their father was an antique-dealer and he owned a house in the city, although it was empty now. Tetsuro, Emiko's thirteen-year-old brother, was at the Manchurian front with the Imperial Army. Her mother was kept busy looking after the children, for her youngest daughter Eiko was sick with heart trouble, and rations were scarce. All of them were undernourished.

6 The night of August 5, 1945, little Eiko was dangerously ill. She was not expected to live. Everybody took turns watching by her bed, soothing her by massaging her arms and legs. Emiko retired at 8:30 (most Japanese people go to bed early) and at midnight was roused to take her turn with the sick girl. At 2 a.m. she went back to sleep.

7 While Emiko slept, the *Enola Gay*, a U.S. B-29 carrying the world's first operational atom bomb, was already in the air. She had taken off from the Pacific island of Iwo Jima at 1:45 a.m., and now Captain William Parsons, U.S.N. ordnance expert, was busy in her bomb-hold with the final assembly of Little Boy. Little Boy looked much like an outsize T.N.T. block-buster but the crew knew there was something different about him. Only Parsons and the pilot, Colonel Paul Tibbets, knew exactly in what manner Little Boy was different. Course was set for Hiroshima.

8 Emiko slept.

9 On board the *Enola Gay* co-pilot Captain Robert Lewis was writing up his personal log. "After leaving Iwo," he recorded, "we began to pick up some low stratus and before very long we were flying on top of an under-cast. Outside of a thin, high cirrus and the low stuff, it's a very beautiful day."

10 Emiko and Hideko were up at six in the morning. They dressed in the uniform of their women's college — white blouse, quilted hat, and black skirt — breakfasted and packed their aluminum lunch-boxes with white rice and eggs. These they stuffed into their shoulder bags as they hurried for the seven-o'clock train to Hiroshima. Today there would be no classes. Along with many women's groups, high school students, and others, the sisters were going to work on demolition. The city had begun a project of clearance to make fire-breaks in its downtown huddle of wood and paper buildings.

It was a lovely morning.   11

While the two young girls were at breakfast, Captain Lewis, over the   12
Pacific, had made an entry in his log. "We are loaded. The bomb is now
alive, and it's a funny feeling knowing it's right in back of you. Knock
wood!"

In the train Hideko suddenly said she was hungry. She wanted to eat   13
her lunch. Emiko dissuaded her: she'd be much hungrier later on. The
two sisters argued, but Hideko at last agreed to keep her lunch till later.
They decided to meet at the main station that afternoon and catch the
five-o'clock train home. By now they had arrived at the first of
Hiroshima's three stations. This was where Hideko got off, for she was to
work in a different area from her sister. "Sayonara!" she called.
"Goodbye." Emiko never saw her again.

There had been an air-raid at 7 a.m., but before Emiko arrived at   14
Hiroshima's main station, two stops farther on, the sirens had sounded
the all-clear. Just after eight, Emiko stepped off the train, walked through
the station, and waited in the morning sunshine for her streetcar.

At about the same moment Lewis was writing in his log. "There'll be   15
a short intermission while we bomb our target."

It was hot in the sun. Emiko saw a class-mate and greeted her. Together   16
they moved back into the shade of a high concrete wall to chat. Emiko
looked up at the sky and saw, far up in the cloudless blue, a single B-29.

It was exactly 8:10 a.m. The other people waiting for the streetcar saw   17
it too and began to discuss it anxiously. Emiko felt scared. She felt that
at all costs she must go on talking to her friend. Just as she was thinking
this, there was a tremendous greenish-white flash in the sky. It was far
brighter than the sun. Emiko afterwards remembered vaguely that there
was a roaring or a rushing sound as well, but she was not sure, for just at
that moment she lost consciousness.

"About 15 seconds after the flash," noted Lewis, 30,000 feet high and   18
several miles away, "there were two very distinct slaps on the ship from
the blast and the shock wave. That was all the physical effect we felt. We
turned the ship so that we could observe the results."

When Emiko came to, she was lying on her face about forty feet away   19
from where she had been standing. She was not aware of any pain. Her
first thought was: "I'm alive!" She lifted her head slowly and looked
about her. It was growing dark. The air was seething with dust and
black smoke. There was a smell of burning. Emiko felt something
trickle into her eyes, tasted it in her mouth. Gingerly she put a hand
to her head, then looked at it. She saw with a shock that it was covered
with blood.

She did not give a thought to Hideko. It did not occur to her that   20
her sister who was in another part of the city could possibly have been
in danger. Like most of the survivors, Emiko assumed she had been
close to a direct hit by a conventional bomb. She thought it had fallen
on the post-office next to the station. With a hurt child's panic, Emiko,

streaming with blood from gashes in her scalp, ran blindly in search of her mother and father.

21   The people standing in front of the station had been burned to death instantly (a shadow had saved Emiko from the flash). The people inside the station had been crushed by falling masonry. Emiko heard their faint cries, saw hands scrabbling weakly from under the collapsed platform. All around her the maimed survivors were running and stumbling away from the roaring furnace that had been a city. She ran with them toward the mountains that ring the landward side of Hiroshima.

22   From the *Enola Gay*, the strangers from North America looked down at their handiwork. "There, in front of our eyes," wrote Lewis, "was without a doubt the greatest explosion man had ever witnessed. The city was nine-tenths covered with smoke of a boiling nature, which seemed to indicate buildings blowing up, and a large white cloud which in less than three minutes reached 30,000 feet, then went to at least 50,000 feet."

23   Far below, on the edge of this cauldron of smoke, at a distance of some 2,500 yards from the blast's epicentre, Emiko ran with the rest of the living. Some who could not run limped or dragged themselves along. Others were carried. Many, hideously burned, were screaming with pain; when they tripped they lay where they had fallen. There was a man whose face had been ripped open from mouth to ear, another whose forehead was a gaping wound. A young soldier was running with a foot-long splinter of bamboo protruding from one eye. But these, like Emiko, were the lightly wounded.

24   Some of the burned people had been literally roasted. Skin hung from their flesh like sodden tissue paper. They did not bleed but plasma dripped from their seared limbs.

25   The *Enola Gay*, mission completed, was returning to base. Lewis sought words to express his feelings, the feelings of all the crew. "I might say," he wrote, "I might say 'My God! What have we done?'"

26   Emiko ran. When she had reached the safety of the mountain she remembered that she still had her shoulder bag. There was a small first-aid kit in it and she applied ointment to her wounds and to a small cut in her left hand. She bandaged her head.

27   Emiko looked back at the city. It was a lake of fire. All around her the burned fugitives cried out in pain. Some were scorched on one side only. Others, naked and flayed, were burned all over. They were too many to help and most of them were dying. Emiko followed the walking wounded along a back road, still delirious, expecting suddenly to meet her father and mother.

28   The thousands dying by the roadside called feebly for help or water. Some of the more lightly injured were already walking in the other direction, back towards the flames. Others, with hardly any visible wounds, stopped, turned ashy pale, and died within minutes. No one knew then that they were victims of radiation.

29   Emiko reached the suburb of Nakayama.

Far off in the *Enola Gay*, Lewis, who had seen none of this, had been 30 writing, "If I live a hundred years, I'll never get those few minutes out of my mind. Looking at Captain Parsons, why he is as confounded as the rest, and he is supposed to have known everything and expected this to happen. . . ."

At Nakayama, Emiko stood in line at a depot where riceballs were 31 being distributed. Though it distressed her that the badly maimed could hardly feed themselves, the child found she was hungry. It was about 6 p.m. now. A little farther on, at Gion, a farmer called her by name. She did not recognize him, but it seemed he came monthly to her home to collect manure. The farmer took Emiko by the hand, led her to his own house, where his wife bathed her and fed her a meal of white rice. Then the child continued on her way. She passed another town where there were hundreds of injured. The dead were being hauled away in trucks. Among the injured a woman of about forty-five was waving frantically and muttering to herself. Emiko brought this woman a little water in a pumpkin leaf. She felt guilty about it; the schoolgirls had been warned not to give water to the seriously wounded. Emiko comforted herself with the thought that the woman would die soon anyway.

At Koi, she found standing-room in a train. It was heading for Otake 32 with a full load of wounded. Many were put off at Ono, where there was a hospital; and two hours later the train rolled into Otake station. It was around 10 p.m.

A great crowd had gathered to look for their relations. It was a night- 33 mare, Emiko remembered years afterwards; people were calling their dear kinfolk by name, searching frantically. It was necessary to call them by name, since most were so disfigured as to be unrecognizable. Doctors in the town council offices stitched Emiko's head-wounds. The place was crowded with casualties lying on the floor. Many died as Emiko watched.

The town council authorities made a strange announcement. They 34 said a new and mysterious kind of bomb had fallen in Hiroshima. People were advised to stay away from the ruins.

Home at midnight, Emiko found her parents so happy to see her that 35 they could not even cry. They could only give thanks that she was safe. Then they asked, "Where is your sister?"

For ten long days, while Emiko walked daily one and a half miles to 36 have her wounds dressed with fresh gauze, her father searched the rub- ble of Hiroshima for his lost child. He could not have hoped to find her alive. All, as far as the eye could see, was a desolation of charred ashes and wreckage, relieved only by a few jagged ruins and by the seven estuarial rivers that flowed through the waste delta. The banks of these rivers were covered with the dead and in the rising tidal waters floated thousands of corpses. On one broad street in the Hakushima district the crowds who had been thronging there were all naked and scorched cadavers. Of thousands of others there was no trace at all. A fire several times hotter than the surface of the sun had turned them instantly to vapour.

37   On August 11 came the news that Nagasaki had suffered the same fate as Hiroshima; it was whispered that Japan had attacked the United States mainland with similar mysterious weapons. With the lavish circumstantiality of rumour, it was said that two out of a fleet of six-engined trans-Pacific bombers had failed to return. But on August 15, speaking for the first time over the radio to his people, the Emperor Hirohito announced his country's surrender. Emiko heard him. No more bombs! she thought. No more fear! The family did not learn till June the following year that this very day young Tetsuro had been killed in action in Manchuria.

38   Emiko's wounds healed slowly. In mid-September they had closed with a thin layer of pinkish skin. There had been a shortage of antiseptics and Emiko was happy to be getting well. Her satisfaction was short-lived. Mysteriously she came down with diarrhoea and high fever. The fever continued for a month. Then one day she started to bleed from the gums, her mouth and throat become acutely inflamed, and her hair started to fall out. Through her delirium the child heard the doctors whisper by her pillow that she could not live. By now the doctors must have known that ionizing radiation caused such destruction of the blood's white cells that victims were left with little or no resistance against infection.

39   Yet Emiko recovered.

40   The wound on her hand, however, was particularly troublesome and did not heal for a long time.

41   As she got better, Emiko began to acquire some notion of the fearful scale of the disaster. Few of her friends and acquaintances were still alive. But no one knew precisely how many had died in Hiroshima. To this day the claims of various agencies conflict.

42   According to General Douglas MacArthur's headquarters, there were 78,150 dead and 13,083 missing. The United States Atomic Bomb Casualty Commission claims there were 79,000 dead. Both sets of figures are probably far too low. There's reason to believe that at the time of the surrender Japanese authorities lied about the number of survivors, exaggerating it to get extra medical supplies. The Japanese welfare ministry's figures of 260,000 dead and 163,263 missing may well be too high. But the very order of such discrepancies speaks volumes about the scale of the catastrophe. The dead were literally uncountable.

43   This appalling toll of human life had been exacted from a city that had been prepared for air attack in a state of full wartime readiness. All civil-defence services had been overwhelmed from the first moment and it was many hours before any sort of organized rescue and relief could be put into effect.

44   It's true that single raids using so-called conventional weapons on other cities such as Tokyo and Dresden inflicted far greater casualties. And that it could not matter much to a victim whether he was burnt alive by a fire-storm caused by phosphorus, or by napalm or by nuclear

fission. Yet in the whole of human history so savage a massacre had never before been inflicted with a single blow. And modern thermonuclear weapons are upwards of 1,000 times more powerful and deadly than the Hiroshima bomb.

The white scar I saw on Emiko's small, fine-boned hand was a tiny 45 metaphor, a faint but eloquent memento.

• •

Explorations:

Kildare Dobbs, *Reading the Time*
John Hershey, *Hiroshima*
Ernie Regehr and Simon Rosenblum, eds., *The Road to Peace*
John Whittier Treat, *Writing Ground Zero: Japanese Literature and the Atomic Bomb*
http://www.csi.ad.jp/ABOMB
http://www.dannen.com/decision
http://www.lclark.edu/~history/HIROSHIMA
http://www.doug-long.com
http://www.dannen.com/hiroshima_links.html

Structure:

1. Identify Dobbs' THESIS STATEMENT, the principle from which his argument is *deduced*. In what very direct way does the rest of this selection teach us to apply that principle?
2. "The Scar" is mostly a *narrative*, in fact two parallel narratives. How do the stories of Emiko and of Captain Lewis complement each other? How does each focus differently on nuclear war?
3. Dobbs' argument is a short essay enclosing a long narrative. Where does each part join the next? And what is the strategy behind this plan?

Style:

1. In his log Captain Lewis writes "it's a very beautiful day" (par. 9), and in paragraph 11 Dobbs adds "It was a lovely morning." What effect do these pleasant words have in the context of the situation? What literary device underlies their power?
2. Captain Lewis writes in his log, "There'll be a short intermission while we bomb our target" (par. 15). Do these words seem peculiar? If so, why?
3. In referring to the first operational nuclear bomb as "Little Boy" (par. 7), what does Dobbs add to the force of his narrative?

4. Paragraphs 23, 24, 27 and 36 are filled with gruesome details that show the effects of "Little Boy." Does this help Dobbs' argument? Do these details spur the reader to oppose nuclear weapons? Or, in their dreadfulness, do they lead the reader to drop the subject and think of other things?
5. What qualifies the SYMBOL of Emiko's scar to close the essay?

Argumentation and Persuasion:

1. Dobbs' argument is *deductive*, based on his opening premise that "To think about thermonuclear war in the abstract is obscene. To think about any kind of warfare with less than the whole of our mind and imagination is obscene. This is the worst treason" (par. 3). Identify five passages where he shuns abstraction to dwell on the CONCRETE and personal experience of nuclear war. Does he apply his own thesis by using "the whole of [his] mind and imagination"?
2. Point out three passages where Dobbs shows Captain Lewis' abstract view of nuclear war to be "obscene." Does the *contrast* between Lewis' bird's-eye view and Emiko's ground-level view develop Dobbs' premise?
3. Does Dobbs make his point mostly through *argumentation* or *persuasion*? To what extent does he *argue* through objective logic, fact, and example? To what extent does he *persuade* through IRONY, loaded words, fright or other appeals to emotion?
4. In the closing, why does Dobbs shift from specific examples to generalizations and statistics (pars. 42–44)?

Ideas for Discussion and Writing:

1. Albert Einstein, discoverer of the mathematics behind the atomic bomb, said that if he had foreseen the results of his work, he would have chosen to be a shoemaker. Do you hold Einstein and the scientists who worked on "Little Boy" responsible for the carnage in Hiroshima? Or should the scientist pursue abstract truth and leave the application to others?
2. The Cold War and the Arms Race between East and West are said to be over. Can we stop dreading nuclear weapons and war now? How dangerous is the new post-9/11 terrorism compared to the old arms race? Give *examples.*
3. In her book *A Matter of Survival: Canada in the 21st Century*, the Canadian economist Diane Francis states, "Already a global government has formed through the auspices of the United Nations and the G-7 process." Do you believe her? Would a true global government prevent war? To what extent could you see Canada functioning as the "police" of a future global government, through its peacekeeping missions?

4. **PROCESS IN WRITING:** *Politicians often state that one letter received from a citizen is worth a thousand votes. Decide whether you think Canada should spend more or less on its military. Now write to the Minister of Defence, arguing your point* deductively. *Apply your premise to a specific example or examples, such as tanks, fighter planes, submarines, destroyers, military bases, the pay rate of personnel, etc. As you look over your "discovery draft," see whether you have specialized in either* argumentation *or* persuasion. *If your treatment seems too extreme, modify it in your second draft with a dose of the other approach, to produce a combined treatment like that of Dobbs. In your final draft edit for conciseness (the best letters to politicians are short). Finally, send your email or letter (you need no stamp to mail a letter to any member of Parliament).*

Note: See also the Topics for Writing at the end of this chapter.

JOY KOGAWA

Grinning and Happy*

With three published books of poetry to her credit — The Splintered Moon (1967), A Choice of Dreams *(1974) and* Jericho Road *(1977) — Joy Kogawa had become a respected minor poet. But in 1981 she created a sensation with her first novel.* Obasan *represented a new step for Kogawa as a writer and as a person: in it she explored her own past and one of the most dubious events of Canadian history. Born in Vancouver in 1935, Kogawa was a child during World War II when the federal government classified Japanese-Canadians as "enemy aliens." Her parents' house in Vancouver was seized, and the family was moved first to a relocation camp in Slocan, B.C., then to the sugar-beet fields of southern Alberta, which are the setting of our selection from the novel. Our narrator is modelled after Kogawa herself, Stephen is the narrator's brother, Obasan is the narrator's silent and suffering aunt, and "Aunt Emily" is modelled after Muriel Kitagawa, a Japanese-Canadian activist whose letters Kogawa studied in the National Archives in Ottawa. These same characters returned in* Naomi's Road *(1986), a children's adaptation of* Obasan, *then in Kogawa's 1992 sequel for adults* Itsuka, *about the struggle of Japanese-Canadians to gain redress for the wrongs described in* Obasan. *Her third novel,* The Rain Ascends *(1995), looked to new subject matter, the unmasking of a respected Protestant minister as a sexual abuser of children. Yet its themes echo those of* Obasan *and* Itsuka, *as the sins of the fathers are visited upon new generations. Then in 2000 appeared another book of poems,* A Song of Lilith, *and in 2003 her selected poems,* A Garden of Anchors. *Though her recent work is well regarded, it is still* Obasan *that places Kogawa among our major Canadian writers.*

1   There is a folder in Aunt Emily's package containing only one newspaper clipping and an index card with the words "Facts about evacuees in Alberta." The newspaper clipping has a photograph of one family, all smiles, standing around a pile of beets. The caption reads: "Grinning and Happy."

2   **Find Jap Evacuees Best Beet Workers
    Lethbridge, Alberta, Jan. 22.**

3   **Japanese evacuees from British Columbia supplied the labour for 65% of Alberta's sugar beet acreage last year, Phil Baker, of Lethbridge, president of the Alberta Sugar Beet Growers Association, stated today.**

---

* Editor's title.

"They played an important part in producing our all-time record   4
crop of 363,000 tons of beets in 1945," he added.

Mr. Baker explained Japanese evacuees worked 19,500 acres of   5
beets and German prisoners of war worked 5,000 acres. The
labour for the remaining 5,500 acres of Alberta's 30,000 acres of
sugar beets was provided by farmers and their families. Some of
the heaviest beet yields last year came from farms employing
Japanese evacuees.

Generally speaking, Japanese evacuees have developed into   6
most efficient beet workers, many of them being better than the
transient workers who cared for beets in southern Alberta before
Pearl Harbor. . . .

Facts about evacuees in Alberta? The fact is I never got used to it and   7
I cannot, I cannot bear the memory. There are some nightmares from
which there is no waking, only deeper and deeper sleep.

There is a word for it. Hardship. The hardship is so pervasive, so   8
inescapable, so thorough it's a noose around my chest and I cannot
move any more. All the oil in my joints has drained out and I have been
invaded by dust and grit from the fields and mud is in my bone marrow.
I can't move any more. My fingernails are black from scratching the
scorching day and there is no escape.

Aunt Emily, are you a surgeon cutting at my scalp with your folders   9
and your filing cards and your insistence on knowing all? The memory
drains down the sides of my face, but it isn't enough, is it? It's your
hands in my abdomen, pulling the growth from the lining of my
walls, but bring back the anaesthetist turn on the ether clamp down the
gas mask bring on the chloroform when will this operation be over
Aunt Em?

Is it so bad?   10

Yes.   11

Do I really mind?   12

Yes, I mind. I mind everything. Even the flies. The flies and flies and   13
flies from the cows in the barn and the manure pile — all the black flies
that curtain the windows, and Obasan with a wad of toilet paper, spish,
then with her bare hands as well, grabbing them and their shocking
white eggs and the mosquitoes mixed there with the other insect corpses
around the base of the gas lamp.

It's the chicken coop "house" we live in that I mind. The uninsulated   14
unbelievable thin-as-a-cotton-dress hovel never before inhabited in winter by human beings. In summer it's a heat trap, an incubator, a dry
sauna from which there is no relief. In winter the icicles drip down the
inside of the windows and the ice is thicker than bricks at the ledge. The
only place that is warm is by the coal stove where we rotate like chickens
on a spit and the feet are so cold they stop registering. We eat cloves of
roasted garlic on winter nights to warm up.

15   It's the bedbugs and my having to sleep on the table to escape the nightly attack, and the welts over our bodies. And all the swamp bugs and the dust. It's Obasan uselessly packing all the cracks with rags. And the muddy water from the irrigation ditch which we strain and settle and boil, and the tiny carcasses of water creatures at the bottom of the cup. It's walking in winter to the reservoir and keeping the hole open with the axe and dragging up the water in pails and lugging it back and sometimes the water spills down your boots and your feet are red and itchy for days. And it's everybody taking a bath in the round galvanized tub, then Obasan washing clothes in the water after and standing outside hanging the clothes in the freezing weather where everything instantly stiffens on the line.

16   Or it's standing in the beet field under the maddening sun, standing with my black head a sun-trap even though it's covered, and lying down in the ditch, faint, and the nausea in waves and the cold sweat, and getting up and tackling the next row. The whole field is an oven and there's not a tree within walking distance. We are tiny as insects crawling along the grill and there is no protection anywhere. The eyes are lidded against the dust and the air cracks the skin, the lips crack, Stephen's flutes crack and there is no energy to sing any more anyway.

17   It's standing in the field and staring out at the heat waves that waver and shimmer like see-through curtains over the brown clods and over the tiny distant bodies of Stephen and Uncle and Obasan miles away across the field day after day and not even wondering how this has come about.

18   There she is, Obasan, wearing Uncle's shirt over a pair of dark baggy trousers, her head covered by a straw hat that is held on by a white cloth tied under her chin. She is moving like a tiny earth cloud over the hard clay clods. Her hoe moves rhythmically up down up down, tiny as a toothpick. And over there, Uncle pauses to straighten his back, his hands on his hips. And Stephen farther behind, so tiny I can barely see him.

19   It's hard, Aunt Emily, with my hoe, the blade getting dull and mud-caked as I slash out the Canada thistle, dandelions, crab grass, and other nameless non-beet plants, then on my knees, pulling out the extra beets from the cluster, leaving just one to mature, then three hand spans to the next plant, whack whack, and down on my knees again, pull, flick flick, and on to the end of the long long row and the next and the next and it will never be done thinning and weeding and weeding and weeding. It's so hard and so hot that my tear glands burn out.

20   And then it's cold. The lumps of clay mud stick on my gumboots and weight my legs and the skin under the boots beneath the knees at the level of the calves grows red and hard and itchy from the flap flap of the boots and the fine hairs on my legs grow coarse there and ugly.

21   I mind growing ugly.

I mind the harvest time and the hands and the wrists bound in rags to 22 keep the wrists from breaking open. I lift the heavy mud-clotted beets out of the ground with the hook like an eagle's beak, thick and heavy as a nail attached to the top of the sugar-beet knife. Thwack. Into the beet and yank from the shoulder till it's out of the ground dragging the surrounding mud with it. Then crack two beets together till most of the mud drops off and splat, the knife slices into the beet scalp and the green top is tossed into one pile, the beet heaved onto another, one more one more one more down the icy line. I cannot tell about this time, Aunt Emily. The body will not tell.

We are surrounded by a horizon of denim-blue sky with clouds clear 23 as spilled milk that turn pink at sunset. Pink I hear is the colour of llama's milk. I wouldn't know. The clouds are the shape of our new prison walls — untouchable, impersonal, random.

There are no other people in the entire world. We work together all 24 day. At night we eat and sleep. We hardly talk anymore. The boxes we brought from Slocan are not unpacked. The King George/Queen Elizabeth mugs stay muffled in the *Vancouver Daily Province*. The camera phone does not sing. Obasan wraps layers of cloth around her feet and her torn sweater hangs unmended over her sagging dress.

Down the miles we are obedient as machines in this odd ballet with- 25 out accompaniment of flute or song.

"Grinning and happy" and all smiles standing around a pile of beets? 26 That is one telling. It's not how it was.

● ●

Explorations:

Joy Kogawa,
  Obasan
  Itsuka
Barry Broadfoot, *Years of Sorrow, Years of Shame: The Story of Japanese Canadians in World War II*
Ken Adachi, *The Enemy That Never Was: A History of the Japanese Canadians*
Ann Sunahara, *The Politics of Racism: The Uprooting of Japanese Canadians During the Second World War*
Roy Miki, *Redress*
Joy Kogawa (video, 1998, 45 min., Sleeping Giant Productions)
http://www.writersunion.ca/k/kogawa.htm
http://quarles.unbc.ca/kbeeler_html/research/kog1.html
http://www.najc.ca
http://www.lib.washington.edu/subject/Canada/internment/intro.html
http://www.jcnm.ca/Jchist.htm

Structure:

1. Why does Kogawa "frame" her argument by citing the newspaper article in both her opening and closing?
2. How does the device of *contrast* help organize this selection?
3. What percentage of *examples* has Kogawa reached in the content of this selection? Is it enough? Do you use enough?
4. How important is *description* to the success of this passage? Give examples.
5. Most THESIS STATEMENTS are placed early in an argument. Why is Kogawa's put in the very last line?

Style:

1. Until *Obasan*, Kogawa was best known as a poet. What poetical qualities do you see in this sample of her PROSE?
2. To what extent does Kogawa communicate by SENSE IMAGES? Cite one case each of appeals to sight, hearing, touch, taste and smell.
3. The poet Kogawa fills her prose with FIGURES OF SPEECH. Point out three good SIMILES and three good METAPHORS.
4. In paragraphs 14 through 17, how many times does the contraction "it's" appear at or near the beginning of a sentence? Is the *repetition* accidental or deliberate? What is its effect?
5. How many words long is the first sentence of paragraph 19? How many times does it use the word "and"? Is this run-on sentence accidental or deliberate? What is its effect?

Argumentation and Persuasion:

1. As a member of a persecuted minority, Kogawa's narrator rejects a *deductive* stance; she shuns the official "telling" of the newspaper article, and instead produces her own eyewitness "telling." Point out at least ten pieces of evidence that lead *inductively* to her own conclusion that the newspaper's version of the truth is "not how it was."
2. Does Kogawa rely more on *argumentation* or on *persuasion*? To what extent does she communicate through reason, and to what extent through emotion?
3. Analyze Kogawa's tools of *persuasion*: point out at least five loaded words, five SENSE IMAGES and five FIGURES OF SPEECH that build emotion. Identify one case of deliberate repetition, and one of extreme sentence length, both of which build emotion. Does all this persuasion put you on guard? Or does it convince you?

Ideas for Discussion and Writing:

1. How often are you, like Kogawa's narrator, caught between two or more views of the truth? Cite a recent case. Did you act *deductively*, accepting a view already held by yourself or others, or did you move *inductively* to a new conclusion?

2. The narrator and her family are Canadian citizens of Japanese descent, removed by our federal government from the coast of British Columbia during World War II for fear they would betray Canada to enemy Japan. (Not a single case of such betrayal was ever found.) Many families were separated and their property taken. Attack or defend these official actions against citizens like Kogawa's fictional family. Have such acts occurred in Canada before? Since? Can you imagine them happening in future to any group you belong to?

3. During the war the Canadian government confiscated an island off British Columbia, compensating its Japanese-Canadian owner with $2000. Two generations later his granddaughter, a university student, estimated the worth of this property at 200 million dollars. In 1988 the Canadian government officially apologized to the Japanese-Canadians and offered each survivor of the epoch $21,000. Has the wrong been righted? Attack or defend our government's actions.

4. You are the student in question 3 above. Write to the Prime Minister, arguing either *deductively* or *inductively* that the island be restored to the heirs of its original owner. *Or* you are the present owner. Write to the prime minister, arguing either *deductively* or *inductively* that your island should not be seized and given to descendants of the man who once owned it.

5. **PROCESS IN WRITING:** *Name a group that you think has been badly treated by Canadian society (for example the disabled, the elderly, Native people, farmers, immigrants, refugees, AIDS victims, single parents, etc.). Take notes, then write an* inductive argument *giving the evidence that led to your belief. In a further draft, fine-tune the balance of* argumentation *and* persuasion. *Now share this version with a small group of classmates, and apply their best advice. Edit. Finally, read your good version aloud to the whole class, and be ready to defend your view.*

Note: See also the Topics for Writing at the end of this chapter.

MARGARET ATWOOD

Letter to America

Novelist, poet, essayist, social and literary critic, Margaret Atwood has had a long and distinguished career. She is the leading light of Canadian literature. Born in Ottawa in 1939, she spent much of her childhood with her parents in the wilds of the Canadian North, where her father did biological research. After studies at the University of Toronto and at Radcliffe, she published several books of poetry that explored the inability of language to express reality, and the alienation of women in society. Then her feminist vision found even broader scope in a long series of success-ful novels, such as The Edible Woman *(1969),* Surfacing *(1972) and* The Handmaid's Tale *(1985), which became an international bestseller and was made into a feature film and an opera. The novel already shows her preoccupation with America. Set in Boston, it portrays a future United States, ruined by nuclear pollu-tion, in which a right-wing theocracy has reduced women to the status of slaves. The main characters flee north towards Canada, as did slaves before the Civil War. Of Atwood's ten novels so far,* Alias Grace *(1996), a polished work investigating a notorious murder in 19th-century Canada, has also been widely admired. By now Atwood's collected poems, stories, essays and her novels total well over 30 books, and she has been translated into more than two dozen languages. Our selection, "Letter to America," expresses an unease with current American government and society. It first appeared April 14, 2003 in the American journal* The Nation, *then on March 28 in* The Globe and Mail, *and finally in the new collection of Atwood's essays,* Moving Targets: Writing with Intent, *1982–2004.*

1 **D**ear America:
This is a difficult letter to write, because I'm no longer sure who you are. Some of you may be having the same trouble.

2 I thought I knew you: we'd become well acquainted over the past fifty-five years. You were the Mickey Mouse and Donald Duck comic books I read in the late 1940s. You were the radio shows — Jack Benny, *Our Miss Brooks*. You were the music I sang and danced to: the Andrews Sisters, Ella Fitzgerald, the Platters, Elvis. You were a ton of fun.

3 You wrote some of my favourite books. You created Huckleberry Finn, and Hawkeye, and Beth and Jo in *Little Women*, courageous in their dif-ferent ways. Later, you were my beloved Thoreau, father of environmen-talism, witness to individual conscience; and Walt Whitman, singer of the great Republic; and Emily Dickinson, keeper of the private soul. You were Hammett and Chandler, heroic walkers of mean streets; even later, you were the amazing trio, Hemingway, Fitzgerald, and Faulkner, who traced the dark labyrinths of your hidden heart. You were Sinclair Lewis

and Arthur Miller, who, with their own American idealism, went after the sham in you, because they thought you could do better.

You were Marlon Brando in *On the Waterfront*, you were Humphrey Bogart in *Key Largo*, you were Lillian Gish in *The Night of the Hunter*. You stood up for freedom, honesty, and justice; you protected the innocent. I believed most of that. I think you did, too. It seemed true at the time.

You put God on the money, though, even then. You had a way of thinking that the things of Caesar° were the same as the things of God: that gave you self-confidence. You have always wanted to be a city upon a hill, a light to all nations, and for a while you were. Give me your tired, your poor, you sang, and for a while you meant it.

We've always been close, you and us. History, that old entangler, has twisted us together since the early seventeenth century. Some of us used to be you; some of us want to be you; some of you used to be us. You are not only our neighbours: In many cases — mine, for instance — you are also our blood relations, our colleagues, and our personal friends. But although we've had a ringside seat, we've never understood you completely, up here north of the 49th parallel. We're like Romanized Gauls° — look like Romans, dress like Romans, but aren't Romans — peering over the wall at the real Romans. What are they doing? Why? What are they doing now? Why is the haruspex° eyeballing the sheep's liver? Why is the soothsayer wholesaling the Bewares?

Perhaps that's been my difficulty in writing you this letter: I'm not sure I know what's really going on. Anyway, you have a huge posse of experienced entrail sifters who do nothing but analyze your every vein and lobe. What can I tell you about yourself that you don't already know?

This might be the reason for my hesitation: embarrassment, brought on by a becoming modesty. But it is more likely to be embarrassment of another sort. When my grandmother — from a New England background — was confronted with an unsavoury topic, she would change the subject and gaze out the window. And that is my own inclination: keep your mouth shut, mind your own business.

But I'll take the plunge, because your business is no longer merely your business. To paraphrase Marley's ghost,° who figured it out too late, mankind is your business. And vice versa: when the Jolly Green Giant

---

° the things of Caesar: In Luke 20:22–25 the priests said, "Is it lawful for us to give tribute unto Caesar, or no?" Jesus asked them to show a coin with the emperor's image, then said: "Render therefore unto Caesar the things which be Caesar's, and unto God the things which be God's."

° Gauls: The early inhabitants of what is now France, who had been conquered by the Romans.

° haruspex: A soothsayer or fortune-teller who discovered the will of the gods by reading the entrails of sacrificed animals.

° Marley's ghost: In Charles Dickens' famous story "A Christmas Carol," the ghost of Scrooge's business partner repents his former selfish ways, saying "Mankind was my business. . . . The dealings of my trade were but a drop of water in the comprehensive ocean of my business!"

goes on the rampage, many lesser plants and animals get trampled underfoot. As for us, you're our biggest trading partner: We know perfectly well that if you go down the plughole, we're going with you. We have every reason to wish you well.

10   I won't go into the reasons why I think your recent Iraqi adventures have been — taking the long view — an ill-advised tactical error. By the time you read this, Baghdad may or may not be a pancake, and many more sheep entrails will have been examined. Let's talk, then, not about what you're doing to other people but about what you're doing to yourselves.

11   You're gutting the Constitution. Already your home can be entered without your knowledge or permission, you can be snatched away and incarcerated without cause, your mail can be spied on, your private records searched. Why isn't this a recipe for widespread business theft, political intimidation, and fraud? I know you've been told that all this is for your own safety and protection, but think about it for a minute. Anyway, when did you get so scared? You didn't used to be easily frightened.

12   You're running up a record level of debt. Keep spending at this rate and pretty soon you won't be able to afford any big military adventures. Either that or you'll go the way of the USSR: lots of tanks, but no air conditioning. That will make folks very cross. They'll be even crosser when they can't take a shower because your shortsighted bulldozing of environmental protections has dirtied most of the water and dried up the rest. Then things will get hot and dirty indeed.

13   You're torching the American economy. How soon before the answer to that will be not to produce anything yourselves but to grab stuff other people produce, at gunboat-diplomacy prices? Is the world going to consist of a few mega-rich King Midases,° with the rest being serfs, both inside and outside your country? Will the biggest business sector in the United States be the prison system? Let's hope not.

14   If you proceed much further down the slippery slope, people around the world will stop admiring the good things about you. They'll decide that your city upon the hill is a slum and your democracy is a sham, and therefore you have no business trying to impose your sullied vision on them. They'll think you've abandoned the rule of law. They'll think you've fouled your own nest.

15   The British used to have a myth about King Arthur. He wasn't dead, but sleeping in a cave, it was said; and in the country's hour of greatest peril, he would return. You too have great spirits of the past you may call upon: men and women of courage, of conscience, of prescience. Summon them now, to stand with you, to inspire you, to defend the best in you. You need them.

• •

° King Midas: In Greek legend, the king of Phrygia who could turn all he touched into gold.

Explorations:

Margaret Atwood,
> *Moving Targets: Writing with Intent,* 1982–2004 (essays)
> *The Journals of Susanna Moodie* (poems)
> *The Handmaid's Tale* (novel)
> *Alias Grace* (novel)

Michael Adams, *Fire and Ice: The United States, Canada and the Myth of Converging Values*

http://www.owtoad.com

http://www.mscd.edu/~atwoodso

http://www.web.net/owtoad/english.html

Structure:

1. The essay as a letter has a long and rich history. Does any other author in the book use this device? What advantages of this format has Atwood exploited in "Letter to America"?
2. Atwood presents a flood of *examples*. And Ray Guy, in his essay "Outport Menu," gives even more non-stop examples. Do you put enough of them into your own essays? Is there any upper limit?
3. What gives so much power to Atwood's final words, "You need them"?

Style:

1. Margaret Atwood knows how to say more with less. In paragraph 6 she writes, "Some of us used to be you; some of us want to be you; some of you used to be us." Find five other examples of extreme CONCISENESS in her essay.
2. Writing shortly before the American invasion of Iraq, Atwood says, "By the time you read this, Baghdad may or may not be a pancake. . . ." (10). Does this METAPHOR make you uneasy? Does it seem sarcastic or even cruel? Or is it supposed to shock, and thus support the author's criticisms of the new U.S. foreign policy? Find five other METAPHORS and/or SIMILES, and comment on them as well.

Argumentation and Persuasion:

1. Atwood's essay both affirms and criticizes America. Are these thoughts derived mostly through DEDUCTION (applying an overall principle to specific examples) or INDUCTION (letting specific examples lead to the principle)?
2. Read paragraphs 2 and 3 aloud in class. Why are certain phrases repeated so many times? And why are the first words of paragraphs 11, 12 and 13 repetitious? Does this show weak style or strong style? What is the effect? Are we looking at ARGUMENTATION or PERSUASION here?

3. What other examples of PERSUASION do you see in this selection? (Review the list of persuasive techniques in the introduction to this chapter.) All in all, is "Letter to America" based mostly on PERSUASION or ARGUMENTATION?

Ideas for Discussion and Writing:

1. In paragraphs 2–4 Atwood admires many American singers, writers, actors, etc. who influenced her in the past. Name ten Americans you would put on your own list for today, and for each one tell why.

2. "I thought I knew you," says Atwood in paragraph 2. Do you agree with her that the United States is changing? And if so, what are the changes you, yourself, notice? And to what extent do these seem caused by the World Trade Center terrorist attack of September 11, 2001? (See also "Your New Job, Your New Life," by Gordon Pitts in this book.)

3. In paragraph 6 Atwood builds an *analogy*: "We're like Romanized Gauls — look like Romans, dress like Romans, but aren't Romans — peering over the wall at the real Romans." Is this a true portrait of Canadians? In what ways do you feel most "like" Americans? In what ways do you feel most different from them?

4. The three most specific criticisms Atwood makes are of the "recent Iraqi adventures" (par. 10), the "gutting" of the Constitution (11) and the "record level of debt" that will "torch" the U.S. economy (12–13). Study those paragraphs. Do you agree with Atwood's analysis? If not, why not? Or if so, what concrete steps do you believe the U.S. could take to begin solving each of these problems?

5. **PROCESS IN WRITING:** *Margaret Atwood writes a "Letter to America." Now imagine yourself looking north across the border and write a "Letter to Canada." First* freewrite *or* brainstorm *for 10 or 15 minutes, then search these notes for points and a topic. (For example, is Canada getting better or worse? Fairer or less fair to minorities? Stronger or weaker economically? Greener or more wasteful environmentally? More respected or less respected internationally? And so on.) Write a first draft, then look it over. Have you lived up to the model of Atwood's letter: Do you say more with less? Are the points concrete, with* examples? *Do they all support the overall main point? Do they rise in importance to a* climax? *Now look at your logic: is it mostly* deductive *or* inductive? *(Write which it is at the top.) Mostly* argumentative *or* persuasive? *(Write which it is at the top.) If it is* argumentative, *are your points real and fair? If it is* persuasive, *does the feeling all contribute to the overall tone and the overall point? If not, revise. Finally, edit for correctness and read your letter to the class.*

Note: See also the Topics for Writing at the end of this chapter.

NAOMI KLEIN

Local Foreign Policy

The Times *of London once called her "probably the most influential person under the age of 35 in the world." Through her speeches and her writing, Naomi Klein is fast becoming the voice of a new world movement whose goals could be summed up in the title of her 2000 international bestseller* No Logo: Taking Aim at the Brand Bullies. *Though she confesses to being a "mall rat" and a slave to fashion while a teen, Klein now fights transnational corporations such as Nike, Reebok, Disney, Benetton and The Gap, which pay a pittance to workers in poor countries but spend fortunes in advertising to sell brand-name clothes at high prices in rich countries. She speaks at major anti-globalization rallies, appears often on television, and writes prolifically for newspapers and magazines. Born in 1970 in Montreal, as a teen Klein rebelled against her social activist parents. But when her mother had a life-threatening heart attack, Klein was shocked into a renewal of her own values. Suddenly a feminist and activist, she edited the University of Toronto's socially conscious student newspaper* The Varsity. *Going on to marry broadcaster Avi Lewis, son of activist parents Stephen Lewis (former Canadian ambassador to the United Nations) and columnist Michele Landsberg, Klein enlarged her own political connections even further. Then after four years of research and writing, Klein published her blockbuster* No Logo, *now translated into 27 languages and considered the bible of anti-globalization forces. "Local Foreign Policy" is a self-contained section of one of its chapters. Then in 2002 she published* Fences and Windows: Dispatches from the Front Lines of the Globalization Debate, *and in 2004, with Avi Lewis, produced a documentary film,* The Take, *about the effects of political and corporate greed in Argentina.*

"**O**kay, I need people on each door. Let's go!" shouted Sean   1
Hayes in the distinctive clipped baritone of a high-school basketball coach, which, as it happens, he is. "Let's go!" Coach
Hayes bellowed again, clapping his meaty hands loud enough for the
sound to bounce off the walls of the huge gymnasium of St. Mary's
Secondary School in Pickering, Ontario (a town best known for its prox-
imity to a nuclear power plant of questionable quality).

Hayes had invited me to participate in the school's first "Sweatshop   2
Fashion Show," an event he began planning when he discovered that the
basketball team's made-in-Indonesia Nike sneakers had likely been man-
ufactured under sweatshop conditions. He's an unapologetic jock with a
conscience and, together with a handful of do-gooder students, had
organized today's event to get the other two thousand kids at St. Mary's
to think about the clothes they wear in terms beyond "cool" or "lame."

3   The plan was simple: as student models decked out in logowear strutted down a makeshift runway, another student off to the side would read a prepared narration about the lives of the Third World workers who made the gear. The students would quickly follow that with scenes from *Mickey Mouse Goes to Haiti* and a skit about how teenagers often feel "unloved, unwanted, unacceptable and unpopular if you do not have the right clothes." My part would come at the end, when I was to give a short speech about my research in export processing zones, and then facilitate a question-and-answer period. It sounded straightforward enough.

4   While we were waiting for the bell to ring and the students to stream in, Hayes turned to me and said, with a forced smile: "I hope the kids actually hear the message and don't think it's just a regular fashion show." Having read the students' prepared narration I couldn't help thinking that his concern sounded, frankly, paranoid. True, fashion shows have become such a high-school stalwart that they now rival car washes as the prom fundraiser of choice. But did Hayes actually think his students were so heartless that they could listen to testimony about starvation wages and physical abuse and expect that the clothing in question would be on sale at a discount after the assembly? Just then, a couple of teenage boys poked their heads in the door and checked out the frantic preparations. "Yo, guys," one of them said. "I'm guessing fashion show — this should be a joke." Coach Hayes looked nervous.

5   As two thousand students piled onto the bleachers, the room came alive with the giddiness that accompanies all mass reprieves from class, whether for school plays, AIDS education lectures, teachers' strikes or fire alarms. A quick scan of the room turned up no logos on these kids, but that was definitely not by choice. St. Mary's is a Catholic school and the students wear uniforms — bland affairs that they were nonetheless working for all they were worth. It's hard to make gray flannel slacks and acrylic navy sweaters look like gangsta gear but the guys were doing their best, wearing their pants pulled down halfway to their knees with patterned boxer shorts bunched over their belts. The girls were pushing the envelope too, pairing their drab tunics with platform loafers and black lipstick.

6   As it turned out, Coach Hayes's concerns were well founded. As the hip-hop started playing and the first kids bounded down the runway in Nike shoes and workout wear, the assembly broke into cheers and applause. The moment the young woman saddled with reading the earnest voice-over began, "Welcome to the world of Nike . . . " she was drowned out by hoots and whistles. It didn't take much to figure out that they weren't cheering for her but rather at the mere mention of the word Nike — everyone's favorite celebrity brand.

7   Waiting for my cue, I was ready to flee the modern teenage world forever, but after some booming threats from Coach Hayes, the crowd finally quieted down. My speech was at least not booed and the discussion that followed was among the liveliest I've ever witnessed. The first question (as at all Sweatshop 101 events) was "What brands are sweatshop-free?" — Adidas?

they asked. Reebok? The Gap? I told the St. Mary's students that shopping for an exploitation-free wardrobe at the mall is next to impossible, given the way all the large brands produce. The best way to make a difference, I told them, is to stay informed by surfing the Net, and by letting companies know what you think by writing letters and asking lots of questions at the store. The St. Mary's kids were deeply skeptical of this non-answer. "Look, I don't have time to be some kind of major political activist every time I go to the mall," one girl said, right hand planted firmly on right hip. "Just tell me what kind of shoes are okay to buy, okay?"

Another girl, who looked about sixteen, sashayed to the microphone. "I'd just like to say that this is capitalism, okay, and people are allowed to make money and if you don't like it maybe you're just jealous." 8

The hands shot up in response. "No, *I'd* just like to say that you are totally screwed up and just because everyone is doing something doesn't mean it's right — you've got to stand up for what you believe in instead of just standing in front of the mirror trying to look good!" 9

After watching thousands of Ricki and Oprah episodes, these kids take to the talk-show format as naturally as Elizabeth Dole. Just as they had cheered for Nike moments before, the students now cheered for each other — dog-pound style, with lots of "you-go-girls." Moments before the bell for next period, Coach Hayes made time for one last question. A boy in saggy slacks sauntered across the gym holding his standard-issue navy blue sweater away from his lanky body with two fingers, as if he detected a foul odor. Then, he slouched down to the mike and said, in an impeccable teenage monotone, "Umm, Coach Hayes, if working conditions are so bad in Indonesia, then why do we have to wear these uniforms? We buy thousands of these things and it says right here that they are 'Made in Indonesia.' I'd just like to know, how do you know they weren't made in sweatshops?" 10

The auditorium exploded. It was a serious burn. Another student rushed to the mike and suggested that the students should try to find out who makes their uniforms, a project for which there was no shortage of volunteers. When I left St. Mary's that day, the school had its work cut out for it. 11

• •

Explorations:

Naomi Klein, *No Logo:*
    Taking Aim at the Brand Bullies
    Fences and Windows: Dispatches from the Front Lines of the Globalization
      Debate
Madeleine Drohan, *Making a Killing: How and Why Corporations Use*
    Armed Force to Do Business
Mickey Mouse Goes to Haiti (video, 17 min., by the National Labor
    Committee)

http://www.nologo.org
http://www.guardian.co.uk/Columnists/Archive/0,5673,-991,00.html
http://www.commondreams.org/views/092300-103.htm
http://www.alternet.org/story.html?StoryID=14175
http://www.adbusters.org/home

Structure:

1. Naomi Klein's bestseller *No Logo* often uses passages of *narration* to argue and persuade. Show how this selection does so. How does telling of the school assembly illustrate the problem of sweatshop labour, and the difficulties North Americans face in doing something about it? Where in this selection do we also see use of *example*? Of *description*? Of *cause and effect*? Of *comparison and contrast*? And of *process analysis*?
2. One of the strongest techniques of an essayist is to build the argument up to a CLIMAX. Has Klein done this? How?

Style:

1. Why does Klein use SLANG or COLLOQUIAL terms such as "jock" (par. 2), "cool" (2), "lame" (2), "gangsta" (5) and "a serious burn" (11)? Are these too racy for a serious argument, or do they work with Klein's subject and format?
2. What kind of AUDIENCE do you believe Klein is writing for? Give reasons.

Argumentation and Persuasion:

1. Is Klein's argument based mostly on *deduction* (a principle applied to specific cases) or *induction* (evidence that leads to a principle)? Support your answer with reasons.
2. To what extent does Klein base this selection on reason (*argumentation*) and to what extent on appeals to emotion (*persuasion*)? Cite examples to defend your view.

Ideas for Discussion and Writing:

1. Look at the clothing you have on right now. Tell the class whether any of it is by Adidas, Reebok, The Gap, or other big name-brand companies. Then try to explain all the factors that led you to choose each item. Cost? Durability? Performance? Or image? Now look at the labels. Where was each item made? What is your estimate of the hourly wage made by the worker in each location?

2. Review the passage on branding in the introduction to Naomi Klein. Better yet, read her book. What are your views so far on this issue? Is it exploitation for big transnational companies to pay workers in Indonesia or Malaysia a tiny fraction of what the running shoes or other clothes will sell for here? Or is it just good business? Is it fair to make them work long hours in special zones patrolled by armed guards? Or are companies doing them a favour by creating employment?

3. Elsewhere Naomi Klein has stated "People come up to me and say, 'I read your book and burned all my Nike clothes.'" Attack or defend their reaction, giving reasons.

4. In paragraph 8 a student states, "I'd just like to say that this is capitalism, okay, and people are allowed to make money and if you don't like it maybe you're just jealous." In paragraph 9 a classmate replies, "No, *I'd* just like to say that you are totally screwed up and just because everyone is doing something doesn't mean it's right — you've got to stand up for what you believe in instead of just standing in front of the mirror trying to look good!" With which student do you most agree? Defend your choice with reasons.

5. What does the title mean? How can "foreign" policy be "local"? What is a PARADOX? Is this title one?

6. **PROCESS IN WRITING:** *Choose one of the two students from question 4 just above as a hypothetical AUDIENCE for your own essay. Now brainstorm a page of notes on the topic of transnational companies producing at low wages in one country and selling at high prices in another. When you realize your own point of view on the topic, put it into a THESIS STATEMENT. Next decide how much reason* (argumentation) *and how much emotion* (persuasion) *are needed to reach your reader. Finally, write a discovery draft, filling it with examples from your own experience and reading. The next day look it over. Does everything contribute to your overall main point? Is the argument appropriate for your chosen AUDIENCE? Have you gone so far using emotion that you're just playing on the reader's feelings? Or is your pure logic so dry it has no life? Then adjust. Finally, edit, print, and share with the class.*

Note: See also the Topics for Writing at the end of this chapter.

RITA SCHINDLER

Thanks for Not Killing My Son

All we know about Rita Schindler is what she herself says in her letter. It was a student who noticed "Thanks for Not Killing My Son" in the "Have Your Say" feature of the December 30, 1990 Toronto Star. *He tore it out and brought it to his writing teacher, exclaiming what a fine argument it was. The teacher agreed. By the time the editor of this book tried to reach Ms. Schindler, though, the* Star *had discarded her address. None of the many Schindlers listed in the Toronto phone book knew her, and the hospital mentioned in her letter would not divulge information. As this new edition was being put together we tried again to find her, but could not. But finally, Access Canada, the Canadian Copyright Licensing Agency, gave permission to reprint the letter, as it can do in such cases. We sincerely believe that Ms. Schindler would want her eloquent and highly principled argument made available to more persons of her son's generation. If you happen to know her, please show her this book and ask her to contact the publisher, who will direct her to the agency office where her author's fee is waiting.*

1   I hope you will print my letter of gratitude to the strangers who have affected our lives.

2   Sometime between 1:30 p.m., Dec. 8, and 1 a.m., Dec. 9, a young man was viciously attacked — beaten and kicked unconscious for no apparent reason other than walking by you on a public sidewalk.

3   He was left lying in a pool of blood from an open head wound — in the Victoria Park-Terraview area. He was found around 1 a.m. and taken to Scarborough General Hospital where ironically his mother spent 48 hours in labor before giving him birth, 23 years earlier.

4   His mother is angry of course, but thankful for the following reasons.

5   First of all — his eye socket was shattered and hemorrhaging but his eyesight will not be affected. Thank you.

6   His ear canal was lacerated internally from a tremendous blow to the side of his head. The cut could not be stitched and the bleeding was difficult to stop. But his eardrum seems to be undamaged — thank you.

7   He required numerous stitches to his forehead, temple and face but your boots didn't knock one tooth out — thank you. His head was swollen almost twice its size — but Mom knew that his brain was intact — for he held her hand for six hours as he lay on a gurney, by the nurses station, I.V. in his arm — his head covered and crusted with dried blood — waiting for x-ray results and the surgeon to stitch him up.

8   So, thank you for this eyesight, his hearing and his hands which you could have easily crushed.

His hands — human hands — the most intricately beautiful and complex instruments of incredible mechanism — the result of billions of years of evolution — and you people used yours to beat another human being. Five guys and two girls to beat one person. Who do I thank? Did you know he was a talented young musician with a budding career — and that playing his keyboards and piano mean more to him than my words can say. 9

And when his friends were talking about revenge, I heard him say, "No, I don't want someone else's mother to go through what mine has." That's who you were kicking in the head. And so — I thank you for not causing the most horrible and devastating thing that can happen to any parent — that is — the untimely tragic loss of a child — at any age. 10

You could have kicked him to death but you only left him to die, thank you. A person found him and called for help. 11

I am his mother — and I have been given a second chance — thanks to you. 12

I hope that someday you'll have children and love them as much as I love mine — but I wouldn't wish on your child what you did to mine. 13

Rita Schindler
Scarborough

● ●

Explorations:

Anthony Burgess, *A Clockwork Orange*
Dan Korem, *Suburban Gangs: The Affluent Rebels*
Frederick Mathews, *Youth Gangs on Youth Gangs*
http://www.bullying.org
http://www.cln.org/themes/youth_violence.html
http://www.wsd1.org/PC_LMS/pf/youthgangs.htm
http://www.bullyonline.org
http://www.bullybeware.com

Structure:

1. Schindler's argument is cast as a letter. For what *audience* is it meant? The youths who attacked her son? All the readers of the *Toronto Star*? How well does her "letter" work as an essay?
2. Schindler organizes her letter by examining in turn each injury inflicted on her son. Point out each. What proportion of the letter's content is given to these *examples*? Could the point have been made without them?
3. After all her ironic "thanking," Schindler ends more literally: "I wouldn't wish on your child what you did to mine." Is her closing weak because it drops the IRONY, or strong because it caps the point?

Style:

1. Six of Schindler's paragraphs have only one sentence. Give reasons. Is this style effective?
2. How CONCISE is this selection? Try to find a passage of deadwood that could have been cut.
3. How FORMAL or INFORMAL is Schindler's TONE? Give examples. Does the tone fit the content? Why or why not?

Argumentation and Persuasion:

1. "You could have kicked him to death, but you only left him to die, thank you," writes the victim's mother in paragraph 11. Her letter of "thanks" is *persuasion* as strong as any in this book. Explain the IRONY of Schindler's "thanking" her son's attackers.
2. Find and explain at least 10 more IRONIES in this selection.
3. The author might have called her son's attackers "thugs," "goons" or worse. Would this openly *persuasive* mode be more effective than the "thanks" she gives? Defend your answer with reasons.
4. In addition to *irony*, the introduction to this chapter lists *repetition*, *fright* and *climax* as techniques of persuasion. How does Schindler use each? Respond with examples.
5. Does Schindler make her point *deductively* (through an innate rejection of violence) or *inductively* (through the many examples she cites, leading to her point)? Can an argument go both ways at once? Would this be a failure of logic?

Ideas for Discussion and Writing:

1. Does Schindler attempt only to heap shame on her son's attackers, or do you also detect, for example in the closing, a desire for reconciliation?
2. When his friends desired revenge, the son said, "No, I don't want someone else's mother to go through what mine has" (paragraph 10). What would *you* have said? Defend your answer with reasons.
3. How much do techniques of nonviolent resisters such as Mahatma Gandhi and Martin Luther King have in common with the responses of Rita Schindler and her son? Is their way ultimately weaker or stronger than the way of those who defend themselves through violence? Give examples.
4. Think of a time when you witnessed bullying at school. Tell the story to the class. Was the incident resolved, and if so, how?
5. Is there violent crime at your school or campus? Give examples. Defend or attack the "zero tolerance" policy of some school boards that permanently expel students who commit violent offences. Are there other solutions?

6. Are public forums such as the letters to the editor column or Internet chatrooms good vehicles for promoting our own ideas? Do others actually read and heed what we say?

7. **PROCESS IN WRITING:** *Read the crime news in your newspaper or hear it on radio or TV. Choose one violent act that provokes your anger or concern. Consider how, like Rita Schindler, you can respond to it through IRONY to persuade your audience to take your side. Make notes, look them over, then write a rapid first draft of a letter to the perpetrator, or to the public, or to both. The next day look it over. Will it startle and persuade the AUDIENCE by meaning the opposite of what it says? (Remember Schindler's "thanking" the attackers, or in Chapter 8 Stephen Leacock's "advice" on how to live to be 200.) Is the ironic TONE consistent? Is the letter concise, like Schindler's? If not, revise. Finally, check the spelling and grammar. When you have produced your good draft, send it as a letter to the editor of the newspaper you read. Or post it with an appropriate discussion group on the Internet. Check either for responses. Collect them, then show them, with the original letter, to the class.*

NOTE: See also the Topics for Writing at the end of this Chapter.

DIONNE BRAND

Job

Born in Trinidad in 1953, Dionne Brand came to Canada in 1970, and that year experienced the frustrating event described in "Job." Since then she has become a strong voice in the fight against racism and sexism in our society. After a B.A. in English and philosophy, an M.A. in education, and then more work in women's studies, all at the University of Toronto, Brand put her egalitarian values into action. She has worked at the Immigrant Women's Centre and the Black Youth Hotline; has been a community relations worker for the Board of Education; and helped found Our Lives, *a community newspaper, and the International Coalition of Black Trade Unionists. She has also worked with the Women's Committee of the Ontario Federation of Labour, and the Metro Labour Council Anti-racism Conference, and has been on the board of a shelter for battered women. In 1983 while Brand was doing community development in Grenada, the United States invaded the little Caribbean country and she was evacuated. Brand has made several documentaries for the National Film Board, such as* Older, Stronger, Wiser *(1989), and* Sisters in the Struggle *(1991). Dozens of her socially conscious poems and stories have appeared in periodicals and anthologies, and Brand has also published over a dozen books of her own, among them* Bread out of Stone *(essays, 1994),* In Another Place, Not Here *(novel, 1996),* Land to Light On *(1997, Governor General's Award for Poetry),* No Language Is Neutral *(poems, 1998),* At the Full and Change of the Moon *(novel, 1999),* A Map to the Door of No Return *(memoir, 2001), and* Thirsty *(long poem, 2002). Our selection is from* Bread out of Stone.

1   It was that tiny office in the back of a building on Keele Street. I had called the morning before, looking for a job, and the man answering remarked on that strong Scottish name of my putative father and told me to come right in and the job would be mine. Yes, it was that tiny office in the back of a building on Keele when I was turning eighteen, and I dressed up in my best suit outfit with high heels and lipstick and ninety-seven pounds of trying hard desperate feminine heterosexuality, wanting to look like the man on the phone's imagination so I could get the job. When I went to that tiny office and saw the smile of the man on the phone fade and the job disappear because all of a sudden it needed experience or was just given to somebody else and, no, there would be no interview and if it were today I would have sued the pig for making me walk away with my eighteen-year-old self trying not to cry and feeling laughter, that laughter that Black people get, derisive and self-derisive rising inside my chest. Yes, it was that man on the phone, that office on

Keele Street, that man's imagination for a Scottish girl he could molest as she filed papers in the cabinets in the tiny office, it was that wanting to cry in my best suit and high heels I could barely walk in and the lipstick my sister helped me to put on straight and plucked my eyebrows and made me wear foundation cream in order, I suppose, to dull the impact of my blackness so that the man in the tiny office would give me that job. What propelled my legs back to the subway was shame. That I could ever think of getting such a job, even so small and mean a job, that some white man could forget himself and at least see me as someone he could exploit, and I was willing to be considered as someone to exploit. It was 1970. A kitchen then, maybe, but not an office. My sister worked the kitchens of hospitals, and that is where I did find a job the next week, and that is where we waited out the ebb and flow of favour and need in this white place.

● ●

Explorations:

Dionne Brand,
>   *Bread out of Stone*
>   *In Another Place, Not Here*
>   *Land to Light On*

Francis Henry, *The Caribbean Diaspora in Toronto*
http://www.nlc-bnc.ca/3/8/t8-5002-e.html
http://www.library.utoronto.ca/canpoetry/brand
http://www.griffinpoetryprize.com/shortlist_2003.php?t=2#a2
http://www.femmenoir.net/Leaders-Legends/DionneBrand.htm
http://voices.cla.umn.edu/vg/Bios/entries/brand_dionne.html

Structure:

1. "Job" is one long paragraph. Why has Brand not broken it up? Do you see reasons for her strategy?
2. What organizational technique does Brand employ when she closes on the words "in this white place"?

Style:

1. Brand begins four key sentences and phrases with the words "It was." Do you think this repetition is accidental or deliberate? What effects does it achieve?
2. Count the words in Brand's fourth sentence. Would you write one so long? Why does she? What are the effects?

Argumentation and Persuasion:

1. Review the list of *persuasive* devices on pages 274–276 of this chapter's introduction. Which ones does Brand use here? Give an example for each of your answers.
2. Does "Job" also have an *argumentative* dimension? If so, is it *deductive* or *inductive*? Tell how.

Ideas for Discussion and Writing:

1. Dionne Brand had recently arrived in Canada when she lived the event she writes of here. How much have things changed since 1970, when she was 18? Would this scene be possible in Toronto today? In your own town or city? If it did happen, what legal recourse is now available?
2. Brand and her sister "waited out the ebb and flow of favour and need in this white place," working in kitchen hospitals, till things changed. Why, in our time, does she still remember the racist who refused her an interview over 30 years ago? Should she try to forget? Or will remembering serve her better in the present and future? How?
3. Our author calls the man who refused her interview a "pig." Do you consider this name-calling justified? Or, in labelling her enemy, does she begin to share his attitudes? What would you do?
4. Every group in Canadian society is now a minority. Has yours suffered unfairness? Illustrate, as Brand has done, with an incident.
5. **PROCESS IN WRITING:** *Use persuasion in the act of writing, as Brand has done, to expose an unfairness that happened to you. Close your eyes and recall the incident, then freewrite on it for several minutes. Look over what you have produced, then work the best of it into a fast discovery draft, adding IMAGES and details (remember Brand "showing" us her high heels and lipstick, the man's smile fading, the difficult walk back to the subway). Later look over the nine devices of persuasion listed on pages 274–276 of our chapter introduction; what do you see that will strengthen your message? Use it. Now edit for style and correctness, then read the piece aloud, with feeling, to the class. Finally, ask for reactions. Which passages communicated most strongly, and why?*

Note: See also the Topics for Writing at the end of this chapter.

ROBERT CHRISTY

Life with Cerebral Palsy

In the essay that follows, from the February 5, 2001 Maclean's, *Robert ("Bob") Christy tells much of his life story. Here are a few more facts: In 1940 he was born to parents who, though he had cerebral palsy and stuttered, taught him to believe he was not disabled. He learned the lesson well, emerging as a lifelong optimist whose motto is "To Look Beyond What You See." In 1963 Christy earned a B.A. in commerce, economics and math from Queen's, and in 1965 an M.B.A. from the University of Toronto. Then during a successful 30-year career in the federal public service in Ottawa and Regina, he was social policy researcher, analyst, advisor and writer. Now retired and a grandfather, Christy writes on issues of physical disability, while living with his wife Gail, who also has cerebral palsy and is an ordained minister in the United Church of Canada.*

Much of Christy's essay deals with a famous legal case. In 1993 Saskatchewan farmer Robert Latimer put his 12-year-old daughter Tracy, severely disabled and in pain from cerebral palsy, into the cab of his truck. He then filled the cab with exhaust fumes till she died. Always known by friends and neighbours as a loving father, Latimer said he did it to end her pain. The court cases that followed were widely covered in the news: In 1997 a judge granted Latimer a constitutional exemption in order to give him a sentence of only two years — with just one year to be served in jail. Supporters were overjoyed, while groups representing the disabled were enraged. A higher court then overturned the verdict, and finally in 2001 the Supreme Court of Canada upheld the second-degree murder charge with a life sentence and no chance of parole for ten years. The debate continues: who is right, the friends and neighbours who think Latimer did a kindness for Tracy, or opponents of mercy killing who guard the rights of the disabled?

My name is Bob, and I am living a wonderful life as a son, brother, husband, father, father-in-law and grandfather. I have studied at three post-secondary institutions, received bachelor's and master's degrees from two of Canada's top universities, and had a 30-year career with the federal government. But people may want to tell me what's best for me, because I have cerebral palsy. When I was young, I was popular in the community and at school, received high grades through working hard and exercising an agile mind, and did everything other kids my age did. Yet a close relative thought I should have been "destroyed at birth," because of my condition. I'm a raging extrovert, energized by people, and humorous when I am with them. Yet those who paid my salary put me into jobs away from the public eye, doing research and policy writing, refusing me the chance to do the things I could do best. When I didn't shine or meet the potential that those who knew me thought I should achieve, people could justifiably say: "What do you expect? He has cerebral palsy."

2   Among the many people I know from all walks of life are a professor, now dead, who taught in a major Canadian university, an Anglican priest and her spouse, a water resources economist who is listed in *Who's Who*, and my wife, a clergywoman who is one of the leaders of the largest Protestant denomination in Canada. We all have cerebral palsy. I've travelled, stood on the Great Wall in China and cruised down the Yangtze River, through the Three Gorges. I've been on safari, swum in the Indian Ocean and played golf in Kenya. I've walked the beaches of Trinidad, stood in the main square of Lima, driven a car in England, Scotland, Ireland (north and south) and Wales, and prayed at the Western Wall of the Second Temple in Jerusalem. I paid for it all myself, through writing contracts, even though I have cerebral palsy.

3   But now I cry. For the plight of Robert Latimer and his family, who will suffer for 10 long years because in their frustration, ignorance and — grudgingly, I'll say — love, they followed their own pigheadedness, apparently did not listen to the wisdom of others and did not grasp the help that was there for their daughter Tracy, whom he killed because he said he could not stand her pain.

4   I also weep for the lack of knowledge of people in our so-called high-literacy nation that think cerebral palsy hurts. It doesn't. What hurts is atrophy when muscles are not used: as the saying goes, use them or lose them. Physiotherapy and patterning help blood flow and ease any pain. Another thing that hurts is the attitude of others. I weep for the many people who, in their ignorance, think Latimer did the "right thing" — who, think, perhaps, that murder, if committed in love to save someone from a "horrible life," is OK if it's a disabled person who dies. Would they feel that way if a person killed another out of love to save the "loved one" from a horrible life as a street person? And I cry for politicians who have forgotten the promises made in 1981, the International Year of Disabled Persons. They are the ones who could be easily tempted to listen to whoever makes the loudest noise, regardless of right or wrong.

5   But maybe I cry most of all for me; in spite of my cleverness, diligence and successes now and in future, will I only be judged in a negative, non-flattering way as "Bob, the man with cerebral palsy"?

• •

Explorations:

Elaine Geralis, ed., *Children with Cerebral Palsy: A Parents' Guide*
http://www.cerebralpalsy.org
http://www.iaetf.org/iua23.htm
http://www.chninternational.com/default.html

http://www.cbc.ca/news/background/latimer/index.html
http://www.hawking.org.uk/home/hindex.html
http://www.stevenfletcher.com/profile.php

Structure:

1. Why does Christy give his name, Bob, in both the opening and closing sentences? What are the effects?
2. Identify Christy's THESIS STATEMENT. Why is it placed toward the middle of the essay?
3. Paragraph 2 is stuffed with a series of quick and colourful *examples*. Are there enough? Is it possible to have too many? Does Christy? What are the effects?
4. Christy ends his argument with a question. Is it a real question? If not, what is its purpose?

Style:

1. In question 2 above, we looked at Christy's thesis statement, "But now I cry," which begins paragraph 3. Now identify every place in the rest of the essay where he writes "I cry" or "I weep." Is this *repetition* accidental or deliberate? What are its effects?
2. For what AUDIENCE do you believe Christy is writing? What challenges does he face in communicating with non-disabled readers? Point out everything he does to teach them the facts of his own condition.

Argumentation and Persuasion:

1. To what extent is "Life with Cerebral Palsy" *induction*, based on *examples* that lead to its author's points? Identify at least ten such examples.
2. Does Christy's essay also employ *deduction*, applying a general principle to specific cases?
3. Does Christy's essay work only through logical thought (*argumentation*) or do we also feel *persuasion*? We have already seen the large amount of evidence he presents to argue his case; now look for places where emotion is used as a tool to help us accept his views.

Ideas for Discussion and Writing:

1. In the introduction to this essay, review the case of Robert Latimer, who in 1993 killed his daughter Tracy to end her pain from cerebral palsy. Do you view this mercy killing as a crime? Does Latimer deserve the minimum ten-year prison sentence he is now serving? Are disability

organizations right in supporting this court decision, so that future disabled persons will be safer? Or do you view Latimer as a loving parent who did the best for his child, and then was unjustly punished? Defend your answers with reasons.

2. In paragraph 3, Christy "cries" for the Latimer family, despite his viewing Latimer's act as "murder." Does this attitude weaken or strengthen his overall argument?

3. One of the world's most brilliant physicists and astronomers, Stephen Hawking, is severely disabled by amyotrophic lateral sclerosis. Visit his official home page at *www.hawking.org.uk/home/hindex.html.* Find out how he goes about his work despite his disability, then tell the class.

4. Are you disabled, or do you have a family member or friend who is? Report to the class on the challenges of the disability, and how to face them.

5. Stephen Fletcher had won Manitoba's kayaking championship, had canoed thousands of miles of northern rivers, and was working as an engineer. Then in a highway collision with a moose, he became a paraplegic. Visit his blog at *www.stevenfletcher.com/profile.php,* to read how Fletcher became an MP in the 2004 federal election, and Senior Health Critic for the Conservative Party. Report to the class on how he has achieved this success despite a severe physical disability.

6. In Canada we often see special facilities for the disabled: elevators, ramps, Braille signs in elevators, audible signals at traffic lights, seeing-eye dogs, etc. Is this enough? Do you have suggestions for what more might be done?

7. **PROCESS IN WRITING:** *Do an Internet search on Saskatchewan farmer Robert Latimer, and spend a couple of hours reading and taking notes (or printing materials) on his famous court case mentioned above. Now decide whether you support or condemn Latimer's act of mercy killing. Write a short outline of your argument, then do a quick discovery draft. Look it over. Is it mostly* deduction *(beginning with a principle you believe in strongly, then applied to make sense of the facts)? Or is it mostly* induction *(examining the facts of the case, then using them to arrive at an overall THESIS STATEMENT)? Examine also your TONE: Do you argue rationally, using mostly fact to support your* argumentation? *Or has this controversial topic made you emotional, so that you in turn use emotion as your main way to* persuade *the reader? At the top of the page, label your essay DEDUCTION or INDUCTION, and also label it ARGUMENTATION or PERSUASION. Now make sure your approach is consistent. Revise and polish. Finally, join with a small group of your classmates to share each other's papers and your reactions to them.*

Note: See also the Topics for Writing at the end of this chapter.

LT.-GEN. ROMÉO DALLAIRE, WITH MAJOR BRENT BEARDSLEY

Cri de coeur[*]

Making peace can take more courage than making war. In 1993 the United Nations named Canadian Lieutenant-General Roméo Dallaire commander of an international peacekeeping force with a tough mandate: to stop an ethnic conflict in the tiny African country of Rwanda. (The career soldier from Quebec seemed a natural choice for operations in a French-speaking nation.) Out of old resentments stemming from the Belgian colonial era, the majority Hutus had begun a persecution of their former masters, the Tutsis. Dallaire saw genocide coming. He alerted the UN, the United States, France and other key players. He requested, then demanded, more troops and weapons. When the slaughters began in spring of 1994, he hounded the major UN countries to save the Tutsis — but they all declined to help, because they saw in Rwanda no strategic value and no oil. So Dallaire and his tiny force went into action: they moved thousands of Tutsis to safety behind the front lines of a rebel Tutsi force; they used moral suasion to defy the governing Hutus; and the apparently fearless General personally intimidated members of the government to obey terms of the peace treaty they had signed. But when the dust settled after 100 days of butchery, some 800,000 men, women and children had died. Dallaire blamed himself, and sank into depression. But over the next decade the world has acknowledged its own guilt, and his heroism. At least seven books, documentaries and feature films now tell the story (see "Explorations"). The best of these is Dallaire's own book Shake Hands with the Devil: The Failure of Humanity in Rwanda *(2003). Our selection is the book's introduction to this harrowing story. The memoir has become an international bestseller, and has been called the most important Canadian book of the decade. Though Dallaire himself seems not to believe it, these pages portray a true Canadian, and world, hero.*

I t was an absolutely magnificent day in May 1994. The blue sky was cloudless, and there was a whiff of breeze stirring the trees. It was hard to believe that in the past weeks an unimaginable evil had turned Rwanda's gentle green valleys and mist-capped hills into a stinking nightmare of rotting corpses. A nightmare we all had to negotiate every day. A nightmare that, as commander of the UN peacekeeping force in Rwanda, I could not help but feel deeply responsible for.

1

---

[*] *Cri de coeur*: Editor's title, in French meaning "a cry from the heart."

2   In relative terms, that day had been a good one. Under the protection of a limited and fragile ceasefire, my troops had successfully
escorted about two hundred civilians — a few of the thousands who had
sought refuge with us in Kigali, the capital of Rwanda — through many
government- and militia-manned checkpoints to reach safety behind the
Rwandese Patriotic Front (RPF) lines. We were seven weeks into the
genocide, and the RPF, the disciplined rebel army (composed largely of
the sons of Rwandan refugees who had lived over the border in camps
in Uganda since being forced out of their homeland at independence),
was making a curved sweep toward Kigali from the north, adding civil
war to the chaos and butchery in the country.

3   Having delivered our precious cargo of innocent souls, we were
headed back to Kigali in a white UN Land Cruiser with my force commander pennant on the front hood and the blue UN flag on a staff
attached to the right rear. My Ghanaian sharpshooter, armed with a new
Canadian C-7 rifle, rode behind me, and my new Senegalese aide-de-
camp, Captain Ndiaye, sat to my right. We were driving a particularly
dangerous stretch of road, open to sniper fire. Most of the people in the
surrounding villages had been slaughtered, the few survivors escaping
with little more than the clothes on their backs. In a few short weeks, it
had become a lonely and forlorn place.

4   Suddenly up ahead we saw a child wandering across the road. I
stopped the vehicle close to the little boy, worried about scaring him off,
but he was quite unfazed. He was about three years old, dressed in a
filthy, torn T-shirt, the ragged remnants of underwear, little more than a
loincloth, drooping from under his distended belly. He was caked in
dirt, his hair white and matted with dust, and he was enveloped in a
cloud of flies, which were greedily attacking the open sores that covered
him. He stared at us silently, sucking on what I realized was a high-pro-
tein biscuit. Where had the boy found food in this wasteland?

5   I got out of the vehicle and walked toward him. Maybe it was the condition I was in, but to me this child had the face of an angel and eyes of
pure innocence. I had seen so many children hacked to pieces that this
small, whole, bewildered boy was a vision of hope. Surely he could not
have survived all on his own? I motioned for my aide-de-camp to honk
the horn, hoping to summon up his parents, but the sound echoed over
the empty landscape, startling a few birds and little else. The boy
remained transfixed. He did not speak or cry, just stood sucking on his
biscuit and staring up at us with his huge, solemn eyes. Still hoping that
he wasn't all alone, I sent my aide-de-camp and the sharpshooter to look
for signs of life.

6   We were in a ravine lush with banana trees and bamboo shoots, which
created a dense canopy of foliage. A long straggle of deserted huts stood
on either side of the road. As I stood alone with the boy, I felt an anxious knot in my stomach: this would be a perfect place to stage an
ambush. My colleagues returned, having found no one. Then a rustling

in the undergrowth made us jump. I grabbed the boy and held him firmly to my side as we instinctively took up defensive positions around the vehicle and in the ditch. The bushes parted to reveal a well-armed RPF soldier about fifteen years old. He recognized my uniform and gave me a smart salute and introduced himself. He was part of an advance observation post in the nearby hills. I asked him who the boy was and whether there was anyone left alive in the village who could take care of him. The soldier answered that the boy had no name and no family but that he and his buddies were looking after him. That explained the biscuit but did nothing to allay my concerns over the security and health of the boy. I protested that the child needed proper care and that I could give it to him: we were protecting and supporting orphanages in Kigali where he would be much better off. The soldier quietly insisted that the boy stay where he was, among his own people.

I continued to argue, but this child soldier was in no mood to discuss the situation and with haughty finality stated that his unit would care and provide for the child. I could feel my face flush with anger and frustration, but then noticed that the boy himself had slipped away while we had been arguing over him, and God only knew where he had gone. My aide-de-camp spotted him at the entrance to a hut a short distance away, clambering over a log that had fallen across the doorway. I ran after him, closely followed by my aide-de-camp and the RPF child soldier. By the time I had caught up to the boy, he had disappeared inside. The log in the doorway turned out to be the body of a man, obviously dead for some weeks, his flesh rotten with maggots and beginning to fall away from the bones. 7

As I stumbled over the body and into the hut, a swarm of flies invaded my nose and mouth. It was so dark inside that at first I smelled rather than saw the horror that lay before me. The hut was a two-room affair, one room serving as a kitchen and living room and the other as a communal bedroom; two rough windows had been cut into the mud-and-stick wall. Very little light penetrated the gloom, but as my eyes became accustomed to the dark, I saw strewn around the living room in a rough circle the decayed bodies of a man, a woman and two children, stark white bone poking through the desiccated, leather-like covering that had once been skin. The little boy was crouched beside what was left of his mother, still sucking on his biscuit. I made my way over to him as slowly and quietly as I could and, lifting him into my arms, carried him out of the hut. 8

The warmth of his tiny body snuggled against mine filled me with a peace and serenity that elevated me above the chaos. This child was alive yet terribly hungry, beautiful but covered in dirt, bewildered but not fearful. I made up my mind: this boy would be the fourth child in the Dallaire family. I couldn't save Rwanda, but I could save this child. 9

Before I had held this boy, I had agreed with the aid workers and representatives of both the warring armies that I would not permit any exporting of Rwandan orphans to foreign places. When confronted by such 10 requests from humanitarian organizations, I would argue that the money to move a hundred kids by plane to France or Belgium could help build, staff and sustain Rwandan orphanages that could house three thousand children. This one boy eradicated all my arguments. I could see myself arriving at the terminal in Montreal like a latter-day St. Christopher° with the boy cradled in my arms, and my wife, Beth, there ready to embrace him.

11   That dream was abruptly destroyed when the young soldier, fast as a wolf, yanked the child from my arms and carried him directly into the bush. Not knowing how many members of his unit might already have their gunsights on us, we reluctantly climbed back into the Land Cruiser. As I slowly drove away, I had much on my mind.

12   By withdrawing, I had undoubtedly done the wise thing: I had avoided risking the lives of my two soldiers in what would have been a fruitless struggle over one small boy. But in that moment, it seemed to me that I had backed away from a fight for what was right, that this failure stood for all our failures in Rwanda.

13   Whatever happened to that beautiful child? Did he make it to an orphanage deep behind the RPF lines? Did he survive the following battles? Is he dead or is he now a child soldier himself, caught in the seemingly endless conflict that plagues his homeland?

14   That moment, when the boy, in the arms of a soldier young enough to be his brother, was swallowed whole by the forest, haunts me. It's a memory that never lets me forget how ineffective and irresponsible we were when we promised the Rwandans that we would establish an atmosphere of security that would allow them to achieve a lasting peace. It has been almost nine years since I left Rwanda, but as I write this, the sounds, smells and colours come flooding back in digital clarity. It's as if someone has sliced into my brain and grafted this horror called Rwanda frame by blood-soaked frame directly on my cortex. I could not forget even if I wanted to. For many of these years, I have yearned to return to Rwanda and disappear into the blue-green hills with my ghosts. A simple pilgrim seeking forgiveness and pardon. But as I slowly begin to piece my life back together, I know the time has come for me to make a more difficult pilgrimage: to travel back through all those terrible memories and retrieve my soul.

15   I did try to write this story soon after I came back from Rwanda in September 1994, hoping to find some respite for myself in sorting out how my own role as Force Commander of UNAMIR interconnected with the international apathy, the complex political manoeuvres, the deep well of hatred and barbarity that resulted in a genocide in which over 800,000 people lost their lives. Instead, I plunged into a disastrous mental health spiral that led me to suicide attempts, a medical release from

---

° St. Christopher: a fearless martyr of the third century, patron saint of travellers.

the Armed Forces, the diagnosis of post-traumatic stress disorder, and dozens upon dozens of therapy sessions and extensive medication, which still have a place in my daily life.

It took me seven years to finally have the desire, the willpower and the stamina to begin to describe in detail the events of that year in Rwanda. To recount, from my insider's point of view, how a country moved from the promise of a certain peace to intrigue, the fomenting of racial hatred, assassinations, civil war and genocide. And how the international community, through an inept UN mandate and what can only be described as indifference, self-interest and racism, aided and abetted these crimes against humanity — how we all helped create the mess that has murdered and displaced millions and destabilized the whole central African region.   16

A growing library of books and articles is exploring the tragic events in Rwanda from many angles: eyewitness accounts, media analyses, assaults on the actions of the American administration at the time, condemnations of the UN's apparent ineptitude. But even in the international and national inquiries launched in the wake of the genocide, the blame somehow slides away from the individual member nations of the UN, and in particular those influential countries with permanent representatives on the Security Council, such as the United States, France and the United Kingdom, who sat back and watched it all happen, who pulled their troops or didn't offer any troops in the first place. A few Belgian officers were brought to court to pay for the sins of Rwanda. When my sector commander in Kigali, Colonel Luc Marchal, was court-martialled in Brussels, the charges against him were clearly designed to deflect any responsibility away from the Belgian government for the deaths of the ten Belgian peacekeepers under my command. The judge eventually threw out all the charges, accepting the fact that Marchal had performed his duties magnificently in a near-impossible situation. But the spotlight never turned to the reasons why he and the rest of the UNAMIR force were in such a dangerous situation in the first place.   17

It is time that I tell the story from where I stood — literally in the middle of the slaughter for weeks on end. A public account of my actions, my decisions and my failings during that most terrible year may be a crucial missing link for those attempting to understand the tragedy both intellectually and in their hearts. I know that I will never end my mourning for all those Rwandans who placed their faith in us, who thought the UN peacekeeping force was there to stop extremism, to stop the killings and help them through the perilous journey to a lasting peace. That mission, UNAMIR, failed. I know intimately the cost in human lives of the inflexible UN Security Council mandate, the pennypinching financial management of the mission, the UN red tape, the political manipulations and my own personal limitations. What I have come to realize as the root of it all, however, is the fundamental indifference of the world community to the plight of seven to eight million black Africans in a tiny country that had no strategic or resource value to any world power. An   18 overpopulated little country that turned in on itself and destroyed its own people, as the world watched and yet could not manage to find the political will to intervene. Engraved still in my brain is the judgment of a small group of bureaucrats who came to "assess" the situation in the first weeks of the genocide: "We will recommend to our government not to intervene as the risks are high and all that is here are humans."

19   My story is not a strictly military account nor a clinical, academic study of the breakdown of Rwanda. It is not a simplistic indictment of the many failures of the UN as a force for peace in the world. It is not a story of heroes and villains, although such a work could easily be written. This book is a *cri de coeur* for the slaughtered thousands, a tribute to the souls hacked apart by machetes because of their supposed difference from those who sought to hang on to power. It is the story of a commander who, faced with a challenge that didn't fit the classic Cold War–era peacekeeper's rule book, failed to find an effective solution and witnessed, as if in punishment, the loss of some of his own troops, the attempted annihilation of an ethnicity, the butchery of children barely out of the womb, the stacking of severed limbs like cordwood, the mounds of decomposing bodies being eaten by the sun.

20   This book is nothing more nor less than the account of a few humans who were entrusted with the role of helping others taste the fruits of peace. Instead, we watched as the devil took control of paradise on earth and fed on the blood of the people we were supposed to protect.

● ●

Explorations:

Lt.-Gen. Roméo Dallaire, with Major Brent Beardsley, *Shake Hands with the Devil: The Failure of Humanity in Rwanda*
Gerald Caplan, Rwanda: *The Preventable Genocide*
Gil Courtemanche, *A Sunday at the Pool in Kigali* (novel)
Joseph Conrad, *Heart of Darkness* (novella)
Gwynne Dyer, *Future: Tense: The Coming World Order*
Hotel Rwanda (feature film, 2004)
Ghosts of Rwanda (PBS documentary)
The Last Just Man (documentary film, 2002)
Shake Hands with the Devil: The Journey of Roméo Dallaire (documentary film, 2005)
http://en.wikipedia.org/wiki/Rom%C3%Ao_Dallaire#Early_life_and_education
http://www.thirdworldtraveler.com/Heroes/Gen_Romeo_Dallaire.html
http://tanadineen.com/COLUMNIST/Columns/Dallaire.htm
http://www.pbs.org/wgbh/pages/frontline/shows/ghosts/interviews/dallaire.html

Structure:

1. Read the opening paragraph aloud. How does Dallaire prepare us for his topic, in telling of the "absolutely magnificent day," the "gentle green valleys" and the "mist-capped hills" of Rwanda?
2. The logic of *cause and effect* plays a large part in Dallaire's argument. Point out five examples of it in these pages.
3. To what extent is "*Cri de coeur*" a *narrative*?
4. In not fighting over "one small boy," the general follows military good sense. But he goes on to say, "in that moment, it seemed to me that I had backed away from a fight for what was right, that this failure stood for all our failures in Rwanda" (12). Point out all the ways in which this selection is an *analogy* to larger things.

Style:

1. The author's first language is French. Apart from the term *Cri de coeur*, chosen from paragraph 19 as our title, do you see any effects of this fact on his style?
2. Read paragraph 8 aloud, if you can. What overall technique lies behind its power to evoke horror?

Argumentation and Persuasion:

1. Examine the logic of this selection. Is it mostly *deduction* (extending a principle to explain individual cases) or *induction* (letting examples lead to a point)?
2. To what extent does the General's *cri de coeur* (cry from the heart) use emotion, or *persuasion*, to make its points? Give examples. And to what extent does it work through logic, or *argumentation*? Can it draw on both at once?

Ideas for Discussion and Writing:

1. After an 11-year-old boy found his 5-year-old sister near the corpses of their parents, he said, "I will hunt the killers to the end of the world. I will kill their children when I grow up. I know the killers; even 70 years from now, I will remember how they and their children look" (*The Ottawa Citizen*, July 13, 2000). What conclusions would you draw from this *example*?
2. Are genocides inevitable or can they be stopped? As this book was going to press, 10 years after the events in Rwanda, another major one had begun in the Sudan, a country with almost no central government and with no Roméo Dallaires to intervene. What could have been done, and when, and who should have done it?

3. After contemplating the downward spiral of his own mental health, the General concludes, "It is time I tell the story from where I stood . . ." (18). Why did it take nine years for him to put it on paper? Do you believe writing and sharing his "story" will bring him peace? Is Sylvia Fraser (p. 29) correct in saying "Writing is healing"? And do the acts of writing that you perform help lead your own conflicts toward peace?

4. At one hopeless point during the conflict, Dallaire was asked, "What in the hell are you doing here? Why are you staying?"

He replied, "If I can save one life, then it's worth it."

"Yeah, but there are tens of thousands being slaughtered every day."

The General concluded, "Then maybe if I could be a witness, maybe I'll have a chance to tell everything that we've been seeing."

Now tell of the time you, too, were a "witness," and what it accomplished.

5. Dallaire entitled his book *Shake Hands with the Devil.* In the documentary film that has the same title, he describes the cold, Devil-like handshake of extremist leaders, and the inhuman quality of their gaze. But he goes on to say, "If I had been able to literally shake hands with the Devil, it only seems absolutely logical that there is another entity. Because there is that extreme of evil, there is the other extreme of the purest good." Who and what, in Rwanda, represented this "purest good"?

6. **PROCESS IN WRITING:** *Like Roméo Dallaire, use persuasion to "tell the story" of the worst conflict you have ever been in. First close your eyes and remember the situation or incident, then freewrite for several minutes. Look over these notes and work the best of them into a rapid first draft. Be sure to state your THESIS STATEMENT, the overall main point. Later review the nine devices of persuasion listed in pages 274–276 of our chapter introduction, and add them wherever they will strengthen your message. Add SENSE IMAGES, as Dallaire has, to bring the scene alive. Add TRANSITIONS (such as "then," "next" and "finally") to speed the narrative, and add logic signals to sharpen your thoughts. Finally, edit for STYLE and correctness, then read the piece aloud, with feeling, to the class. Later, think about Sylvia Fraser's comment "Writing is healing." Has it been true for you?*

Note: See also the Topics for Writing at the end of this chapter.

Topics for Writing

CHAPTER 9: ARGUMENTATION AND PERSUASION

Develop one of the following topics into an essay of argumentation and/or persuasion, choosing the side you wish to take. If you wish, modify the topic so it says more exactly what you think. (See also the guidelines that follow.)

1. Pit Bulls Should Be (Allowed/Outlawed).
2. Talking on a Cell Phone While Driving Should Be (Permitted/ Outlawed).
3. Racism in Canada Is (Increasing/Decreasing).
4. Our Country's Health Care System Is (Better/as Good as/Worse Than) It Was Ten Years Ago.
5. Car Insurance (Should/Should Not) Cost the Same for Males and Females.
6. NHL hockey Is (Better Than/as Good as/Worse Than) It Was a Generation Ago.
7. Television Has Been a (Good/Neutral/Bad) Influence on My Life.
8. Adopted Children (Should/Should Not) Be Told Who Their Birth Parents Are.
9. My Neighbourhood Is Becoming (Safer/Less Safe).
10. Class Sizes at My School Are (Acceptable/Too Large).
11. The Use of Cars in the Centre of Big Cities Should Be (Abolished/ Restricted/Maintained).
12. Compulsory Retirement at 65 Should Be (Maintained/Abolished).
13. The School Library Is (Terrible/Fair/Mediocre/Good/Excellent).
14. The Great Majority of Films Shown in Canadian Theatres Are Foreign, Mostly American. Should Theatres Be Required to Show a Higher Percentage of Our Own Films?
15. Drunk Drivers (Should/Should Not) Lose their Licences Permanently.
16. With Computerization, Employees Are Now Working (Less/As Much/More).
17. Irradiation of Food Is (Safe/Dangerous).
18. It (Is/Is Not) Important for New Canadians to Pass Their First Language On to Their Children.
19. Knowing (French/Spanish/Cantonese/or Another Language) (Will/Will Not Be) Important in My Future Career.
20. Putting Money into the Stock Market Is (a Dangerous Gamble/a Calculated Risk/a Good Way to Get Rich).
21. Clearcutting of Old-Growth Forests Should Be (Permitted/ Regulated/Outlawed).
22. The School Computer Facilities Are (Terrible/Fair/Mediocre/ Good/Excellent).

23. Tax Policy (Should/Should Not) Promote Better Fuel Mileage in Vehicles.
24. Companies (Should/Should Not) Be Held Liable for Their Own Pollution.
25. Cloning of Humans (Should/Should Not) Be Outlawed.
26. The Canadian Senate Should Be (Maintained/Changed/Abolished).
27. There (Is/Is Not) Life in Outer Space.
28. Extreme Sports Are (Good Fun/Risky but Worth It/Foolhardy).
29. Food in the School Cafeteria Is (Terrible/Fair/Mediocre/Good/Excellent).
30. Canada Should (Maintain/Abolish) Its Ties to the Monarchy.

Note: See also the Process in Writing topics after each selection in this chapter.

Process in Writing: Guidelines

Follow at least some of these steps in writing your essay of argumentation and/or persuasion (your teacher may suggest which ones).

1. *Choose a good topic, if necessary customize it, then go to either 2 or 3 below.*

2. **DEDUCTION:** *Do you already know your point of view because of a moral or intellectual principle you hold? First examine that principle, the foundation of your argument: Is it extreme, or is it reasonable enough (and clear enough) that your* AUDIENCE *can accept it? If the latter, proceed. Make notes, then do a rapid first draft showing how the principle supports your point.*

OR

3. **INDUCTION:** *Did experience or observation teach you the point you wish to make? First generate a page of notes. Then put these experiences or observations into the order that led you to your conclusion. Now transfer this argument to a rapid first draft.*

4. *You have probably organized your draft through a pattern we studied in an earlier chapter.* Cause and effect *is a natural for either deduction or induction, and so is* comparison and contrast. *You have surely used* examples, *perhaps* narrating *or* describing *them. You might also have* classified *your subject, or cast your logic in a* process analysis. *Apart from analogy, which appeals more to emotion than to logic, all the approaches we have studied so far can serve deduction or induction. Use whatever works. If your first draft makes partial use of a major pattern, consider revising to extend the pattern and strengthen its effect.*

5. *As you look over your first draft, add any missing examples, especially if your argument is inductive (the more evidence, the better). Heighten your logic with signals such as "however," "therefore," "as a result" and "in conclusion."*

6. *Now judge how* argumentative *or* persuasive *your approach has been so far. Does your cold logic need a little colour and life? If so, add it, consulting pages 274–276 on techniques of persuasion. Or do emotions dominate your argument? Do they even encourage the audience not to think? If so, revise toward a more blended stance in your second draft.*

7. *Now cut all deadwood. Check for spelling and punctuation before printing out your best version.*

GLOSSARY

Abstract   Theoretical, relying more on GENERALIZATION than on facts and examples. Abstract writing may lack interest and force, because it is hard to understand and the ideas are hard to apply. *See also* the opposite of abstract, CONCRETE.

Allegory   In poetry or PROSE, a passage or an entire work that has two levels of meaning: literal and symbolic (*see* SYMBOL). Like a parable, an allegory draws such numerous or striking parallels between its literal subject and its implied subject that, without ever stating "the moral of the story," it leads us to perceive a moral or philosophical truth. An allegory, though, is longer and more complex than a parable. It also differs from an analogy in that it does not openly identify and compare the two subjects.

Allusion   An indirect reference to a passage in literature or scripture, to an event, a person, or anything else familiar to the reader. An allusion is a device of compression in language, for in a few words it summons up the meaning of the thing to which it refers, and applies that meaning to the subject at hand. Critics of big government, for example, often *allude* to Big Brother, the personification of governmental tyranny in George Orwell's novel *1984.*

Anecdote   A short account of an interesting incident. An anecdote can be a joke or a true story about others or oneself, and is often used as an example to introduce an essay, close an essay, or illustrate points within an essay.

Audience   The reader or readers. One of the essayist's crucial tasks is to match the level and strategy of an argument to the needs and qualities of the particular audience that will read it. *See* the section "Who is my audience?" in this book's introductory essay, "The Act of Writing," p. 1.

Bias words   Terms which, either subtly or openly, encourage strong value judgments. SUBJECTIVE language is a vital ingredient of much good writing, especially in description and in persuasion; to avoid it completely is difficult and often undesirable. The important thing is to avoid blatantly loaded language in an essay: terms like "jerk," "slob," "cretin," "geezer," "Hogtown," "Newfie," "tree hugger" or "neocon" will inflame an uncritical reader and offend a critical one. Note that many bias words are also SLANG.

Cliché   A worn-out expression that takes the place of original thought: "sadder but wiser," "bite the bullet," "hustle and bustle," "been there, done that," "the bottom line" and "no pain, no gain." All clichés were once fresh, but like last year's fad in clothing or music, have lost their appeal and may even annoy.

Climax   In an essay, the point where the argument reaches its culmination, its point of greatest intensity or importance. The closing of an essay is normally a climax; if it is not, it may give the impression of trailing feebly off into nothingness.

Colloquial   Speech-like. Colloquial expressions like "cop," "guy," "kid," "nitty gritty" and "okay" are often used in conversation but are usually avoided in essays, especially FORMAL essays. Though lively, colloquialisms can be inexact: "guy," for example, can refer to a rope as well as a person, and "kid" can refer to a goat as well as a child. *See also* SLANG.

Conciseness   The art of conveying the most meaning in the fewest words. A concise essay does not explain its topic less fully than a wordy one; it just uses words more efficiently. Concise writers get straight to the point and stay on topic. They are well enough organized to avoid repeating themselves. They give CONCRETE examples rather than pages of ABSTRACT argument. They use a short word unless a long one is more exact. And most concise writers, to achieve these goals, revise extensively.

Concrete   Factual and specific, relying more on examples than on abstract theory. Concrete language makes writing more forceful, interesting and convincing by recreating vividly for the reader what the writer has experienced or thought. SENSE IMAGES, ANECDOTES, FIGURES OF SPEECH and CONCISENESS all play a part in concrete language and are usually lacking in its opposite, ABSTRACT language.

Deduction   A kind of logic that accepts a general principle as true, then uses it to explain a specific case or cases. *See* "Deduction," p. 272, and its opposite, "Induction," p. 273.

Dialogue   The quoted conversation of two or more people. Normally a new paragraph begins with each change of speaker, to avoid confusion as to who says what. A bit of dialogue can lend colour to an essay, but heavy use of it is normally reserved for fiction and drama.

Economy   See CONCISENESS.

Epigram   A short, clever, and often wise saying. The best-known epigrams are proverbs, such as "What can't be cured must be endured" and "To know all is to forgive all."

Epigraph   A short introductory quotation prefixed to an essay or other piece of writing.

Essay   Derived from the French term *essai*, meaning a "try" or "attempt," the word "essay" refers to a short composition in which a point is made, usually through analysis and example. While most essays are alike in being limited to one topic, they may vary widely in other ways. The *formal essay*, for example, is objective and stylistically dignified, while the *familiar essay* is subjective, anecdotal and sometimes colloquial.

Euphemism   A polite expression that softens or even hides the truth: "pass away" for "die," "senior citizens" for "old people," "low-income neighbourhood" for "slum," "gosh darn" for "God damn," "perspire" for "sweat," "terminate" for "kill," and "de-hire" or "select out" for "fire." Euphemisms have become more and more common in uses ranging from personal kindness to advertising to political repression.

Fable   A tale, usually about animals, that teaches a moral truth or lesson meant for humans. Examples range from the classical Greek fables of Aesop about animals such as the tortoise and the hare, to modern fables such as Basil Johnston's selection in this book, "Modern Cannibals of the Wilds."

Fiction   Imaginative literature written in PROSE. Consisting mainly of novels and short stories, fiction uses invented characters and plots to create a dramatic story. Most ESSAYS, by contrast, rely on literal fact and analysis to create an argument. There is of course an area of overlap: some fiction is very factual and some essays are very imaginative.

Figures of speech   Descriptive and often poetic devices in which meaning is concentrated and heightened, usually through comparisons:

A. **Simile:** A figure of speech in which one thing is said to be *like* another. ("With its high buildings on all sides, Bay Street is like a canyon.")
B. **Metaphor:** A figure of speech, literally false but poetically true, in which one thing is said to *be* another. ("Bay Street is a canyon walled by cliffs of concrete.")
C. **Hyperbole:** Exaggeration. ("The office buildings rise miles above the city.")
D. **Personification:** A figure of speech in which a non-human object is described as human. ("At night the empty buildings stare from their windows at the street.")

Formal   Formal writing is deliberate and dignified. It avoids partial sentences, most contractions, colloquial expressions and slang. Instead its vocabulary is standard and its sentences are often long and qualified with dependent clauses. It follows accepted rules of grammar and principles of style. *See also* INFORMAL.

Generalization   A broad statement of overall principle, as opposed to an explanation using specific examples. Although an essay needs generalizations, especially in places such as the THESIS STATEMENT and the CONCLUSION, most arguments that lack concrete examples are dull and difficult to understand.

Hyperbole   *See* FIGURES OF SPEECH.

Image   In literature, a mental picture triggered by words. Because they strongly stimulate thought and feeling, yet take little space, well-chosen images are vital ingredients of writing that is CONCRETE and has CONCISENESS. *See also* SENSE IMAGES.

Induction   A kind of logic that derives a general principle from the evidence of specific examples. *See* "Induction," p. 273, and its opposite, "Deduction," p. 272.

Informal   Informal writing resembles speech and, in fact, is often a representation of speech in writing. It may contain partial sentences, many short sentences, contractions, COLLOQUIAL expressions and sometimes SLANG. *See also* its opposite, FORMAL. Academic essays avoid almost all informal language.

Irony   A manner of expression in which a statement that seems literally to mean one thing actually means another. "Wonderful!" is a literal remark when said by a dinner guest enjoying the pie, but an ironic complaint when said by a driver who has backed into a tree. In a larger sense, *irony of situation* is a contrast between what is expected to happen and what does happen. It is this that creates our interest in the national leader who is impeached, the orphan who becomes a millionaire, or the evangelist convicted of tax fraud. Irony is a powerful tool of argument and especially of SATIRE.

Jargon   Technical language or language that seeks to impress by *appearing* difficult or technical. Specialized terms can hardly be avoided in technical explanations: How could two electricians discuss a radio without words like "capacitor," "diode" and "transistor"? But these same words may need defining when put in an essay for the general reader. Other jargon uses technical-sounding or otherwise difficult words to seem important. An honest essayist will try to avoid "input," "output," "feedback," "interface," "knowledgeable," "parameters" and other ugly words of this sort when writing for the general reader.

Juxtaposition   The deliberate placing together of two or more thoughts, IMAGES or other elements that emphasize each other, usually by contrast.

Metaphor   *See* FIGURES OF SPEECH.

Neologism   A newly invented word. Some new terms are accepted into our standard vocabulary. For example, the word "laser" quickly became standard because we needed it to label a new and important invention. Most newly minted words are nuisances, though, meaningless to the many readers who do not know them.

Objective   The opposite of SUBJECTIVE. In objective writing the author relies more on hard evidence and logical proof than on intuitions, prejudices or interpretations.

Onomatopoeia   A poetical device in which language sounds like what it means. Some onomatopoetic words, such as "boom," "bang" and "crash," are obvious sound effects; others, such as "slither," "ooze" and "clatter," are more subtle. Onomatopoeia can be achieved not only through word choice but also through larger aspects of style. A series of short sentences, for example, gives an impression of tenseness and rapidity.

Paradox   A statement that seems illogical but that in some unexpected way may be true. The Bible is full of paradoxes, as in "Blessed are the meek, for they shall inherit the earth."

Personification   *See* FIGURES OF SPEECH.

Prose   Spoken or written language without the metrical structure that characterizes poetry. Conversations, letters, short stories, novels and essays are all prose.

Pun   A play on words. A pun is based either on two meanings of one word or on two words that sound alike but have different meanings. Often called the lowest form of humour, the pun is the basis of many jokes. (Why did the fly fly? Because the spider spider.)

Quotation   The words of one person reproduced exactly in the writing or speech of another person. A well-chosen quotation can add force to an argument by conveying the opinion of an authority or by presenting an idea in words so exact or memorable that they could hardly be improved upon. Quotations should be reproduced exactly, placed in quotation marks, and attributed to their source. In writing research papers, there are whole systems of presenting and documenting quotations.

Reduction to absurdity   A technique of SATIRE in which the subject is belittled through being portrayed as absurd. A favourite device of humorists, such as Stephen Leacock.

Sarcasm   Scornful and contemptuous criticism, from the Greek word *sarkazein* ("to tear flesh").

Satire   Humorous criticism meant to improve an individual or society by exposing abuses. In TONE, satire can range from light humour to bitter criticism. Its main tools are wit, IRONY, exaggeration, and sometimes SARCASM and ridicule.

Sense images   Descriptive appeals to one or more of the reader's five senses: sight, hearing, touch, taste and smell. Sense images are vital in helping the reader to experience, at second hand, what the writer has lived in person. CONCRETE language has many sense images; ABSTRACT language does not.

Simile   *See* FIGURES OF SPEECH.

Slang   Racy, unconventional language, often limited to a certain time, place or group. Slang is the extreme of colloquial language, terminology used in conversation but hardly ever in an ESSAY except for dialogue or special effects. One reason to avoid a slang term is that not everyone will know it: expressions like "swell," "square" and "far out" have gone out of use, while expressions like "bug juice," "croaker," "jointman" and "rounder" are known to only one group — in this case, prison inmates. *See also* COLLOQUIAL.

Stereotype   An established mental image of something. Most stereotypes are of people and are based on their sex, race, colour, size or shape, economic or social class, or profession. Jokes about mothers-in-law, "Newfies," absent-minded professors, woman drivers or short people are

all examples of stereotyping. While they may provoke humour, stereotypes are anything but harmless: they prevent recognition of people's
individuality and they encourage prejudices which, at their extreme, can
result in persecution like that of the Jews in Nazi Germany.

Style   In general, the *way* something is written, as opposed to *what* it is
written about. Style is to some extent a matter of TONE — light or serious, INFORMAL or FORMAL, ironic or literal. It is also a matter of technique. Word choice, FIGURES OF SPEECH, level of CONCISENESS, and
characteristics of sentence structure and paragraphing are all ingredients of style. Although a writer should pay close attention to these matters, the idea that one deliberately seeks out "a style" is a mistake that
only encourages imitation. An individual style emerges naturally as the
sum of the writer's temperament, skills and experience.

Subjective   The opposite of OBJECTIVE. In subjective writing the author
relies more on intuitions, prejudices or interpretations than on hard evidence and logical proof.

Symbol   One thing that stands for another, as in a flag representing a
country, the crescent representing Islam, or a logo representing a company. Symbols in word form appear frequently in poetry, drama, fiction
and also essays.

Thesis statement   The sentence or sentences, usually in the introduction,
which first state the main point and restrict the focus of an essay.

Tone   The manner of a writer toward the subject and reader. The tone
of an essay can be light or serious, INFORMAL or FORMAL, ironic or literal.
Tone is often determined by subject matter; for example an essay about
parties is likely to be lighter and less formal than one about funerals. An
innovative writer, though, could reverse these treatments to give each of
the essays an ironic tone. The identity of the reader also influences tone.
An essay for specialists to read in a technical journal will tend to be more
OBJECTIVE and serious than one written for the general reader. The main
point for the writer is to choose the tone most appropriate to a particular essay and audience, then maintain it throughout.

Transition   A word, phrase, sentence or paragraph that moves the
reader from one part of the essay to the next. Transitions even as short
as "next," "then," "as a result," "on the other hand," "in conclusion" or
"finally" are crucial not only to speeding the argument along, but also to
pointing out its logic.